2007

Excellence
in Practice:
Moving the Goalposts

**Innovation and Excellence in Business
Process Management and Workflow**

2007 Excellence in Practice:
Moving the Goalposts

Innovation and Excellence in Business Process Management and Workflow

LAYNA FISCHER

Future Strategies Inc.
Lighthouse Point, Florida, USA

2007 Excellence in Practice: Moving the Goalposts (Print Format)
Innovation and Excellence in Workflow and Business Process Management

Copyright © 2007 by Future Strategies Inc.

ISBN10: 0-9777527-5-5

ISBN13: 978-0-9777527-5-1

09 08 07 7 8 9

Published by Future Strategies Inc., Book Division

2436 North Federal Highway, #374
Lighthouse Point FL 33064 USA
954.782.3376
954.782.6365 fax
http:// www.futstrat.com
books@futstrat.com

Publisher's Cataloging-in-Publication Data

ISBN: 978-0-9777527-5-1

Library of Congress Control Number: 2007906361

2007 Excellence in Practice: Moving the Goalposts (Print Format)
Innovation and Excellence in Workflow and Business Process Management
/Layna Fischer

p. cm.

Includes bibliographical references and appendices.

1. Technological Innovation. 2. Organizational Change. 3. Business Process Management.
4. Information Technology. 5. Total Quality Management. 6. Management Information systems.
7. Office Practice-Automation. 8. Knowledge Management. 9. Workflow. 10. Process Analysis

Fischer, Layna.

TABLE OF CONTENTS

Section 4: Pacific Rim

Section 5: South America

Section 6: Appendix

Moving the Competitive Goalposts

Layna Fischer, Editor and Awards Executive Director

The prestigious annual **Global Excellence Awards for BPM and Workflow** are highly coveted by organizations that seek recognition for their achievements. Now evolved into their 17th year, starting with, and moving through, imaging, documentation, knowledge management and more, as our industry moved forward, these awards not only provide a spotlight for companies that truly deserve recognition, but also provide tremendous insights for organizations wishing to emulate the winners' successes.

These winners are companies that moved the goalposts for their industries.

The criteria for submitting an entry are fairly simple: the project should have been operational for six months prior to nomination, and have been installed within the past two years. The submission guidelines, however, are more detailed. To be recognized as winners, companies must address three critical areas: excellence in *innovation*, excellence in *implementation* and excellence in strategic *impact* to the organization.

Innovation encompasses the innovative use of technology for strategic business objectives; the complexity of the underlying business process and IT architecture; the creative and successful deployment of advanced workflow and imaging concepts; and process innovations through business process reengineering and/or continuous improvements.

Hallmarks of a successful *implementation* include extensive user and line management involvement in the project while successfully managing change during the implementation process. Factors impacting the level of difficulty in achieving a successful implementation include the system complexity; integration with other advanced technologies; and the scope and scale of the implementation (e.g. size, geography, inter-company processes).

Impact is the bottom line, answering the question, "What benefits do BPM and workflow deliver to MY business? Why should I care?"

Examples of potential benefits include: productivity improvements; cost savings; increased revenues; product enhancements; improved customer service; improved quality; strategic impact to the organization's mission; enabling culture change; and—most importantly—changing the company's competitive position in the market. The visionary focus is now toward strategic benefits, in contrast to marginal cost savings and productivity enhancements.

While successes in these categories are prerequisites for winning a Global Excellence Award, it would reward all companies to focus on excelling in *innovation*, *implementation* and *impact* when installing BPM and workflow technologies. Companies must recognize that implementing innovative technology is useless unless the organization has a successful approach that delivers—and even surpasses—the anticipated benefits.

True visionaries are not content with merely achieving benefits; they are proactively driven to raise the standard for excellence in their industry—in essence, *moving the competitive goalposts*.

Section 1: Europe

BARCLAYS, FRANCE,   17

Finalist 2006, Europe; nominated by W4, France

This is not the first workflow application at Barclays France. Since 2004, the bank has been reshaping its loan allocation application for its entire sales network, as well as for its back-office staff. Today, this application, called "loan workflow", manages loan requests, from the opening of the file at the branch to the issue of the offer, and includes automatic routing between the various players in charge of decision-making. The computerisation of the file management process has helped to eliminate paperwork and also offers customer-relationship managers better traceability of operations. Every request may be identified at each step in the process and authorised users may access files and keep customers informed of the progress of their request. Furthermore, it offers management a clear and homogenous view of the operations carried out. Finally, automation helps to maintain a history of all the steps in the procedure, including the reasons for loan refusal. It is on the strength of this solution that Barclays France decided to extend the workflow process to exchange flows and steps in the account life.

MODELO CONTINENTE HIPERMERCADOS PORTUGAL, EUROPE   37

Gold Award 2006, Europe; nominated by
iProcess and Tlantic SI, Portugal

This paper presents the experience of the implementation of workflow technology in Modelo Continente Hipermercados (MCH), the largest retailer in Portugal. Started in the later 90's, motivated by the challenge to take advantage of the best technologies available, MCH´s experience involves more than 23 automated processes covering virtually all business areas. The company has adopted workflow technology in a corporate and strategic way, establishing a new management paradigm. The benefits obtained are way beyond the expected, resulting in expressive efficiency gains for the company. Workflow technology contributes to MCH's strategic goals, building concrete competitive advantages.

THE SPIDER BPM SOLUTION AT TELENOR, NORWAY   49

Silver Award 2006, Europe; nominated by
auSystems (now Cybercom), Sweden

This case study illustrates the approach taken by Telenor to establish a new network infrastructure rollout organization and a supporting IT system. The approach is based on the idea of a portfolio of standardized infrastructure products and automated business processes supporting all types of infrastructure networks (IP, mobile, fixed and cable TV) in a convergent fashion and also including integration of partners in the process to supply the civil engineering work necessary to build a telecommunications network.

The IT system is realized using an application framework for Business Process Management with support for reusable process components. This document will cover the business drivers and organizational challenges for initiating, executing and launching the project. The technical solution and project experiences will also be presented and finally share some thought of the future usage possibilities. The system is named "Spider" and was put in production in mid 2005 at Telenor, Norway.

Section 2: Middle East and Africa

PAYMENTCENTRIC, JORDAN   67

Gold Award 2006, Middle East and Africa;
nominated by Telaterra LLC, Jordan

The purpose of this document is to layout the overall success elements of implementing the Merchant Management Application at PaymentCentric (PC) located in Amman, Jordan.

In the following sections you will unfold the innovations accomplished on various levels, the challenges overcome, the competitive advantages the project has added to PC as the end user organization and the vendor's experience. Future plans to upgrade the project are numerous since PC are in continuous expansion throughout the region and beyond; changes depending on the business needs for each different region will be incorporated. Adding to that the increased fierce competition within the market forces PC to excel in and optimize its services.

TRACKER SYSTEM, SOUTH AFRICA   81

Silver Award 2006, Middle East and Africa;
nominated by TIBCO, South Africa

The TRACKER System was developed in the USA by LoJack where it has been operational since 1986. It was specifically developed to assist the police in curtailing vehicle theft. To date there are more than two million units fitted throughout 25 countries in the world including the USA, UK, Hong Kong, Russia, Korea, Mexico, Brazil, Argentina and Colombia. In South Africa, TRACKER has been operational since October 1996. The company enjoys strong financial backing and has invested millions in establishing its own network and providing the police with the technology to fight vehicle crime. Tracker also has its own recovery teams based throughout South Africa.

TRACKER is a jointly owned by FirstRand (32.5 percent), VenFin (31 percent), The Mineworkers Investment Company (26.5 percent) and a Private Investment Consortium (10 percent).

AMMAN CHAMBER OF INDUSTRY, JORDAN   93

Gold Award 2005, Middle East and Africa;
nominated by Telaterra Software LLC, Jordan

The purpose of this document is to layout the overall success elements of implementing the eChamber project at the Amman Chamber of Industry (ACI) located in Amman, Jordan.

In the following sections you will unfold the innovations accomplished on various levels, the challenges overcome, the competitive advantages eChamber has added to ACI as the end user organization and the vendor's experience. Future plans to upgrade the eChamber are various since major changes to the chambers regulations in Jordan are to be introduced in the near future, forcing ACI to become even more competitive.

Silver Award 2005, Middle East and Africa;
nominated by TIBCO Software, South Africa

A market leader in many areas, Nedbank understands that in a highly competitive market, it is essential to focus energy both on customer retention and on acquiring new business. But in a market characterised by product parity, it is service which sets one Bank ahead of its competitors, in the minds of both new and existing clients. When choosing between financial institutions, the deciding factor for clients is not the intrinsic product benefits alone, but the efficiency with which applications are dealt, the speed with which they are granted finance and the efficacy with which staff are able to act. In short, the Bank's ability to manage the credit process is paramount to its success, meaning that in addition to presenting clients with an outstanding range of products and services, it's imperative that those products and services be accessible in the most convenient and in the quickest way possible, if prospective clients are to be converted to actual clients. Motivated by the principles explained above, Nedbank Retail Banking Credit Assessment department - which grants credit to both personal clients and small business - implemented an innovative BPM solution (TIBCO Staffware Process Suite – TIBCO SPS), in conjunction with consultants from Idea Junction, to help it attain its goal of processing credit applications more effectively, thereby increasing business for the bank.

Section 3: North America

Gold Award 2006, North America; nominated by
TIBCO and Siemens, USA

The healthcare industry has been slower to adopt Business Process Management (BPM) than other industries. However, The Chester County Hospital (CCH) has distinguished itself by not only implementing workflow management technology in a healthcare setting, but by customizing and supplementing that technology with its own home-grown applications. The result is a workflow system that integrates clinical, operational and financial processes to support patient-centered care. In addition to meeting the primary goal of providing safer, more efficient care to patients, BPM has enabled CCH to improve working conditions for employees, dramatically increase productivity, achieve higher levels of cost optimization, and become a competitive force to reckon with in the local healthcare community.

Silver Award 2006, North America; nominated by
Lombardi, USA

Hasbro is the second largest toy maker in the world, with 2005 revenues of $3.1 billion. Hasbro brands and products include G.I. Joe, Transformers, Play Doh, Tonka, Nerf, Playskool, Milton Bradley, Parker Brothers and Magic, The Gathering, to name a few.

With such a diverse line of products, Hasbro relies in part on outsourced manufacturers for some of its toy and game production. Of course, managing a supply chain comprised of many diverse suppliers and numerous large orders a day required a team of people to manage vendor relationships and individual request for quotes (RFQs). Before Hasbro adopted a business process management (BPM) solution from Lombardi, almost all of the processes for determining an order and its supplier were paper based and manually intensive. Hasbro began its eConnect program with a clear mission statement:

Hasbro e-Connect delivers a collaborative e-business platform designed to connect business partners. It enables secure, self-service business transactions with business partners via the Internet, with seamless integration into our systems. The result is a streamlined business processes that save time and money.

NAS CHEETAH PROJECT, USA   133

Finalist 2006, North America; nominated by Green Square Inc, USA

Sometimes you need to run like a Cheetah. In 2003 Congress passed sweeping changes to the nation's Medicare program. Noridian Administrative Services, LLC. (NAS), one of the largest Medicare contractors in the country had only a short time to prepare for these changes. One of their key Medicare contracts was the first selected for competitive bid. NAS executives challenged a number of areas within the company to offer innovative approaches that could better position NAS to win and execute future contracts. Business Process Management (BPM) and workflow were identified as critical technologies that could enable the innovation. A team was quickly formed to dramatically expand the existing workflow environment. In the spring of 2005, the Cheetah project was established to take on this challenge. Cheetah's mission was to expand workflow/BPM into every operational team, a feat that would require the implementation of 20 workflows in 13 departments for over 350 users in just 20 weeks. This case study focuses on the possibility and reality of massively parallel workflow implementations.

GROUPO FINANCIERO UNO, USA   139

Gold Award 2005, North America; nominated by
Ultimus, USA

Grupo Financiero Uno, headquartered in Miami, FL, is the leading financial service provider for Central America, with locations in seven Latin American Countries, including Mexico, Guatemala, El Salvador, Honduras, Nicaragua, Costa Rica and Panama. The company realized that with its continued success and steady growth, it was about to face a major challenge with its credit card approval process. It was taking 15 days to process a single request due to the many manual administrative tasks and approval cycles. Additionally, the approval process was highly susceptible to human error, including applications sitting in in-boxes for extended periods of time and often getting lost in the shuffle. Today Grupo Financiero Uno is now able to process 470 percent more credit card applications and credit card disputes with the same number of staff per year while client growth continues to clip along at 30 percent year-over-year.

Section 4: Pacific Rim

ASIA VITAL COMPONENT CO. LTD., TAIWAN   149

*Silver Award 2006, Pacific Rim; nominated by
Flowring Co. Ltd., Taiwan*

The article describes the BPM planning and implementation of AVC (Asia Vital Component Co. Ltd.) using BPM suite. The processes covered in the article includes: PDP (product design procedures), QIT (quality issue tracking), MAS (material approval system) and OA (office automation). The target workflow applications integrate legacy ERP/PLM/PDM application system and work together to provide smooth and quick product design activities coordination among R&D teams (from AVC and business partners), as well as the compliance with environmental protection regulation (i.e. RoHS).

KTF CO. LTD., KOREA   163

*Gold Award 2006, Pacific Rim; nominated by
HandySoft*

The telecom market is faced with a sharp increase in the number of service subscribers to such a degree that demand exceeds supply. In the past, the industry's information systems consisted mostly of calculating a customer's telephone traffic and sending a bill. But severe competition and the growing availability of products in the market space has forced the providers to leverage state-of-the-art technologies to improve customer service and satisfaction. In order to remain competitive, information systems had to address this sharp change to customer focus.

MAX NEW YORK LIFE, INDIA   175

*Finalist 2006, Pacific Rim; nominated by
Newgen, India*

The company operates in a fiercely competitive and rapidly growing Life Insurance industry in India. The advent of several private insurance players—most of them collaborations involving international Insurance giants—has broken the monopoly of the monolithic state insurance agency—Life Insurance Corporation of India. With most of the new players in the Insurance market offering more or less the similar type of basic products, key differentiations can be achieved through automation of processes that enhance customer service. As a result, Max New York Life (MNYL) became one of the earliest insurance players in India to adopt Business Process Management (BPM). The phased implementation of BPM solution has enabled the company to rapidly expand its customer base, continuously enhance product offering, and stay well on course of realizing its vision of being the most admired life insurance company in India.

ACBEL POLYTECH, TAIWAN   183

*Silver Award 2005, Pacific Rim; nominated by
Flowring, Taiwan*

The intention of this case study is to present the business process modeling and implementation effort that was invested in the past years to deploy an integrated information systems at AcBel. The goal of the target information system is to enhance and extend the capability of AcBel legacy ERP system by introducing a full-function workflow system. From the functional view, it constructs a software system for AcBel's ISO quality assurance system, and provides computer-guided standard operating procedures for the product design and manufacture processes.

SAMSUNG HEAVY INDUSTRIES, KOREA   199

**Gold Award 2005, Pacific Rim; nominated by
HandySoft Global, Korea**

Due to a dramatic increase in the quantity of orders received since 2000, Samsung Heavy Industries (SHI) realized the necessity of implementing business process management (BPM) technology for more efficient management and monitoring of our international shipbuilding operations. Today, the implemented BPM system has improved and efficiently manages not only processes such as order placement management, contractor process management, production management, and quantity management related to shipbuilding outsourcing, but has also improved the business processes related to the materials supplied to subcontractors of the various shipyards. Using this system, the e-ouTEr Assembly Management System (e-TEAMS) processes were visualized. This visualization allowed us to optimize the fabrication management process, enable employees to manage and monitor the priority and status of various business processes in real-time, and provide an alarm notification function for process delays. e-TEAMS was the first instance of the application of BPM technology supporting business processes in the Korean shipbuilding industry.

Section 5: South America

ALLIANZ, VEHICLE INSURANCE OPERATION, COLOMBIA DIVISION   213

**Gold Award 2006, South America; nominated by
Bizagi, Colombia**

This document, describes the successful implementation of the Allianz Colombia BPM model on the vehicle insurance division "The Power on Your Side". Today, the system has literally given the power to third parties involved on the business; engaging agents, brokers, CNCs, call centers, work shops, lawyers and the back office in more than 1.500 activities starting from the underwriting of the policy until the disbursement of a claim. This has increased the integration, visibility, productivity and profitability of the whole operation of the auto-insurance Allianz Colombia division.

METROVÍAS, ARGENTINA   221

**Finalist 2006, South America; nominated by
PECTRA Technology, Inc., Brazil**

METROVÍAS is a company that operates a major public transportation net in Buenos Aires city, Argentina. The net comprises five subway lines, two streetcar branches and one railroad branch. Nowadays, METROVÍAS has 3,000 employees working on 70Kms of rails through 108 stations and yearly carries 300 millions passengers in its 692 cars.

METROVÍAS started operating on January 1st, 1994 facing the challenge of changing a traditionally deficit activity into an efficient and profitable business. By applying modern and competitive entrepreneurial criteria, accordant to the theories of contemporary management, METROVÍAS strives to turn the service into a customer-oriented one.

GRUPO PÃO DE AÇÚCAR   233

Silver Award 2006, South America; nominated by iProcess, Brazil

This paper describes the experience of the implementation of workflow technology in Grupo Pão de Açúcar(GPA), the largest retail group in Brazil. Motivated by the necessity of adjustment to the Sarbanes-Oxley act, and of acceleration of critical processes execution, GPA began the usage of workflow technology. There are three developed workflow systems: the first, Investment Approval Workflow, being deployed in May, 2005. The benefits of workflow technology were quickly perceived, with the reduction of 80 percent of average process time and great increase of control effectiveness. For this reason, GPA is not only expanding the use of workflow technology, but also connecting IT and process disciplines, building a solid path into BPM direction.

LA VOZ DEL INTERIOR, ARGENTINA   245

Gold Award 2005, South America; nominated by PECTRA Argentina, SA.

La Voz del Interior is the most prestigious regional newspaper in the Argentine Republic. It is currently owned by the Grupo Clarín, the main mass media holding in Argentina, and one of the most important mass media organizations in the Spanish-speaking world. With a history spanning more than 100 years, La Voz del Interior tops the list of the daily newspapers that are edited in the interior of the country, and is ranked third in Argentina, vis-a-vis advertising revenues. Its average daily circulation is 60.000 copies (Mondays to Saturdays) and 85.000 copies on Sundays. Due to the successful implementation of the solution, which showed excellent results, the company has optimized the distribution of additional material and achieved significant cost-reductions and tighter control in the traceability of its processes.

UNIVERSIDADE DE SANTA CRUZ DO SUL, BRAZIL   255

Gold Award 2005, South America; nominated by Cryo Technologies, Brazil

The University of Santa Cruz do Sul—UNISC, based on the commitment to keep its characteristics of a Community University - institution of not-state public nature – expressed by administrative and financial transparency, democratic management and its insertion in community's life, searched through the use of Workflow technology to afford a tool to its managers that guarantee the essential characteristics so that the information becomes a strategic resource. This technology allowed the accompaniment and the management of the work flows and the access to information on a safe, online and integrated form, reflecting transparency and agility in processes and also reduction of people and paper's traffic.

Section 1

Europe

Barclays France

Portail des Opérations Project

Finalist 2006, Europe; nominated by W4, France

EXECUTIVE SUMMARY

This is not the first workflow application at Barclays France. Since 2004, the bank has been reshaping its loan allocation application for its entire sales network, as well as for its back-office staff. Today, this application, called "loan workflow", manages loan requests, from the opening of the file at the branch to the issue of the offer, and includes automatic routing between the various players in charge of decision-making. The computerisation of the file management process has helped to eliminate paperwork and also offers customer relationship managers better traceability of operations. Every request may be identified at each step in the process and authorised users may access files and keep customers informed of the progress of their request. Furthermore, it offers management a clear and homogenous view of the operations carried out. Finally, automation helps to maintain a history of all the steps in the procedure, including the reasons for loan refusal. It is on the strength of this solution that Barclays France decided to extend the workflow process to exchange flows and steps in the account life.

OVERVIEW

Allowing customer relationship managers to devote themselves to sales activities, improving speed and traceability of operations and reducing manual back-office

(BO) tasks, are some of the bank's objectives for initiating paperless processes and the automation of exchange flows between branches and the back-office. It is an ambitious project which started in December 2005 and the first step has already been completed. The objective was to identify all the types of instructions for operations and to create forms accessible on the bank's Intranet, available to all branch staff on their work terminals. Until then, exchanges between branches and head office were conducted through forms sent by fax, e-mail and post after completion of the approval and signature chain. In order to ensure that all those concerned are involved, a project group, comprising staff members from all operations in the computing department, branches and organisation, set up and controlled the management of this project.

The first step consisted of describing and formalising procedures, followed by the creation of forms. The second included the setting up of a paper process automation platform, for which the bank chose the W4 workflow software. The platform manages forms, procedures and the follow-up actions required for processing the request from start to finish, in particular, according to the roles and functions of users. For this, the existing corporate staff directory was integrated into the system. One of the major steps was successfully integrating the application into the databases, in order that the information is well presented to users.

From March 2006, 11 forms were available on-line: domestic payment requests, user code changes, applications for reversals of bank charges or account management fees, etc. By mid-July 2006, 33 forms were available. These included new operations, such as requests for money transfers, international payments and securities trading. "At present, we process 500 requests per day and we have an application which is able to manage several thousand daily operations", explains Hubert Locqueville, Barclays France' Chief Operations Officer.

Once the form has been entered by the branch staff, if he or she is entitled to sign it, the application is sent directly to the back-office. If the approval of another person is required, the form is transferred automatically to that person's task in-tray. "Some applications require the involvement of several signatories", explains Hubert Locqueville. Once processed, the form is routed automatically to the BO. The automation of the entire chain allows users to follow the progress of the application on their screens in real time. "This process allows us to eliminate paperwork and also offers a complete audit trail for the entire chain", explains Hubert Locqueville. Furthermore, the W4 application is connected to central systems, which makes it possible to keep a record of the history of all the customers' operations. If the BO refuses the operation, the information is sent to the customer relationship manager's in-tray and he or she closes the task, keeping a note of the customers' history.

BACKGROUND INFORMATION

Company

With a presence in France since 1917, Barclays France is a multi-specialist bank with a business portfolio covering affluent and private banking, commercial banking operations, its mortgage specialist Barclays *Financement Immobilier*, and the asset and investment management company, Barclays Asset Managers. Barclays France manages more than €12 billion of assets for 150,000 customers and is developing a complete offering of products and services for an affluent, wealthy and international clientele, as well as for private investors, institutional organisations and SME.

People

Today, Barclays France has a network of 54 branches and 15 Barclays Finance offices, representing a total of almost 500 customer advisors.

Furthermore, Barclays Contact, the call center (middle-office) comprising 20 people, is responsible for gathering and launching customer requests.

Existing applications

The main core business applications rely on an IBM MVS Mainframe based in the UK. It hosts applications for French, Spanish and Portuguese subsidiaries. At the same site, an AS/400 specialises in the management of loans and mortgages.

Alongside this production environment, a front-office management tool was developed (PowerBuilder/Oracle): "*Branch Platform*". It records all customer data and references information gathered at different meetings with the financial advisor, customer profiles (assets outside of the bank) and even the notion of profitability or customer segmentation. The data from the database is used by other applications, in particular, the different processes in place at Barclays France.

THE KEY BUSINESS MOTIVATIONS BEHIND THE PROJECT

The automation of information exchange flows between branches and the back-office are part of a paperless project for exchanging instructions on internal operations. By equipping itself with an application which meets the needs of its profession, Barclays France is ensuring that it can secure flows (less paper and data entry errors) and coordinate operations from the loan chain to the management of the account life.

The project group needed a tool which could merge progressively with the overall Intranet groupware and the extranet architecture, to meet the following objectives:

- Improve reliability, scalability and normalisation of the processes
- Promote better collaboration and consistency between the various departments and be able to manage a complex organisation
- Replace paper forms
- Facilitate use and ease of learning
- Maximise monitoring of processes and deadlines
- Optimise the cost of operations, deployment and administration

In order to strengthen its presence on the market and, through improving customer satisfaction, Barclays needed to remain loyal to its values, be flexible and succeed in modernisation its processes. In this respect, the following lines of development were seen as a priority:

- modernise the services provided and anticipate customers' needs
- improve service quality and reliability
- be a factor in customer satisfaction
- increase performance and enhance competitiveness

Financial issues

With this new strategic direction, Barclays France focused on driving down costs to achieve tangible productivity savings. To improve the speed of response and, therefore, competitiveness, Barclays France constantly needed to adapt processes to the changing environment.

Flexibility reflects directly on the services offered. By optimising its front-office banking processes, time to market has been reduced significantly. Delays have been eliminated. The period required for answering customers has also been reduced and guaranteed.

Customer services also need to be speeded up and customised in order to increase customer loyalty. This is vital today because of the fierce competition which exists as a result of new regulations and the Internet. Customisation also develops cross sales.

Within this strategy, Barclays France needed to:
- eliminate organisational malfunctions, in order to solve problems related to the quantity and geographical distribution of the different units and players
- eliminate document exchanges between the various entities (branches, back-office and head-office)
- reduce data entry operations and the risk of error, by avoiding the loss of tasks and preventing time wasting and a lack of information
- reduce the amount of paper

Strategic issues

The acquisition of ING Ferri and ING Private Banking in July 2005 and the wish to position itself among the leading banks in its segments in France led Barclays to rethink its information system and its services across its banking, investment banking and asset management activities. Redesigning services to anticipate the growth in activity became a priority. In order to increase competitiveness and create value, Barclays France had to address two main issues: on the one hand, their expertise, which had to be formalised in a process description and, on the other hand, the streamlining of their processes.

Formalization of processes

By memorising and formalising process definitions in a documented business repository and updating them quickly and methodically, the company was able to clarify and identify its intellectual capital, which, could therefore be shared and kept independent. Consequently, it can be adapted constantly to meet market changes. Increased know-how and optimal use of the information system were reflected in the quality of services.

The company was then able to differentiate itself by offering better service quality or by extending its services. By improving customer satisfaction, the company is able to develop customer loyalty, strengthen its image and win market share.

Additionally, employees were more efficient, satisfied and customer-focused, allowing them to concentrate on their core business. This new workflow application was a key element in the company's overall data history. All current or past customer applications are stored in a central database and may be accessed quickly by every employee involved.

Streamlining of processes

In order to solve the problem caused by the quantity and geographical distribution of branches, Barclays France needed to improve and streamline process management to create one single centre. With this new strategic organisation, the ambition was to eliminate any double entries and contribute to better cohesion and coordination between all employees, whether they are working in front-office or back-office functions.

THE KEY INNOVATION

Barclays France's key innovation was to automate all exchanges between back and front offices, creating a link between 54 branches and the central site. Another innovation was in the scope of processes covered: more than 30 processes, previously managed by paper-based procedures, have been automated. Users now manage these through a "to-do" list, which has been tailored to meet their needs and which shows immediate priority tasks.

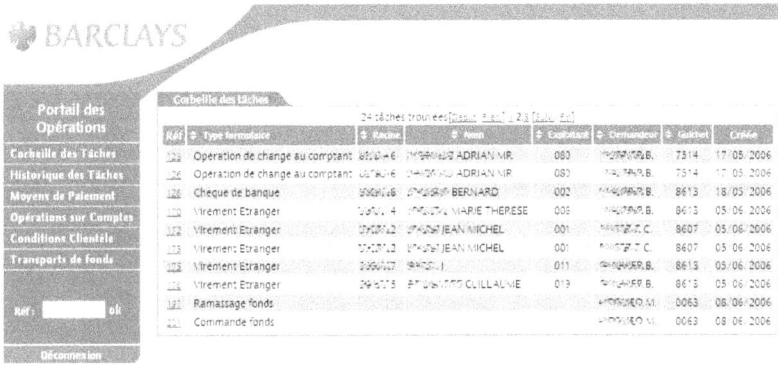

Figure 1: The user's To-do list in the application

BUSINESS

A new relationship has been established between front and back offices, offering better service to the final customer, a more comfortable user interface and a reduction in delays when moving information from one site to another. The result is improved response time for any incoming request. Now, all customer requests are managed by electronic forms transferred via a workflow solution, thus removing the need for paper, fax or e-mail.

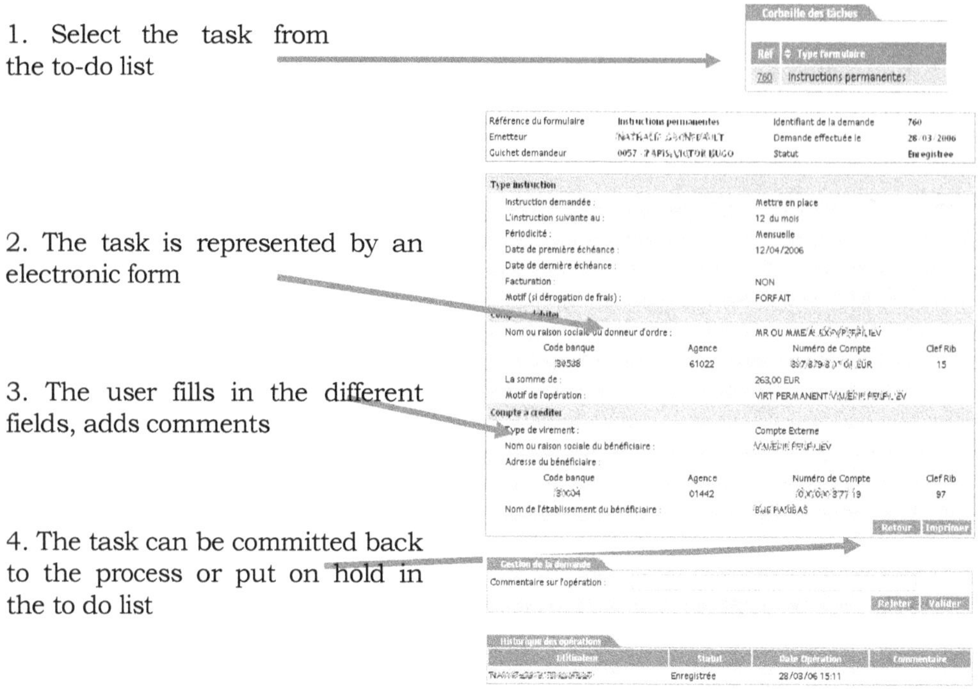

1. Select the task from the to-do list

2. The task is represented by an electronic form

3. The user fills in the different fields, adds comments

4. The task can be committed back to the process or put on hold in the to do list

Figure 2: Application global kinematics

SEVERAL BUSINESS PROCESSES, ONE WORKFLOW PROCEDURE AND MULTIPLE FORMS

During the specification period, each form and its process have been analyzed separately. All of them have been designed graphically, as a form/process pair.

Here are three examples of the result of the specification phases:

Certified Cheque

The process

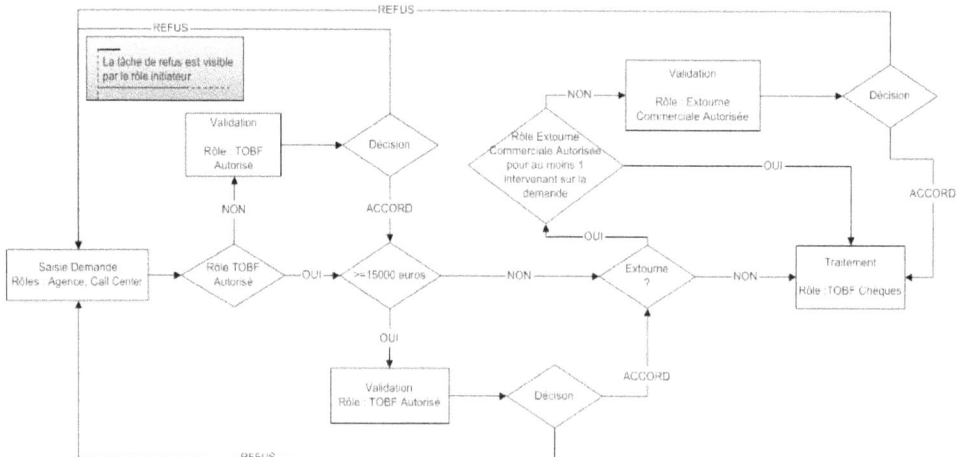

Figure 3: The certified cheque process

The related form

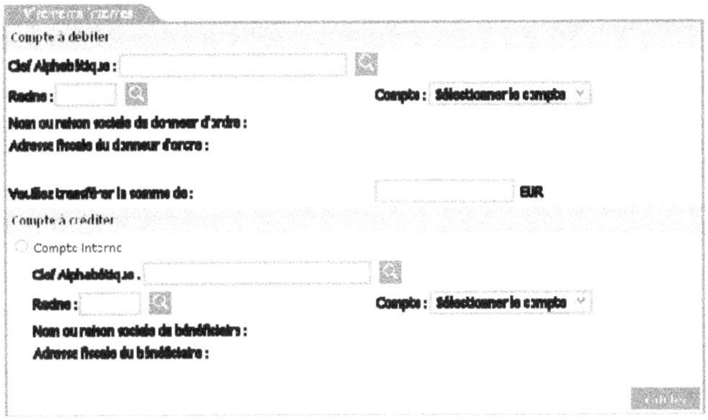

Compte à debiter

Clef Alphabétique :

Racine : Compte : Sélectionner le compte

Nom ou raison sociale du donneur d'ordre :

Adresse fiscale du donneur d'ordre :

Veuillez transférer la somme de : EUR

Compte à créditer

Compte Interne

Clef Alphabétique :

Racine : Compte : Sélectionner le compte

Nom ou raison sociale du bénéficiaire :

Adresse fiscale du bénéficiaire :

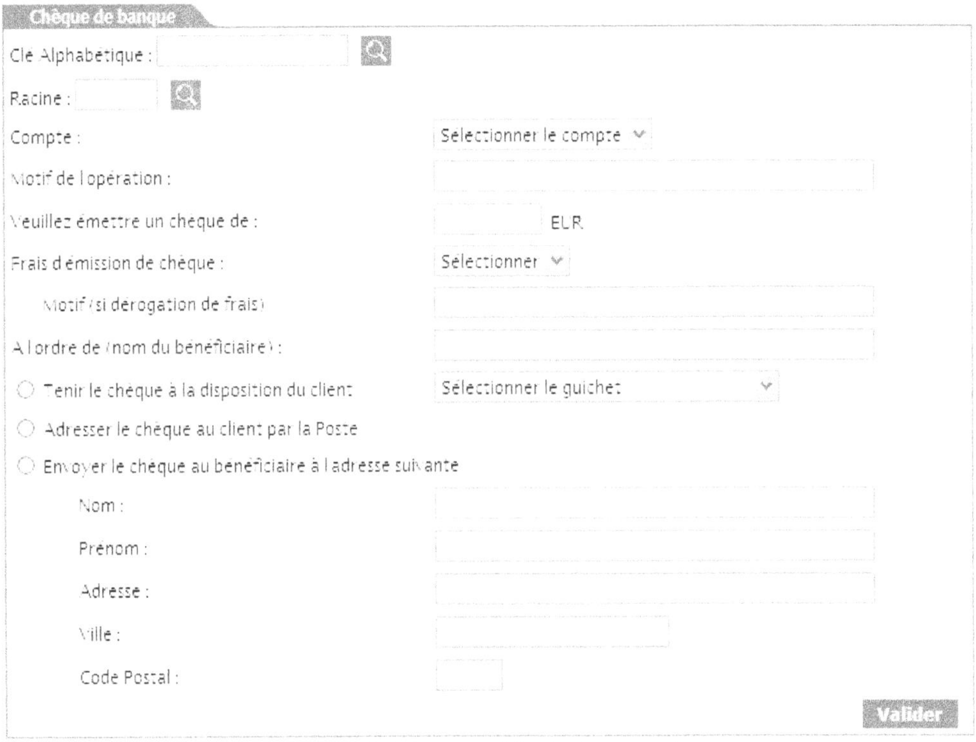

Chèque de banque

Clé Alphabétique :

Racine :

Compte : Sélectionner le compte

Motif de l'opération :

Veuillez émettre un chèque de : EUR

Frais d'émission de chèque : Sélectionner

Motif (si dérogation de frais)

A l'ordre de (nom du bénéficiaire) :

Tenir le chèque à la disposition du client — Sélectionner le guichet

Adresser le chèque au client par la Poste

Envoyer le chèque au bénéficiaire à l'adresse suivante

Nom :

Prénom :

Adresse :

Ville :

Code Postal :

Valider

Figure 4: The certified cheque form

Internal transfer

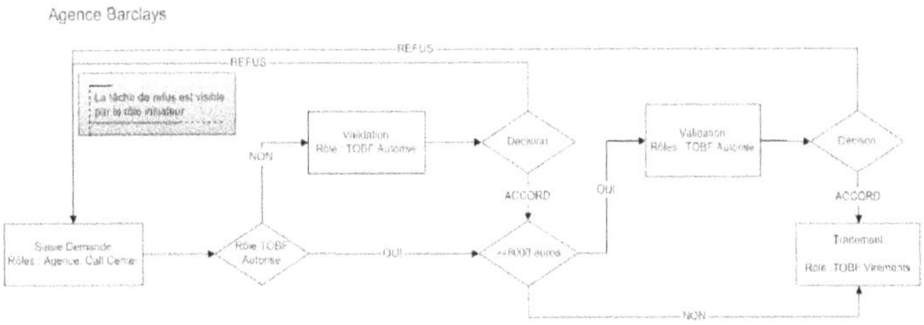

Figure 5: Internal transfer process and related form

Account Root attachment

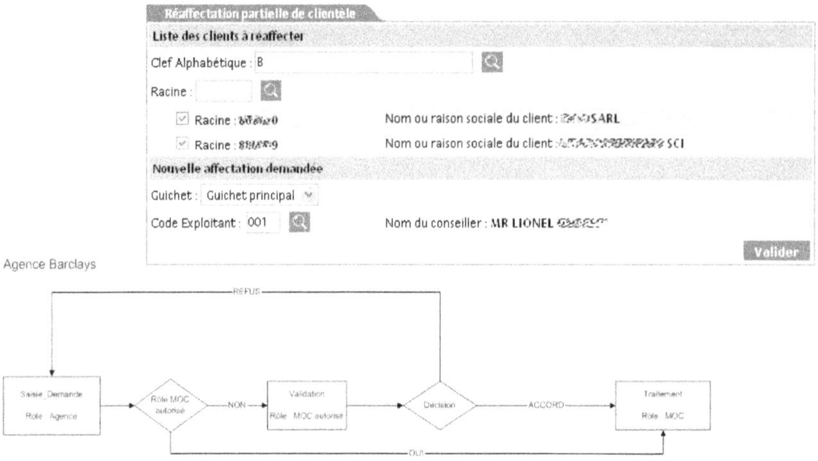

Figure 6: Account Root attachment process and related form

The global workflow process

Even if all the processes look very different, they are all based on the same work-flow procedure definition at the server level. The rules have been externalized, as well as the role definition management.

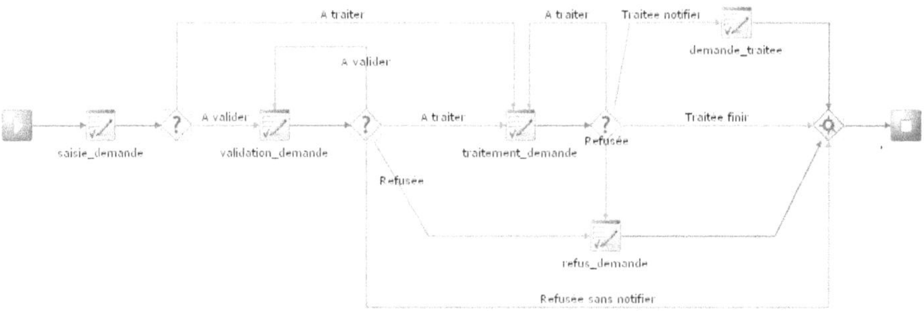

Figure 7: The global workflow procedure

In this environment, creating and deploying a new form in the organization takes a little time, about 1 day. This factor of success has been a key motivation for the definition of the development framework now in place.

Roles management

As a complement to the workflow definition, a tailored interface has been de-signed to manage the roles, in accordance to the workflow process. The applica-tion administrators are allowed to modify the roles assignments, in addition to the information coming from the LDAP directory.

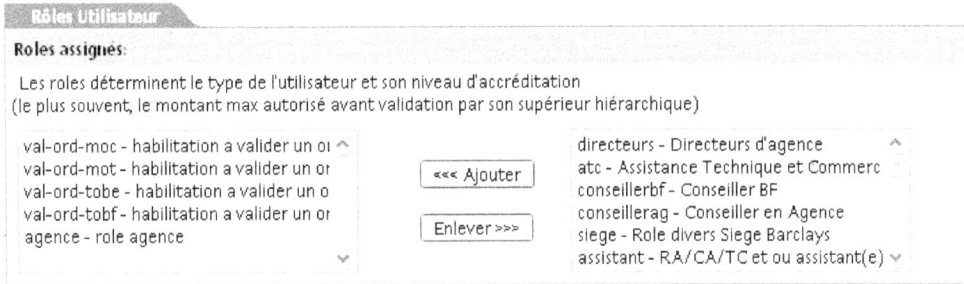

Rôles Utilisateur

Roles assignés:

Les roles déterminent le type de l'utilisateur et son niveau d'accréditation
(le plus souvent, le montant max autorisé avant validation par son supérieur hiérarchique)

val-ord-moc - habilitation a valider un or	directeurs - Directeurs d'agence
val-ord-mot - habilitation a valider un or	atc - Assistance Technique et Commerc
val-ord-tobe - habilitation a valider un o	conseillerbf - Conseiller BF
val-ord-tobf - habilitation a valider un or	conseillerag - Conseiller en Agence
agence - role agence	siege - Role divers Siege Barclays
	assistant - RA/CA/TC et ou assistant(e)

`<<< Ajouter`   `Enlever >>>`

Figure 8: Role administration user interface

Technology – The PoPs application.

The implementation solution relies on the use of user terminals' Web navigators. The PoPs application is based entirely on W4 Suite technology, which combines a workflow engine and a presentation layer which uses Web technology. These elements permit the integration of new applications, based on underlying processes, into an existing portal.

The operations management portal (POPS) set up is an unchanging space which includes the banner showing Barclays colours and a side menu, accessible at all times. This is designed around the main points of access:

- The task in-tray, which leads to the list of tasks to be dealt with by the user
- The task history, for searching for files in progress
- Request entry: sorted by type, it allows the customer relations manager or any other operator to enter the data from the customer's initial request form
- Search for and follow-up of a request: in progress or closed requests are accessible via a search interface which presents the selected request's complete history

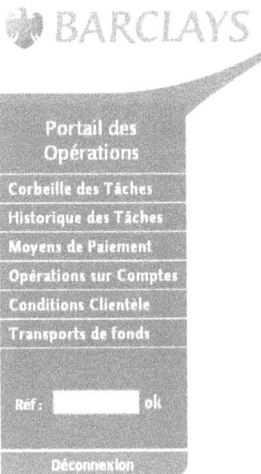

Figure 9: PoPs main menu

Requests in-tray

Once the user has been authenticated, he or she is directed to the requests in-tray. This screen offers access to the list of tasks allocated to the user (validation, processing).

The list of requests displayed depends on the role and the authorisations granted to the user.

- The authorisations are the same as those defined in "Branch-Platform".
- The roles are the same as those defined in the corporate directory application.

The tasks are presented in ascending order (date and priority). Sorting is possible for each field in the list.

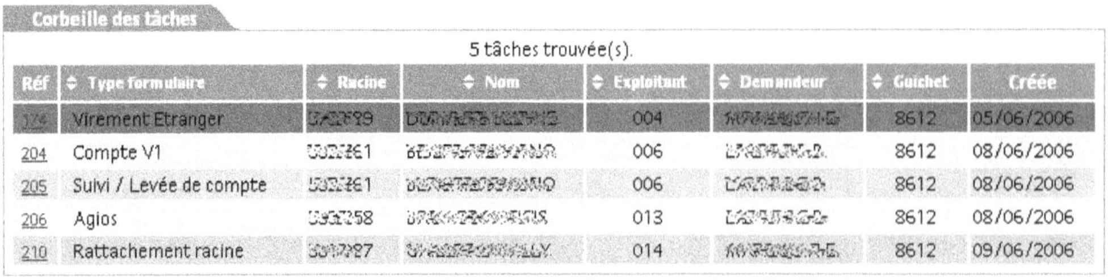

Réf	⬍ Type formulaire	⬍ Racine	⬍ Nom	⬍ Exploitant	⬍ Demandeur	⬍ Guichet	⬍ Créée
174	Virement Etranger	░▓░▓89	░▓░▓░▓░	004	░▓░▓░▓░	8612	05/06/2006
204	Compte V1	░░░261	░▓░▓░▓░	006	░▓░▓░	8612	08/06/2006
205	Suivi / Levée de compte	░░░261	░▓░▓░▓░	006	░▓░▓░	8612	08/06/2006
206	Agios	░░░258	░▓░▓░▓░	013	░▓░▓░	8612	08/06/2006
210	Rattachement racine	░░░787	░▓░▓░▓░	014	░▓░▓░	8612	09/06/2006

Corbeille des tâches — 5 tâches trouvée(s).

Figure 10: The colored in tray (to-do list)

A link to the form allows the user to access the application directly. Once the application is displayed, the user may validate (process), or refuse the request. After each action, the form status is updated automatically. The date of the most recent update and the operator's surname and first name are also recorded.

Référence du formulaire	Chéquiers. RIB	Identifiant de la demande	12
Emetteur	IULIANA ░▓░▓░	Demande effectuée le	02/03/2006
Guichet demandeur	0057 - ░▓░▓░▓░	Statut	Rejetée

Compte :	░▓░▓░▓░ EUR
Guichet :	0057 - ░▓░▓░▓░
Nom du Client :	MADAME PAULETTE ░▓░▓
Veuillez préparer :	
1 Carnet(s) de chèques en EUR	F25 - PORTEFEUILLE
Mise à disposition :	
Tenir le chéquier à la disposition du client au guichet :	0057 - ░▓░▓░▓░

Retour Imprimer

Gestion de la demande

Commentaire sur l'opération :

Clôturer

Historique des opérations

Utilisateur	Statut	Date Opération	Commentaire
Colette ░▓░▓	Rejetée	02/03/06 16:46	Veuillez nous confirmer accord renouvellement automatique
JULIANA ░▓░▓	Enregistrée	02/03/06 16:41	

Figure 11: Validation form

Requests history

The user may consult the requests history at any time. This screen offers access to the list of the most recent requests, as well as details on the status and date of the most recent modifications.

The list of requests displayed depends on the user's authorisations. Thus, a branch advisor will only have access to requests entered by his or her branch, whereas central services will be able to view all branches' requests. Authorisations for the history screen are the same as for those defined in the "Branch-Platform".

By default, only requests dating from the past 30 days will be presented. Sorting is possible for each field in the list.

Recherche par date de création

Depuis le :	Jusqu'au :	
01 03 2006 (jj mm aaaa)	02 03 2006 (jj mm aaaa)	Valider

Historique des demandes

24 demandes trouvées [Début Préc.] 1 2 [Suiv. Fin]

Réf	⇕ Type formulaire	⇕ Racine	⇕ Demandeur	⇕ Guichet	⇕ Statut	Créée	Modifiée
506	Rattachement racine		ELISABETH BEMI	0066	Traitée	01/03/06	01/03/06
505	Rattachement racine		ELISABETH BEMI	0066	Clôturée	01 03 06	01 03 06
504	Rattachement racine		ELISABETH BEMI	0057	Clôturée	01/03/06	01/03/06
503	Rattachement racine		RAVISHANKER		Traitée	01 03 06	01 03 06
502	Rattachement racine		CHRISTIAN BARGGEMI		Traitée	01/03/06	01/03/06
501	Rattachement racine		CHRISTIAN		Clôturée	01 03 06	01 03 06
500	Rattachement racine		JULIANA	0057	Clôturée	01/03/06	01/03/06
499	Rattachement racine		JULIANA	0057	Traitée	01 03 06	01 03 06
498	Rattachement racine		JULIANA	0057	Traitée	01/03/06	01/03/06
497	Rattachement racine		JEAN PIERRE	0057	Traitée	01 03 06	01 03 06
496	Rattachement racine		JEAN PIERRE	0057	Clôturée	01/03/06	01/03/06
495	Intervention compte		ELISABETH BEMI	0057	Traitée	01 03 06	01 03 06
494	Intervention compte		ELISABETH BEMI	0066	Clôturée	01/03/06	01/03/06
493	Intervention compte		ELISABETH LEMI	0066	Traitée	01 03 06	01 03 06
492	Intervention compte		RAVISHANKER	2418	Traitée	01/03/06	01/03/06

Figure 12: Request search result

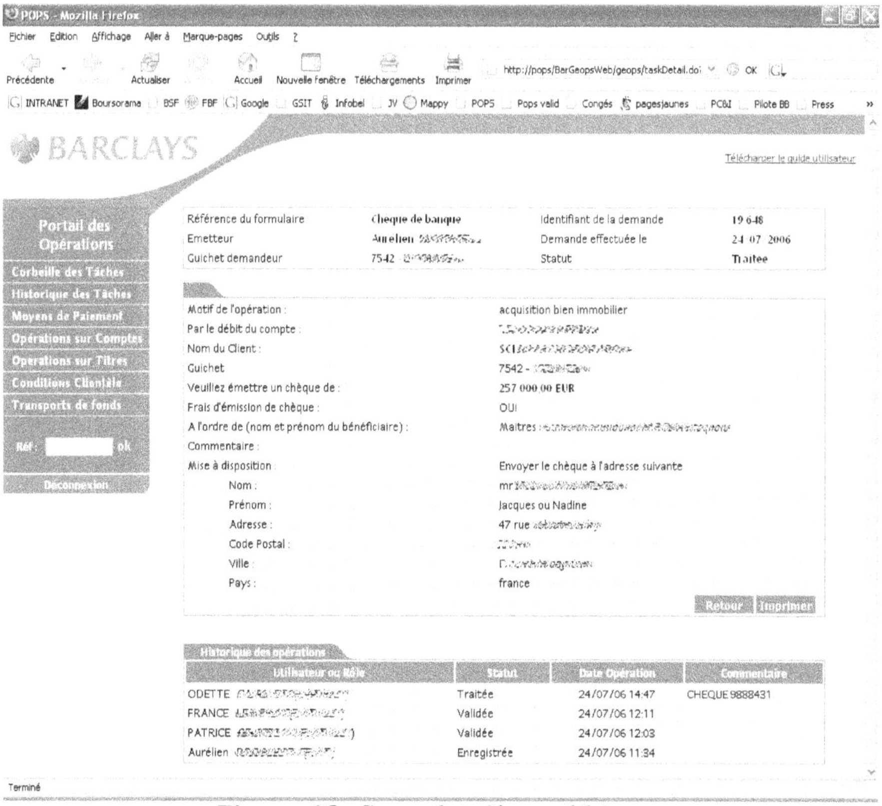

Figure 13: Case details and history

Entering an application

Screen kinematics, such as those described below, explains a user's way of working.

Selection of the request form by type.

The Operation portal offers users a browsing menu with categories and content adapted to the agent's roles. Request forms are grouped together by type (account operation, payment method, etc.) and can be accessed by a simple search.

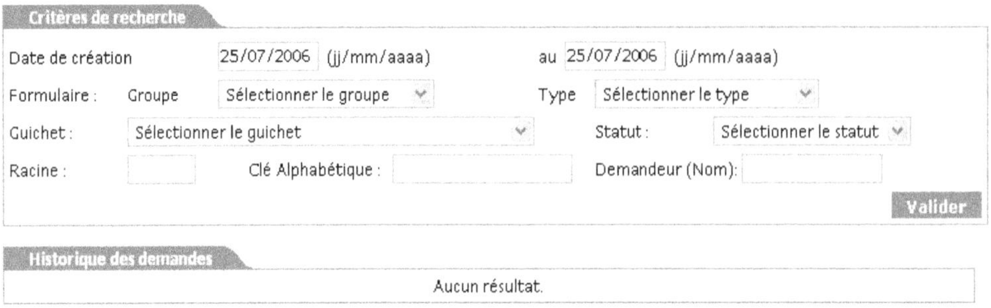

Figure 14: Form search screen

Entering a root or an alphabetic key (if applicable)

Once the request form has been selected, a data entry screen is offered to the user. In general, the first step involves searching for the account to attach to the operation. An engine allows users to search a list of accounts on the basis of a root or an alphabetical key. Once the request form has been selected, a data entry screen is offered to the user.

Figure 15: Customer information search criteria

Search for authorised roots and feeding an account list

The portal uses the "*Branch-Platform*" repository. The search rules which apply to the operations portal are the same as those implemented in *Branch*. Movement of the magnifying glass offers access to the root selection screen (primary sorting by alphabetical key). Sorting by root, Title and counter columns are also available.

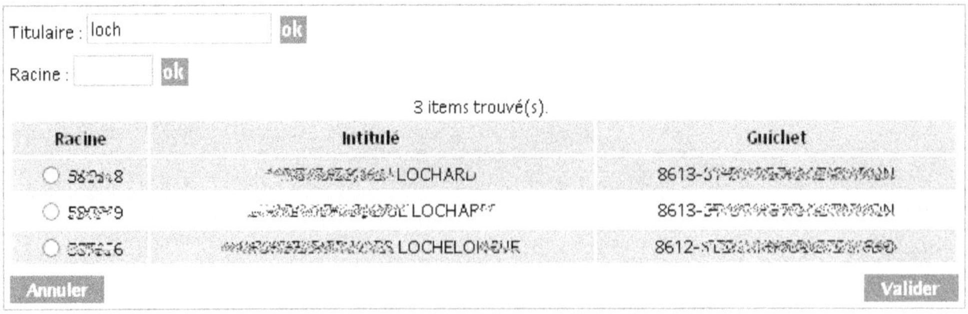

Figure 17: Root account search screen

The selection of a root permits loading of all the customer's information (accounts, list of bank cards, etc.).

Selection of an account and automatic entry of the account's characteristics

Accounts are presented in ascending numerical order. When an account is selected, some of the form's fields are completed automatically with data such as bank code, sorting code, etc. passed on automatically by the "Branch-Platform" repository.

If there is only one account, it will be selected by default.

Figure 17: account selection upon the root number

Checking the form's mandatory fields

To be registered, the user must complete all or part of the form's fields. A data entry check is carried out to validate the form. Checks are conducted to ensure the presence of a data entry (numerical or alphanumerical).

Figure 18: Typical entry form (Certified cheque)

Confirmation of the operation request

Once the data entry check has been completed, a confirmation screen provides details of the request. At the top of the form, a box contains information about the user (surname, first name, counter, applicant).

- The confirm button registers the application.
- The modify button sends the user to the data entry form.
- The cancel button sends the user to the request in-tray

| Emetteur : | JEAN PIERRE ~~~~ |
| Cuichet demandeur | PARIS-~~~~ |

Chèque de banque

Motif de l opération :	Achat Vehicule
Par le débit du compte :	~~~~
Cuichet :	0057 - ~~~~
Veuillez émettre un chèque de :	15 000,00 EUR
Frais d émission de chèque :	OUI
A l ordre de (nom du bénéficiaire) :	Carage Renault
Mise à disposition :	Tenir le chèque à la disposition du client au guichet : 0063 - ~~~~

Modifier | Annuler | Confirmer

Figure 19: Operation confirmation screen

Registering the request

When the confirm button is clicked the request is registered and a unique username is allocated to the request. Depending on the user's authorisations and the type of form, this is sent to the branch manager for validation, or transferred directly to central services for processing.

Following an application

The operator may find out about the state of his or her request at any time. The request is accessible from the task history or, directly, via the search engine by entering the username. At the bottom of the screen, a history table shows the validation steps and the remarks of each person involved.

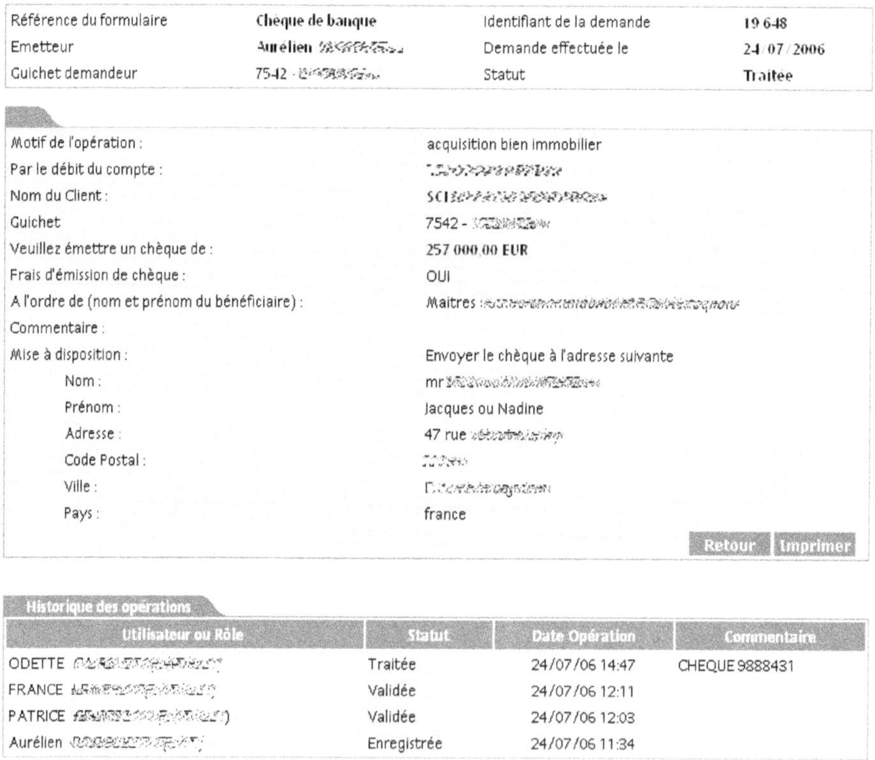

Référence du formulaire	Chèque de banque	Identifiant de la demande	19 648
Emetteur	Aurélien ~~~~	Demande effectuée le	24/07/2006
Guichet demandeur	7542 - ~~~~	Statut	Traitée

Motif de l'opération :	acquisition bien immobilier
Par le débit du compte :	~~~~
Nom du Client :	SCI~~~~
Guichet :	7542 - ~~~~
Veuillez émettre un chèque de :	257 000,00 EUR
Frais d'émission de chèque :	OUI
A l'ordre de (nom et prénom du bénéficiaire) :	Maitres ~~~~
Commentaire :	
Mise à disposition :	Envoyer le chèque à l'adresse suivante
Nom :	mr ~~~~
Prénom :	Jacques ou Nadine
Adresse :	47 rue ~~~~
Code Postal :	~~~~
Ville :	~~~~
Pays :	france

Retour | Imprimer

Historique des opérations

Utilisateur ou Rôle	Statut	Date Opération	Commentaire
ODETTE ~~~~	Traitée	24/07/06 14:47	CHEQUE 9888431
FRANCE ~~~~	Validée	24/07/06 12:11	
PATRICE ~~~~	Validée	24/07/06 12:03	
Aurélien ~~~~	Enregistrée	24/07/06 11:34	

Figure 20: Case details and history screen

THE IMPACT ON USERS OF THE SYSTEM

"For sales network staff, this is a modern tool which allows them to save time and, also, to access the operations' history and details of the people in charge of validation and processing. Thus, they will be able to improve coordination of their work and serve customers better on a daily basis", explains Hubert Locqueville.

Also, the advantages are felt in back-office functions: at last, Back-Office staff see their work being recognised thanks to the fact that the operator's name is visible at each step in the processing of operations. "He or she is also relieved of some manual tasks, such as deciphering written documents and checking for signatures, in order to be able to concentrate on other activities with higher added value", he adds, underlining that the redesign of the process has permitted the development of a closer relationship between branches and head office.

Historique des opérations			
Utilisateur ou Rôle	Statut	Date Opération	Commentaire
ODETTE	Traitée	24/07/06 14:47	CHEQUE 9888431
FRANCE	Validée	24/07/06 12:11	
PATRICE	Validée	24/07/06 12:03	
Aurélien	Enregistrée	24/07/06 11:34	

Figure 21: Case history with all participant names (front and back office)

Ease of learning

In order to ensure the involvement of its 54 branches and BO users of the system, Barclays France set up a special training programme, including a user's handbook and Intranet access to the workflow tool. "A half hour telephone conference with a project team member was organised for each branch", explains Hubert Locqueville. Back-offices were not forgotten and they received personalised training sessions.

Furthermore, the online user manual summarises all the necessary information in just fifty pages in order to be easily accessible to all.

THE NEW SYSTEM CONFIGURATION

The global environment is based on an IBM MVS 3090+ mainframe which hosts 80% of banking professions' key application software for Portugal, France and Spain. It is based in the UK and uses an Adabas database (Software AG); The processes which must interact with this application software may be carried out via middleware, in this case EntireX from Software AG. It is the same as with the AS/400 which manages mortgages and loans. The "Branch Platform" application software uses an Oracle platform. This is accessed by standard JDBC type layers from the application software, in particular, through forms managed by W4.

The W4 Suite program is deployed in an IBM AIX environment, Oracle database and IBM Web Websphere. The 1,500 users of the PoPs application software are distributed automatically between two servers in complete redundancy, hosted on two different sites, in accordance with computer safety rules defined by the bank. In the event of a problem on one of the servers, users are redirected automatically to the other server, thus enabling the maintaining of all the application's functions.

THE BIGGEST HURDLES OVERCOME

In order to ensure that all professions are involved, a project group, comprising staff members from all operations in the computing department, branches and organisation, set up and controlled the management of the project. The first step consisted of describing and formalising procedures, followed by the creation of forms. The second included the setting up of a paper process automation platform, for which the bank chose the W4 workflow program. The platform manages forms, procedures and the follow-up of actions required for processing the request from start to finish, in particular, according to the roles and functions of users.

The project itself has been driven in an iterative way: rather than writing detailed specifications, Barclays France chose to start from a general specifications document, defining needs and the main user forms, and to rely on the iterative application-generating capacity of the chosen tool, W4 Suite. The processes have been finely tuned directly with business user representatives and each process has been validated within a short time span.

Management

The project was launched under the initiative of the operations division, of which Hubert Locqueville is the Director. The main difficulty encountered at this level has been the availability of people in the branches, who did not initially necessarily accept the project. But, over time and, in particular, during the prototype phases, the project was adopted very quickly. At the end of July 2006, no fewer than 20,000 applications were processed.

Business

On this point, given the method used, which is based on interactivity in defining processes and associated forms, there have been no noticeable difficulties. On-lining of forms has meant that many of them have been updated: with the operations division being directly involved, forms which were used the least have been done away with and those which posed problems have been modified. This has led to greater efficiency in the solution set up, without the need for a re-

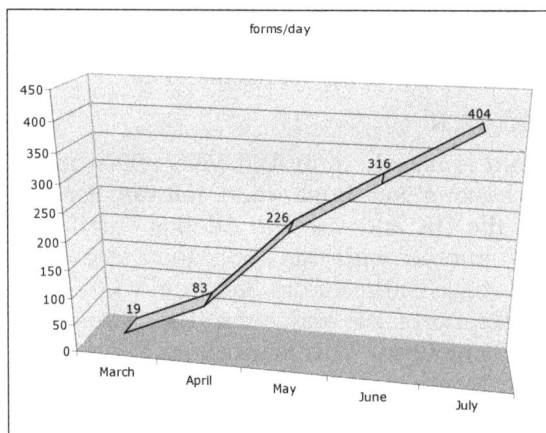

Figure 22: Forms usage evolution

engineering phase which might have been long and fastidious. The important point is the guarantee given to customers that requests are processed and replied to more quickly.

Technology

This new application was carried out in a known technological environment. From this point of view, the specific points to implement had been defined clearly.

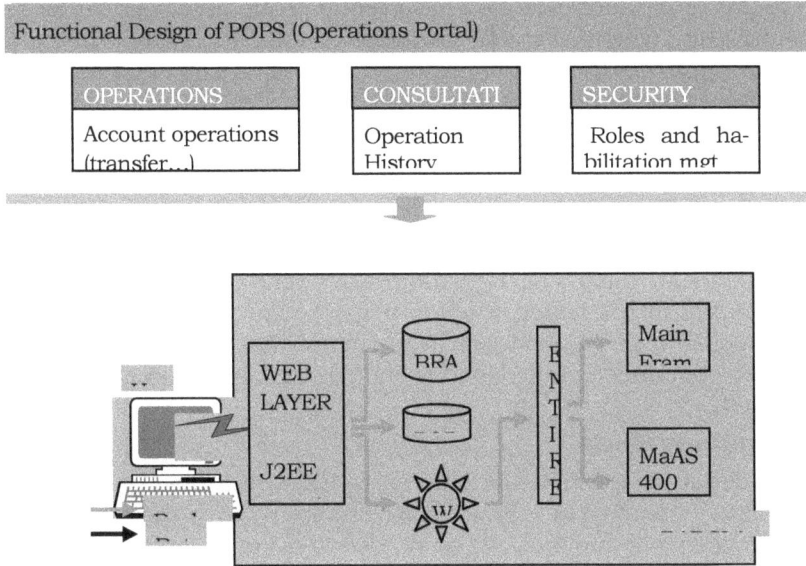

Figure 23: Overall application architecture

LDAP (corporate directory) authentication and checking of the agents' roles

For the needs of the project a LDAP directory was set up to manage access to the operations portal (and any future products), as well as the allocation of roles. This directory was initialised according to the organisation defined in the Intranet portal. Users' roles are entered using the corporate directory. Daily processing updates the LDAP directory according to the input and output of each of the two databases.

Integration with the IS applications

Generally, the different procedures set up lead to an operation on the central systems. All that has to be done is to add a "robot" step in the flow of tasks for sending updating orders, since the data has been validated by the processes themselves. Technical aspects of integration have been resolved for other applications already in production, in particular, through the use of middleware-based technologies.

The automatic completion of forms, once minimum data had been entered (account holder, account number), was made possible thanks to reusable components, with database connections being managed by the *"Branch Platform"* tool.

The advantages offered by the W4 Suite software allow the integration of new forms in record time, approximately one day, whilst respecting the group's computer applications compliance regulations.

Modernisation of the IS

A number of forms were based on groupware software which is coming to the end of its life span, but which is still used by the group. The shift to Web technologies in the framework of this project has permitted the freeing of the IS of the management of these outdated platforms

BENEFITS

Cost savings

The set up of this application software has permitted the redeployment of several posts, by doing away with tasks with low added value, such as checking signatures or account numbers. Now, staff are more focused on customer relations and this level of service is starting to bear fruit, with a greater ability to attract a new clientele.

Barclays France measured a global return on investment for the PoPs' 6 month project.

Increased revenues

Branch sales staff now have 5 to 10% more sales time, because data computer entry operations are much faster, thanks, in particular, to assisted data entry. Whereas on paper forms it was necessary to ensure that all the information was correct, now, the customer's name alone is enough to find the necessary information to be entered.

Productivity improvements

From an operational perspective, the processing time for a request has been cut from approximately one day to a little under one hour, with the guarantee that the process has been followed and can be verified at every stage thanks to it being based on a workflow engine. Each user can now benefit from a global view of the operations relating to the client that he is dealing with. The information is more reliable to make decisions more rapidly and with more relevance.

The time gains that were obtained come from a time saving in handling documents (in between paper folders transfer), from savings in time required to fill in documents (through assisted data entry), savings in time required to execute the process, and quicker answers to customer inquiries.

COMPETITIVE ADVANTAGES

Branches can now commit themselves to time limits and guarantees in transmission times which the application offers is reassuring to agents who now feel completely confident. Forms, which used to be sent by fax or turnaround mail, are processed by back-offices immediately and the customer relationship manager who has requested the operation only has to check on the central system that the operation has been completed, thus allowing him or her to free up even more time. Today, the result is greater reliability in processing of banking operations and an absence of requests failing as a result of a breakdown in transmission between services.

Since all requests (bank cheques, transfer, etc.) trigger an operation which is tracked in a repository unique to the entire company, each bank employee may, at any time, have an overall view of the customer he or she is dealing with and, thus, adapt his sales approach to suit.

IMMEDIATE AND LONG-TERM PLANS

Barclays France is not planning on stopping there. "In view of the tool's power and the speed and ease of setting it up, we are intending to introduce new forms", explained Hubert Locqueville. Furthermore, at present, the bank is working on the deployment of an electronic document management tool (EDM) to automate processing of the account life (opening, changes and closing), which, for example, takes into account the management of a file's documents of proof via digitising. The bank will combine the W4 Suite product already in production with Hummingbird Enterprise™ DM. Barclays France has chosen BT as the system integrator. This system should be operational by the end of 2006.

The other line of development under consideration is the opening of applications to the Internet, by offering customers the opportunity to make requests themselves (for example, overseas transfers) a service, which, today, is carried out either in the branch or through Barclays Contact call centre. This expansion is planned for 2007 and will require an architecture which meets the bank's security regulations.

The project's success has generated interest among the group's other departments and new applications will see the light of day in human resources and marketing, for campaign management.

"Our approach is pragmatic. We prefer to progress by steps rather than by launching ourselves into the total redesign of the system, in view of the inherent risks involved in this type of project", concluded Hubert Locqueville.

Modelo Continente Hipermercados Portugal, Europe

Gold Award 2006, Europe; nominated by iProcess and Tlantic SI, Portugal

EXECUTIVE SUMMARY

This paper presents the experience of the implementation of workflow technology in Modelo Continente Hipermercados (MCH), the largest retailer in Portugal. Started in the later 90's, motivated by the challenge to take advantage of the best technologies available, MCH´s experience involves more than 23 automated processes covering virtually all business areas. The company has adopted workflow technology in a corporate and strategic way, establishing a new management paradigm. The benefits obtained are way beyond the expected, resulting in expressive efficiency gains for the company. Workflow technology contributes to MCH's strategic goals, building concrete competitive advantages.

OVERVIEW

MCH is a diversified retail company that executes a huge amount of business processes. Due to several reasons mentioned in the next section, there is a great interest to make them more efficient, faster and under control.

The first workflow system started to be developed in late 90's. The good results stimulated the development of new systems, reaching the number of 22 systems in production on August 1, 2006 (20 on February 1, 2006), while six other are presently in pilot production or being developed. These systems have automated processes as distinct as product repair, goods transfer, contract management, travel request and purchase order approval. They encompass a total of 1750 process activities, of which 647 are human activities and 1103 are automated steps (the average process has around 80 steps).

Despite the variety of developed systems, it is easy to find common benefits to all of them. Process control, increased productivity, improved service and cost reduction were the reasons of the success of MCH´s experience. The company used workflow technology to connect all parties of its business processes – customers, employees, managers and suppliers – creating totally virtual processes. In a dispersed organization as MCH, this was the key to overcome the obstacles to productivity, efficiency and control.

These common benefits came from a set of process improvements. Among them we can find faster customer response, task automation, process rules enforcement, paper elimination, reduced store stocks, automatic integration with legacy systems and better employee organization.

In this movement towards massive adhesion of workflow technology, a basic element was user involvement. In all the stages of the development, end users were present and made decisions about each system. User satisfaction with workflow can be measured by the usage and new developments required in a proactive way.

Thus, the current experience of MCH portrays a new and powerful culture of work in the corporation. This powerful culture, stimulated by strong user participation, places MCH in the front line, becoming consistently more efficient and competitive.

THE KEY BUSINESS MOTIVATIONS BEHIND THE PROJECT

MCH is the largest retail company in Portugal, and currently has 342 stores distributed in more than 60 cities. Its total selling area is more than 500,000 square meters. In 2005, its sales reached € 3.1 billion (US$ 3.95 billion). Food retail sales were around € 2.3 billion and non-food retail sales were € 771 million. MCH is also the largest employer in Portugal, joining more than 20,000 employees. MCH belongs to Grupo Sonae (Sonae Group), Portugal's largest private group. Grupo Sonae operates in several different industries such as retail, manufacturing, real estate, telecommunications, media, software development, tourism, logistics and venture capital. The company is in 8 countries from 3 continents.

Several reasons led MCH to implement workflow technology. Some were external, defined by the market, while others were internal. Besides that, as the use of the technology expanded, the benefits of the systems became clearer, and stimulated even more the implementation of new workflow systems. The following subs-sections illustrate these motivations.

Accelerated expansion requires process consolidation

Since its foundation, MCH has experienced a fast expansion. The business diversified from food into a multitude of food and nonfood formats.

It is clearly not viable to sustain such growth rate without adequate processes and tools in place. Only they can guarantee the standardization of best practices, bring maximum operational efficiency and give managers a precise picture of the actual business performance. Naturally, MCH first focused the automation of basic core processes through the ERP packages for back and frontoffice. After these had been adequately handled, the next target was set for the vast amount of MCH-specific processes.

Search for innovation leads to workflow technology

MCH has always been an innovative company. When it started its operations, in 1985, MCH brought to Portugal a new concept for the local market – the hypermarket. Later, in the mid-90s, MCH was also a pioneer in the development of new non-food retail formats. This innovative spirit, shared by the whole company, leads the MCH´s IT Department to continuously evaluate the best technologies available, looking for ways to bring practical advantages to the business. The company started to evaluate workflow technology in the late 90s, defining a strategic vision on *business process virtualization*, which allowed for connecting people and legacy systems.

KEY BUSINESS INNOVATION

Workflow technology impacted MCH´s business in several ways. The next chapters highlight some of the innovations and benefits brought by workflow.

Greater customer convenience

One of the advantages brought by workflow technology was the improvement of customer convenience. Certainly the best example comes from the Product Repair Workflow. This workflow manages the complete process of repairing a product (whether it was purchased in a MCH store or not). From the customer's perspective, this is a time-sensitive process, since he/she generally wants to recover the product as soon as possible.

Workflow technology allowed to completely reengineer the service provided. On average, the total repair time fell by 37 percent.

Increasing convenience is also one of the goals of the Suggestions & Claims Workflow. This system allows for faster response times and more effective solutions for any customer demand.

Improved collaboration with business partners

Efficient collaboration with suppliers and other business partners was a significant achievement. Once more, the Product Repair Workflow is a good example. After the goods reception, a multitude of different partners (logistic operators, repairers, manufacturers, product component resellers etc.) may participate in the process, according to the established business rules. These rules are workflow system controlled and may define, for instance, that a product within warranty will be sent to its manufacturer instead of a repairer. Service level agreements (e.g. time to repair a TV) are defined and monitored by the system.

All these partners interact directly with the workflow system through a *Repairer Portal*. This allows real-time communication among all parties, with process traceability. The system is so well accepted that today more than 500 repair-related partners use it, executing around 35,000 instances per month.

Better partner collaboration was also the goal of the Goods Devolution-Supplier Workflow. This workflow controls the reverse logistics process of returning goods from a store directly to the supplier. A clear understanding of each party (MCH store, MCH central stock management and supplier) duties is enabled, streamlining the process and having proper exception handling.

Also, the Item Creation Workflow improved the interaction with suppliers. Using this workflow a supplier can easily suggest new items to be added to the company's retail product range. The workflow assists the evaluation of the suggestion and helps correct classification and registry in the retail front-end ERP.

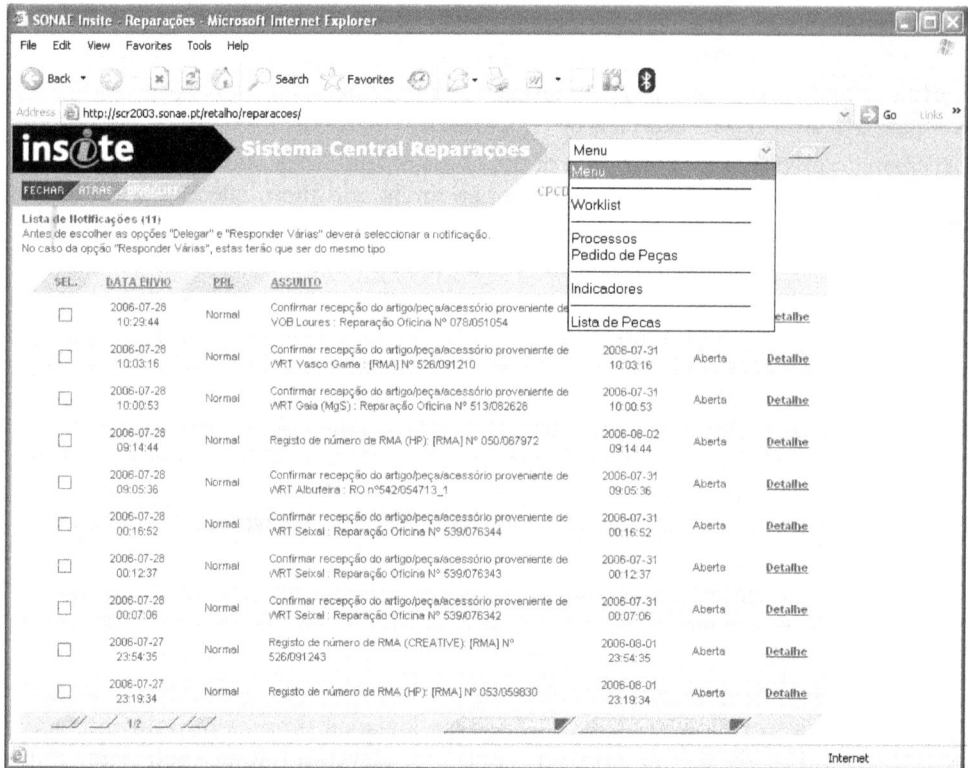

Figure 1. Repairers can log in the Repairer Portal and check their work-list. They can also monitor process status and initiate new ones.

Optimized stock management

Stock management is one of the most impacting issues for a retailer's profitability. MCH was able to optimize it through a variety of workflow systems, namely: Goods Devolution-Distribution Center, Goods Devolution-Supplier, Goods Transfer and Quality Problem. Several reasons can origin the start of a process in these workflows:

- a store wants to return goods to the distribution center
- the Central Stock Manager decides to balance goods among stores with excess and lack of stock
- the manufacturer issues a product recall and the related goods have to be collected
- there are excess goods after a marketing campaign

The handling of these situations in an efficient way can be complex. For instance, frequently it is cheaper to destroy a product than to send it back to the supplier or to the Distribution Center. A correct evaluation has to consider factors such as the type of product, the location where it is, the amount that has to be transferred, environmental rules and commercial agreements. The best decisions are the ones that allow the company to maintain the lowest possible stock, without stock-outs, and with less management costs.

The developed workflows guarantee that all these complex processes are followed in a controlled and disciplined way, allowing MCH to effectively optimize its stock management. With these workflows, the best practices were shared and available to all stock managers, and a significant stock reduction was achieved.

Improved employee interaction

Streamlined employee interaction is an important issue for any company. This was the goal of a group of workflow systems: Vacation Scheduling, Internal HR Recruitment and Work Contract Change. All of them fit into the concept of a *self-service portal*, allowing employees to start requests and have the related decisions formalized and implemented. As known, one important reason of employee dissatisfaction is not receiving appropriate feedback regarding their demands.

The Internal HR Recruitment Workflow is an excellent example of the impact brought by workflow in the relationship of MCH with its employees. This system allows any employee to apply for any open position within the company. The results are better process consistency – all approvals and validations are correctly made – and transparency – the rules and steps are known by everyone. This guarantees that the selection process is fair and that company policies prevail over any personal preferences.

Effective indicator-based process management

Workflow technology facilitates automatic process data generation and recording. MCH soon realized that the collected information was precious to improve process management. Indicators were defined and automatically generated for key processes. These indicators are monitored using a tool called *Indicators Portal*, where process managers can apply filters and see information in different formats (tables, graphs etc.). This feature expanded the perception of managers, which did not have accurate information in the past to take the best decisions.

KEY PROCESS INNOVATION

Workflow technology brought several innovations to MCH´s processes. With workflow, processes became faster, more efficient and better controlled. The next sections explain these innovations in further detail.

Intelligent Process virtualization

Intelligent process virtualization was one of the main process innovations brought by workflow technology. Virtualization, in this sense, means the elimination of all possible restrictions of location and time, imposed to process performance, joined with intelligent automation. In practical terms, it involves:

- substitution of paper forms by Web applications and digitizing of paper documents
- automatic data and business rules validation, increasing productivity and avoiding rework
- automatic process routing, eliminating the need for physical document transfer and/or manual process forwarding
- access to worklist through the enterprise portal
- centralized database, keeping all forms, document and workflow information
- workflow activity UI (user interface) tuned for user productivity
- extensive use of alerts to minimize activity deadline loss
- automatic data and transaction integration with legacy systems
- ability to monitor processes regardless of the store or department where they are being executed

Intelligent process virtualization was applied to all the workflows, and has allowed MCH to achieve gains such as: greater agility, reduce human work/rework (freeing several employees to more value-added activities), reduce the use of paper (reducing both costs and ecological impacts), increase user productivity and improve management control.

Back-office processes, such as Invoice Validation, Travel Request, Purchase Order Approval, Reimbursement and Expenses Approval, were the most benefited with intelligent virtualization. Some of the results were:

- 6,400-hour annual saved in the Purchase Order process
- 60 percent reduction in the Invoice Validation process time
- automatic invoice validation in Travel Invoice Validation grew from 20 percent to 65 percent
- near-zero rework in all processes
- These benefits will be described below in further detail.

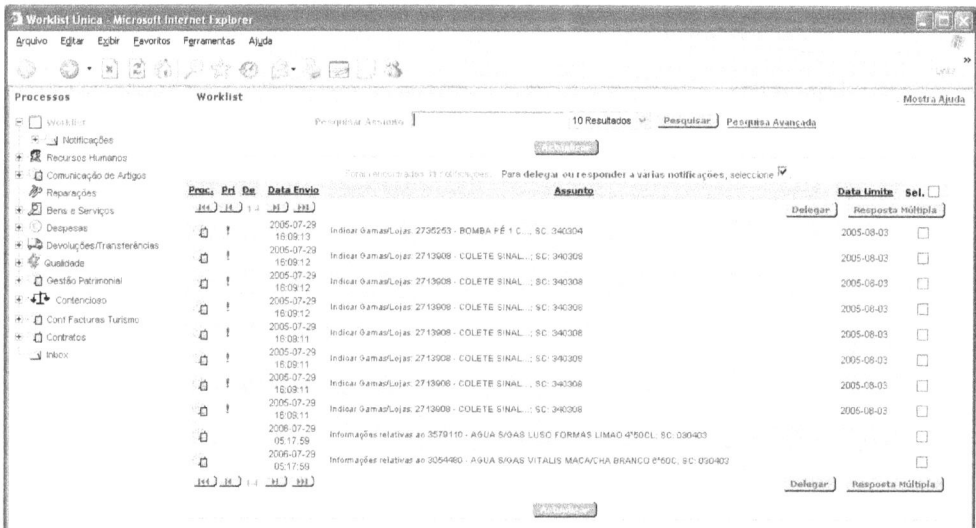

Figure 2. Unified User Worklist showing tasks from all workflow systems. The left pane shows all workflow systems available, each one with specific options.

Increased flexibility to improve processes

Creating and maintaining alignment among a large number of people about process definitions is certainly a challenge for any company. In the traditional way, process definitions have to be communicated through normative documents, and often audited to verify proper execution. This also means that any change to current processes requires a reasonable amount of work and re-training. In some situations, this effort may even become an inhibitor to process change and evolution.

MCH soon discovered that the resources provided by workflow technology made process evolution much easier than before. Since systems are designed to 'guide' users through the process, it is necessary just to update them to reflect the desired process changes. The required training is much shorter, and the new process can begin to operate in a very short time and to a large audience, with minimal flaws. This flexible behavior has stimulated business users to take effective control of their processes, running a continuous cycle of analysis and improvement.

KEY TECHNOLOGICAL INNOVATION

Workflow technology success in MCH was only possible due to several technological innovations. The topics below present some of the most important facts.

Heavy investment in usability

Since its conceptualization, workflow technology was thought as a tool for user productivity. Thus, heavy investment has been made in interface usability, focusing on minimizing user's effort; having a pleasant look-and-feel and enforcing consistent behavior among all systems.

Reduced user's effort was achieved through a series of interface design decisions, such as:

- automatic consolidation of information from several systems, avoiding the need to use several applications
- automatic pre-validation of business rules, highlighting topics for user's attention and suggesting actions
- allowing user to act on several tasks at once (batch)
- The picture below, from the Goods Devolution Workflow, illustrates this approach.

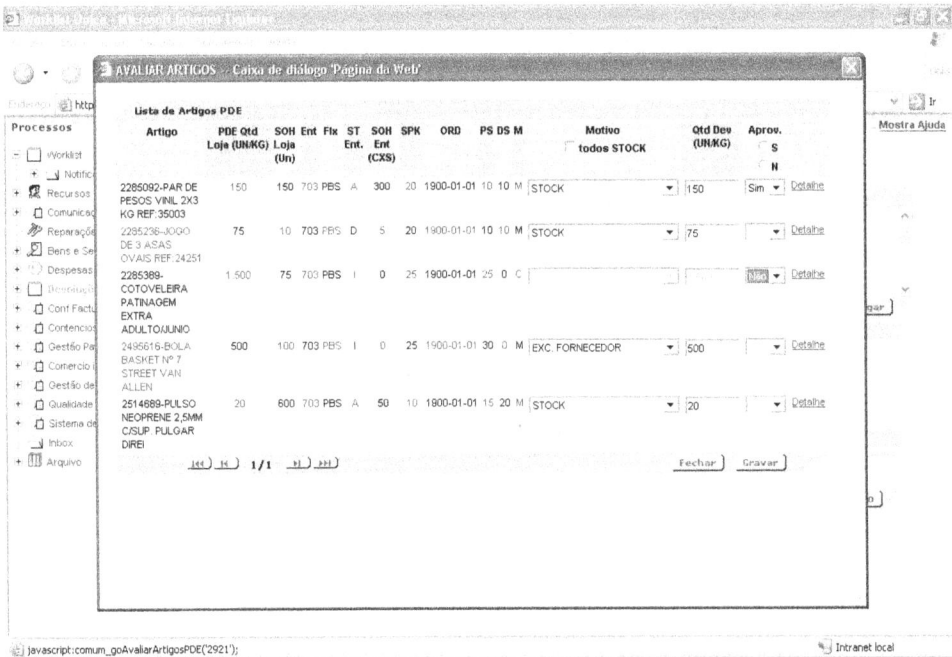

Figure 3. The stock manager receives a screen consolidating information from Retail Front-End ERP and the workflow system itself. Business rules are pre-validated and an action is automatically suggested. The user can easily act on several instances in batch (worklist in the background).

Extensive technology integration

As any large company, MCH uses a multitude of different systems and technologies. Integrating all of them in an organized, coherent way is critical for two main reasons:

- to allow the creation of "virtual work environments" where users can receive all necessary information without having to logon to several systems

- to allow a high level of process automation, eliminating manual tasks as much as possible

The most important systems and technologies integrated were:
- Oracle Workflow: workflow management engine
- Retek: retail ERP, stores all product and inventory information
- SAP: financial and accounting data
- MS SharePoint: enterprise portal framework
- IXOS: document digitalization and storage
- Crystal Reports: workflow reporting
- LDAP (MS Site Server): stores user and profile information
- ASP, .NET, XML and XSL for application development
- Web Services and RPC for application integration

To assure appropriate reuse, these integrations were bundled in a *workflow framework*, and are accessible to any workflow system developed in MCH.

New methodologies for offshore development

In 2004, MCH started to offshore workflow system development to Tlantic, a Sonae-owned software company based in Brazil. Obviously, this required the revision of the development methodology in place. The main changes were:
- adoption of a formal software development process (Tlantic is currently CMMI Level 2 certified)
- more precise definition of project phases and artefacts
- clearer separation of MCH's and software company's duties. More business-related activities (e.g. process redesign) were left to MCH while technology-related ones were left to Tlantic
- detailed project planning to assure that workflow analyst can complete his/her work in 2-3 weeks (average time spent in a Brazil-Portugal travel)
- software test team prepared to detect language flaws in user interface

These actions have achieved the desired results, and offshore development has been a great success. Currently, all MCH workflow systems are being developed in Brazil.

THE SYSTEM USERS AND WHAT THEIR JOBS NOW ENTAIL COMPARED TO PRE-INSTALLATION

The large-scale workflow usage at MCH affected the work of almost every employee. The most important changes were:
- greater organization at work, because one can easily check his or her worklist to see pending activities. This was very appreciated by business partners who often couldn't be easily communicated about a new task;
- access to documents and tasks anytime, anywhere. Fundamental to include business partners in the process;
- transition from paper documents to electronic documents, allowing several data validations, easing cooperation and speeding the process;
- transformation of manual tasks into automated ones, such as ERP validations and transactions;
- process transparency, making full history available and allowing one to know who's delaying the process;
- greater awareness about task deadlines due to work item information and to alerts;
- general feeling of control and organization.

THE BIGGEST HURDLES OVERCOME IN MANAGEMENT, BUSINESS AND TECHNOLOGY

Management

Considering the size and variety of workflow systems, management hurdles were smaller than expected. Some hurdles were faced, especially in the first workflow systems, due to the lack of a process culture among certain employees. This led to situations such as users printing all process documents before starting to work. After some months of training and supervision these obstacles were overcome, and users started to feel very comfortable with the virtual process.

Another hurdle was the practical complexity of offshore development. Besides the physical distance and time zone difference, there are significant variances in terms of culture and language between Brazil and Portugal. To overcome this, several measures were taken, such as extensive use of Web collaboration tools (web conferencing, MSN); conference calls to discuss document interpretation; formal document approvals and creation of glossaries to clarify word meaning.

Business

Customer-related workflows, such as Product Repair required an increased focus in the training and support of the front-line employees serving the clients. This is also a process heavily affected by seasonality, peaking after Christmas and Easter. Besides the tuning of usability issues and the right-sizing and monitoring of the IT platform, special care was taken in the management of change.

Technology

Several technological hurdles had to be overcome to ensure systems' success. One of the major ones was the need to accommodate different usability needs (directors, managers, employees, suppliers etc.). The solution was found in the creation of different user interfaces for suppliers and MCH-personnel, with several configurations that are automatically applied according to user profile.

Due to the diversity of technologies integrated, it is also a challenge to maintain and upgrade the systems. Since the workflow database is very large, any change operation has to be carefully planned.

Legacy system integration also presented some challenges, especially because, at the time of the first integrations, ERP vendors did not provide very open connectivity mechanisms.

THE NEW SYSTEM CONFIGURATION

The system infrastructure is divided in 3 main components:
- Workflow Server: a 4-processor (3 GHz), 8 GB RAM Intel machine running Red Hat 3.0, Oracle Database Server 9.2.0.6 and Oracle Workflow Server 2.6.3. External storage is used (150 GB)
- Application Servers (not dedicated to workflow): 2 servers, each a 2-processor (3 GHz), 4 GB RAM Intel machine running Windows 2003 and MS IIS. Internal storage is used (36 GB)
- External Application Servers (not dedicated to workflow): 2 servers, each a 2-processor (2 GHz), 512 Mb RAM Intel machine running Windows 2003 and MS IIS. Internal storage is used (36 GB)
- Legacy systems servers: Retek Server, SAP Server, IXOS Server, Exchange Server

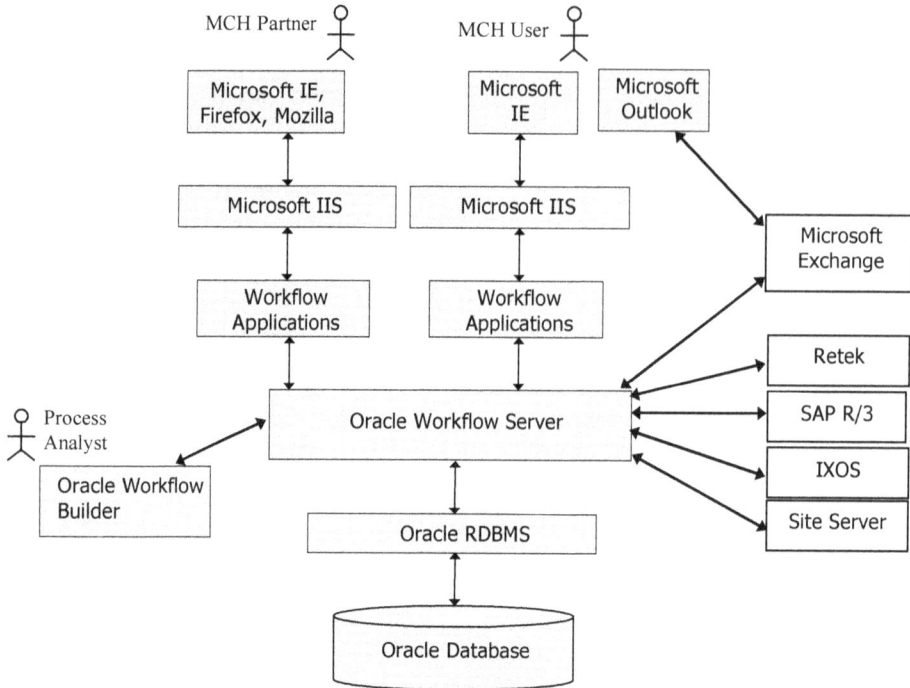

Figure 4. Global system architecture

Due to security reasons, all external access (e.g. business partners) is made through External Application Servers.

COST SAVINGS, INCREASED REVENUES, AND PRODUCTIVITY IMPROVEMENTS

Workflow technology has brought several tangible and intangible benefits to MCH. The table below shows some of the direct financial benefits achieved, and estimates the total savings obtained since the system entered in operation until August 1, 2006:

Workflow	Impact
Product Repair	more than 200,000-hour annual savings
Goods Devolution	several million Euros of store stocks reduction
Devolution Request	2000-hour annual saving (freeing time from stock managers)
Invoice Validation	3200-hour annual saving (reduced staff due to automation)
Purchase Order	6400-hour annual saving (reduced staff due to automation)
Reimbursement, Travel Request	12-minute saving per instance due to user productivity
Other workflows	10,500-hour annual saving (reduced staff due to automation)

Other benefits of a more intangible nature are generally connected to quality of service. Some of them had a significant impact:

Workflow	Performance Improvement
Product Repair	• 37 percentage process time reduction • increased revenue due to increased customer satisfaction and loyalty
Goods Devolution	• guarantee that devolution processes will have the lowest possible operational cost
Goods Transfer	• increased revenue due to increased customer satisfaction
Invoice Validation	• 60 percentage process time reduction
Travel Invoice Validation	• increased automation allows VAT (value-added tax) to be recovered earlier
Reimbursement, Travel Request	• safer, simpler and quicker approval
Internal HR Recruitment	• increased chance to find the best employee to the open position

IMMEDIATE AND LONG-TERM PLANS TO SUSTAIN COMPETITIVE ADVANTAGE

Workflow technology has conquered a very important place in MCH, thanks to the concrete business benefits brought by it. Since its introduction there is a permanent cycle of workflow usage expansion. Beyond the 23 systems already in production, 6 other are under development and 5 other are planned to start soon.

This pace is only possible because MCH has reached an extremely high maturity level in workflow usage. IT management has a perfect understanding of the technology and knows exactly when workflow should be used. There are mature methodologies to cover all the phases of systems development, turning workflow expansion an easier task.

Beyond the automation of new business processes, plans related to workflow and BPM comprise:

- development of a central database to extract better management information from process execution data
- technological alignment with SOA (service-oriented architecture)
- increased connection between process analysts and IT analysts
- expansion of BPM vision by transforming functional-oriented competencies and tasks into process-oriented structures

The Spider BPM solution at Telenor, Norway

Silver Award 2006, Europe; nominated by auSystems (now Cybercom), Sweden

EXECUTIVE SUMMARY

This case study[1] illustrates the approach taken by Telenor to establish a new network infrastructure rollout organization and a supporting IT system. The approach is based on the idea of a portfolio of standardized infrastructure products and automated business processes supporting all types of infrastructure networks (IP, mobile, fixed and cable TV) in a convergent fashion and also including integration of partners in the process to supply the civil engineering work necessary to build a telecommunications network.

The IT system is realized using an application framework for Business Process Management with support for reusable process components. This document will cover the business drivers and organizational challenges for initiating, executing and launching the project. The technical solution and project experiences will also be presented and finally share some thought of the future usage possibilities. The system is named "Spider" and was put in production in mid 2005 at Telenor, Norway.

OVERVIEW

Telenor is Norway's leading telecommunications company with a strong position in the Scandinavian market for broadband services with over 1,4 million subscriptions, and the largest provider of commercial TV services to the Scandinavian market. Telenor is also one of the world's largest mobile operators, with more than 123 million mobile subscriptions world wide. The company has a workforce of more than 32 150 man-years with 10,000 employees within Telenor Nordic. The revenues for 2006 are 91.1 billion NOK, and the company is listed on Oslo Stock Exchange.

In 2003 Telenor established one common build net unit across Fixed, Mobile Cable TV handling all tactical planning and roll out for these three business areas. The new "Build net unit" was given responsibility to implement a new converged process for the Nordic region and as its strategic initiative to realize this goal the Spider project was started. To establish an IT system to support this process and organization, the Spider system was designed as a BPM application within Telenor with functionality to reach out to all its subcontractors within civil engineering.

Integrating the Operational planning and build business processes at Telenor with the business processes of the subcontractors performing civil work for Telenor was one major goal for the organization and the Spider system as Telenor has about 4 major subcontractors in the Nordics and about 30 smaller regional

---

[1] This case study was written by Jon Omund Revhaug of Telenor Nordic Operations, Norway, with co-author Per Skenhall of auSystems (now Cybercom), Sweden.

subcontractors. The Spider system executes both Telenor's internal workflow and handles the public processes for effectively B2B communication with the subcontractor's business process.

In April 2005 Telenor established the new Nordic operation and merged the previously diverged Tactical planning units in Fixed and Mobile, enabling the operation for additional convergence of the mobile and fixed infrastructure process. The new organization is illustrated in the figure below.

"Telenor Nordic" organizes all of Telenor's business units within mobile and fixed communications in the Nordic region. This involves all sales & marketing activities and also all planning, building, fulfillment and assurance of infrastructure.

"Operations" is the common Telenor Nordic unit for all infrastructure operations. This includes planning, building and assurance of all Nordic mobile and fixed networks. The unit has 2200 employees located in Norway, Sweden and Denmark.

This document will describe the business and technical aspects of the Spider system and the processes it supports.

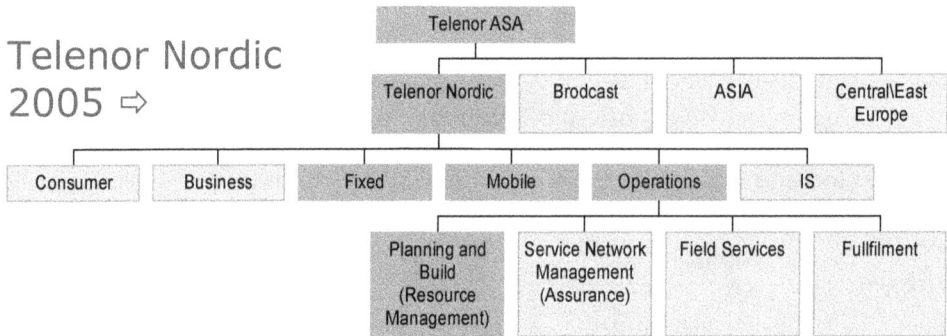

Figure 1: Telenor's organization as per April 2005.

THE KEY BUSINESS MOTIVATIONS BEHIND THE PROJECT

In the latter part of the 1990's Telenor, and most European telecom operators invested intensively in transport and core capacity in the telecommunication networks. As a result the marked experienced surplus capacity by 2000- 2001. In addition the marked generally slowed down, strengthening the surplus trend.

A generally slower marked initiated a stronger focus on base line operational costs and product profitability. Also, Telenor was listed on the stock exchange in year 2000 which caused somewhat stronger focus on cost savings and better margins.

Telenor aimed to lower operating cost, increase exploitation ratio for core and transport infrastructure capacity and utilize scale advantages better in the Norwegian marked through better business process modelling within the resource management area.

In 2003 Telenor started the established one common build net unit handling Fixed, Mobile and cable TV infrastructure roll out in Norway. In April 2005 this was expanded to the Nordic region. This common unit aimed to supply Telenor with the best build network processes within the telecom business. The business processes focused on five central business drivers for change listed below:
- The process should support a reactive customer driven investment portfolio in infrastructure
- The process should increase efficiency of order handling and completion time.

- The process should enable for synergies across business units, Mobile, Fixed and Cable TV.
- Utilize scale advantages towards the subcontractor market used for all civil works.
- Create and maintain a competition among a handful of larger suppliers in the subcontractor market, to stimulate process improvements and cost reductions.

The Spider project was the Build Network unit's strategic initiative to ensure that the unit met its goals.

THE KEY INNOVATION

The chapters below demonstrate the impact of the Spider project on the categories Business, Process and Architecture.

BUSINESS

The build net unit handles approximately 50,000 projects per year, whereas the durability and size of the projects vary;

- 1/3: 10 days – 3 months
- 1/3: 3 – 9 months
- 1/3: 9 – 18 months (some big scale projects are even longer, but rarely over 24 months)

The build net unit established a close cooperation to all three business units that represented the unit's principals being Mobile product house, Fixed product house and cable TV product house. The basic idea was (and still is) to standardise and simplify the interfaces through the use of standardised products and specifications, as apposed to the previous where extended use of case by case specifications and case tailoring was used.

Further the unit established a business to business (hereby B2B) interface with pre- selected contractors used for civil work and engineering. Also in this interface Telenor aim to simplify through extensive use of standardised products. The B2B interface enables Telenor and contractors to have an interactive order exchange solution. This enables contractors to respond quickly upon order handling, and also enables for shorter time processed in change management.

Through standards and common products the unit could focus upon increasing efficiency by automation of the unit's private business processes.

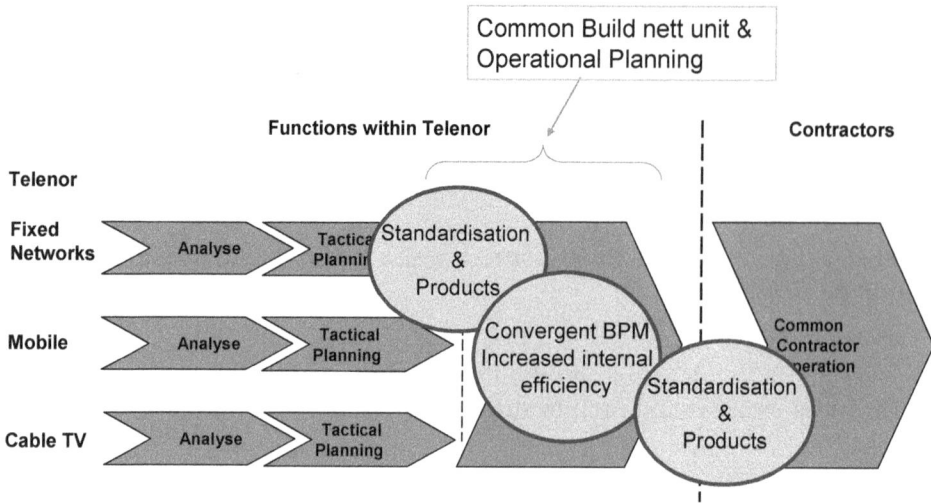

Figure 2: Through standardisation and products the interface to the build net unit's principals and the contractor marked is simplified, and enables automation in the build net units private business processes.

PROCESS

The pre-Spider process situation

The Spider project addresses the telecommunications process area "Resource capability delivery" within "Resource Development" as defined in eTOM[2].

Before the initiative was started the organisation had a variety of internal processes to handle the different build net and roll out functions. This is illustrated in the figure below; Fixed Networks, Mobile and Cable TV all have different processes and separate contractor framework agreements.

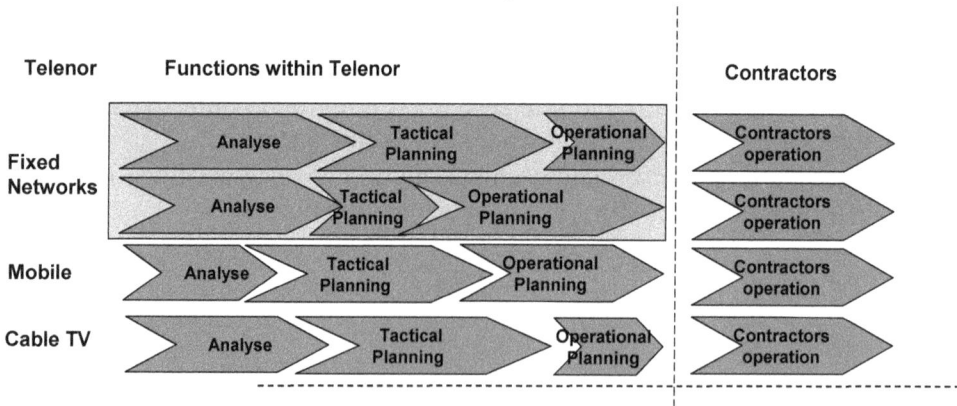

Figure 3: Pre-Spider process situation

Conclusion of Pre-Spider process situation:
- All Telenor business units have their own infrastructure processes.
- Divergent value added in each phase across the business units.
- All units have their own contractor framework agreement.

---

[2] eTOM – Enhanced Telecommunication Operations Map. For more information on eTOM browse to http://www.tmforum.org/browse.aspx?catID=1647

The after-Spider process situation

A goal of the Spider project was to have one common build network operation for all Telenor business units and a common contractor framework agreement.

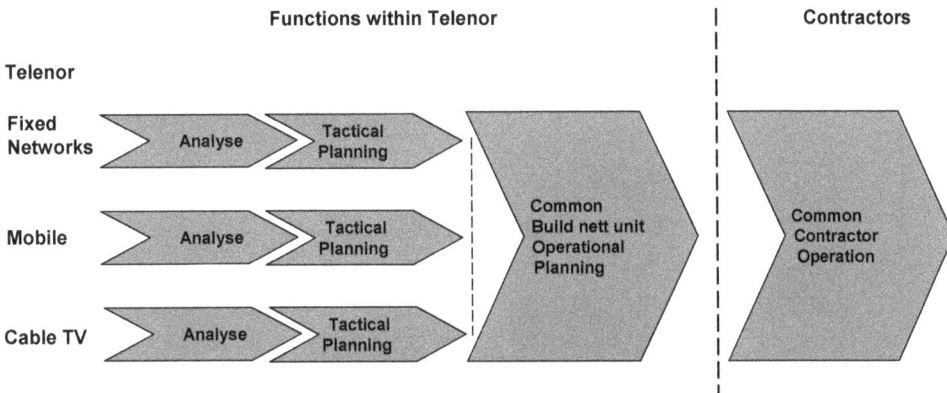

Figure 4: After-Spider process situation

To obtain this process the following project & solution approach was used:
- Standardized products
  - Build products (interfaces the tactical planning with the common build net unit illustrated by the *left* dotted line in the figure above).
  - Subcontractor products (interfaces the common build net unit with the common contractor operation, illustrated by the *right* dotted line in the figure above).
- Processes (instead of one-off project approach)
- Technology specific competences should be only limiting factor of resource flexibility in the organization.
- The process design should represent "best practice" that is executed each time.

Conclusion of After-Spider process situation:
- One common Build network operation for all Telenor business units.
- One convergent process for fixed & mobile build network operation.
- One convergent contractor framework agreement.

The Spider project solution

The Buyer's view in Figure 5 below illustrates the view of the Tactical Planning unit. The Tactical Planning unit dynamically creates build assignments at order entry time by selecting required build products. The build products are selected from a product catalogue. Dependencies between build products are handled using milestones and synchronization points in the processes.

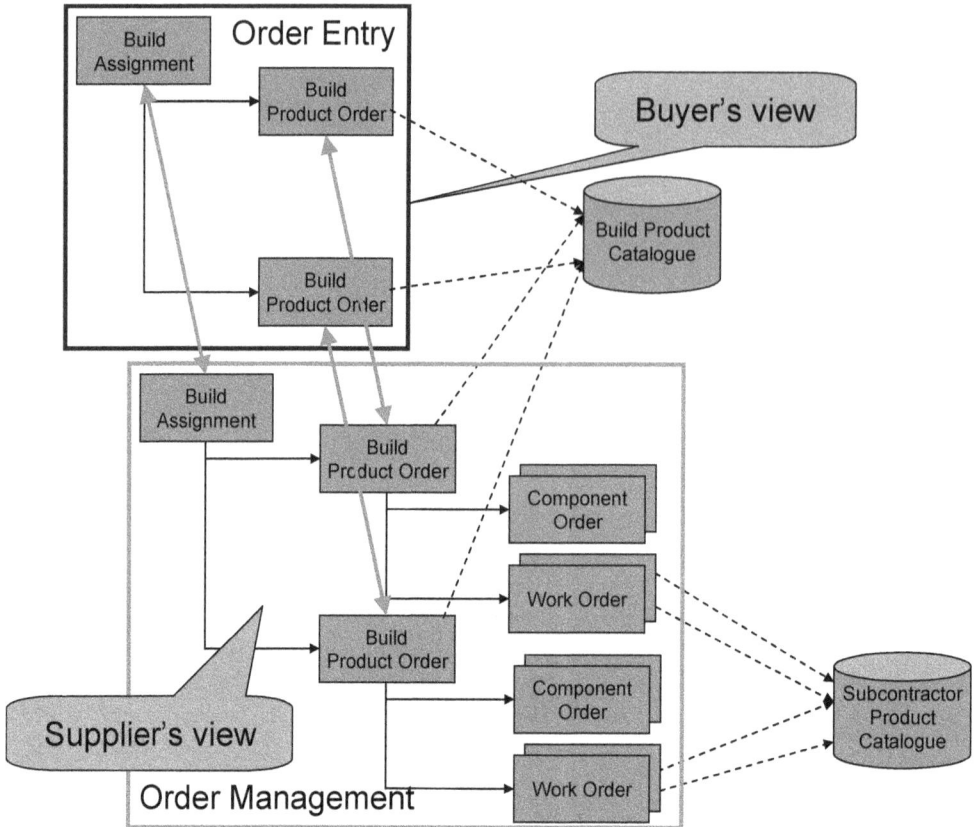

Figure 5: Decomposition of orders

As illustrated in Figure 5 the supplier's view is created by expanding the buyer's view. To be more specific; component orders and work orders are added. Every order in the Buyer's view has a corresponding order in the Supplier's view.

The Supplier's view on the order structure (Build Assignment, Build Product Orders, Component and Work Order) is executed by processes. These processes form a hierarchy of pre-designed processes. I.e. instead of uniquely planned projects, pre-designed processes are used with a well-defined platform for further process improvements.

In the design of processes in Spider there exists an isolation of process design in two layers:

- **Assignment & Product processes** – executes Build Assignments and Build Product Orders.
  - Selected based on business rules and order data, e.g. product category. Defines the process for one or more build products and the assignment. Uses component processes to realize part of the product process. Easy introduction of new products by re-use or copying existing product processes
- **Component process** – executes Component Orders and Work Orders.
  - Responsible for a well-defined function in the build process. Handles all communication towards external systems. The component processes are **reusable** across all build processes. Improvement in one component impacts all uses of the component

Solution Properties

The Spider solution reuses a BPM framework at Telenor called FLOW Foundation and a methodology with templates for process design and specifications. This framework and the methodology contain the building blocks for further process improvements.

Using a BPM platform enables a close relationship between the designed processes (using the methodology and the templates) and the implemented process (BPM and Business Rules). This in turn enables natural process design where business specialists participate in process design.

A "Super User"-forum has been established where experts working in the Build Net process improve the solution based on best-practice. The design specifications are and the implementation processes are updated continuously based on the input of the "Super Users".

The solution also provides:
- Seamless mixture of automatic and manual tasks
- Dynamic processes at runtime
- Organizational freedom to give business flexibility
  - Manual tasks assigned through roles, not organization

Closing the process lifecycle

The Spider BPM solution is build for change by trying to isolate hot-spots of change of three categories:
- Process
- Business Rules
- Information model

Each of these categories should be able to be changed and deployed independently of each other to allow changes without massive impacts.

Through the separation of the "hot-spots for change", analyzing the actual process outcome and feeding the results back as improvement requirements helps to close the loop, for future continuous process improvements.

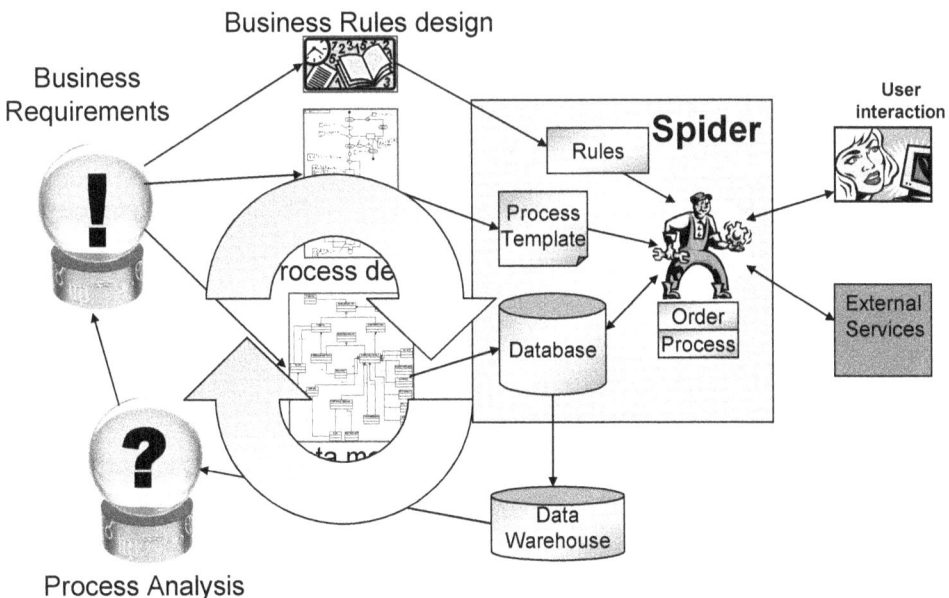

Figure 6: Closing the process lifecycle

TECHNOLOGY

Figure 7 below shows the logical architecture of the Spider solution and its modules. In chapter 0 there is a description of the technical design and components of the system.

The system typically has four types of "actors" communicating with the system:

1. **Buyers** – using a web based Order Entry module the buyer may enter an assignment consisting of one or many products selected from a common product catalogue, called the Build Product Catalogue. When the assignment is created as desired it is sent for execution to the Order Management module. The Order Management module starts the processes for completing the order based on the associated process definitions of the build products included in the assignment.

2. **Workflow Users** – this type of users are attached to a number of groups in the system depending on the roles (competences) they individually have for performing network rollout activities. From the build product processes started in the Order Management module, from the component processes started in the Component Delivery module and from the work order processes started in the External Ordering module, the workflow users receive the valid tasks for processing depending on individual competences. The Spider system also has the capability to do load-balancing among groups based on pre-defined business rules.

3. **Subcontractors** – communication with the Spider system (and Telenor) can be achieved using two different technical protocols – a propriety legacy protocol (HA) and a new standard based protocol (NeBI). The collaboration with subcontractors contains protocol functionality for:
   - Sending, answering and negotiating quotations.
   - Grouping collections of work orders in batch transactions.
   - Sending single work orders, updates, status replies.

4. **External system** – Spider currently integrates to 10 different support systems within Telenor to read and write information. The integration is based on a standard J2EE integration framework at Telenor called Metro. On Metro Spider both publishes its services to be used by other systems and called the published services from other systems. The processes executed in Spider uses automatic tasks to call on these services and update the network build order with its results.

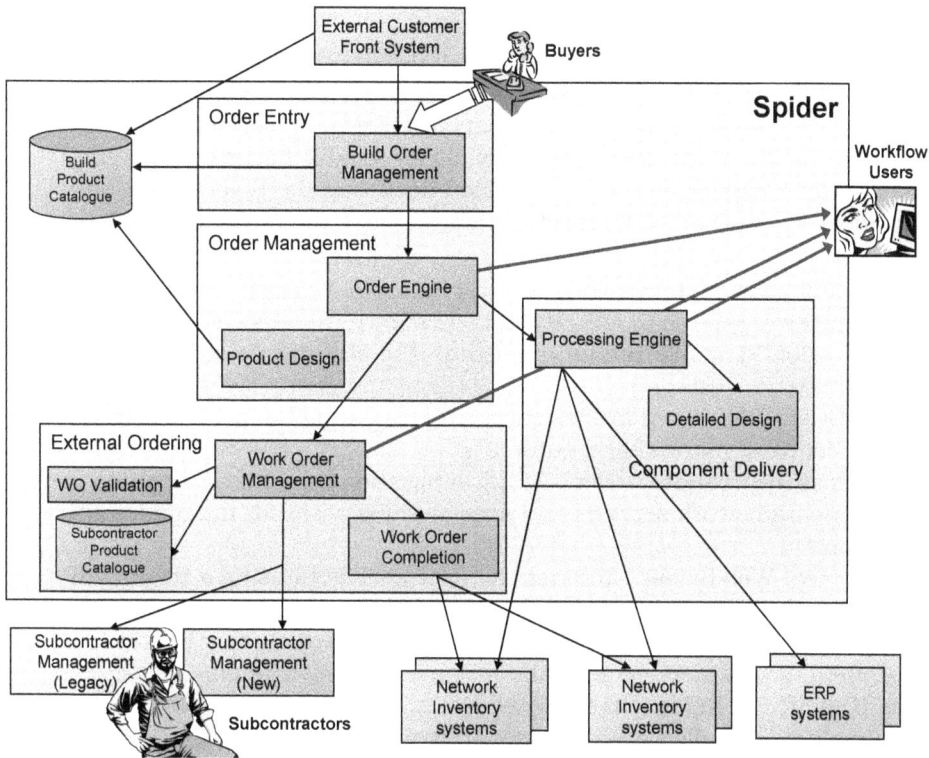

Figure 7: Overview Spider system architecture.

THE IMPACT ON USERS OF THE SYSTEM

The build net unit was established with people from different business units and the unit is geographically distributed. This has been challenging to create one standard business process and a good working environment for the users.

Before,

- Personal skills define the business process each project. Different user groups, different business areas and different projects can have different processes.
- Similar task in different business areas (Mobile/Fixed/Cable TV) require different resources due to separate routines and processes. Knowledge as to how things are done in the user's "own" business area separate tasks even if there is a common goal (the network) and practical commonalities.
- Same information inserted several places – The lack of a common process engine and many different support systems requires the same information to be entered in several places.
- No systematic as to ensure that best practiced is done every time

After;

- The solution carries the business process. It tells you how things are done for the specific project.
- Only technical skills differentiate employees. Its easier/possible for employees to perform tasks in all business areas
- Information follow the order (system). The system supports the interaction with other support systems and inventory systems. This reduce the risk of inconsistent data
- Employees are "problem solvers" focusing only on value adding activities.

THE NEW SYSTEM CONFIGURATION

The Spider system reuses a BPM framework developed by auSystem from Telenor in a project called FLOW. The FLOW system is used at Telenor to automate the delivery process of telecommunication services like broadband (xDSL) access. The core part of the FLOW system is designed as a reusable framework for BPM applications called *FLOW Foundation*, and when designing the Spider solution it was a key element to reuse this existing framework to reduce development time and costs.

The Flow Foundation framework is built using a layered architecture starting from a number of generic COTS products as shown in the lowest platform layer in the figure below. The five products used as the starting point of the framework are:

- TIBCO BPM – Used for designing and executing the processes and its tasks, both manual and automatic.
- JBoss Application Server – J2EE application server that executes the generic framework services and specialized services for the Spider application.
- Tomcat Web Server – Renders all user interfaces using a Struts JSP framework, including both the end user view with inbox, task forms, search operations and the administrative view including user management, group management and parameter configuration.
- ILog JRules Rules Server – Executes all separated business logic rules evaluations called from the executing processes in TIBCO BPM product.
- Oracle Database Server – Separate storage for both process data and order data.

On top of the generic COTS platform layer the FLOW Foundation framework adds common components used at Telenor to support quicker development of BPM applications in a telecommunications environment. This includes components for workflow functionality, system communication/integration, user interface design etc.

Before this framework is ready to be used in building BPM applications at Telenor, another layer is added to the framework: Module patterns. This layer contains reference designs and architectural guidelines of how to build applications on top of the COTS products and framework components to ensure future maintainability and configurability.

Finally the layer of applications is added. The Spider application is built from four application modules:

- Order Entry – for creating and managing orders
- Product Master – the master storage of product definitions on what can be ordered with what SLA and cost.
- Spider Order Manager – executing a selected product process based on the product order in Order Entry, integration both human and automatic systems.
- Spider Component Delivery – executing component processes called from the product process, to allow for a dynamic hierarchical process execution.

Additionally the Spider application makes use of two common modules (External Ordering and Subcontractor Management) that are shared with the FLOW application to communicate work orders to subcontractors performing civil work.

These modules contain the public B2B process definitions and the agreements/products used for ordering across the B2B interface.

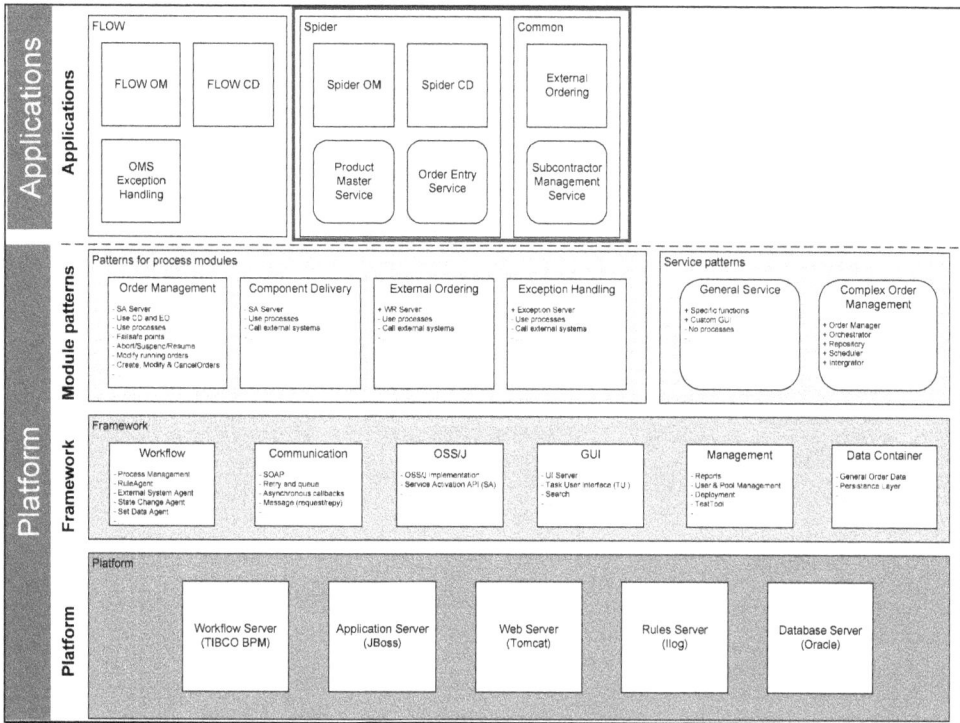

Figure 8: The FLOW Foundation framework reused in Spider.

The system hardware configuration used to run the Spider application is shown in the picture below. The two servers running the Spider application are located within a Telenor internal domain (TID) together with and existing server for the time reporting application Trackview. The Spider application server integrated to all other (external) systems within Telenor and to the external partners (B2B) via a central integration environment at Telenor called Metro. Finally B2B integration towards partners available via the Internet is managed securely via a dedicated B2B gateway located in a demilitarized zone (DMZ).

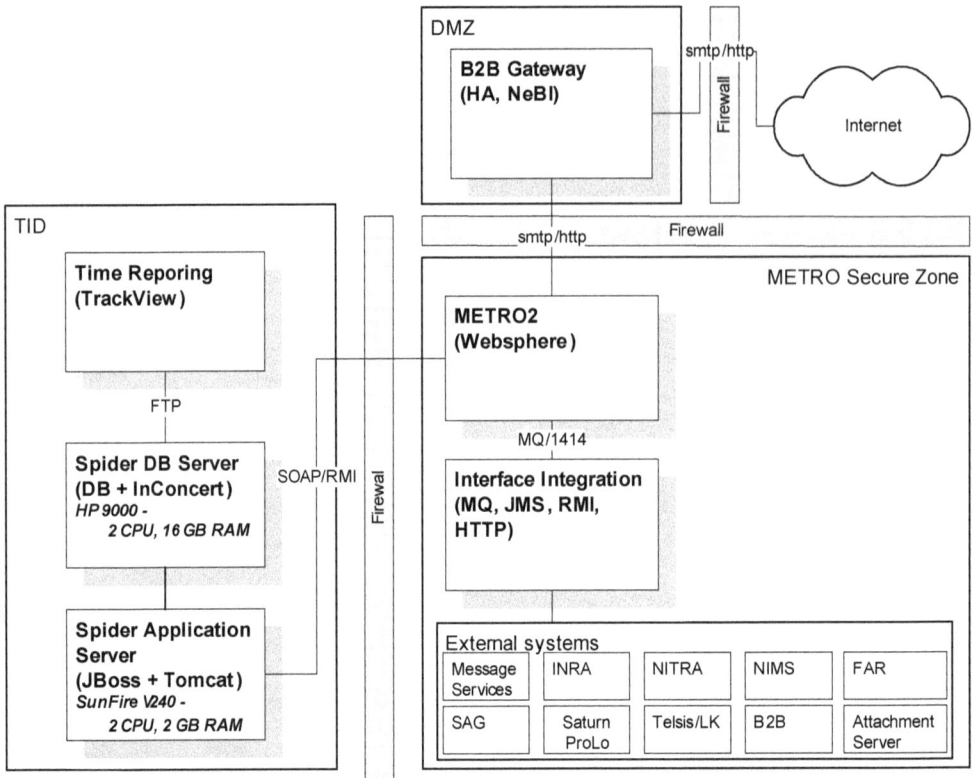

Figure 9: The Spider system hardware platform.

THE BIGGEST HURDLES OVERCOME DURING THE PROJECT

The Spider project was executed using a multi phased project plan. In the initial phase requirements was gathered, validated and documented together with an overview to-be process design. For the delivery phases auSystems (Teleca) was chosen as the supplier based on the BPM applications and framework previously delivered to Telenor. Each delivery phase conducted detailed process design, user interface design and application development. Each delivery phase was concluded by a test phase of both integration testing and acceptance testing.

MANAGEMENT

From the management view the project was confronted with and overcame the following hurdles:

- Financing – As budgets always are tight and infrastructure is a large cost for any telecom operator, the business case for Spider had to be thoroughly documented and positive.
- Internal resources – One of the cornerstones of Telenor's BPM methodology is to involve the users – the experts in their field – in process design. It is obviously so that the same resources are also the most wanted in the daily business.
- Removal of "sub cultures" – When introducing centralized process definitions some local sub cultures and strong local leadership has to give way for a unified way of working.

BUSINESS

From the business view the project was confronted with and overcame the following hurdles:

- How detailed should the business expert users be involved in designing the detailed processes – and how much should be left to IT people? This is a tricky question to balance as the more business experts know about the details of the process design the more they can influence and improve, but on the other hand - the more of their time must be devoted to process design, risking to loose their expert knowledge of the actual business. This has been resolved by introducing a Specification Maturity Model that governs how much detail that needs to be added at each stage in designing a process for execution.
- When procuring a BPM solution that should contain a to-be process not designed in detail, how to handle flexibility vs. fixed price from supplier of a configurable BPM solution? This was jointly constructed and negotiated with the main supplier auSystems (Teleca).
- Spider is also a multi vendor project due to a common integration platform (Metro). All the different support systems within Telenor that needs to be integrated with Spider required separate procurements from the different system suppliers.

TECHNOLOGY

From the technology view the project was confronted with and overcame the following hurdles:

- As Spider is a multi vendor project, care must be taken when specifying interface design to allow parallel development and finally successful integration testing across the interfaces.
- When introducing a new BPM application it may be hard to predict the usage profile of the system during testing, which may cause capacity and stability problems in the production environment. The remedy is to find ways to do simulating and testing with a relevant load model of the BPM system.

QUANTIFICATIONS OF BENEFITS

There are many ways to quantify the benefits of a BPM system – both hard metrics and softer ones related to the users perception of a more stimulating and productive environment. Listed below are some areas of benefits and their outcome due to Spider.

Particular interesting is that the Build Net unit has been able to increase its order handling capacity by 400 percentage, while reducing the staff by 30 percentage in the same time period.

COST SAVINGS

- Telenor has realized cost savings through common contractor agreements
- 2000- 2003; Reduced prices by 40 percentage.
- 2003- 2005; Reduced prices by 5 percentage annually.
- Telenor now handles increased volume of orders with less resources
- 2001- 2005; Reduced employee resources by 30 percentage

INCREASED REVENUES

The Spider solution addresses lower operational cost and therefore increased revenues would come as a consequence. This metric are therefore not applicable in this case study.

PRODUCTIVITY IMPROVEMENTS
- Telenor has reused the same BPM platform as used for service fulfilment
- Establish a new BPM application:
  - FLOW: Foundation 5 months, Application 4 months / product area
  - Spider: Foundation extensions 3 months, Application 3 months / increment
- Introduce new product process in 1 month for Spider (February 2006)
- Telenor handles increased volume of orders with less resources
  - 2001- 2005: Increased order volume by 400 percentage (x4)
- Telenor has created a flexible unit for handling Mobile and Fixed operations using the same recourses
  - Better resource utilization & load balancing

COMPETITIVE ADVANTAGES GAINED

The Spider project has realized benefits within all business drivers for the project. The advantages of the solution are:
- Standardization of processes and products
  - Enables convergent business process between Mobile & Fixed operations
  - Enables automation
- Increased order handling efficiency enables better customer driven investment strategies
- BPM platform enables shorter introduction time of new product processes

Telenor is now taking new steps as to converge more functions in the infrastructure process, and is using part of the same business drivers and goals as were used when the common build net unit was established.

PLANS TO SUSTAIN COMPETITIVE ADVANTAGE

In order for Telenor to sustain, in short-term, its current competitive advantage there is a number of activities that could be done. One significant area of improvement may be to extend the BPM platform to allow for a larger degree of user configured business logic using e.g. dynamic parameter values in business rules to allow extremely short cycle times for updates in business logic.

In order for Telenor to sustain in long-term its current competitive advantages in the area of telecommunications infrastructure rollout, the next step was initiated during 2005 when Telenor established one common unit for tactical planning as illustrated in the figure below.

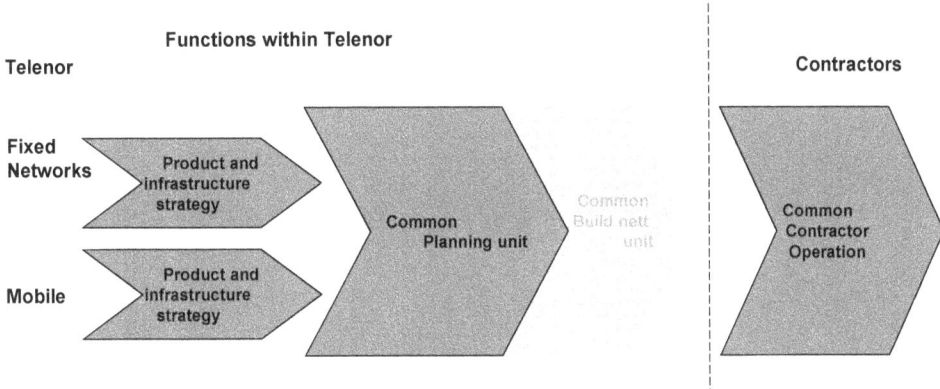

Figure 10: Future step by introducing a common planning unit.

This increase of process area will allow Telenor to further increase resource utilization, but also removing non-value adding steps in the process when information is retyped into different systems.

After that, there is also the possibility to take this convergence approach even one step further and introduce converged processes for product and infrastructure strategy. If Spider and BPM technology are the right IT tools to take convergence so far has jet to be investigated.

Section 2

Middle East and Africa

PaymentCentric, Jordan

Gold Award 2006, Middle East and Africa; nominated by Telaterra, Jordan

SUMMARY

The purpose of this document is to layout the overall success elements of implementing the Merchant Management Application at PaymentCentric (PC) located in Amman, Jordan.

In the following sections you will unfold the innovations accomplished on various levels, the challenges overcome, the competitive advantages the project has added to PC as the end user organization and the vendor's experience. Future plans to upgrade the project are numerous since PC are in continuous expansion throughout the region and beyond; changes depending on the business needs for each different region will be incorporated. Adding to that the increased fierce competition within the market forces PC to excel in and optimize its services.

The following terms are used throughout the document:

PC-Payment**C**entric

ITD–**I**nformation **T**echnology **D**epartment

BBD–**B**usiness **D**evelopment **D**epartment

FD–**F**inancial **D**epartment

OD–**O**perations **D**epartment

Merchant **M**anagement **A**pplication-**MMA**

OVERVIEW

PaymentCentric is a clearing house that is currently focused on providing Electronic Bill Payment and Presentment (EBPP) within the region. We offer several services, two of which are relevant and are summarised as follows:

- **eJABY** enables all bill issuing entities to allow their customers to inquire and pay their postpaid, prepaid, and incidental bills at trusted eJABY payment "Depots" spread throughout the country; securely, efficiently, and in real time.
- eJABY interconnects with payees to allow presentment and ePayment of their issued bills within the network. On the other side, certified payment depots interconnect with eJABY in order to allow their customers to inquire about and pay their bills.
- **eSAL** enables all prepaid card issuers to sell their prepaid cards electronically via **PaymentCentric's network** of eSAL merchants via EFT POS devices and mobile handset software provided to such merchants.

PC's systems are highly automated. However, for the eSAL service, appointing a merchant and terminating him used to be a painstakingly manual process, which leaves a long paper trail. Several employees from four departments are involved in this process. Automating the process in a human-centric workflow system was essential to the growth of PC since the company appointed 100 merchants in Jordan per month on the manual system, but was expecting to appoint 1200 per month in Saudi Arabia.

One of the main success factors behind this project was the leadership at the top. Although some re-engineering occurred while automating the workflow, the line managers' input was very professional.

PROJECT PARTICIPANTS

Merchant Management implementation team possessed a diverse skill set that proved to be very effective in covering and fulfilling all aspects of the project's requirements. They are:

- **PC ITD,** contributed in bridging the gaps between the business and technical requirements, as well as made sure that the new developed application integrates with current applications and PC core technology. The ITD did a huge effort in analysis and design of the different features of the application.

- **PC BDD,** contributed to the overall business concepts of the application developed. BDD is represented by the Sales team that initiates the process.

- **PC OD,** contributed to the overall business concepts of the application developed. Operations are represented by the Customer Care Unit as well as Technical Support Unit that are main contact entity for communication with the Merchants through the CRM module.

- **PC FD,** contributed to the overall business concepts of the application developed. Financial Department is represented by the Accountants that are main contact entity for all financial transactions within the process.

- **Telaterra,** Merchant Management technical developers, a Jordanian company specializing in Internet-enabled software application development were responsible for the development life cycle of the project.

IMPLEMENTATION PROCESS & METHODOLOGY ADVANTAGES

The Merchant Management Application was built in compliance with Telaterra Software methodology which is by itself based on ISO 12207 and PMI Standards for Project Management. Meeting these standards had a great effect on the flow of the project within its several phases. A key milestone in the project was early on during the workshop meetings, where all stakeholders at PC contributed to shape the road map for the project covering the procedures and business processes to be covered in the automated system, profoundly impacting the speed and ease of subsequent phases that were handled through out the change management process issued against schedule, cost and solution. The project was built using rapid approach whereby prototypes have been developed first with the help of the designated department, subsequently it was shown to the department to get a feel of the application and help shape the flow to make sure it streamlines with their approach, finally the prototype was developed into an actual application. This approach helped the buy-in process from the Line Managers and ensured a successful end result.

KEY MOTIVATIONS FOR INSTALLING THE MMA

Operations at PC before MMA

Prior to the installation of **MMA,** existing operations were manually run against a predetermined set of instructions and procedures; data entry was used to store the merchant's information and documents were physically stored in a physical folder cabinet creating a massive paper-trail. The process and procedures were rendered to be of a complex nature with numerous openings for improvement. A significant number of instructions were skipped or not followed in the correct manner creating friction between involved departments, as well as the difficulty in capturing fraudulent Merchants and Black Listed ones.

To add to that, many transactions were associated with a time-line which management was not able to oversee in most of the cases, keeping them from identifying the bottlenecks or reasons delaying the application's progress. Not forgetting the difficulty an employee would deal with if attempting to generate a statistical or performance report for executive management taking several days to complete.

In addition, the manual process presented limitations to the expansion plans of the whole organization as it would have been close to impossible to appoint 1200 merchants in the Saudi market, as it was already difficult to deal with the increased number of registration/termination applications in an efficient manner in Jordan.

No documentation of Sales leads was present, thus follow-up on sales leads was dependant on the sales person with no realistic futuristic look presented to the executive team or proper channeling of sales leads.

A workflow system was the answer to PC business requirements. It was internally acknowledged that some of the major concerns were manipulating the application forms, going through the privileged personnel for approvals, monitoring progress, not skipping part of the process, overlooking legislations, and getting the merchant operational in due time just to mention a few. The proposed solution at that early stage of the project was to insure the correct flow of operations and the flexibility of making changes to the procedures by PC IT Staff.

Why PC needed a workflow application?

The main objective behind installing MMS was the executive management realization of the need of expansion regionally and internationally. This requirement created a need whereby the process of managing their Merchants needed to be dramatically enhanced to cope with the new business need and market share. Thus the handling of Merchant Services needed to integrate seamlessly with PC existing core technology through the proper authorization channels.

The need for a "workflow" based system was very apparent from the beginning. The company's processes are very well mapped and documented. However, this particular process grew organically as the company adapted to market conditions. The process also kept being manually driven for 3 years simply because it had changed a lot and management was worried that a workflow system would need more time to be adapted programmatically, than if it was implemented manually. However management became convinced with time that the advantages that MMA would bring outweigh by far the advantages of the manual system. Furthermore, the chameleon side of the manual system started being more of ineffectiveness rather than a convenience.

Overall Business Innovation

MMA Business Requirements

Following is the list of the system objectives which were implemented in the delivered solution:

- Re-engineering of the merchant management processes by identifying needless steps (waste) and modifying existing processes. The system should improve efficiency reduce/eliminate manual processes and paperwork, as well as eliminate redundancies. It should also enhance PC internal communication.
- Development of standard business rules that serve the processes at PC, also creating the flexibility in the system to cope with changing business rules as per the market needs
- The system should maintain an accurate up-to-date electronic record of all registered merchants and should be used as a central database to integrate all merchant information, including photocopied document images.
- Present PC Staff with a complete web-based cycle for all Merchant Management services from registration to operational support through integration

with their existing administration modules, thus giving a single sign on for all services.

- Full integration between the new web-based application and PC core technology.
- Making use of available technology investments within PC, ex Linux platform and Oracle, as well as some of the existing licenses.
- Having a one organization information hub, between PC headquarters and its branches without the need to install the application at every location.
- Assist PC management to audit, evaluate, monitor and escalate all of the process tasks external as well as the internal ones.
- Assist PC management in overall control of the procedures, by providing statistics that identify bottlenecks thus giving management a clearer view in their endeavor to increase work efficiency and most importantly effectiveness.
- The system should track the status of all merchants and provide a tool to continuously communicate with the merchants to enhance merchant management activities and increase their satisfaction level.
- The system should enable the assignment of processes/procedures to the correct staff/role responsible to carry out the tasks of these specific procedures. It should take into consideration staff redundancy which is needed when employees take vacations and are replaced by their colleagues.
- The system should be able to identify fraudulent merchants or black listed ones on the fly; since we are dealing with critical financial information.
- The system should provide an interface to document Sales Leads and Monitoring Sales Activities, as well as issue notifications and reminders for proper follow up. This is a simple format of a CRM system.
- The system should integrate with the current POS Tracking System to automatically monitor and keep track of POS Machines.
- Integration of several loose modules dealing with merchant registration, whereby all initiation and handling of these modules is currently done automatically within the Merchant Management Application; this includes POS Tracking, Financial Information, and Support Requests.

Merchant Management Business Components
Following are the core business components of the MMA:
- **Merchant Registration**: This module deals with registration of Merchants to become PC Merchants and be able to sell prepaid cards to their customers.
- **Merchant Termination**: This module deals with the termination of the Merchants contract with PC.
- **Merchant CRM**: This module deals with the merchant relationship management, where the Customer Care staff are able to correspond with their merchants, measure their satisfaction, send /receive surveys and present them with competitive offers and full support.
- **Document Archiving:** Each of the modules listed above had a number of needed attachments to be supplied from the merchants indicating the need for a document management system. A simple document archiving system was developed to cover the needs of PC in storing and retrieving of documents electronically.
- **ePayment:** All payments during registration/termination or through any other service are currently entered within the application and integrated with a previously installed financial application (JAMSHEED).

- **Business and Statistical Reporting:** More than 10 very comprehensive reports were designed to cater for all business reporting needed by PC both internally and externally. A good part of those reports contained statistical and historical information to help evaluate and enhance the efficiency of PC through its entire departments as well as comprehensive charts.

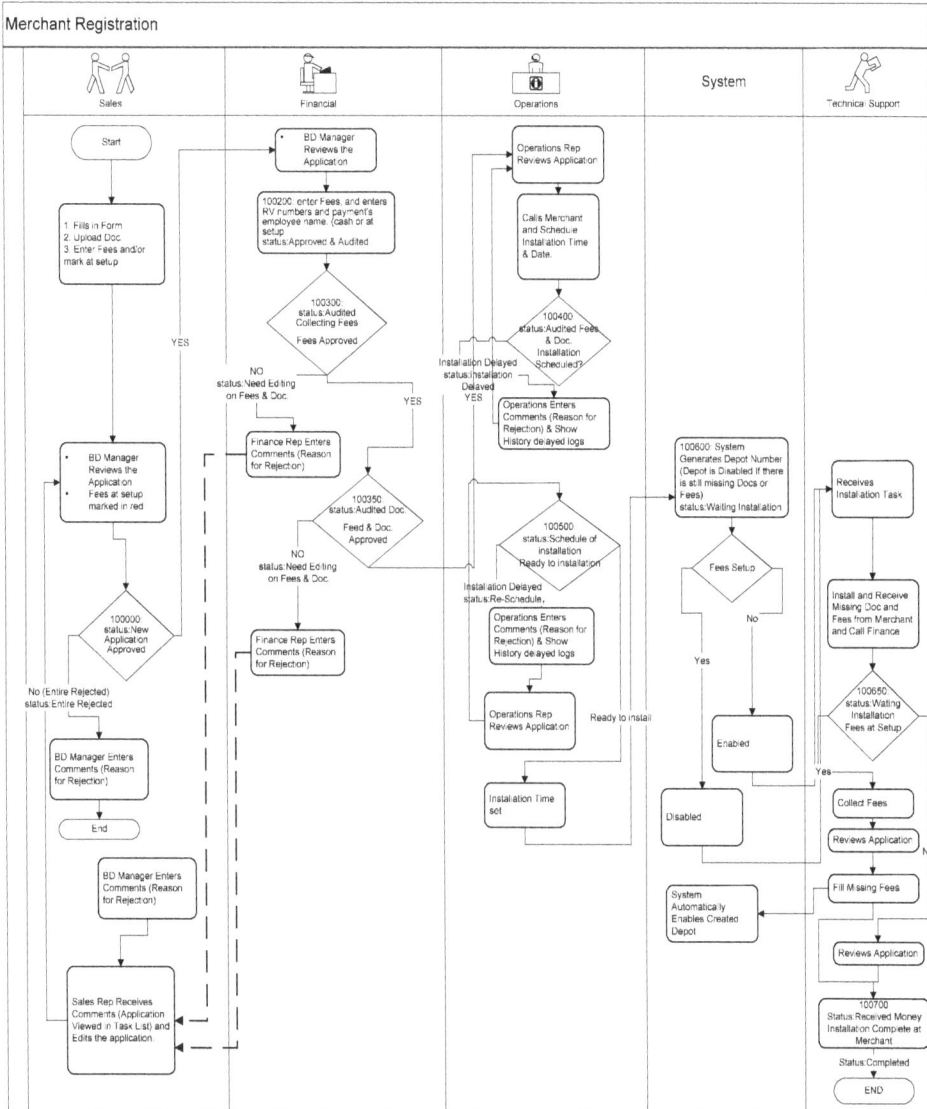

PC Merchant Management Business Process FlowchartsBusiness Innovation Impact

THE BUSINESS INNOVATION IMPACTS OF INSTALLING THE MMA

Faster Merchant Registration

The management wanted to speed up the process of registering a new merchant, by decreasing the time from signing up the merchant until a POS is installed at his location, from 3 working days to 1. Since the market is still young and there are thousands of merchants to be assigned, speed played a decisive factor in gaining market share. The company is now gaining a very healthy market share at the expense of its competitors. With that said, the merchant selection activities were very important for maintaining a certain target 'profitability per merchant'. Without such vision, POS dumping would cause the company to blindly build its market share.

Less Waste

Before we started, the company had started a "Lean Consumption" revision of the merchant registration process. The management identified which activities were of "no or little value" to the customer, and hence tried to reduce them, or eliminate them entirely. The company applied the Lean Solutions methodology and succeeded in re-engineering the processes effectively.

Streamlining the decision process

A lot of decisions were taken at each activity along the way within the process. The sales person holding the registration papers had to pass through several offices, talk to the employee with authority, get the proper signature, and then deposit the papers in the In-tray. This took at least 1 or 2 days. We estimated the time that it took the sales person at 4 hours, which were not utilized in acquiring new merchants. The MMA took into consideration the pooling of authorized persons who can approve an activity within the process. Employees receiving a task on their screen could respond much faster with a few clicks to give approvals, while the sales person is in the field acquiring more merchants.

One of the outcomes of this policy was "empowering" the frontline employees since the decision process was segregated into finer tasks.

Adapting systematically

The market changes continuously with incremental changes that are usually small; most of the time these changes will require modifications on the MMA. So far, such changes have been putting a small burden on the development and QA teams. The cycle of change has been very short so far, and did not entail any friction between the departments, which was something that occurred frequently in the past.

The overall impact was to enable the company to expand into regional markets without fear of scalability. Mostly, the company subsidiary in Saudi Arabia would not have been able to handle 1200 merchant registrations per month without an automated human-centric workflow application.

The complexity lies in the fact that some activities within the process were kept pending till the end of the process. For example, if the merchant did not pay the deposit upon signing the contract, the process of collecting the deposit could wait till the installation of the POS at the merchant location, which meant that the merchant would not be able to transact till the financial department employee could actually confirm receipt of the deposit.

Another complexity factor came from the number of departments involved in the design phase; each wanting to impose its own set of rules that further complicated the tasks downstream.

Overall Technological Innovation

The Merchant Management Application has helped PC move this process from a manually run operation into an electronic workflow-based within a period of one month of deployment. Furthermore, it seamlessly integrated within PC current "admin" module inheriting the same look & feel and navigation style. It also integrated with the core technology providing a single comprehensive area for merchant management.

Merchant Management Application Architecture

All processes and procedures were translated into an XML format using the "Business Process Modeling Language" (*BPML*) version 2.0 standard, which is an

Extensible Markup Language (XML)-based meta-language developed by the Business Process Management Initiative (BPMI.org) as a means of modeling business processes, much as XML is, itself, a meta-language with the ability to model enterprise data. BML allowed PC both conformity with worldwide standards for business process definition as well as enabling high flexibility in adjusting MMA for future changes in process and activities. PC now uses BPML as the main modeling language for all of its business processes.

The solution was built using Macromedia ColdFusion MX through the creation of ColdFusion Components (CFCs) representing the business layer, HTML/CFML (ColdFusion Markup Language) for the GUI layer, and Oracle 9i for the database layer amongst other layers.

The following diagram shows each layer within the web application. Telaterra utilized a methodology named Fusebox to separate the GUI layer from the business logic layer.

Following is a diagram depicting the different layers according to the technologies within the project.

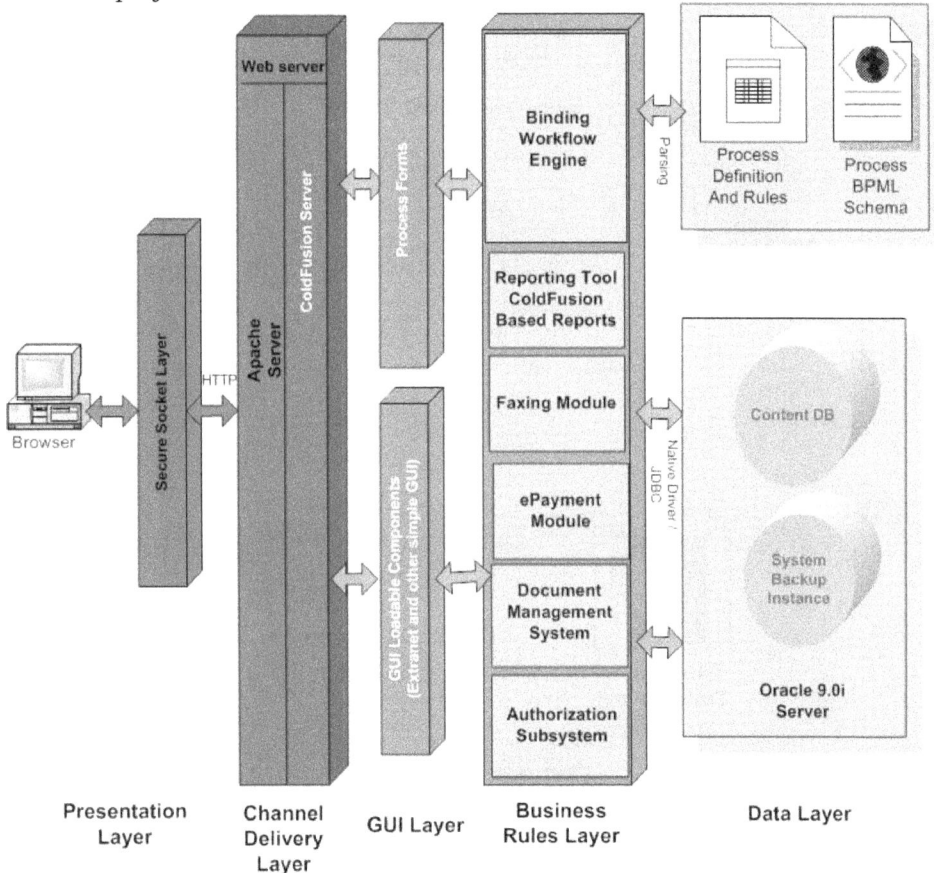

BINDING WORKFLOW ENGINE (BWE)

BWE is a **human-centric** workflow; which depends to a greater extent on the people in an organization. Human-centric as opposed to process-centric; requires a high level of interactivity between the person and the solution in order to feed the correct information into the activity a person is responsible for, which facilitates processing any of the services a person is in charge of to feed the next set of activities and so forth. The BWE coordinates and binds all of the components (See

Components View diagram below) in order to work through the process instantiating each activity or atomic activity as it occurs. It is also responsible for binding the components to create a single instance.

Telaterra Software developed the Binding Workflow Engine (BWE) which was utilized to parse the BPML-based XML.

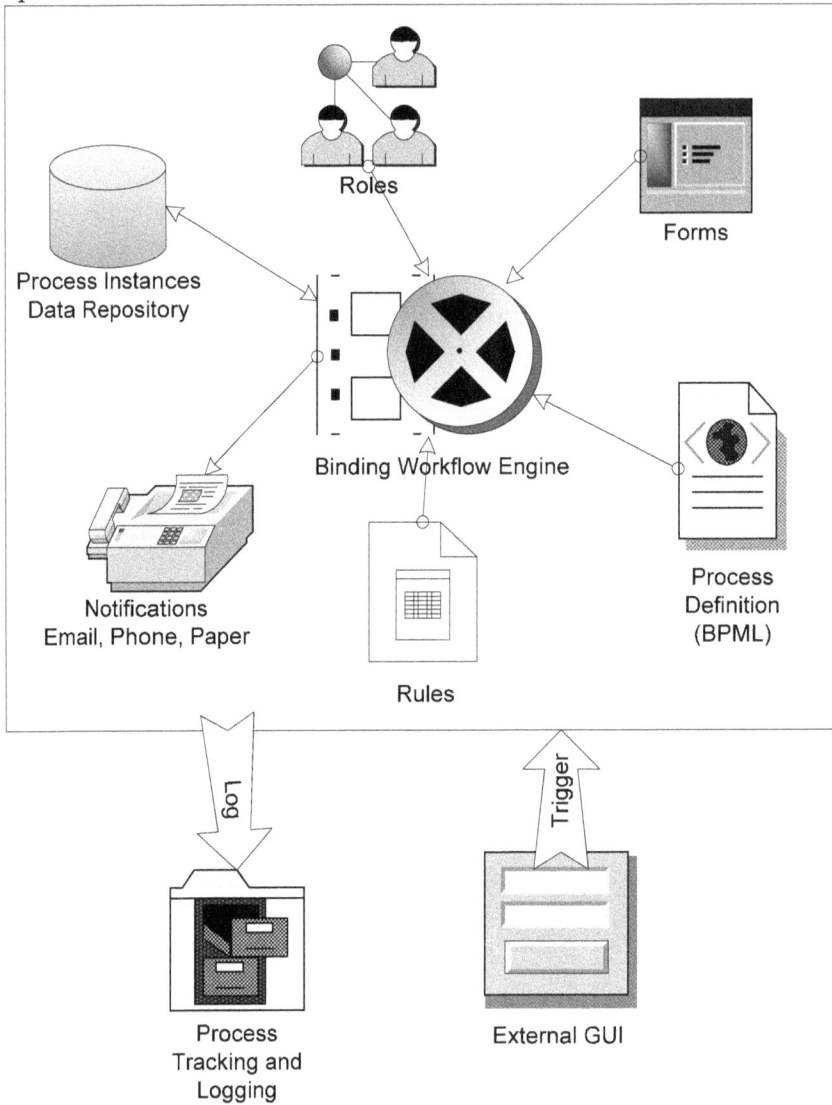

Components View

The diagram below demonstrates how the BWE binds the system components:

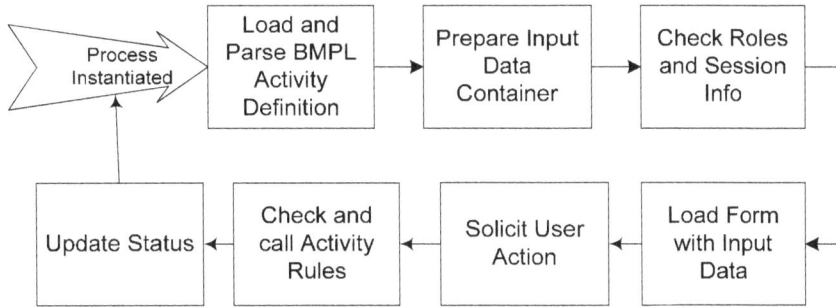

Each activity is modeled as per the following diagram:

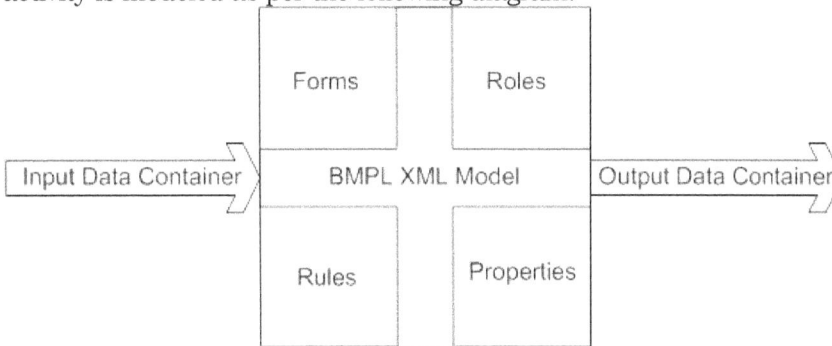

Furthermore, Telaterra developed a process editor and builder interface that offers maximum flexibility for the client. Using this tool, the client can modify and create different processes to expand his process flow or modify it with no programming experience, thus having full ownership and control over his process flow. He/She can modify process attributes such as (Process Type, Next Process, Category, Documentation, etc). A graphical view displaying the process in association with its location within the flow is presented to ensure correctness. The processes are saved in the Database in xml format and then parsed by the BWE upon usage. Following screen shot represent this tool:

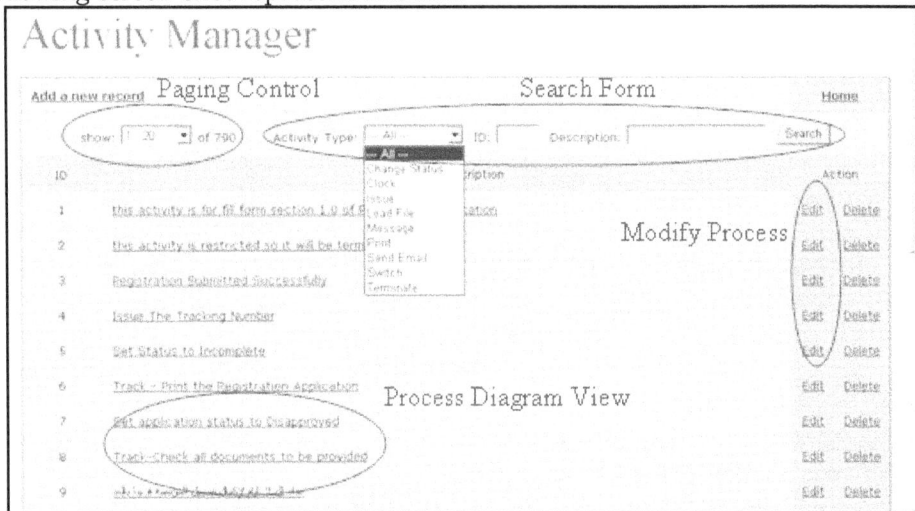

Process Manager

System:	☑
Authority Section:	☐ Registration ☐ Permitting
Property:	Status ▾
Status:	Approval on Plans ▾
Next Activity Number:	2 Search
Save	Cancel

Process Details Page

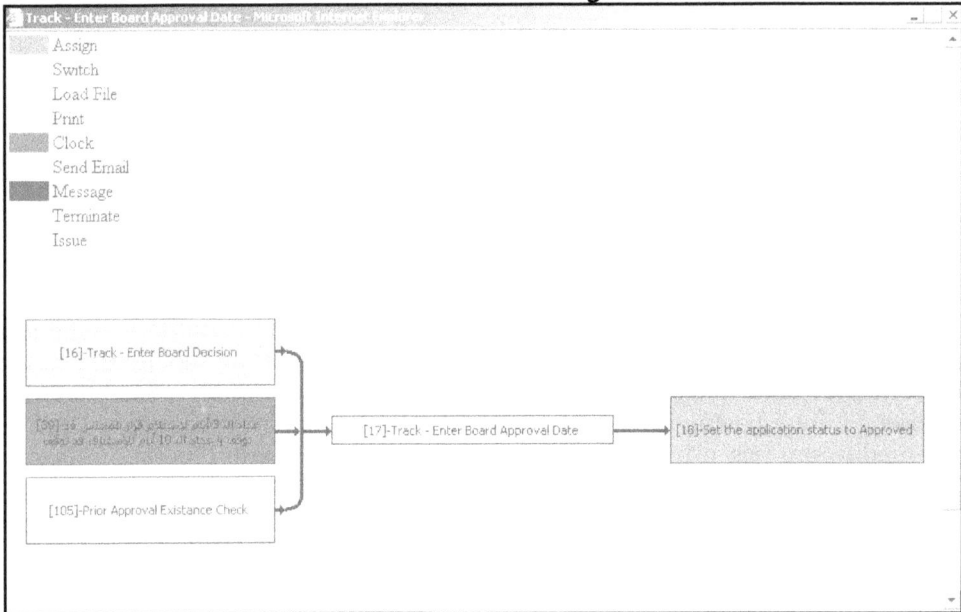

Track - Enter Board Approval Date - Microsoft Internet Explorer

Assign
Switch
Load File
Print
Clock
Send Email
Message
Terminate
Issue

[16]-Track - Enter Board Decision

[17]-Track - Enter Board Approval Date

[18]-Set the application status to Approved

[105]-Prior Approval Existance Check

GUI Representation of the Processes

SYSTEM USERS

The following table illustrates the different states at PC before and after MMA:

Before MMA	MMA System Users
• Long paper trail for all merchant registration and applications, including supporting documents	• Ability to store and retrieve documents through the integrated document archiving system
• Loose procedures and standardization of processes	• Ease of use (User Friendly)
• Loose modules handling the registration of the merchants (Merchant Information, Merchant Financials, POS Inventory, Merchant Communications)	• Ability to locate the pending point of the merchant application being processed
	• Viewing pending application details per user
• Manual Archiving of contracts and related documentation	• Strong management monitoring capability to determine exactly where the bottleneck obstacle exists per application per user
• Difficulty of following up on a	

pending application and point reached or covered so far	• Effortless correspondence between departments.
• General indications of pending application status through verbal feedback	• Reduction to minimal time spent on correspondence
• Immense efforts of follow up and communication between departments and with merchants.	• Single application to deal in the backend with several modules for the registration of merchants
• None existent management monitoring capabilities of applications standing point per user	• All information dealing with merchants is stored and easily retrieved by staff whenever needed
• Immense efforts to generate reports to management	• System caters for 1200 new Merchants per month
• System barely caters for 100 new Merchants per month.	• Ease of communication with merchants on a daily basis with mass distribution features available.

BIGGEST HURDLES OVERCOME

	Merchant Management Project Challenges
Managerial Level	• Buy-In of Line Managers and finding the middle ground • Managing the top Management Decisions
Business Level	• Re-engineering the registration of Merchants and setting up the rules and standards • Training PC staff to embrace the system and use it proactively in their daily work • Training PC Administrators on the process editor and how to study the impacts of the changes done to the process across the board
Technology	• Creating interfaces to maintain PC core-technology as a separate layer • Maintaining Security since we are dealing with financial data

The system deployment was considerably a smooth process due to the fact that most users were involved in the design phases of the application. The two major issues that were encountered during and after the implementation were as follows:

• **Resistance from the sales staff**–as they were now forced to do a lot of data entry to the application to initiate the process of registration; a task that they did not have to do earlier. This was soon solved by PC management by, minimizing the registration form data.

• **Friction between departments**–automatic integration between departments work and the ability of application refusal/returning between departments created friction between line managers during early usage of the system. Executive management had to intervene to impose strict inter-department rules. No technical work needed to be done here, as the system offered the flexibility of modifying the process flow though the Process Editor.

NEW SYSTEM CONFIGURATION

The system configuration and architecture used to deploy MMA was founded on existing infrastructure at PC. Client workstations consist of 24 PCs running Windows XP Professional and accessing the system through MS-Internet Explorer 6 being authenticated using database-based authentication.

The following are all off –the-shelf software products which the system utilizes:

* Macromedia JRUN 4 as ColdFusion MX 6.1 Application Server
* Apache 1.327 with SSL as the Web Server
* Oracle 9.0i as the Database Server
* Suse Linux latest version
* SMTP as the Email sending protocol
* Microsoft Windows XP professional as the client PC's operating system

CONFIGURATION VIEW

The following diagram displays the current system configuration:

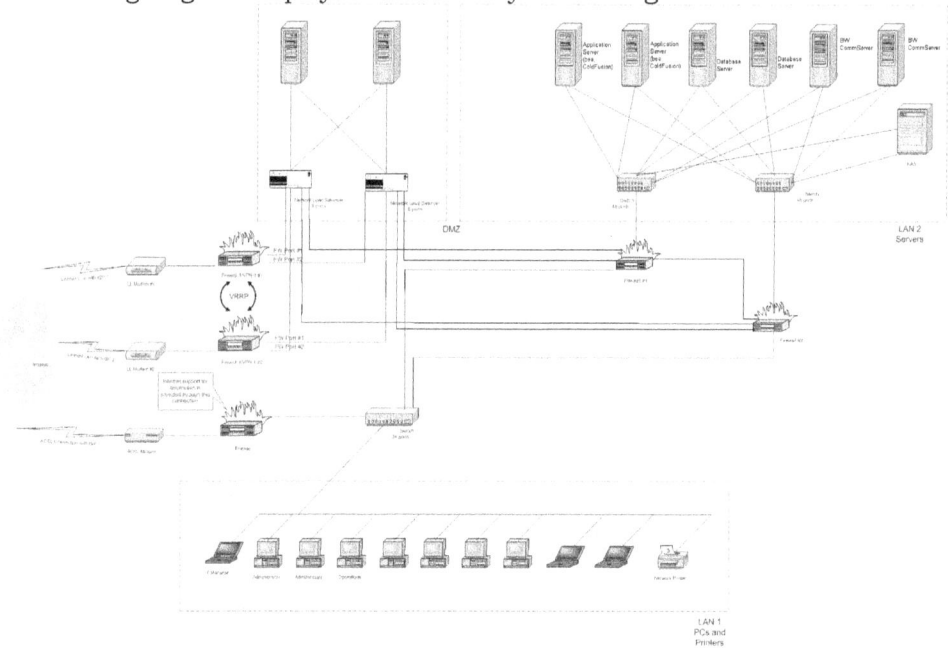

SAVINGS, REVENUE & PRODUCTIVITY

The following are direct factors that were measured 3 months after the MMA was implemented:

* Merchant Registration is down from 3 to 1 business day
* Merchant acquisition cost decreased by JD18
* There were no directly measured financial revenues from the project due to the fact that several projects that could impact revenue had taken place. However, we list the following KPI's that were measured 4 months after implementing the MMA:
* Market share in Jordan increased by 11 percent
* Monthly processed volumes increased by 6 percent

COMPETITIVE ADVANTAGES

Business Oriented Advantages

The main competitive advantage that we were able to capture is faster merchant acquisition, which led to higher market share within a relatively short period of time. Moreover, our process enabled us to be more selective of merchants, which meant higher monthly volumes.

In general, merchants who sign up to the service have to pay a deposit. They would like to see this deposit utilized within a very short period of time. If one of our salespersons approached a merchant at the same time when a competitor reached him, we would usually assign the merchants because we offer slightly better features, and much faster merchant activation.

One of the decisive factors that increased merchant acquisition was a side effect from this process. Apparently, merchants did not want too much paperwork, and they liked computer generated paperwork. Promotion by word of mouth constitutes more than 40 percent of our sales lead generation, and thus we were always receiving good customer referrals.

Immediate and Long Term Plans

The most important next step is to implement the system on the same servers, to be utilized by our staff in Saudi Arabia. The workflow will need to change slightly to accommodate regions within Saudi.

One of the issues we are contemplating at this stage is how to increase productivity by another large factor, which is data capturing. In this case, we feel that a PDA could be very useful for the salesperson entering the data at the merchant shop, thus decreasing the need for salespersons to have to come back to the office for data entry. This could very well work in Saudi, and would introduce large savings.

When the salespersons are in the field, they visit a lot of shops. Only such merchants who pay the deposit are actually enrolled in the service and a registration form and contract are filled. The MMA started by gathering information on non-interested merchants but not in a fully-fledged CRM system. We feel that we will be able to extend the initial data entry screens to crease a more comprehensive CRM system.

The MMA will also be able to integrate with other extensions to the eSAL service; such as the Mobile eSAL channel. In this channel, merchants are not required to sign a contract and are enrolled via a very short term process. However, merchants on the system are all alike. Registering Mobile eSAL merchants through the MMA should be able to enhance the enrolment process for both the merchant and PC.

TRACKER System, South Africa

Silver Award 2006, Middle East and Africa; nominated by TIBCO, South Africa

ABOUT TRACKER

The TRACKER System was developed in the USA by LoJack where it has been operational since 1986. It was specifically developed to assist the police in curtailing vehicle theft. To date there are more than two million units fitted throughout 25 countries in the world including the USA, UK, Hong Kong, Russia, Korea, Mexico, Brazil, Argentina and Colombia. In South Africa, TRACKER has been operational since October 1996. The company enjoys strong financial backing and has invested millions in establishing its own network and providing the police with the technology to fight vehicle crime. Tracker also has its own recovery teams based throughout South Africa.

TRACKER is a jointly owned by FirstRand (32.5 percent), VenFin (31 percent), The Mineworkers Investment Company (26.5 percent) and a Private Investment Consortium (10 percent).

BUSINESS REQUIREMENTS

The Tracker Credit Control call centre receives approximately ±350 Client customer calls a day. These calls are currently handled manually and emails, faxes and physical mail are scanned into the system. The Business Process Management (BPM) implementation was necessary to automate this manual process and make is simpler for the consultants to complete their tasks.

The main business objectives:

Queries
- Automation of query process.
- To increase productivity in terms of handling incoming calls.
- To get better insight into the amount of work done by each consultant and to enable quality checks on the work.
- To be able to draw detailed reports on all the calls handled by the call centre.
- To be able to revise the call centre process when needed to suit business.

Collections
- Automation of collection process.
- Proactive management of the Tracker collection process.
- Optimise the collection process regarding contact, correspondence and feedback to the customer.
- To have efficient follow-up on PTPs by utilising a diary action follow-up system within TIBCO BPM.
- To manage the process of collections more efficiently by sending customers reminders to pay and by setting deadlines to check if payments are done.
- To save money on outgoing call costs by sending an SMS instead.
- To obtain management information on customers that were contacted due to arrears.

Reports
- Management information regarding customers that are in arrears.

- Management reports regarding customer query trends, risks and individual performance of Tracker credit control consultants.
- Management reports regarding collection trends, risks and individual performance of Tracker credit control consultants.
- Productivity reports.

BUSINESS REQUIREMENTS

At the core of the solution are automated business processes which are defined in, and controlled by, TIBCO's BPM Software. TIBCO's BPM Software applies business rules to determine each step in the processes and activities, who should conclude the activity and when it should be completed. This automation of processes and activities enforces a high degree of consistency, allowing for the smooth handling of customer calls and resulting in more efficient management of the query and subscription collection process.

User interaction is facilitated through a customised out-of-the-box Web client. Time sensitive tasks are controlled by deadlines and priorities, and escalation activities (such as a simple reminder) are initiated automatically by TIBCO BPM when a deadline expires. This reduces delays in the process and improves service levels.

Control and visibility of the process is provided automatically. All work in progress is recorded in TIBCO BPM, and work items (tasks) are delivered into work queues which are accessed by the TIBCO BPM work queue manager. Suitably authorised users easily perform tasks, such as processing customer calls. TIBCO BPM also provides an automatic audit trail of every activity.

The results (driven by business requirements) were:

- Creating a positive professional customer experience;
- Ensuring that TIBCO BPM enforces Tracker's procedures seamlessly;
- Delivery of accurate trends and management reports regarding the query and collection process;
- The enablement of effective, easy handling and resolution of customer calls;
- Better management of the process and people that are required to help resolve queries.

THE MEASUREMENT OF BENEFITS

In order to demonstrate that the proposed solution delivered significant business benefit, it was recommended that measures be identified. TIBCO BPM generates raw data from which these measures can be derived, extracted and analysed.

However, it can often be difficult to construct tangible measures for some benefits. A pre-requisite for determining how TIBCO BPM has improved the process is to benchmark measures in the existing process.

The following means of identifying the success of the proposed solution were put forward and used in measuring the benefits:

- Improvement in end-to-end process time, as opposed to a manual system.
- Reduction in errors.
- Internal satisfaction surveys.
- Audit trails for accountability.
- Improvement of process efficiency.
- Process time-frame reduction.
- Number of queries received and resolved.
- Number of collections received and resolved.

The User Interface Layer

In a BPM solution, the user interface layer performs the following functions:

- It provides a work queue manager where a user is notified of work that needs to be done, and selects a work item to do.
- It provides a task manager - some form of dialogue and information display that guides a user through the performance of the task or tasks represented by individual work items.

The BPM Layer

The BPM layer is the dominant component of a BPM solution. It consists of one or more TIBCO BPM procedures, each of which automates a defined business process. This means the rules of the business process are both defined and implemented using TIBCO BPM. TIBCO BPM controls who does what and when - i.e. it delivers work to the appropriate person. It also automatically takes control of the process if work does not get carried out within defined timescales.

As part of the BPM layer, there are usually one or more BPM triggers which take the form of interfaces to other applications, triggering certain TIBCO BPM procedures to start automatically when an event takes place, such as scanning in a document, writing a record to a database, or the receipt of a data file.

The Middleware Layer

The middleware layer consists of black box interfaces which are called by TIBCO BPM procedures in order to retrieve data from, or write data to, other applications. These black boxes are normally created as bespoke interfaces for each BPM solution and are re-usable. The design and development of these generic, parameter-driven interfaces is a one-off activity, resulting in black boxes which are re-used in many different TIBCO BPM procedures. This reduces development time and saves the customer money.

The Application Layer

The application layer consists of all the other applications, databases and documents which contain information that needs to be delivered to a user during the processing of a case or a TIBCO BPM procedure, or which needs to be updated automatically by TIBCO as the case progresses. Each component of the application layer is normally made accessible to TIBCO by a black box interface in the middleware layer. For example, a generic SQL interface allows TIBCO BPM procedures to retrieve or update information in a relational database such as SQL or Oracle Server.

Components of the TIBCO BPM Solution

This section adapts the generic BPM Layered Model, presented in the previous section, to present the components of a BPM solution which are specific to the requirements of Tracker. Figure 2 represents these components diagrammatically, and the remainder of this section describes the individual components within the context of each layer in the BPM Layered Model.

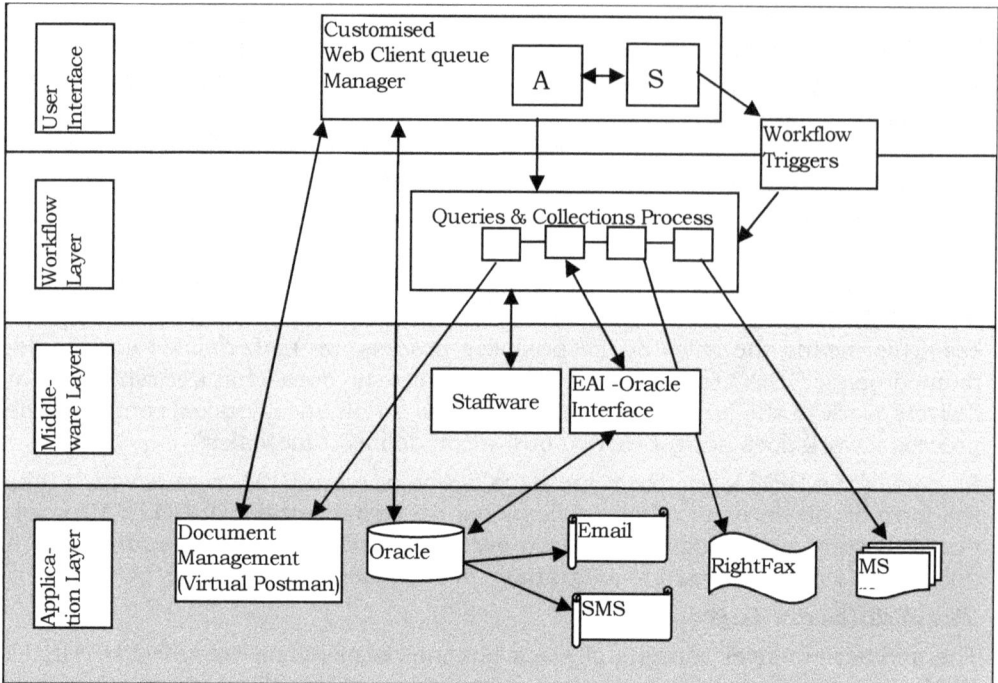

Figure 2 The components of the proposed TIBCO BPM solution
Components of the User Interface Layer

Customised/Standard Web Client

This project did not require a specialised user interface, which means the "out the box" Web client supplied by TIBCO could be used. This simplifies third-party developer defined integration, along with deployment and training.

Tabs on the TIBCO BPM Web client work item pages allow Tracker to display client information extracted from the Oracle database as well as documents from the document management system. This information is extracted in real-time and is displayed on the Web client screen in different tabs.

The following interfaces were required:

- Oracle access (CDS and Willow) through the EAI Oracle Adapter.
- Document Management Interface - Virtual Postman (Faxes, Scanned Docs, Emails and Word documents)
- RightFax
- Microsoft Office Products.
- Administration (for Administrators and Supervisors)

The TIBCO BPM Web client runs on standard windows based workstations through the browser and uses ASP pages that communicate to the TIBCO BPM process objects server. The TIBCO BPM Web Client runs on IIS on either the TIBCO BPM servers.

The output of the Web server is standard HTML, with little or no client side scripting and DHTML. The TIBCO BPM Web Client runs on Internet Explorer 5.5 and upwards.

Process Triggers

Process triggers allow for new cases to be started in a procedure without human intervention. This allows for external systems (such as a Virtual Postman) to initiate a trigger and allow the broker to create new cases in the TIBCO BPM engine. In the Tracker scenario, a broker starts the necessary cases for new incoming correspondence. This is to add newly created word documents and attached to specific cases.

Components of the BPM, Middleware and Application Layers

The following diagrams provide an overview of the implemented processes.

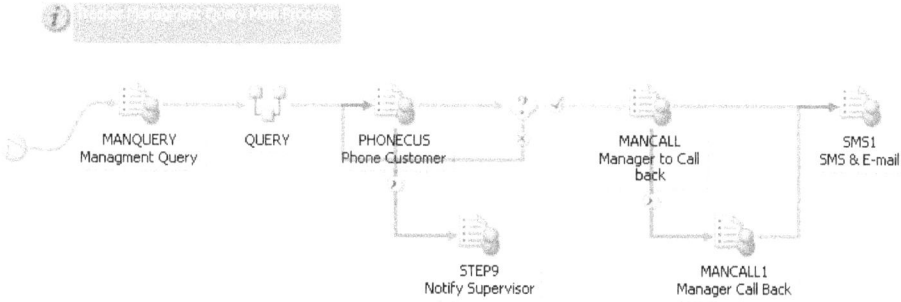

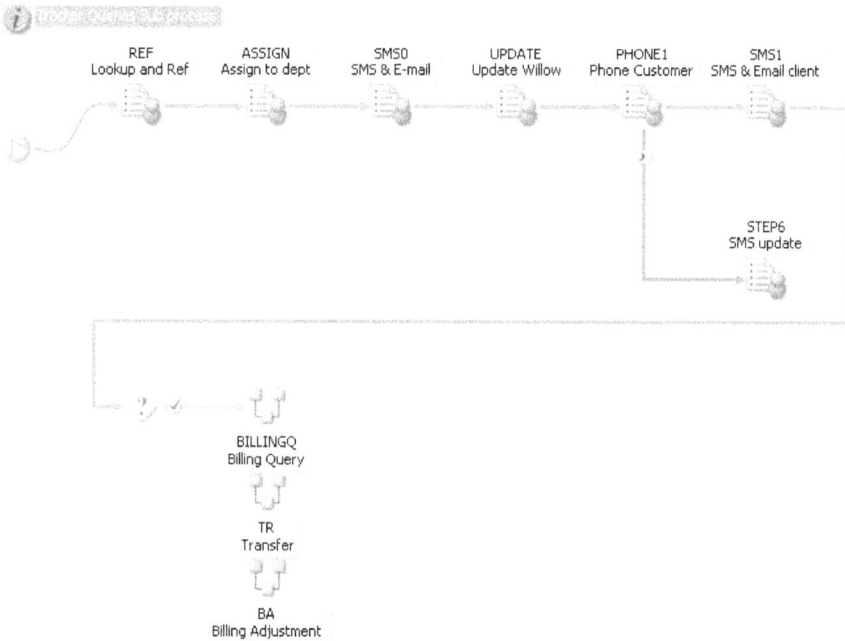

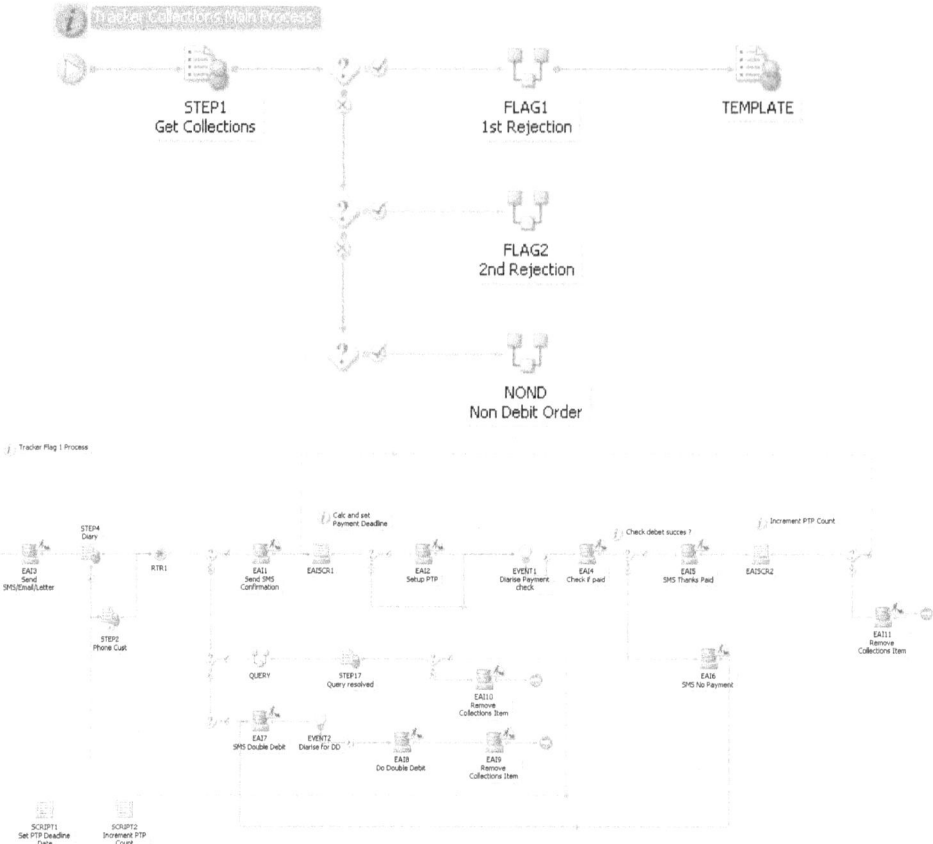

Explanatory notes

The diagram is divided into four sections, **Process Definition** defines the process flow from a business perspective, **User Interface** defines what the user sees at each stage in the process, **Architecture** defines how the system is put together, and **Backend Systems** defines what third party interfaces are needed.

Process Definition

Customer queries

Tracker receives incoming client queries on a daily basis. When a query arrives, the call centre evaluates the query and starts a BPM case that facilitates the resolution of the query and notifies the customer on a regular basis throughout the process via email or SMS of the status of the query.

Queries are also captured on the Tracker BPM system electronically. These methods include Fax, email, scanned documents (a result of manual paper – letters or faxes). An electronic broker integrated into the Virtual Postman system, picks up any new electronic customer communications and starts a new BPM case in TIBCO BPM. As soon as the customer is identified (after the indexing step), the system notifies the customer that the correspondence was received and also supplies the customer with a case reference number.

Once the BPM case is started, the BPM system ensures that the query is handled and resolved as soon as possible. The process enforces the preset deadlines and ensures that the process SLA is adhered to and maintained.

The first step in the process is indexing. This step identifies the work item by assigning a client account number, ID number or car registration number to the work item. Once the indexing step is complete, the system populates the other outstanding information from the Oracle database using an Enterprise Application Integration (EAI).

If the query originated from a document entering the system, the document is stored in Tracker's document management system and a reference is carried through the process to the location of the document. When the call centre consultants need to refer back to the document, it is accessed directly from the BPM client screen.

Any electronic communication from Tracker to the client is controlled and created automatically from the BPM system. The system caters for SMS, email and Faxing. Faxing is done using an electronic broker. SMS and email messages are sent as a result of an entry in the Oracle database which is done through the EAI step. The electronic broker is a Windows service (resident software package on the BPM server) that is developed to handle all electronic functions in the system.

Collections

A TIBCO BPM process is designed to explore the Oracle database on a daily basis for new entries. This process uses the broker to execute a stored procedure which returns all customer account numbers that are in arrears. A TIBCO BPM collections case is then started for every customer that is in arrears.

The collections process sends the customer an SMS message or an email notifying him that the account is in arrears. The work item is diarised for one day after the SMS or email message is sent. This allows the customer to call the call centre and make the necessary arrangements for payment.

If the customer does not call back within one day, he is then contacted by a call centre consultant the following day to make the necessary arrangements.

User Interface

The user gains access to the system by opening a shortcut in the Windows Internet Explorer. A username and password screen is presented to the user. Only users with the necessary access rights are able to log on to the TIBCO BPM Web client.

Each user has access to a personal queue as well as the assigned group queues where the work assigned to them is delivered. Because work items are mainly delivered to group queues, the user sees all the work items that are available. As soon as a work item is opened, the users name is stamped next to the item and from that moment onwards, that work is then performed by that consultant.

Architecture

This section explains in more detail the process of integrating all the systems that TIBCO BPM uses in the Collections and Queries processes.

SMS Messages (Outgoing only)

At this stage SMS message is only outgoing, although this may change in the future.

Outgoing SMS messages are sent using information from the Oracle database. TIBCO BPM writes a record to an Oracle table using an EAI step in the TIBCO BPM process stating the SMS status. The information that is passed to the database is the following.

- Mobile number.

- The message.
- The user name sending the message.

E-Mail Messages

Outgoing

Outgoing email messages are sent the same way as the SMS Message. The necessary information is written to an Oracle database using a TIBCO BPM EAI step. TIBCO BPM only executes a predefined Oracle query and passes the necessary file to the query.

Incoming

Incoming email messages are not handled by TIBCO BPM. The document management system, Virtual Postman, reads all incoming email messages sent to a mailbox intended for the TIBCO BPM processes. Virtual Postman saves the email message in its repository and writes an XML file in a predefined directory where TIBCO BPM software reads it. The XML file contains the URL to the location of the relevant document.

A TIBCO BPM process designed to poll the XML file directory opens the XML file and creates a new TIBCO BPM index case. Where Virtual Postman pre-indexes the email message, TIBCO BPM appends it to an existing case in TIBCO BPM. When a customer is replying with information relating to a specific TIBCO BPM case, the process executes an Event Step in the existing TIBCO BPM case and adds the new document URL to the TIBCO BPM case.

When an Index case is started, someone indexes the email document and adds information to the case identifying the client that the email belongs to. In this case the process also searches the TIBCO BPM database for existing cases. If no case for the current customer exists, a new case is started.

Fax

Outgoing

Outgoing faxes make use of RightFax. RightFax supplies a Com API that allows you to send a fax programmatically. This is done using the TIBCO BPM Broker. If a word document is faxed out, the document is generated and saved to the Virtual Postman. A following step is responsible for sending the word document via the TIBCO BPM Broker Control Service and using the RightFax Com API.

Incoming

Incoming faxes are mailed from RightFax to a mailbox intended for TIBCO BPM. This mailbox is treated like the email inbox. These mails then follow the same path as the normal incoming email messages.

Word Documents

Word documents are created through TIBCO BPM using the MS Word Com API. The MS Word Com API exposes all the functionality to open a predefined MS Word template and inserts BPM specific data.

All required bookmarks in the MS Word template are captured in the TIBCO BPM process. The TIBCO BPM Broker Control Service is used to open the MS Word template from a predefined directory.

Once the population of the MS Word template is complete, the new document is saved to a directory; the TIBCO BPM Broker Control Service mails the new document with all the index values to a mailbox that is monitored by Virtual Postman. Virtual Postman saves the document to the document repository. The document is sent as a normal mail message with an attached MS Word document. The Subject field for the mail message contains the index values. The format for the subject field should be as follows.

- The index field name in this example is displayed as italic characters.
- The index value follows after the comma.
- One index field is separated from another with a pipe (|) character.
- The SW_CASENUM field is the unique case number that TIBCO BPM assigns to each new case.
- The SW_PROCNAM field identifies the procedure type that the case belongs to.

The Virtual Postman reads the email message containing the MS Word document like it does all other incoming email messages. The Virtual Postman identifies the TIBCO BPM case number in the subject field of the email message and adds the rest of the index values to the repository.

The Virtual Postman then writes a new XML to the directory where TIBCO BPM picks up all new incoming documents. The XML file contains the URL for the MS-Word document as well as the rest of the index values. TIBCO BPM then adds the URL to the TIBCO BPM case number supplied in the index values. This is done by triggering a TIBCO BPM event step in the existing TIBCO BPM case.

Document Management

The Virtual Postman is the document management solution that is used in the TIBCO BPM solution. The documents in the Virtual Postman are linked to a TIBCO BPM case with a URL. The URL is saved in a TIBCO BPM field.

Oracle

The database for the Tracker Backend systems is Oracle. All integration to the Oracle database is done via a TIBCO BPM EAI step. The EAI step executes a stored procedure on the Oracle database and responds with the required data.

All the backend systems in the Tracker architecture run on Oracle databases. All integration to the tracker backend systems (CDS and Willow) relating to the process is handled by TIBCO BPM.

IMPLEMENTATION TIMETABLE AND ESTIMATED EFFORT
Implementation Tasks

This section identifies the most significant tasks that were carried out in order to implement the proposed system, and covers the schedule of these tasks.

- Project initiation
    - Confirmation of project plan
    - Allocation of resources
    - Agreement of milestones and responsibilities
- Procurement
    - Identification and acquisition of required hardware
    - Software and services
- Detailed design
    - Scoping study, which provides an overview of the proposed solution
    - Technical specification of middleware components
- Hardware configuration (development, test and production environments)
    - Hardware installation
    - Operating system installation and configuration
- Software configuration

- - Installation and configuration of TIBCO BPM servers
  - Web server in development, test and live environments
  - Installation of any other required software (e.g. RightFax)
- Skills acquisition (TIBCO BPM training)
  - Introduction to TIBCO BPM and Procedure definition (Done)
  - System integration (SPO)
  - System administration
- Development
  - User Interfaces
  - Process development
    - Prototyping of processes for the Collections and Queries
  - Middleware development
- Resilience strategy
  - Strategy to minimise interruption of business in event of system failure
  - Backup strategy
- Testing and Training
  - Integration testing
    - End-to-end testing of BPM procedure and interfaces in target environment
  - Acceptance testing
    - User-defined and conducted tests to verify functionality
  - Resilience testing
    - Verification of recovery procedures identified by resilience strategy
  - End user training
    - Training of analysts, production staff and other potential users
- Roll-out
  - Definition of TIBCO BPM users and groups
  - Deployment of Web server(s), integration components

Other Activities

It was fully expected that additional activities would need to be carried out in order to support the implementation of the proposed BPM system, including:

- Project management
- Network capacity planning
- Design of system topology – location and number of application servers, file servers, network connections, etc
- Design, development and testing of software version control and release mechanisms, if not already in place or not compatible with technical characteristics of the components of the proposed solution
- System administration - definition of users, user attributes and groups in TIBCO BPM, users and passwords in server operating system, backup procedures
- Preparation of acceptance test plans
- Definition and agreement of operational procedures, user guides, training materials
- Definition of management information requirements for monitoring performance, productivity gains, etc.
- Migration planning and optional development of conversion or back-loading components if the existing (manual) workload needs to be incorporated in the automated BPM system

- Skills transfer for ongoing development and support
- Documentation

RISKS CONSIDERED AND MITIGATED BY THE PROJECT

This section identifies a number of risks that are common to BPM projects due to the nature of the technology and the method of its implementation, and includes risks that are specific to the project. All projects carry a degree of risk and by providing advance warning of the risks that are anticipated, these risks were minimised and even removed.

Resistance to Change from Managers and Users

This risk is prevalent in BPM projects because the technology involved is new and unfamiliar to the people who will use the system, but primarily because it has the ability to change the way people work.

The risk was managed by: ensuring that the objectives and benefits of the BPM solution were well-promoted through Project Initiation activities and supplemented by some form of road show where necessary; and by ensuring that users were consulted during the development process by means of significant user participation in RAD sessions.

A valuable tactic for managing resistance to change is to introduce a BPM system in a phased approach by, for example, implementing simple generic processes initially. This still places a lot of responsibility on end users for deciding how a process will be managed. This not only has the benefit of making the effects of change less dramatic, it also means that users gain first hand experience and an understanding of a BPM system which is fed back into the design and development of subsequent phases of the solution.

This risk was not considered to be high in this project.

Technical Viability

This risk is prevalent in BPM projects because they involve many technologies.

The risks were managed by using tried and trusted techniques wherever these were available. If no such techniques were available, a technical proving project was carried out in advance of the main project to prove that there was a viable way of integrating TIBCO BPM with other applications.

This risk was not high in the proposed solution, since most of the components are known and proven, or could be easily developed in the light of relevant experience.

RESULTS OF THE IMPLEMENTATION

TIBCO's BPM software significantly improves the automation and handling of customer and financial requests. Tracker estimates that using TIBCO's BPM solution has reduced the number of outstanding inquiries by 90 percent and the quality of customer service has improved by 200 percent.

Andre Ackerman, Financial Manager at Tracker, said: "We chose TIBCO's BPM suite due to its flexibility, functionality and ease-of-use. Moreover, the independence it provides our staff was an important factor that convinced us that TIBCO was they way to go. We even have the ability to change processes and design new uses without using an outside consultant."

Tracker previously handled customer inquiries manually. However, customer account growth proved to be too much to manage, and the processes became inefficient and cumbersome. The number of outstanding inquiries was getting out of control – up to 2000 at any point in time, hurting the business' customer service and bottom line.

Furthermore, staff performance metrics were not available to help management identify and handle problems in the inquiry process. This made quality control and performance improvement impossible. Tracker concluded that it could realise greater efficiencies by adopting a business process management system to automatically handle financial inquiries and provide information about the department's performance.

Ackerman said: "The solution has paid for itself within 12 months through customer service improvements, better billing and collection, and other business functions. We are very happy with the solution – it exceeded our expectations. In fact, we are planning to take the BPM solution and adapt it across other departments of the company."

Marco Gerazounis, Country Manager, TIBCO South Africa, said: "The flexibility of TIBCO's BPM solution allows Tracker to change processes on a month-to-month basis if necessary. The solution can accept bolt-on applications very easily because of its dynamic and scalable features. This helps Tracker to think about ways to adopt and automate other activities at the same time."

ABOUT TIBCO SOFTWARE

TIBCO Software Inc. (Nasdaq:TIBX) is a leading business integration and process management software company that enables real-time business. Real-time business is about giving organisations the ability to sense and respond to changes and opportunities as they arise. TIBCO has delivered the value of real-time business, what TIBCO calls The Power of Now®, to over 2500 customers around the world and in a wide variety of industries. To learn about TIBCO's solutions for service-oriented architecture, business process management and business optimisation, contact TIBCO at +1 650 846 1000 or on the Web at www.tibco.com. TIBCO is headquartered in Palo Alto, California.

Amman Chamber of Industry, Jordan

Gold Award 2005, Middle East and Africa; nominated by Telaterra Software LLC, Jordan

SUMMARY

The purpose of this document is to layout the overall success elements of implementing the eChamber project at the Amman Chamber of Industry (ACI) located in Amman, Jordan.

In the following sections you will unfold the innovations accomplished on various levels, the challenges overcome, the competitive advantages eChamber has added to ACI as the end user organization and the vendor's experience. Future plans to upgrade the eChamber are various since major changes to the chambers regulations in Jordan are to be introduced in the near future, forcing ACI to become even more competitive.

The following terms are used throughout the document:

ACI—**A**mman **C**hamber of **I**ndustry

ITD—**I**nformation **T**echnology **D**epartment

MSD—**M**embers **S**ervices **D**epartment

OVERVIEW

Based on a human-centric workflow system, **eChamber**, was not only an innovative approach to satisfying **ACI**'s direct requirements of connecting all systems into one that serves all their needs, but also the fastest and most cost effective investment **ACI** contributed towards accommodating the economically growing industrial environment of Amman. Due to the significant impact such a system could add to **ACI**, the project was a heart held effort by all team members to succeed. The power and sophistication of **ACI's** practices were mirrored and signified in the development of the eChamber workflow application.

Being a fairly young country to adopt technology, moving into automated workflow in a semi- government agency is one of the building blocks in the success story of e-government project in Jordan.

Project Participants

eChamber implementation team possessed a diverse skill set that proved to be very effective covering and fulfilling all aspects of the project's requirements. They are:

- **ACI ITD,** developed a mature sense of what an eChamber is all about, and contributed highly in the design and analysis of the project.
- **ACI- MSD,** contributed to the overall business concepts of the services developed, as well as they were the first to use the eChamber.
- **Telaterra,** eChamber technical developers, a Jordanian company specializing in Internet-enabled software application development were responsible for the development life cycle of the project.
- **Computer and Engineering Bureau** supplied ACI with their ImageLink document management system.

- **Business One** supplied ACI with their PayOne online banking solution to connect to a local network of banks in Jordan.

Implementation Process & Methodology Advantages

The eChamber Application was built in compliance with Telaterra Software methodology which is by itself based on ISO 12207. Meeting these standards had a great effect on the flow of the project within its several phases. A key milestone in the project was early on during the workshop meetings, where all stakeholders at ACI contributed to shape the road map for the project covering the procedures and business processes to be covered in the automated system, profoundly impacting the speed and ease of subsequent phases that were handled through out the change management process issued against schedule, cost and solution.

KEY MOTIVATIONS FOR INSTALLING THE ECHAMBER

Operations at ACI before eChamber

One of the main time-consuming challenges that used to face ACI before eChamber was the difference in technology platform and infrastructure, whereby ACI applications were scattered with no integration, thus yielding their maintenance and synchronization a cumbersome task, following were the systems in place:

Internal System—Terminal-server architecture was used to run operations developed using Oracle 7 database along with Oracle forms and reports. Only the following member-related services were processed in this system:

- New membership
- Membership Renewal
- Certificate of Origin
- Teller Transactions

These services served to facilitate ACI members' daily transactions through the issuance of the required certificates and the building of an industrial database comprising a nucleus for the industrial sector.

The data was entered in the MSD at ACI headquarter and branches after which it was classified using industrial coding standards and audited manually at the ITD.

The forms used to enter the application forms for these services lacked business rules, workflow procedures or consistency checks, best described as "Data Entry Forms". Furthermore desktop-based templates were used to generate all certificates and official paper based-communication was stored using a physical folder cabinet.

Web Site and information dissemination: ACI website at the time contained mostly static pages and some dynamic ones linked to a separate oracle database. The website served ACI's communication with the public only (Internet) and provided no special services/information of interest to members. Only ITD were authorized to conduct changes which was mainly done through the authoring of HTML pages or data entry, making changes time-consuming and error prone, thus the frequency of change was minimal, yielding out-dated information.

A workflow-based system was thought of to integrate all the services with member profiles first and then to connect all of these systems to better serve the industrial community ACI serves.

Why ACI needed a workflow application?

The key objective for the eChamber project of The Amman Chamber of Industry (ACI) was to deal with all member incoming requests and applications as well as to provide the chamber's members with an easy online access to its facilities, services and information by establishing a unified communication platform through which ACI members, chamber staff and chamber clients can exchange knowledge, information and services through a Workflow Web Based Services platform.

OVERALL BUSINESS INNOVATION

eChamber Business Requirements

The following is the list of the system objectives which were implemented in the delivered solution:

- Re-engineering of the chamber processes by transforming them into member-centric processes.
- Development of standard business rules that serve the processes at the chamber
- Present ACI members with a complete online cycle for their services from form entry to the issuance of the official certificate/document including the ability to pay the fees online, and delivery.
- Implementing a "One System for all needs" using a unified platform to serve the public (Internet), ACI members (Extranet) and internal staff (Intranet).
- Full integration between the new web-based application and 3rd party solutions such as Document Archiving System.
- Making use of available technology investments within ACI, ex Linux platform and Oracle, as well as some of the hardware.
- Having an identical navigation structure for all users, serving no difference between internal and external views.
- Facilitating an up-to-date, accurate information presentation at ACI website.
- Having a one organization information hub, between ACI headquarters and its branches without the need to install the application at every location.
- Assist ACI management to audit, evaluate and monitor all service transactions external as well as the internal ones.
- Assist ACI management in overall control of the chamber's procedures, by providing statistics that identifying bottlenecks thus giving management a clearer view in their decision-making to increase work efficiency.

eChamber Business Components

Following are the core business components of the eChamber application:

Processing of Chamber Services

Procedures for each service offered by ACI were implemented using a workflow-based approach allowing each of these services to be tracked by the different departments: ITD, MSD and Finance. Due to the level of detail needed to capture and export information, both the forms and the flow of information tended to be of a complex nature.

The services implemented in the eChamber are:

Certificate of Origin (COO): This service deals with the issuance of Industry Certificate of Origin for exporting Jordanian Products. User can issue between 1—100 certificates at once, creating a Multiple COO's copied from the original with minimal data entry, and processing time.

New Membership Registration: This service deals with the issuance of membership certificate for first time registrations.

Renewal of Membership: This is an annual service, whereby registered members renew their membership. Notifications are sent to the members periodically before the actual expiration of the membership. Members can renew online.

Authentication of Signature: This service deals with requesting of Authorization of Signature for the members, whereby ACI verifies its member's signatures with its records.

Request for Bail: This service deals with bail requests by the members from ACI, whereby several rules determine the amount of bail given.

Recommendation: This service deals with requests from members, whereby ACI issues a recommendation certificate stating the standing of its member among other data.

Event Registration: ACI hosts several events throughout the year, these events are publicized on the website and registrations are conducted within the website as well.

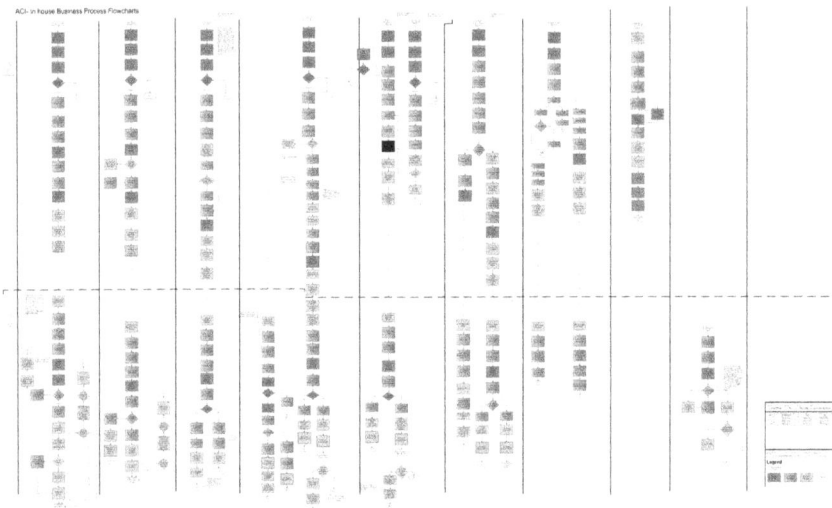

ACI In-house Business Process Flowcharts

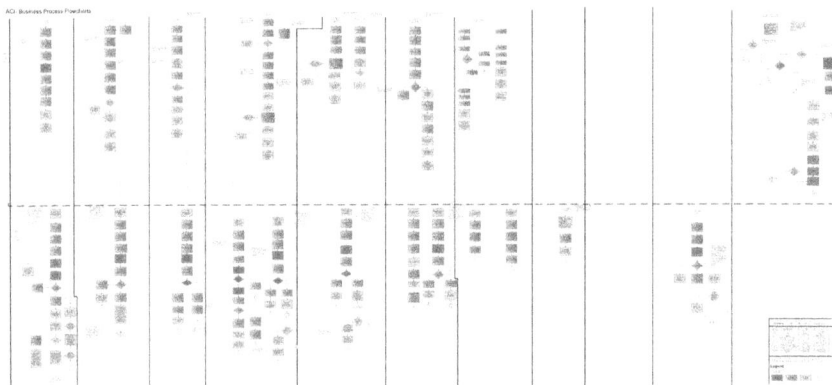

ACI Online Business Process FlowchartsDocument Exchange

Each of the services listed above had a number of needed attachments to be supplied from the member indicating the need for a document management system. ACI utilized CEB's *ImageLink* for that purpose where the technical team had to integrate the eChamber with the Document Management System (DMS) by facilitating the capture, organization, storage, retrieval, manipulation, control and circulation of documents in an electronic format.

Content Authoring

ACI's website was transformed into three main areas: a public website, a member area as well as an internal staff area. All content provided in these three sections was content managed through the development of a specialized Content Management system to help users author and audit content before it is published online.

ePayment

ACI chose an initial ePayment solution which enables ACI members to pay online through existing Bank Networks in Jordan. It solves as an intermediate solution to online banking, since the full model of online banking is not available in Jordan to date. This model has been integrated within the online eChamber thus giving ACI members yet more added value features.

Business and Statistical Reporting

More than 20 very comprehensive reports were designed to cater for all business reporting needed by the chamber both internally and externally. A good part of those reports contained statistical and historical information to help evaluate and enhance the performance of chamber through its entire departments.

Business Innovation Impact

The business innovation impact of installing the eChamber comprised mainly of building a "One System for all" serving the interaction of the:

Public (Internet)

Through their public website (www.aci.org.jo) ACI was able to provide information about the industrial community in Jordan, and Amman in specific in order to promote all products and achievements of this very important economic sector. This information is up-to-date and available 24hrs a day.

Members (Extranet)

Facilitate the interaction of ACI members through adding a member area where authorized users are able to login, request a service, track its status and pay its fees online. Creating an online members area was one of the key objectives of the eChamber, whereby the member can perform all requests within the comfort of his office, at any time, since its available 24hrs. Furthermore, Members receive scheduled / un-scheduled notifications on the status of their requests; this is either done thru an email generation or automated fax generation thru seamless integration with *ImageLink* depending on the members' available data.

Internal Staff (Intranet)

Enable ACI staff from all three locations (Amman, Sahab and Aqaba) to connect through the system and be able to process all member requests either made online or received by hand. After the user logs in, he/she are presented with a customized home page listing all transactions that need further processing with an option to filter by date, service and/or member. Furthermore, the system is designed to send internal notifications to the staff thru emails to ensure timely handling of requests.

Creation of Virtual Offices

The application enables ACI to open virtual office in Aqaba to serve its members needs in that geographical area. Thus minimizing overall operational costs and serving members in distributed geographical areas.

OVERALL TECHNOLOGICAL INNOVATION

eChamber has helped move ACI from a loosely connected set of systems into one connected electronic workflow-based within a period of one month of deployment. It transformed the culture at the ACI from a stateless notion of services into one where the state of each service transacted is known and tracked to insure a high satisfaction rate among serviced members.

With a user friendly interface, eChamber insured a pleasant user experience and a learning ground for ACI and data entry staff where all information was migrated into the new system's electronic database, to serve as the main repository for all information exchanged in the chamber from which statistical and decision-support reports are generated.

eChamber Application Architecture

All processes and procedures were translated into an XML format using the "Business Process Modeling Language" (BPML) standard, which is an Extensible Markup Language (XML)-based meta-language developed by the Business Process Management Initiative (BPMI.org) as a means of modeling business processes, much as XML is, itself, a meta-language with the ability to model enterprise data. BML allowed ACI both conformity with worldwide standards for business process definition as well as enabling high flexibility in adjusting eChamber for future changes in process and procedures. ACI now uses BPML as the main modeling language for all of its business processes.

The solution was built using Macromedia ColdFusion MX through the creation of ColdFusion Components (CFCs) representing the business layer, HTML/CFML (ColdFusion Markup Language) for the GUI layer and Oracle 9i for the database layer amongst other layers.

The following diagram shows each layer within the web application. Telaterra utilized a methodology named Fusebox to separate the GUI layer from the business logic layer.

Following is a diagram depicting the different layers according to the technologies within the project.

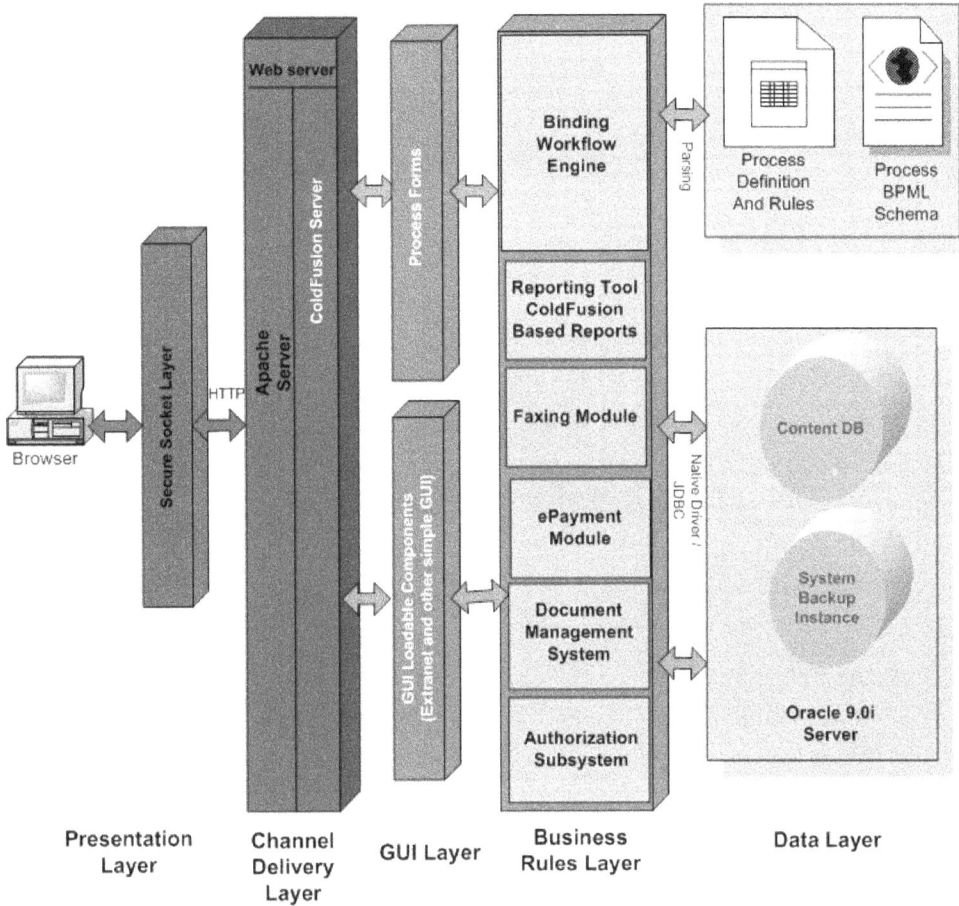

| Presentation Layer | Channel Delivery Layer | GUI Layer | Business Rules Layer | Data Layer |

Binding Workflow Engine (BWE)

BWE is a **human-centric** workflow; which depends to a greater extent on the people in an organization. Human-centric as opposed to process-centric; requires a high level of interactivity between the person and the solution in order to feed the correct information into the activity a person is responsible for, this facilitates processing any of the services a person is in charge of to feed the next set of activities and so forth. The BWE coordinates and binds all of the components (See Components View diagram below) in order to work through the process instantiating each activity or atomic activity as it occurs. It is also responsible for binding the components to create a single instance.

Telaterra Software developed the Binding Workflow Engine (BWE) which was utilized to parse the BPML-based XML.

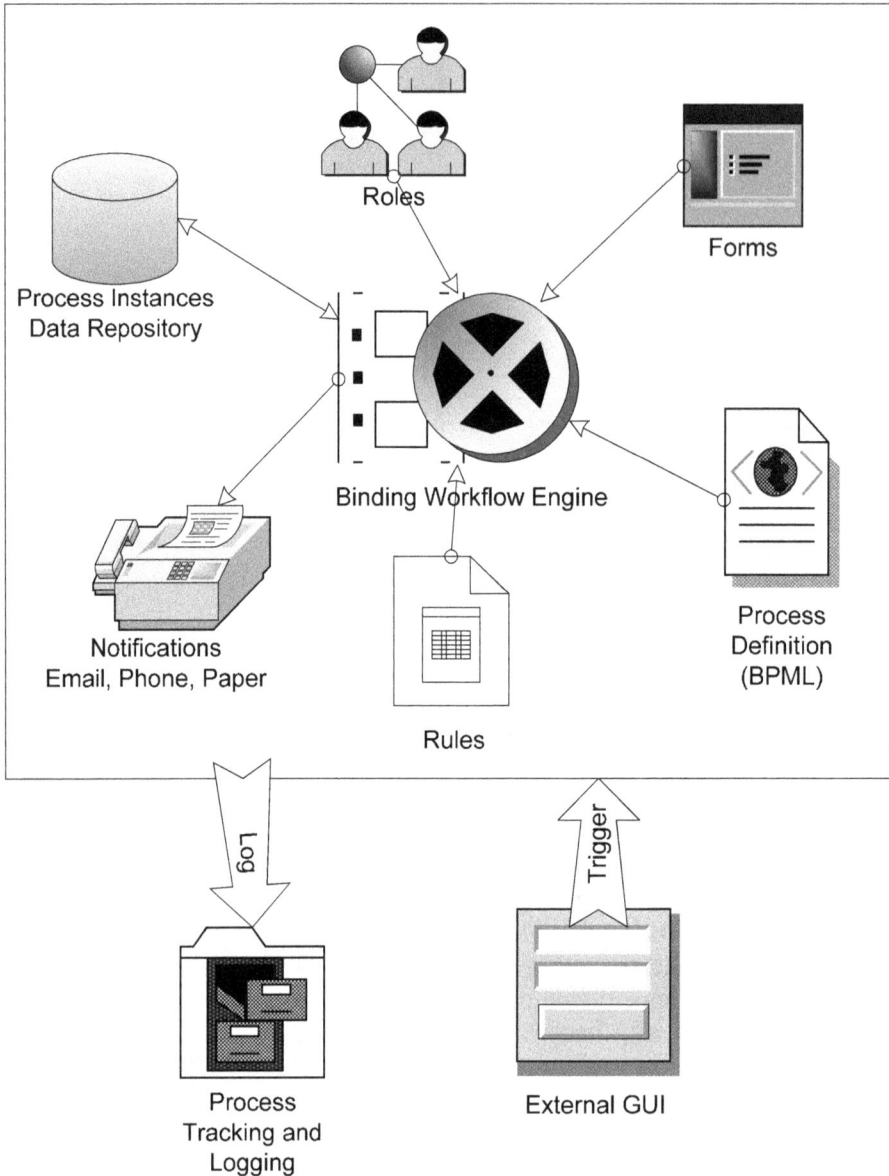

Process Instances
Data Repository

Roles

Forms

Binding Workflow Engine

Notifications
Email, Phone, Paper

Rules

Process
Definition
(BPML)

Log

Trigger

Process
Tracking and
Logging

External GUI

Components View

The diagram below demonstrates how the BWE binds the system components:

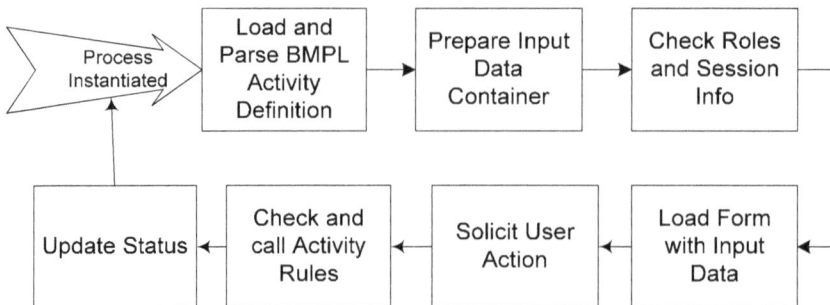

Process Instantiated → Load and Parse BMPL Activity Definition → Prepare Input Data Container → Check Roles and Session Info

Update Status ← Check and call Activity Rules ← Solicit User Action ← Load Form with Input Data

Each activity is modeled as per the following diagram:

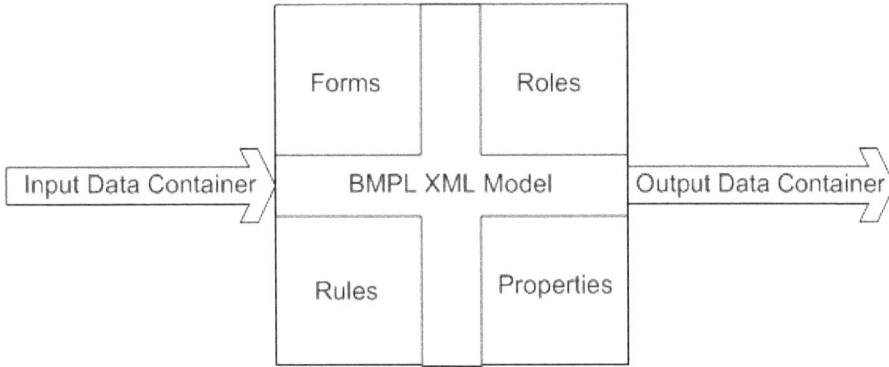

```
          ┌──────────┬──────────┐
          │  Forms   │  Roles   │
          │          │          │
┌─────────┴──────────┴──────────┴─────────┐
│ Input Data   │ BMPL XML Model │ Output Data │
│ Container    │                │ Container   │
└─────────┬──────────┬──────────┬─────────┘
          │  Rules   │Properties│
          │          │          │
          └──────────┴──────────┘
```

SYSTEM USERS

The following table illustrates the difference states at ACI before and after eChamber:

Before eChamber	eChamber System Users
• Document management and filing system for all MSD application processes • Loosely connected legacy systems. • Difficulty of following up on a pending application and point reached or covered so far • General indications of pending application status through verbal feedback • Immense efforts of follow up and communication between departments and with members. • None existent management monitoring capabilities of applications standing point per user • Immense efforts to generate reports to management. • Investors were obliged to apply for the chamber services at ACI offices.	• Ability to store and retrieve documents through the document archiving system integrated with the eChamber • Ease of use (User Friendly) • Ability to locate pending point of application being processed • Viewing pending application details per user • Strong management monitoring capability to determine exactly where the bottleneck obstacle exists per application per user • Effortless correspondence between departments and with members. • Reduction to minimal time spent on correspondence • Current number of users on eChamber is 11; no increase in number of staff at the chamber; the system enabled ACI to process 20 percent more COO's with the same number of staff. • The ability to apply for services from the convenience of their offices.

BIGGEST HURDLES OVERCOME

	eChamber Project Challenges
Managerial Level	• Tight delivery schedule & Budget
Business Level	• Understanding of ACI's processes and

	procedures.
	• Training ACI staff to embrace the system and use it proactively in their daily work.
Technology	• Acceptance phase where using the system included reporting bugs and errors that were detected from as a result of a user's experience of the system
	• Deploying the right hardware that would absorb the load on the system.
	• Integration with 3rd party systems (DMS, ePayment)

The most serious of all issues encountered during and after the implementation of the new system was the **resistance** of the internal staff as well as the industrial community.

From the internal perspective, resistance was mainly initiated because ACI had the need to employ new qualified staff to work on the system in its efforts to be more effective in serving the industrial community. ACI management at all levels were focused in turning the project into a successful one therefore were able to effectively manage this form of resistance and insure the success of the eChamber.

While from an external perspective, resistance from ACI members were evident at the first weeks after the system was deployed for production. The industrial community was very frustrated because of the extra length in time they were faced with before they were able to process their transactions at the Chamber. The situation was tackled quickly by ITD and Telaterra through swiftly implementing the following changes:

1. ITD requested a new server to deal with the unexpected extra load the system faced during first weeks of production.
2. Telaterra made some major performance tuning modification into the system to help decrease the amount of time it took for the forms and home pages to load.
3. Also, the technical team along with ITD designed special forms to facilitate bulk data entry of several Certificate of Origins to save time on the data entry staff.

In less than 2 weeks, the system's performance was significantly enhanced helping the industrial community to accept and move forward in using the system.

NEW SYSTEM CONFIGURATION

The system configuration and architecture used to deploy eChamber was founded on existing infrastructure at ACI MIS Labs. Client workstations consist of 30 PCs running Windows 2000 Professional and accessing the system through MS-Internet Explorer 5.5 and above being authenticated using database-based authentication.

The following are all off –the-shelf software products which the system utilizes:

1. Sun Solaris 9 as the server operation system
2. Macromedia JRUN 4 as ColdFusion MX 6.1 Application Server

3. Apache 1.327 with SSL as the Web Server
4. Oracle 9.0i as the Database Server
5. ImageLink as the Document Management System and Faxing System
6. Microsoft Exchange Server as the Email Server
7. Microsoft Windows 2000 professional as the client PC's operating system

The following diagram displays the current system configuration:

Configuration View

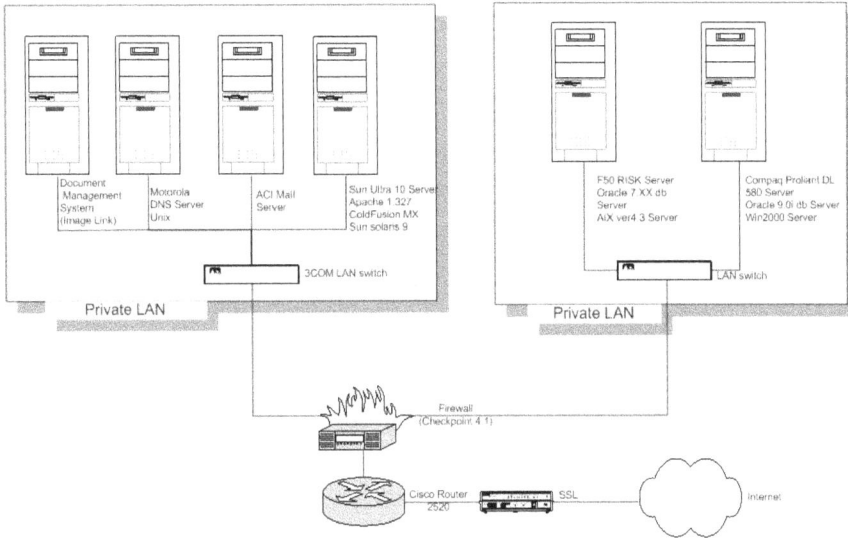

SAVINGS, REVENUE & PRODUCTIVITY

No major economic advantages were thought of relating to the implementation of eChamber however, ACI were able to maintain their internal IT policy by utilizing their existing platform infrastructure to accommodate for the eChamber application with addition of new hardware and software which resulted in a smooth data migration effort into the new system.

The following table illustrates the productivity gains ACI made by implementing the eChamber since the beginning of 2004:

	Total No. of COO –Amman	Total No. of COO –Sahab	Total No. of COO	Total No. of new members	Total No. of Renewal	Total No. of AOS	Total No. of Bails	Recomme ndation	Events (not used)
2001	27,455	5,871	33,326	770	6,249	3,928	150		
2002	20,144	7,686	27,830	647	6,140	4,115	139		
2003	30,614	9,676	40,290	811	6,207	5,546	107		
2004	36,326	11,739	48,065	1,093	6,407	6,153	210		
Year 2004 online (for 4 months)	24,552	9,882	34,748	1,150	6,507	2,006	36	147	

Notes:

1. As shown in the above table the # of COO's has increased rapidly every year, by implementing the e-chamber ACI was able to resolve the approx. 20 percent increase of COO transactions without hiring new staff in addition ACI was able to resolve customer dissatisfaction at the Sahab branch by increasing online transactions by 50 percent and 23 percent of all chamber's transactions.

2. A new virtual branch was inaugurated at Aqaba, where ACI was able to serve its members there through its own virtual office at the Aqaba Special Economic Zone Authority (ASEZA). Previously such an opportunity was un-available.

COMPETITIVE ADVANTAGES

Business Oriented Advantages

- Jordan chambers are corporations regulated by public law with compulsory membership according to the member's location; however that is all going to change in the near future. The chamber will face a competition between different chambers; advanced services of the chamber will attract more members.
- By implementing eChamber, ACI has become the first Jordanian semi-government agency to offer online services
- Connecting ACI with the industrial community in an easy online working environment
- Strengthened communication flow internally and externally
- Enabled ACI maintain its competitive advantage within Jordan and the region aiming to result in attracting foreign investment into the Jordanian industrial sector.

IMMEDIATE & LONG TERM PLANS

ACI eChamber project is envisioned to go through several phases; Phase I (Currently Implemented) focuses on the online-services and content-management-system to ensure an easy and timely communication with the members.

Several future plans are being thought of at the moment:

1. Complementary services through the partnership with several content providers like the Ministry of Information and Communication Technology and the Greater Amman Municipality to name a few.
2. Implement a Member Services Center to better serve ACI members through:
   a. Efficiently managing all the members/customer requests through multiple communication channels the phone, email, the web, chat, and wireless devices.
   b. Record, assign, escalate, track, manage, and report on members/customer requests and issues
   c. Create a complete audit trail of all activities and communications for each members/customer issue and solution
   d. Integrate telephone call management, for efficient, automated call routing
   e. Providing technical support and eChamber focused training to encourage more members to use the eChamber.
3. Integrate and workflow-enable other systems/departments and include them in eChamber like:
   a. Human Resources Procedures
   b. Financial System
   c. Electronic Record Management
4. Work with MoICT and other governmental, legislative and private sector entities to establish a Certificate Authority in order to introduce e-Signature to Jordan and the eChamber respectively.

Nedbank Retail Banking Credit Control Department, South Africa

Silver Award 2005, Middle East and Africa; nominated by TIBCO Software, South Africa

SUMMARY

The need for an efficient Business Process Management (BPM) solution

A market leader in many areas, Nedbank understands that in a highly competitive market, it is essential to focus energy both on customer retention and on acquiring new business. But in a market characterised by product parity, it is service which sets one Bank ahead of its competitors, in the minds of both new and existing clients. When choosing between financial institutions, the deciding factor for clients is not the intrinsic product benefits alone, but the efficiency with which applications are dealt, the speed with which they are granted finance and the efficacy with which staff are able to act. In short, the Bank's ability to manage the credit process is paramount to its success, meaning that in addition to presenting clients with an outstanding range of products and services, it's imperative that those products and services be accessible in the most convenient and in the quickest way possible, if *prospective* clients are to be converted to *actual* clients. Motivated by the principles explained above, Nedbank Retail Banking Credit Assessment department - which grants credit to both personal clients and small business - implemented an innovative BPM solution (TIBCO Staffware Process Suite—TIBCO SPS), in conjunction with consultants from Idea Junction, to help it attain its goal of processing credit applications more effectively, thereby increasing business for the bank.

Bottom Line: The BPM solution has increased the department's processing capacity by 650 percent, reducing organisation risk and leading to significant new business being written.

A look at Nedbank

On 1 January 2003 the new Nedcor Group was formed, combining Nedcor, BoE, NIB and Cape of Good Hope Bank into one legal entity. New management structures came into effect allowing these entities to become a fully integrated business. Nedbank Group (previously known as Nedcor) is one of South Africa' s leading financial organizations, with headline earnings for the 6 month period ended 30 June 2005 of R1,398 million, an increase of 74,3 percent, with banking branches spread across South Africa. A financial institution of this size, with such a decentralised spread of branches, presents clear challenges, but also exciting opportunities, with regard to developing a BPM solution that facilitates optimum efficiency and allows for seamless integration.

OVERVIEW

New growth, reduced costs, increased efficiency—the key to success

Within the banking sector, growth is governed by two major factors: the ability to expand business in the form of credit granted, and the ability to reduce costs and make processes more efficient. As a bank, Nedbank has to manage its risk very carefully in order to remain competitive. Credit risk is the risk that an asset, in the form of a monetary claim against counterparty, may not result in a cash receipt (or equivalent) in accordance with the terms of the contract. Credit risk represents one of the most significant risk exposures of the group. A variety of credit risk management tools and techniques are employed across the group. The Nedbank Retail Banking Credit Assessment Department is responsible for processing applications for credit from personal clients and small businesses. These include applications for a number of products, inter alia current accounts, credit cards, vehicle finance, and scheme vehicle finance. The success of these products is often determined by the speed at which they can be processed. For instance, when a consumer purchases a new vehicle, he would normally apply to between three and five finance houses for vehicle finance. Generally, the first finance house to provide him with approved vehicle finance will get his business.

It is therefore clear why it is essential to enhance the business' ability to process applications quickly and effectively, while simultaneously maintaining an acceptable level of credit risk for the bank.

The BPM solution implemented in Nedbank Retail Banking Credit Assessment provides not only for fast, but also safe and efficient processing of credit applications. The end-to-end process has been automated (credit checking, fraud and vetting, for instance), allowing the process to move as quickly as possible, while maintaining acceptable credit risk levels.

KEY MOTIVATIONS

The decision to move from manual to automated

Within the Nedbank Retail Banking Credit Control Department, which grants credit to both personal clients and small businesses, all applications had previously been handled manually. Nedbank's management team made the decision to move away from the decentralised regional office towards a centralised one. This would have an enormous impact on the way business had been conducted up to that point. The need for process management became apparent, with expected benefits for implementing a business process management solution being:

- Increased productivity without increasing staff levels
- Improved feedback to sales staff at branches
- Reduced queries on applications by sales staff to credit assessment
- Establish and maintain consistently high service levels
- Improved feedback and communication to clients
- Improved turnaround times
- Reduced communication costs
- A standardised customer experience
- Increased staff motivation
- Improved information provided to assessors

The manual process had a number of flaws. Sales staffers were not receiving feedback during the process, service levels were erratic and immediate feedback to clients was virtually impossible. Additionally, sales staff could fax the same application form for assessment more than once, even possibly to different assessors. As a result, a single application could have multiple outcomes.

BUSINESS INNOVATION

Fewer errors, faster turnaround time

There are two main sets of system users: sales staff within the different banks and credit assessment staff. Previously, sales staff would hand application forms to clients and hope that they'd come back with filled-in forms. Forms were not always completed correctly, and were then faxed to credit assessment, sometimes duplicating the process, and leading to a single application having multiple outcomes. Credit assessment staff was required to check behavioural scores, and credit records themselves while assessing an application. Sales staff would also call credit assessment staff to check on the progress of an application, disrupting their work schedule.

The complete credit application, vetting and activation process has been reworked, meaning that all credit applications are now obtained and submitted electronically on the intranet, providing customers with better service levels. To assist sales staff, all forms have built-in checks to ensure all the necessary information is included on the application form before it is sent for assessment. In this way error-free application forms can be more easily generated and incomplete forms would be less likely to be submitted, again saving time in that applications can be processed correctly first time around.

Due to a business rules system, some applications are immediately granted or turned down, improving customer service levels. Automated credit checking and behavioural scoring has simplified credit control staff's working procedures, and an appeals process has meant that individual applications can be reviewed within a controlled environment.

Motivated staff, satisfied clients

The Credit Managers can now manage their business area pro-actively with timely information like the number of applications processed per hour or which user groups are creating bottlenecks within their department. In one Assessment area, 70 percent of all applications received have been processed within half an hour. The improved speed of processing has resulted in a significant increase in customer satisfaction. Approval times have reduced to such an extent that one banker sent Credit Assessment an email asking if the approval he had received was a hoax, as he couldn't believe the turnaround time. Communication between sales staff in branches and Credit Assessment staff has also been improved, while reducing the number of queries on Credit Assessment staff. This has been achieved by making the process transparent on the intranet, allowing sales staff to check on the progress of an application without having to speak to Credit Assessment staff directly. In addition, a Credit Assessment helpdesk has been set up, through which sales staff can query credit decisions.

Overall, staff productivity, morale and motivation have improved dramatically.

Focus on people and not product

The solution has made the bank more customer-focused. Previously, bankers would simply hand potential customers application forms, and ask them to return the completed form. An online application is now completed with the customer giving the banker an opportunity to better understand the customer's needs. Blame shifting is no longer possible because of the end-to-end process control the solution provides. The Credit Assessment staff both accepts responsibility and receive recognition for its improved quality of work.

TECHNOLOGICAL INNOVATIONS

A hand-in-hand approach

The credit control area encompasses two main processes (personal client or small business), each offering five different products (credit card, current account, company card, individual car loans and scheme vehicle finance). Each of the five products has up to 10 different variations making the area a complex one. For instance, the scheme vehicle finance process has to accommodate for an infinite number of individual vehicle owners within a single company. This complexity was heightened by the fact that there was no standard process, particularly within the vehicle finance application process. The project management team had to consult with all parts of the business to compile an automated business process that worked for every aspect of the business. Since there was no universal baseline for the application process, the re-engineering process encompassed the whole bank and changed the way in which it works. As part of the change management process, communication with staff was paramount. Step-by-step instructions and guidelines have been created on the intranet to help sales staff navigate the new process, and a train-the-trainer approach was used to train staff on the new BPM solution. User manuals are available on public folders, and electronic communication has been used to its fullest extent. A national road show was also staged to alert banking staff to the changes credit assessment was making, and explaining how credit assessment would be making life better for banking staff.

After process re-engineering, the credit control process consists of three different areas: document collation and preparation, assessment (including verification and fraud detection) and activation of the account.

In the preparation arena, bankers capture the applicant's information on the intranet. Besides the alarm mentioned above, the electronic application form also automatically activates or declines certain applications on the basis of rules that have been written into the process. The assessment process is kicked off by an automated credit check to major credit bureaus, reducing the time involved in obtaining a potential client' s credit record. Assessment is based on a number of factors, including:

- borrower's current financial condition and repayment capacity;
- borrower's payment history;
- current value of security;
- days overdue in respect of repayment terms; and
- other factors impacting prospects of collection of principal and interest.

All applications are tracked on the system, and sales staff in branches can now check on the progress of an application using the intranet. Credit assessment staff also now have a clear idea of how much time they have spent on a particular application, with deadlines appearing next to the work item displaying the expected service level for the task. Automatic escalations are built in to alert credit assessment staff when deadlines are approaching.

Once an application has been approved or rejected, the system automatically sends the results to sales staff at branches, improving communication dramatically. In the case of a rejected application, the systems allows for reasons for the rejection to be included in the email. This is particularly important, as it forces credit control staff to use standard motivations for rejection of an application, making the service to branches more consistent. The system also allows for appeals against rejection of an application. Since some branches do not yet have access to the intranet, a fax server has been included in the solution. Not only does this mean that branches with lower levels of technology also have access to the improved system, but it keeps track of faxes, overcoming previous duplication issues. Close integration between TIBCO SPS and the intranet means that a user can start an application process on the intranet, and later update the application without logging on to TIBCO SPS first - the TIBCO SPS component is automatically updated. Proxy-based business rules allow the system to automatically check the internal behavioural scoring database and to search credit bureaus. Based on that information, the information is then sent to Transact, which will come back with an offer on all three products, giving the amount of credit the customer has available for current account, home loan and vehicle finance. TIBCO SPS handles appeals by bankers through a manual reassessment process.

SYSTEMS USERS

By automating the communication between the two main sets of system users, namely sales staff within banks and credit assessment staff, the entire credit assessment process is now able to progress quickly without error or duplication. Sales staffers are able to provide better client service, focusing on the client and completing the application form immediately, rather than leaving it for the client to complete and return, and credit assessment staff are ensured the return of complete and accurate application forms.

HURDLES OVERCOME

Possibly the biggest hurdle that had to be overcome was the time pressure. Nedbank had made a decision to centralize its retail banking credit control department, which had previously been decentralized across the country. A single office was to be established, and the project team had six months within which to conceptualise, design and implement the solution, including installing network points and setting up servers. The project went into pilot phase on 13 November 2002 and was rolled out 6 December 2002. The project approach had to comply with the IT department's implementation standards, but be implemented within the six month time frame. All work had to go through quality assurance and change control, and proper functional user acceptance testing. Flowing from this was the requirement to change business processes.

On average, it takes Nedbank two years to change business processes, but this change was achieved within six months, without compromising on the quality assurance process. All corporate governance requirements, as well as business needs and technology implementation requirements were met within the six months. In part, this was due to the fact that an iterative approach was used, where design and development were conducted simultaneously. While subsequent versions of TIBCO SPS support multiple relationships, the version available at the time of the implementation did not. Nonetheless, the solution encompasses both one-to-many and many-to-many relationships. This accommodates the fact that a single person may have up to five credit cards, and means that companies are not limited in the number of credit cards they can hold. Each of these cards could have different card holder information, which is accommodated within the system.

SYSTEM CONFIGURATION

The solution uses TIBCO Staffware iProcess Engine version 10, TIBCO Staffware Process Objects version 10, TIBCO Staffware Process Monitor version 10, a custom-developed Web client, a production server and a development / Quality Assurance server, running on MS Windows 2000. There are 530 PCs accessing the solution from the Credit Control Department, and branches across the country using the system via in-branch PCs.

COST SAVINGS, INCREASED REVENUES AND PRODUCTIVITY IMPROVEMENTS

The Credit Control Department's processing capacity has increased by 650 percent. Prior to the implementation, the department was able to handle between 2000 and 6000 applications per month. Since the TIBCO SPS implementation, these figures have improved dramatically, with 12 000 applications being processed during the first month of the implementation and 15 000 by the fourth month. No additional resources were required to process the increased number of applications. Today the Credit Control Department process in excess of 25 000 application per month on the TIBCO SPS.

Turnaround times on applications have also increased dramatically. The application process used to take two days, but now 80 percent of applications are completed in less than two hours. This includes applying to a banker to load the credit limit and informing the customer of the status of their application. Additional savings were gained through the elimination of paper, creating savings on stationery costs. The simple fact that all information on applications is now available in a single place on the intranet, rather than scattered across desks in different offices, has meant an increase in productivity, as staff knows exactly where to look to find the information they require.

COMPETITIVE ADVANTAGES GAINED

As mentioned earlier, banks cannot really compete on price or special products, but instead have to increase the efficiency of their internal processes and their customer service to gain competitive advantage. Increased productivity is thus a main objective in attaining and maintaining competitive advantage. Through the new solution, the increase in applications processed of 650 percent has led to a 12 percent increase in the current account book. Since turnaround times on applications have improved, customer service has also increased dramatically. The assessment personnel can now make their decisions within an hour 95 percent of the time. Since appeals are now handled through a form available on the intranet, credit control personnel are not interrupted in their work processes.

The customer experience has also been standardized through a choice of standardized replies and the removal of human intervention where possible. Within the context of the current accounts book growing by 12 percent, it is important to note that within the banking community, the current account book is considered one of the most difficult things to grow. In addition, Nedbank ran a marketing campaign which offered an applicant a credit card every time a home loan was granted, decreasing the volume of applications which credit assessment staff had to process. A focus on fraud, which is built into the system, has led to not only reduced exposure for the bank from fraud syndicates, but also to the prosecution of fraud syndicates.

IMMEDIATE AND LONG TERM PLANS TO SUSTAIN COMPETITIVE ADVANTAGE

At the moment, ongoing process improvements and measurements on how fast the process is working and where bottlenecks exist are underway. Through the use of the TIBCO Staffware Process Monitor process are being constantly analysed, improved and refined. This provides Nedbank with a close feedback loop on where and how to improve process inefficiencies through used cases.

Section 3

North America

The Chester County Hospital, USA

Gold Award 2006, North America; nominated by TIBCO and Siemens, USA

EXECUTIVE SUMMARY

The healthcare industry has been slower to adopt Business Process Management (BPM) than other industries. However, The Chester County Hospital (CCH) has distinguished itself by not only implementing workflow management technology in a healthcare setting, but by customizing and supplementing that technology with its own home-grown applications. The result is a workflow system that integrates clinical, operational and financial processes to support patient-centered care. In addition to meeting the primary goal of providing safer, more efficient care to patients, BPM has enabled CCH to improve working conditions for employees, dramatically increase productivity, achieve higher levels of cost optimization, and become a competitive force to reckon with in the local healthcare community.

OVERVIEW

While other industries have embraced BPM, healthcare has been slow to use BPM to reengineer its processes, in large part because the very nature of the industry has not lent itself to such an endeavor. Healthcare is not a finite, stationary industry with clearly defined, static procedures. The constantly changing variables involved in patient care, along with the mobility involved in the administration of that care, make it much more challenging to apply workflow procedures. Ironically, the need for integrated workflow management is probably more vital in healthcare than in virtually any other industry, because in few other industries can such processes mean the difference between life and death as they can in a healthcare setting.

The Chester County Hospital is acutely aware of the need for workflow technology in healthcare, and has made its mark in southeastern Pennsylvania by achieving all-around excellent results in implementing BPM. Located in West Chester, Pa., with roots dating back to 1892, CCH is a provider of a full network of healthcare services including a 234-bed not-for-profit acute care hospital; home care; and many other ancillary services.

Faced with the challenges of increasing patient safety, efficiency and cost-effectiveness, and meeting the demands of increasingly sophisticated and knowledgeable healthcare consumers, CCH discovered that BPM was one of the keys to the survival of a healthcare system in the 21st century.

CCH implemented what would become the foundation for its workflow management portfolio: the Soarian® health information solution from Siemens Medical Solutions, which integrates the TIBCO iProcess Engine into its core functionality. Soarian combines clinical, financial, diagnostic and administrative processes across a healthcare enterprise. CCH's IT staff took Soarian a step further by creating their own, customized applications to add on to Soarian to meet the specific, unique needs of their facility. The result came to be known at CCH as 9ADMIT, a workflow system that integrates patient care with Web platforms, legacy systems, and telephone and paging systems. 9ADMIT can be thought of as a vestibule with various rooms branching off of it; the system launches at Admission and then takes the data that comes in through the Soarian system and routes it to different workflows based on predetermined criteria. Once launched, the system follows the patient through his or her stay, constantly listening for data, displaying that data for the people who need it, and ensuring that the next steps in the process are taken. Like a guardian angel of sorts, the system always knows where the patient is in the continuum, where he or she should be next, and what steps should be taken for his or her care.

Two workflows in particular have yielded enormously valuable results for CCH: Bed Management and Infection Control.

KEY BUSINESS MOTIVATIONS

The primary motivation for adopting workflow management at CCH has been as basic as the very essence of what drives just about every individual who enters the medical field: the desire to make people well, and to do so in the most safe and effective way possible. In addition, other motivating factors have been challenges that CCH, along with the healthcare industry as a whole, has faced in recent years—rapidly escalating costs, aging patient populations and therefore more chronic diseases, human resource shortages and increasingly complicated work environments. Also, patient expectations have dramatically risen over the past several decades, compelling healthcare providers to search for ways of providing increased customer service. As the Baby Boomer population is aging and consequently consuming more healthcare, they are demanding quality and convenience that their parents and grandparents would not have thought to expect. Moreover, the Internet has provided individuals with the ability to access healthcare information on their own, and has created savvy healthcare consumers who are prepared to take their business to the provider who will give them the highest level of service and the greatest probability of recovery.

CCH has discovered that the key to meeting these challenges is integrated workflow management—the process of seamlessly moving patients, information and resources throughout the healthcare continuum in a way that was never before possible.

KEY INNOVATIONS

At its most basic level, workflow management takes the vast amount of scattered, multisource data that is available in a healthcare system and moves that information throughout the enterprise so that key clinical and administrative information can be shared, interpreted and analyzed. The result has been an enormously positive impact on both clinical and business outcomes. For each user at CCH, physician, nurse, executive, etc., the workflow-engineered IT system provides the right information for the task at hand. Rather than having to use a string of systems with clumsy interfaces and multilevel trees and menus, the single, uniform system brings together relevant information, orders and documentation in a meaningful way, from the moment a patient is admitted. It gathers the patient's lab and diagnostic results, vital signs, documentation and orders, and organizes them in a way that is most logical for the patient's condition. In a sense, the system "watches over" the patient throughout his or her stay, constantly capturing data to guide the patient's care from one step to the next.

While CCH has applied a variety of workflows to its processes, and continues to develop new ones, two workflows in particular have reaped important positive outcomes: Bed Management and Infection Control.

Bed Management: Impact on business

The availability of beds and lack thereof is one of the greatest sources of bottle-necks in a hospital environment. Emergency departments and recovery rooms are full of patients who are simply "waiting for beds." Ultimately, these delays have the potential to increase the length of patients' hospital stays and require staff to work over and beyond their normal hours. CCH has used Bed Management work-flows to reduce turnaround time from the moment a patient leaves a bed to the moment the next patient can be admitted to that bed. The hospital's Bed Management system follows patients throughout their stays and alerts key departments, such as Nursing and Environmental Services, regarding transfers and discharges. By reducing wait times for beds, CCH is getting patients to the proper care setting that their conditions require, and providing more satisfying in-patient experiences for them.

Bed Management: Impact on Process

The manual handoff of tasks from person to person is a process that is susceptible to human error. Prior to the use of BPM, the Bed Management process was an extremely complex and inefficient process, encumbered by a host of these manual handoffs and tasks. A unit secretary would need to enter transfer or discharge information into the system and then begin a manual process of documentation and phone calls, notifying several departments and individuals that a patient had vacated the room and the bed needed to be cleaned. Once the bed was cleaned and ready for a new patient, another series of phone calls needed to be made. Additionally, both the unit secretary and housekeeping staff utilized several documents to track the response and steps in the process. This cumbersome system often required nurses to perform many extra steps that took them away from their primary duty of caring for patients.

CCH's Bed Management system has automated many of the manual processes involved in Bed Management and, as a result, the hospital has experienced a 50 percent reduction in the manual processes involved. The improved workflow process begins with the same step as the unautomated process: the unit secretary enters the discharge or transfer order into the system. But that's where the similarity ends. From that point on, the subsequent steps, notifications, monitoring and progress of the workflow are totally automated, ending with the housekeeper entering a numeric code into a telephone, signifying that the bed is cleaned and ready. This has also freed housekeepers from having to respond to overhead pages and find phones to obtain work assignment details, and has diminished nurse involvement in the bed cleaning workflow, allowing them to focus on the care of their patients.

When the bed is emptied, the workflow process automatically starts multiple activities. The Nursing Supervisor is called via a text-to-speech alert to her IP telephone and asked to give the cleaning a priority level: 1= 45 minutes, 2 = 30 minutes, 3 = 15 minutes. The system updates a Web-based electronic "Bedboard" so everyone knows the exact status of the hospital's bed situation. It also accesses reference tables to see which housekeeper to contact based on the floor, day of the week, and shift. The appropriate housekeeper is alerted of the empty bed and its priority via a text pager. The housekeeper indicates that the cleaning is started by dialing to a specific number from the bedside phone and pressing the numeral "1." He indicates the bed cleaning is complete by dialing the same number and pressing "2." The workflow automatically contacts the nursing supervisor and updates the Bedboard when the room is ready. If the bed cleaning is not started within the specified time, the housekeeper is re-paged, along with the Housekeeping supervisor. Both the Nursing and Housekeeping supervisors utilize wireless tablets to have up-to-the-minute status information to manage their people, and to interact with the workflow engine.

The Hospital has also built safety checks and an alert mechanism into its Bed Management workflow in the form of Business Activity Monitoring (BAM). As already mentioned, an escalation path is created so that if a bed is not cleaned in a predetermined amount of time, an alert is sent out at certain time intervals to keep the process moving. Furthermore, the system automatically notifies the IT staff of an issue if the pages do not go out within 15 minutes. Every day the BAM system generates an activity report for the previous day and sends it to the director of housekeeping, the vice president of support services and shift supervisors, who can review the reports and determine if there are bottlenecks in the system and who or what is causing them.

CCH brought in an external consultant to conduct a pre- and post-workflow time and motion study of the bed cleaning process. The consultant chose to focus on the key business issue of bed availability on the hospital unit that had the biggest bottleneck, Telemetry, during the peak discharge times between 2 and 8pm. His study showed that the workflow automation process changes resulted in six beds being available to receive patients an average of two hours earlier than compared to the pre-workflow status.

Bed Cleaning Process Pre-Workflow

The following charts display before and after scenarios of CCH's Bed Management workflow processes. Notice the free floating boxes on the pre-workflow diagram. They represent manual steps that were not connected to the rest of the process.

Bed Cleaning Process Post-Workflow

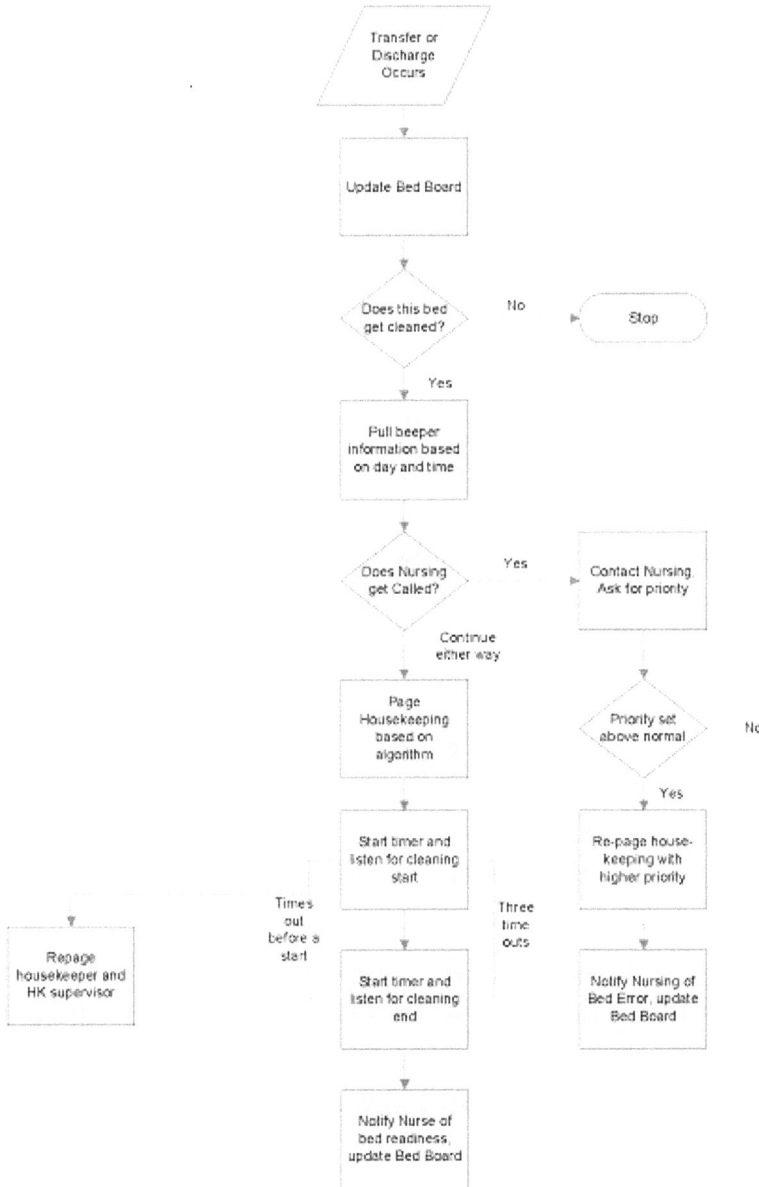

Transfer or Discharge Occurs

↓

Update Bed Board

↓

Does this bed get cleaned? — No → Stop

↓ Yes

Pull beeper information based on day and time

↓

Does Nursing get Called? — Yes → Contact Nursing. Ask for priority

Continue either way

↓   ↓

Page Housekeeping based on algorithm   Priority set above normal — No

↓   ↓ Yes

Start timer and listen for cleaning start   Re-page house-keeping with higher priority

Times out before a start   Three time outs

Repage housekeeper and HK supervisor

↓   ↓

Start timer and listen for cleaning end   Notify Nursing of Bed Error, update Bed Board

↓

Notify Nurse of bed readiness, update Bed Board

The graphic following shows the current main workflow screen for bed management.

Main Workflow Screen for Bed Management

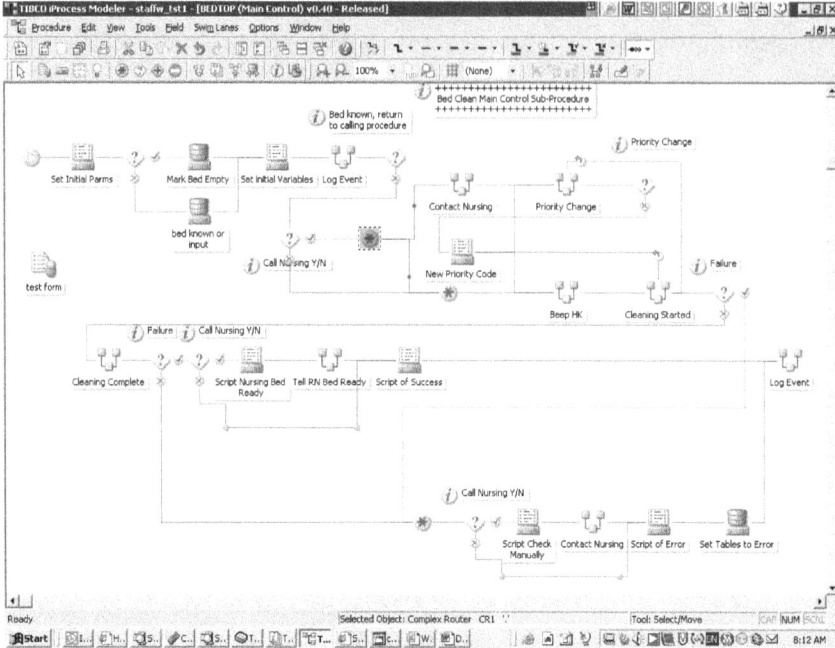

Bed Management: Impact on technology

The original bed cleaning process utilized functionality that required human interaction with every step. It included work lists placed on a clipboard and a nursing census list that was crossed out and edited throughout the day. Pages were made to the housekeeper via an in-house paging system to a numeric pager. This method required someone to manually call the system and insert data for paging. The housekeeper would then need to return the call for information. A work order system created in Microsoft Access was also used. This system would print out a requisition to a designated printer in the housekeeping office, prompting either someone in the housekeeping office or the hospital operator to page the housekeeper again. The nursing supervisor used an IP phone and the housekeeping supervisor used a walkie-talkie. In all cases, information was given or obtained via human-initiated contact.

The BPM automated system utilizes much of the same communication technology, but now the steps are automated. There were several technology changes made to allow this to occur. Numeric pagers were replaced with text pagers, an Intel Dialogic analog telephonic card was purchased, and a Web UI was created to report the status of all beds within the institution. The telephonic card was used to automate pages to the existing paging system, to send text to speech messages to individuals via the telephone, and to receive feedback via the phone's keys. The Access database was removed from the process since the metrics were captured directly within the BPM process. The walkie-talkie was discontinued and wireless tablets were given to the nursing and housekeeping supervisors respectively to view the Bedboard Web UI. This UI was made available to all appropriate personnel and continually updated by the BPM system. In this way, the process, discussed above, was automated and controlled, reducing variation and the potential for human error. Key to the success of this endeavor was the using of existing technology (phones and pagers) while removing manual tasks from the staff's workload.

Infection Control: Impact on business

It is a well-known fact that the longer a patient stays in the hospital, the greater he or she is at risk for hospital-acquired infections. This is particularly significant in facilities like CCH, where 85 percent of the rooms are semi-private. In such an environment, patients are vulnerable to infections potentially carried by their roommates. Hospital rooms are full of objects that provide breeding grounds for bacteria, from telephones to food trays, and from toilets to flower arrangements. Therefore, it is of utmost importance, and in some cases can even mean the difference between life and death, for a hospital to identify as early as possible any patients who are carrying infections that require isolation, and to communicate that fact to all the staff who will be involved in these patients' care. This early identification of patients with isolation-requiring infections not only protects other hospital patients and the hospital staff from contracting infection, but also can reduce the length of stay for the infected patient. Obviously, the sooner the patient is placed in isolation and receiving the proper antibiotics, the sooner he or she will recover.

There are two major infections that, once contracted, cause a patient to be considered a carrier for life: Methicillin Resistant Staphylcoccus Aureus (MRSA) and Vancomycin Resistant Enterococcus (VRE). It is imperative that patients who carry these organisms are properly isolated until their current contagiousness can be determined. If either of these organisms is spread to another person, that person is infected for life. Furthermore, since hospital patients are invariably in a compromised state, any newly acquired infection could cause serious complications or even death. It is tragic when the hospital inadvertently infects the patient. The central reason for creating the isolation workflow was to prevent this from happening.

It is also important to identify patients who, although previously active with a contagious infection, no longer require isolation. Putting a patient in isolation unnecessarily leaves already-scarce isolation rooms unavailable to patients who really need them and causes bottlenecks in bed availability. In addition, due to the extra supplies needed (gowns, masks and gloves) and the additional time involved for staff members to "gown-up" before entering isolation rooms, the hospital incurs extra costs for keeping a patient in isolation—approximately $100 per day.

Infection Control: Impact on process

Before CCH implemented an Infection Control workflow, the identification of patients needing isolation was a hit-or-miss, ineffective process. Admission assessments were done after the patient was placed in a bed. At that point, if the assessment revealed that the patient was a carrier of a contagious infection, the patient had to be moved into isolation, after already having exposed a roommate and the staff to the infection. This also involved having to reclean the contaminated bed, causing more bottlenecks in bed flow. Moreover, the staff that would care for the patient in isolation was caught unprepared, and in some cases was not fully stocked with the proper isolation supplies.

On the flip side, the old IT system would flag cases where cultures were positive, but not those that were negative, since theoretically negative results were not a reason for action. In the case of Infection Control, however, negative results are just as important as positive ones, since knowing that a patient does not need isolation is just as important as knowing that a patient does, for reasons already outlined above.

To determine its effectiveness at Infection Control, the IT staff at CCH conducted a study on patients entering the hospital with MRSA. Four percent of adult patients entering the hospital have a history of MRSA, and they account for 8 percent of patient days. In a study of 30 patients over a four-week period, approximately 25 percent of MRSA patients with prior positive results who should have gone into isolation upon admission were missed at initial bed placement. This necessitated an immediate transfer to isolation status. If they were missed altogether, this would place other patients and hospital workers at risk for the infection.

Now that CCH has implemented an Infection Control workflow, when a patient comes in with a history of a contagious infection, the system places an automated phone call to alert the nursing staff to take precautions, to perform a culture immediately to determine if the patient requires isolation, and to explain the situation to the patient's family members. The system then takes care of all the operational downstream work, such as notifying the Laundry Department to send extra isolation supplies to the patient's room.

The following charts display before and after scenarios of CCH's Infection Control workflow processes.

MRSA Infection Control Process Pre-Workflow

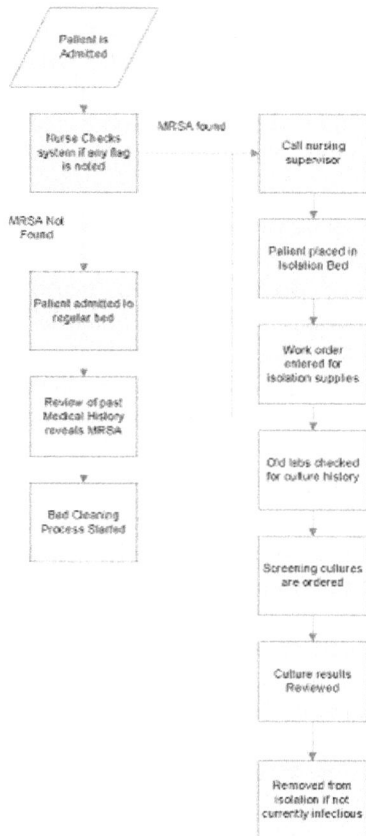

MRSA Infection Control Process Post-Workflow

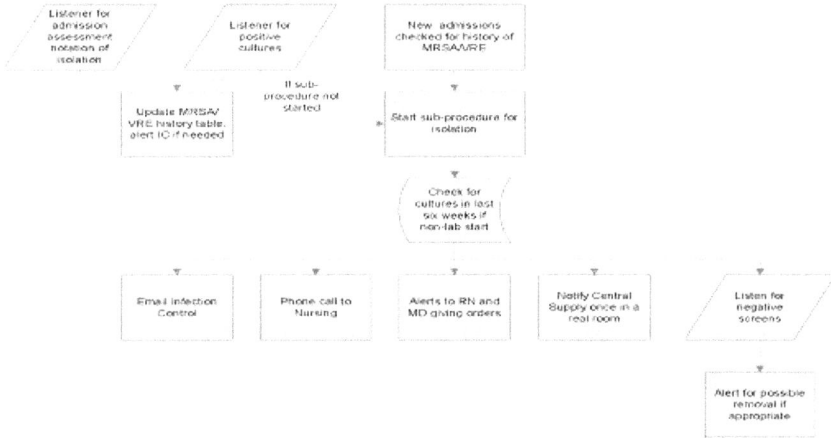

The graphic below shows the current main workflow screen for infection control.

MAIN WORKFLOW SCREEN FOR INFECTION CONTROL

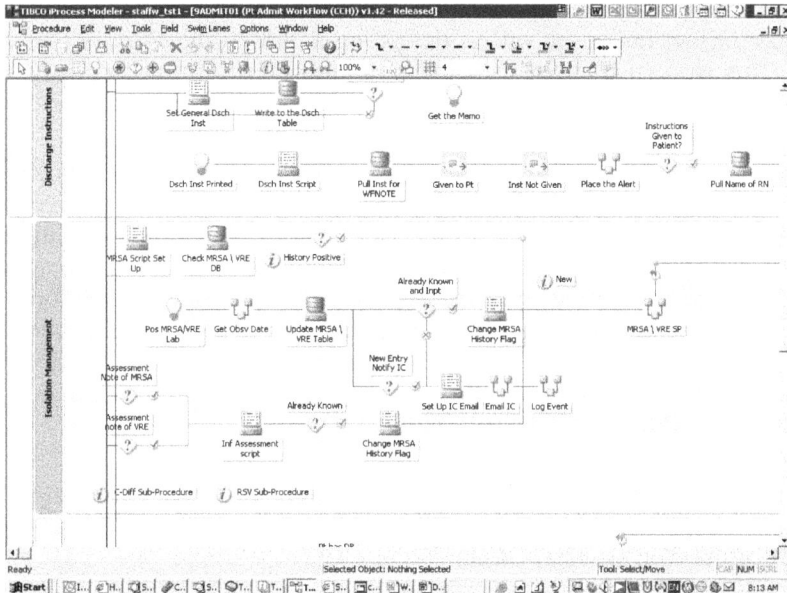

INFECTION CONTROL: IMPACT ON TECHNOLOGY

The original Infection Control process utilized little technology and was heavily dependant on human action at almost every step. Prior to the implementation of the isolation workflow, a database flag was set in the patient registration system if the patient was identified with MRSA or VRE. However, this flag did not appear in any clinical computer screens and therefore clinical staff were unaware of the patient's status. Also, the Infection Control Department manually entered the flag on a periodic basis (often many weeks after the fact). This master list was kept on the Infection Control Department's computer, and was printed out and distributed to clinical staff. As a result, if a patient was newly diagnosed with the MRSA/VRE infection and subsequently readmitted prior to the publishing of the new list, their current status would not have been evident at either admission or during initial review on the floor. Also, new positive lab values were printed to the floor's printer and were to be accompanied by a phone call from the Microbiology Department. Negative lab values were printed and needed to be interpreted by the nurse for potential relevance. In either case, values that needed to be acted upon necessitated a series of phone calls and work orders.

The BPM system was configured to automate these same tasks with little human intervention. The master list of infectious patients was placed in the SQL Server database, updated automatically by the BPM engine, and made available through the institution via a Web UI. Every patient being admitted is checked against the master list and if a match is found, the system performs the necessary steps. A phone call is placed using the above-mentioned telephonic interface to the nursing supervisor. E-mail notification is sent to the Infection Control department via the Microsoft Exchange server. Clinical notifications show up on the Soarian clinical system and on the Bedboard UI noted above. Notifications to ancillary departments, such as Laundry for isolation gowns, occur automatically via printed media. Every new lab value is evaluated for relevance. New labs with critical values are acted upon with proper notifications and the master list is immediately updated. Again, a key technological aspect of this process's success has been the ability to coordinate existing technology with the BPM system and to remove many of the manual steps.

The Impact of Workflow on Users

In the case of both Bed Management and Infection Control, workflow has reduced the number of manual steps within the process of identification, notification and tracking. This in turn has reduced the time and effort of the end users, making them more efficient and productive and allowing them more time for the care of patients rather than spending time on the process.

Bed Management has reduced the number of manual steps by 50 percent. It provides an enterprise-wide, up-to-the-minute status for the care delivery team. It automatically manages nursing alerts, prioritization, and housekeeping staff assignments, and provides the supervisors with an automated departmental management and comprehensive reporting of activity for analysis. Infection Control has assured that every patient with a known MRSA or VRE condition is managed and isolated properly. It assures that isolation bed placement is optimized by appropriately placing all patients in the proper status but only for as long as they need to be there. Proper care is automatically directed, assuring efficient, effective and safer patient care.

The following chart indicates the volume of patients that have been impacted and the automated alerts that have been accomplished by the Bed Management and Infection Control workflows at CCH:

Number of patients monitored at any given time	1,200-1,500
Number of beds cleaned (since October 28, 2004)	37,500+
Admissions checked for MRSA since December 2004	38,500+
Number of pages sent out	181,000+
Number of phone calls	77,500+

System Configuration

Most workflow examples that we have seen are predicated on end-user interaction with a computer terminal. The key to CCH's BPM success was less the choice of technology (which telephonic card or .NET versus Java) but rather configuring the BPM process to interact with the end-user using the technology that they already employed. This is most apparent when BPM is used to manage workflow for support departments that are never in front of a terminal but who need to be able to receive assignments and provide updates to the system.

The chart below provides a description of CCH's BPM system.

The Chester County Hospital

BPM Architecture

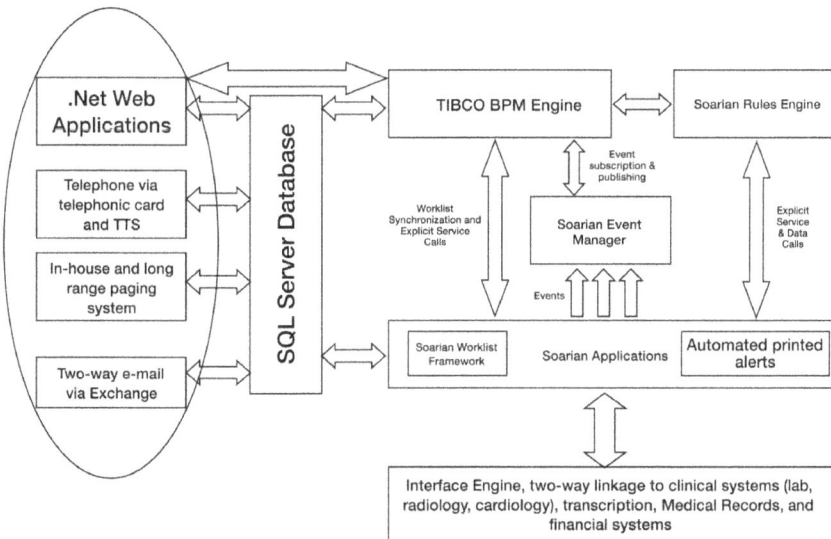

HURDLES OVERCOME

Management hurdles

As CCH began to implement workflow processes, there was an immediate positive buy-in from managers. There were, however, some challenges, the first of which was to educate key members of the hospital on the capabilities and power of the workflow management tools. The next challenge was to determine which processes to analyze and improve upon with workflow management, and to ensure that management was committed to the initiative and able to align the appropriate resources to analyze, design, test and monitor all workflows.

Business hurdles

One of the biggest hurdles that the CCH IT Department encountered in setting up an integrated workflow management system was achieving consensus on the proper protocols to follow, since there is such a huge variation in medicine on how to deal with certain illnesses, etc. Another challenge was determining just how much to automate in the workflow process. Some processes would simply need to be refined, while others would require a complete redesign. It was very important for CCH to get a buy-in from doctors for the workflow design, and to get doctors to trust the system enough to perform functions that had previously been performed by people. The IT staff needed to strike a balance between making processes simpler and more efficient for doctors and yet not automating processes so much that it took away or limited doctors' control.

Another challenge was setting up a workflow system in an environment that is not a stationary setting where workers sit at computers and perform most of their job functions right at their desks or work stations. A healthcare setting by its very nature is very mobile. Employees, from housekeepers to surgeons, do not work in one place, but rather depend on pagers, phones and laptops to carry out their duties. It was challenging to take traditional workflow systems and modify them so that they could be effective in a clinical setting, where workers are like moving targets and the steps involved in performing their job duties vary from hour to hour and are as unique as the patients they serve.

Technology hurdles

In creating its workflow management system, CCH's greatest technological challenge was to build a whole portfolio of workflow modules to add on to the Soarian workflow engine and make those modules work seamlessly together, rather than building standalone pieces that were independent of each other. The next technological hurdle to overcome involved putting a monitoring system in place as a fail-safe for the system. Again, in few other industries does the failure of a workflow system have the potential to mean the difference between life and death, as it does in a healthcare environment. Hospital staff relies on this system, not just during normal business hours, but 24 hours a day, seven days a week, 365 days a year. The IT staff was challenged with building an early warning system for business interruption occurrences that would provide a level of vigilance far beyond anything that was already available out of the box.

As a result, at CCH, there is a built-in escalation management system that goes into action the minute it detects a lock-up or failure in any of the many handoffs to legacy systems. Indeed the stability issue has rarely been with the BPM engine, but rather with these legacy systems. As mentioned in Bed Management, a comprehensive monitoring system using a .NET Web UI, text paging, and e-mail notifications was created to monitor the database and system activity. This monitoring system resides on a separate server and continually "pings" the various processes and hardware for proper operation.

BENEFITS

Cost Optimization/Increased Revenues

In a healthcare setting, particularly a not-for-profit institution such as CCH, the traditional business model of increasing revenues does not directly apply. Most payers pay on a fixed-fee basis, either a certain amount per approved day of care or per case, regardless of the care given. When it comes to financial matters, the focus must be on optimizing cost so that there is a positive margin on each case. So, rather than seeking a "profit," hospitals need to focus on decreasing expenses and then seek to increase the volume of patients. If efficiency is not achieved, the hospital could experience a loss with each patient admission and increasing volume would actually hurt the institution. The constant goal is to provide excellent care, to contribute to a population of healthier people, and to do so in a safe and cost-effective manner. CCH has made great strides in meeting this goal through its workflow management system.

As already discussed earlier in this case study, the workflows that CCH has put into place have helped to ensure that the hospital is making the most of its operating dollars by eliminating waste and spending money where it is most needed. The Bed Management workflow, for example, has eliminated 50 percent of the manual steps involved in the bed cleaning process and increased the timeliness of bed availability. This has decreased the costs associated with overtime hours, lengthy hospital stays, and bottlenecks caused by a shortage of clean beds, which often requires diverting patients to other hospitals. The Infection Control workflow has reduced the extra costs that are incurred from hospital-acquired infections, such as lengthier stays and potential lawsuits. It has also saved money by eliminating the unnecessary use of isolation rooms and isolation supplies which, as stated earlier, costs an additional $100 a day.

The bottom line is that workflow technology has allowed CCH to provide better, safer care to its patients, and thus meet or exceed national regulatory requirements for obtaining the maximum reimbursement from insurance providers.

Productivity Improvements

CCH's Bed Management workflow system has automated many of the manual processes involved in Bed Management. All the steps, notifications, monitoring and progress of the workflow are totally automated, with only the housekeeper needing to enter into a telephone that the bed is cleaned and ready. This has freed housekeepers from having to respond to overhead pagers and find phones to respond to requests, and has diminished nurse involvement in the bed cleaning workflow, allowing them to focus on the care of their patients. It also has diminished the bottlenecks that occur due to a shortage of clean beds, and has reduced patients' wait time to get into a room and begin receiving the proper care.

The Hospital's Infection Control workflow has greatly improved productivity by providing staff with an early warning system to identify patients who need/do not need isolation rooms. The system manages tables that identify which patients have MRSA and VRE, noting the site of initial and last infection, valuable information from a clinical perspective. The ability to immediately identify patients who require isolation allows staff to save time through advance preparation. For example, the Laundry Department is notified to send extra isolation supplies to the patient's room. The ability to identify patients who no longer require isolation has decreased the incidence of using isolation rooms and supplies unnecessarily, saving time and money.

COMPETITIVE ADVANTAGES

The implementation of BPM at CCH has gained competitive advantages for the hospital as both an employer and as a healthcare provider. By becoming a hospital of distinction that has set itself apart from its competitors, CCH has been able to attract the best and the brightest staff, and has become the hospital of choice for the surrounding community.

In light of the current shortage of healthcare workers, the ability to attract quality employees is critical. In general, those who select healthcare as a profession tend to be individuals who are driven to help others. When their jobs are weighed down with non-clinical duties, they tend to become frustrated and dissatisfied. By putting efficient workflows in place, CCH has been able to provide employees with a work environment that allows them to focus on what they enjoy the most: patient care. Demonstrating its workflow efficiency at nursing recruitment venues has given the hospital a definite advantage in attracting prospective nursing employees. Likewise, young physicians who have been educated in a time when workflow has become increasingly important are seeking to affiliate themselves with hospitals that have streamlined processes in place that make it easier for them to practice medicine. Thus CCH has increased its ability to attract physicians to its staff.

Workflow management has also provided CCH with a competitive advantage in attracting patients. As discussed earlier, today's healthcare consumer, particularly Baby Boomers, are much more demanding of quality care, and are much more informed about healthcare issues. Publicly reported data on hospitals is available with the click of a computer mouse, and consumers do their homework in deciding where to go for healthcare services. CCH believes that BPM will help in decreasing not just infection rates but, at the end of the day, reduce morality rates as well. Thus, incorporating BPM into its strategy to increase patient safety has definitely improved CCH's ability to attract patients.

BPM has set CCH apart from competitors, attracting employees and patients alike. In so doing, the hospital has moved competitive goalposts and has caused a healthy drive for other hospitals to stay in the game by following suit with efficient workflow management processes.

PLANS TO SUSTAIN COMPETITIVE ADVANTAGE

CCH continues to develop the BPM workflows. Since the healthcare industry continues to change, CCH has purposely designed its workflow management system with evolution in mind. The IT staff plans on adding pieces to the system so that ultimately there will be workflow procedures in place to not only manage business processes but to manage evidence-based medicine and clinical care wherever possible. The hospital has already added dietary, diabetes, Congestive Heart Failure, admission assessment, outpatient, microbiology results, automated nursing notes, automated discharge instructions, and smoking cessation education workflows. It is currently working on drug management, heart attack, pneumonia, sepsis, radiology test preparation, and Emergency Department workflows. CCH strives for the creation of workflow-enabled patient care processes that cover all aspects of care.

Hasbro, USA

Silver Award 2006, North America; nominated by Lombardi, USA

EXECUTIVE SUMMARY

Hasbro is the second largest toy maker in the world, with 2005 revenues of $3.1 billion. Hasbro brands and products include G.I. Joe, Transformers, Play Doh, Tonka, Nerf, Playskool, Milton Bradley, Parker Brothers and Magic, The Gathering, to name a few.

With such a diverse line of products, Hasbro relies in part on outsourced manufacturers for some of its toy and game production. Of course, managing a supply chain comprised of many diverse suppliers and numerous large orders a day required a team of people to manage vendor relationships and individual request for quotes (RFQs). Before Hasbro adopted a business process management (BPM) solution from Lombardi, almost all of the processes for determining an order and its supplier were paper based and manually intensive. Hasbro began its eConnect program with a clear mission statement:

Hasbro e-Connect delivers a collaborative e-business platform designed to connect business partners. It enables secure, self-service business transactions with business partners via the Internet, with seamless integration into our systems. The result is a streamlined business processes that save time and money.

By automating numerous mission-critical processes in their complex supply chain with Lombardi as a single BPM platform, Hasbro has identified several key areas of benefits:
- Increased supply chain visibility
- Increased supply chain automation
- Increased data quality and integrity
- Leads to lower stock inventory
- Reduced administration processing cost
- Reduced length of supply chain cycle
- Provided value-added customer services
- Centralized all processes onto one standardized platform

Those benefits have firm metrics including reduced staffing costs, reduction in cycle times for RFQs, and a substantial increase in employee productivity. In sum, BPM has significantly improved operational efficiencies and more deeply integrated the Hasbro supply chain into its customers, suppliers, and shipping partners.

INITIAL BUSINESS MOTIVATION

Beginning in 2001, Hasbro launched an enterprise wide initiative to improve supply chain processes and reduce costs. One of the key areas was in the management of outsourced manufacturing vendors, especially vendor order management. Hasbro is a large SAP customer and used SAP to manage all of their transactions, but it wasn't managing the RFQ process, and facilitating them to receive a quote for fulfillment from vendor. Instead, Hasbro's processes were paper based and manually handled. When a large order came in via fax, the team split it up into individual products and faxed separate RFQs to various vendors depending on their capabilities. The decisions were made manually by the Hasbro team. Vendors would fax back their quotes with an expected time to delivery and the team would parse through all these faxes to put together the best way to supply the order. However, often vendors would fax back partial quotes, or would not return quotes on time, or there were errors. To resolve these problems, Hasbro employees were required to hit the phones and fax more requests. They also had to manage any exceptions and handle all of the paper to resolve even the simplest of orders. Once an order was resolved, a fax was then sent to the customer notifying them when they should expect the order to be fulfilled.

At the time, Hasbro was receiving enough orders per day to create a logistical nightmare, with cycle times averaging 12 days. In order to keep up with large customers, especially during peak demand seasons such as the holidays, Hasbro kept a necessary inventory of toys. This practice had a cost associated with it. The process was an ideal candidate for optimization through workflow automation.

PROCESS INNOVATION

Hasbro evaluated several software packages including extending the SAP system with portal technology and other web development tools, but determined that the core problem was in the workflow of their business process itself. The goal was to automate the management of information so that team members could better understand the quote items, the vendor responses, and the optimal sourcing. By eliminating the paper and faxes from the mix, Hasbro could increase productivity and reduce cycle times, especially as it relates to the management of exceptions.

Today, Hasbro now receives orders electronically from its customers directly into the SAP system. Individual quotes are separated and RFQs are sent to the vendors who can supply the items. Each RFQ is sent to a vendor via email, and includes Internet links to a Hasbro web form for that vendor to respond with a quote for fulfillment. Reminders are automatically sent to vendors who are late in responding to minimize manual exception management. All vendor quotes received are then aggregated, sorted and queued for selection based on price and delivery so that the optimal sourcing contract(s) can be identified. At any time, the business user can see the status of the quote on a single screen instead of mulling through hundreds of faxes. Hasbro now has considerable atomic visibility into the status of each quote they receive. Once a quote is finalized, it is committed to SAP via a native BAPI integration from TeamWorks into SAP. Phase I of automating the human workflow was completed and delivered in 90 days.

With a flexible BPM infrastructure in place with TeamWorks, Hasbro realized that it could iterate on the process quickly (and easily) and therefore determined that the next area of improvement for the process was to increase the straight-through processing (STP) of the workflow so that many orders did not ever have to be touched. Business rules were created so that incoming RFQs were split up and sent to outsourcing vendors automatically based on their capabilities. Incoming quotes for most orders could also be automatically parsed and selected based upon business rules that prioritized price or delivery time based upon the type of order, customer, and priority. As a result, the vast majority of incoming orders are now processed automatically without the need for anyone on the Hasbro team to touch them. One of the key lessons learned during the implementation was the importance of adopting a platform that can be continuously improved in short development cycles with minimal impact to existing processes and the option of them inheriting the improvements.

TECHNOLOGY INNOVATION

By implementing TeamWorks as an agile BPM development platform on top of SAP, Hasbro is now able to much more quickly build and iterate supply chain processes. Where as before, Hasbro was managing large sets of code files for development, with TeamWorks, all process flows are defined graphically even at the screen-by-screen level of detail. The graphical development approach not only vastly reduces the amount of code Hasbro needed to develop (and ultimately maintain), but also provides a better framework to ensure business users and IT are on the same page as to the application definition and implementation. Increasing the role of the business analyst in the development process was a crucial aspect of Hasbro's success. The development time for new major process iterations has averaged between 60-90 days as opposed to being measured in months or years.

Hasbro also has a more standards-based infrastructure. TeamWorks is a 100 percent J2EE application that fits completely within the Hasbro technology stack. TeamWorks runs on WebSphere and DB2 and all the interfaces are web based. Since the process model is BPMN-compliant, and the product relies heavily on XML, SQL and JavaScript, there are no proprietary languages that Hasbro had to learn.

TeamWorks natively connected into Hasbro's Active Directory to leverage existing user directories and group definitions, but it also provides them with the flexibility to manage users of the system externally. This capability was crucial so that Hasbro could outsource vendor user management to the vendors themselves. Each outsourced supplier manages their own team's access to the system, thus dramatically reducing the vendor management burden for Hasbro. Setting up a new vendor in TeamWorks is now a one time cost as opposed to a continual maintenance nightmare.

BUSINESS INNOVATION AND IMPACT

The results of implementing TeamWorks to automate the Hasbro supply chain have been outstanding. By automatically the vast majority of orders without manual intervention, the team can focus more on exceptions, high value added transactions, and process improvement opportunities than day to day management of faxes and order processing. In turn, they have become much more productive.

Furthermore, Hasbro is much more tightly integrated into its customers and suppliers. By hooking customers directly into the SAP system, customers' orders are processed more quickly and order status is more available. Hasbro is much more able to respond to rush orders because cycle time has gone from 6 days to 1 or 2 days on average and customer satisfaction is higher.

On the supply side, vendors also have much better visibility into their quotes and acceptances so they can make more intelligent and competitive quotes and realize how their decisions affect their revenue.

The radical change in development productivity and ability to iterate quickly has also improved their corporate agility significantly. After September 11th, the Customs Trade Partnership Against Terrorism (C-TPAT) mandated Hasbro change its shipping procedures and customs documentation. Shipping receipt processes had to be changed, customs notifications had to be more proactive, and the level of detail required to be documented increased. By implementing the process in TeamWorks, Hasbro was able to respond to regulatory requirements within 90 days and more importantly, not a single shipment was left waiting on the docks. Hasbro's response to C-TPAT is just one example of how its supply chain processes have become much more agile because of the TeamWorks BPM infrastructure. Additionally, the business has much more input into the design process and the skill set that is required to help build the applications is less stringent. As a result, business acceptance of the application and overall satisfaction are both significantly higher as well. With TeamWorks, the company also receives new and detailed visibility into their process performance. Hasbro can see bottlenecks and react in real-time, drill down to see performance data specific to a customer, vendor, or even an order level. Such visibility increases Hasbro's ability to manage business and supplier relationships, expedite important orders, identify and quantify exceptions, and improve the process over the long term.

SYSTEM CONFIGURATION

Biggest Hurdles

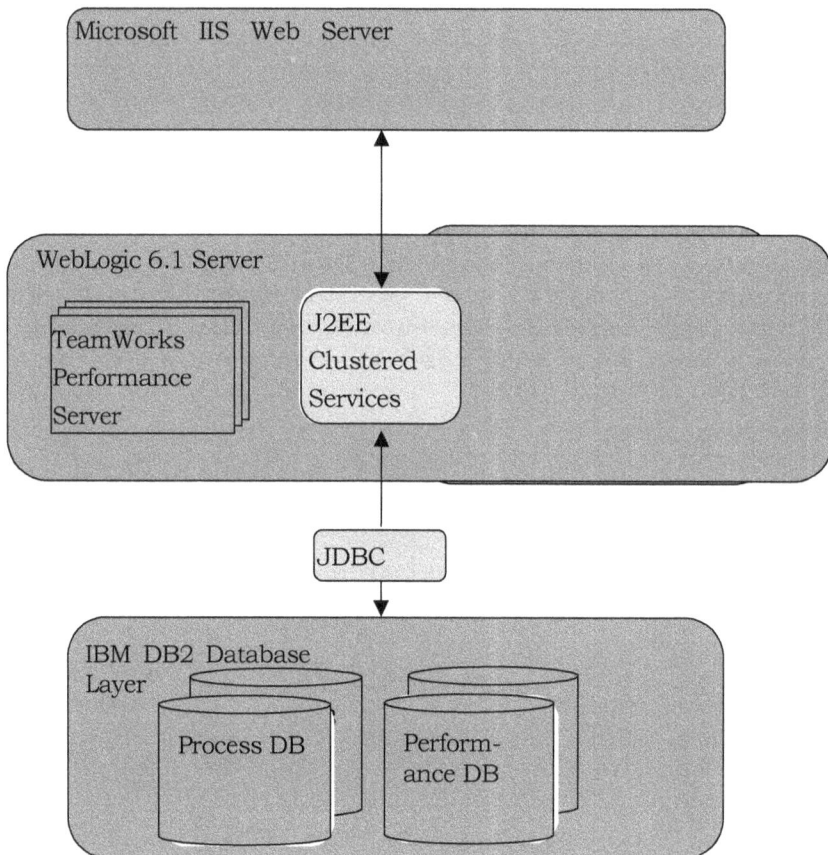

Being such a large user of SAP, it was a difficult technological hurdle for Hasbro to agree to search for an external vendor to augment the SAP system. There were several competitive solutions that potentially could have suited Hasbro's needs, but did not deliver all of the capabilities that the company was looking for. Selecting an emerging start-up such as Lombardi required considerable evaluation, though in the end the capabilities proved to best meet the company's requirements.

Once the initial workflow was in place and the initial results were clearly positive, team members were eager to participate, as the improvements put in place important efficiencies that allowed them to do their jobs more effectively. Similarly, the management challenge was to bring suppliers online and familiarize them with the system as with any new application. Extending such functionality outside of the firewall can be difficult when there are 100 different parties to work with. They also became more involved in the improvement process as they saw the value the system brought to their business, by delivering greater visibility into their quotes, faster response times, and the need for less faxes and phone calls. Hasbro's suppliers provided insightful improvement suggestions such as providing multi-quote views to see all of their commitments, and creating a single vendor management portal across all supply chain processes in TeamWorks. Hasbro's suppliers became extended members of the process improvement team.

BENEFITS SUMMARY

There have been many benefits received by the Lombardi BPM implementation including reduced cycle times, error rates, lost orders, inventory rates, hardware costs (computers, faxes, etc.), paper costs, and increased customer and vendor satisfaction, order volume, and improved accuracy.

"The e-Connect system enables all of HFE vendors and logistics providers to communicate and manage the entire production process through the Internet, resulting in better customer service, improved fulfillment cycles and cost savings. We use e-Connect to automate the vendor process so that inquiries and purchase orders flow through and update SAP, our internal system, with minimal human interaction. By reducing fax and manual communication, these efficiencies enabled HFE operation to absorb a significant increase in volume without adding additional resources." Josephine Lau, Director of Operations and Planning of Hasbro Far East Limited

SUSTAINABLE ADVANTAGE

The TeamWorks advantage has spread virally above and beyond the RFQ process, and it has become a strategic platform for designing, executing, and improving processes within the supply chain.

In 2003, in response to new U.S. customs regulations (C-TPAT), Hasbro was compelled to change the way it accounted for, labeled, and managed their shipments. Changing the shipping operations of such a large manufacturer required changing processes and the data collected and communicated. Because the communications between Hasbro and its vendors had already been automated, adding shipping label changes and easing the vendors through the transition was much easier. Hasbro could send the right labels directly to the vendors themselves to print out. By using Lombardi's TeamWorks, Hasbro was able to respond quickly and not a single shipment was delayed at the docks because of C-TPAT regulations.

In 2004, Hasbro continued to build upon TeamWorks to automate its delivery operations integrating more closely into its forwarders. Customers were continually changing orders and it was difficult to consolidate those changes into a single view of delivery operations. Using Lombardi, eConnect provided a consolidated list of deliveries for the coming six weeks, pending changes, and integrated into the systems of forwarders and suppliers' internal systems to take advantage of changes and consolidate orders. The number of errors resulting from managing changes was drastically reduced, and disruptions in shipments at forwarders could be detected immediately and acted upon. Hasbro also enabled its suppliers to provide better shipping instructions that were validated directly in Hasbro's

SAP system. This, in turn, increased the accuracy of shipment records and reduced cycle times.

In 2005, Hasbro continued to extend its SAP system to its vendors through managing shipping dimensions. Vendors would sometimes disagree with the dimensions of shipments and managing the communication of changes between teams and quality assurance became a cause of errors and delays. Using Lombardi, vendors update final dimensions, with validation in SAP. Vendor changes are then updated in SAP for future shipments and further updated to other Hasbro internal systems: Hasbro's Product Profile System and Customer Quote Sheet System.

Today, Hasbro continues to innovate with Lombardi to streamline manual processes and closely integrate its systems from its customers, suppliers, and shipping partners and has even spread to managing computer access requests for compliance.

By adopting a platform that lets them build processes in 90 days or less and iterate them just as easily, Hasbro can respond to changing market conditions and take advantage of new opportunities faster while empowering the business users to be much better aligned with IT. Through continuous process improvement, Hasbro depends on TeamWorks for a long term sustainable advantage. Josephine Lau, Director of Operations and Planning of Hasbro Far East Limited, explains:

In traditional shipping process which is still commonly used by most companies, the trail of paperwork, files and faxes among shippers, suppliers, 3PL and shipping lines would be a nightmare to manage. Our shipping process including e-bookings, shipping order, shipping manifest, Harmonized Tariff System (HTS), Advance Ship Notice (ASN) etc is all automated on one platform for all parties and data is integrated with SAP. It improves supplier and logistics performance, and supply chain visibility on track and trace.

ABOUT HASBRO

Hasbro, Inc. (NYSE:HAS) is a worldwide leader in children's and family leisure time entertainment products and services, including the design, manufacture and marketing of games and toys ranging from traditional to high-tech. Both internationally and in the U.S., its PLAYSKOOL, TONKA, MILTON BRADLEY, PARKER BROTHERS, TIGER, and WIZARDS OF THE COAST brands and products provide the highest quality and most recognizable play experiences in the world.

NAS Cheetah Project, USA

Finalist 2006, North America; nominated by Green Square Inc, USA

Executive Summary / Abstract

Sometimes you need to run like a Cheetah. In 2003 Congress passed sweeping changes to the nation's Medicare program. Noridian Administrative Services, LLC. (NAS), one of the largest Medicare contractors in the country had only a short time to prepare for these changes. One of their key Medicare contracts was the first selected for competitive bid. NAS executives challenged a number of areas within the company to offer innovative approaches that could better position NAS to win and execute future contracts. Business Process Management (BPM) and workflow were identified as critical technologies that could enable the innovation. A team was quickly formed to dramatically expand the existing workflow environment. In the spring of 2005, the Cheetah project was established to take on this challenge. Cheetah's mission was to expand workflow/BPM into every operational team, a feat that would require the implementation of 20 workflows in 13 departments for over 350 users in just 20 weeks. This case study focuses on the possibility and reality of massively parallel workflow implementations.

Overview

When the Cheetah vision was communicated to the NAS project team in April of 2005, the task of a massively expanding the workflow environment by August 31 seemed ... aggressive. It would require the creation of some totally new processes and technologies. However, it was made perfectly clear that the project was critical to the company. It was time for a bold vision. While it is not the goal of this case study to convince the reader that the Cheetah project, as it came to be known, is on par with man's first trip to the moon, at the time the effort seemed equally daunting.

This case study describes the enterprise-wide, massively parallel implementation approach used by NAS and details its implications, the challenges the NAS team faced, and the benefits gained by the approach. The reader will also see first-hand how workflow automation addresses key issues in the healthcare and insurance industries.

The Challenge:

The root of NAS's growth lies within the expansion of the Medicare program. Currently, there are approximately 42 million people receiving Medicare health care, and the number is continuously increasing. From a small division of Noridian Mutual Insurance Company, which administered the federal Medicare program for one state, the company has grown into a federal contractor processing over 75 million Medicare claims per year, serving 6.3 million Medicare beneficiaries and more than 130,000 Medicare providers in 14 states. Efficient, effective processes are critical to NAS assuring the continued delivery of health services to its customers.

A History of Workflow Success

In 2000, NAS Executive and Information Technology Management took a hard look at their paper-bound processes. A forward-looking strategy was undertaken to explore alternatives that could move NAS toward a less-paper environment. An approach was developed to introduce document management technologies, stopping the paper "at the door" and providing digital access to the documents. The success of these early document management initiatives spawned a move in 2001 to introduce process automation technologies in the form of workflow software.

Cheetah is Born

The competitive landscape for Medicare contracts changed dramatically in 2003. President George W. Bush signed into law the Medicare Prescription Drug Improvement and Modernization Act of 2003 which included far-reaching changes to the nation's Medicare program. All Medicare contracts would be competitively bid over a 24 month period starting in 2005. One of NAS' key contracts was to be the first in line for this competitive process. NAS Executive Management challenged the information technology and business areas to devise a method as rapidly and broadly as possible that expands document management and workflow technology. In early 2005, the Cheetah Project was born.

NAS' history of success with document management and workflow technologies was fairly prototypical. Methodical, department-by-department evaluations were completed and workflow was deployed in the areas with the greatest needs. While the success was evident, delivering significant financial and operational benefits, it was also evolutionary. Evolutions are slow. What NAS needed was a workflow revolution. The question that confronted the NAS team was—is there an alternative to slow, methodical implementations? Can enterprise workflow be widely and rapidly deployed with high quality and value to the organization?

In April of 2005 a team was assembled to answer these questions. Executive Management at NAS challenged the team to have a workflow solution deployed to every operational department by the end of August. To achieve this goal, the team would have to invent a new way of deploying workflow; it would need to move like a Cheetah.

The Cheetah Project's goals were clear.
- Implement imaging and workflow for 20 processes in 13 departments for 350 employees located in five different locations for production on September 1, 2005
- Improve performance in each affected process without a negative impact on quality
- Create a consistent, reusable and systematic workflow project process and methodology that NAS could leverage in future projects

THE KEY BUSINESS MOTIVATIONS BEHIND THE PROJECT.

NAS has established a bold vision: To be the benchmark by which all other Medicare and Medicaid contractors are measured. The competitive landscape of Medicare contracts undoubtedly drove the speed of change at NAS, but the core motivations behind the Cheetah project are rooted in this vision of excellence.

With that vision as the standard, the Cheetah project's values and principles were established: performance, quality, cost and agility. These were the drivers for the Cheetah project.
- **Performance**—Highest performance based on customer-oriented metrics
- **Quality**—Sustained, systematic quality in every NAS process
- **Cost**—Unparalleled technology-driven reduction in costs
- **Agility**—Flexible, scalable, and radically adaptive processes that embrace change

In order to achieve the vision of being the industry benchmark by which all other Medicare and Medicaid contractors are measured, NAS will have to lead in the area of technical innovation. For operationally-oriented companies like NAS and other Medicare contractors, this innovation is found in customer-centric process automation that delivers on themes of performance, quality, cost and agility.

It remains to be seen whether projects like Cheetah will help NAS achieve sustained competitive advantage. It is clear, however, that Cheetah and similar projects at NAS are delivering real value to Medicare beneficiaries and providers today through faster customer service response times, lower costs and fewer errors.

THE KEY INNOVATION

The key innovation for the Cheetah project was agility. Agility is an often-quoted term used by various industry luminaries and vendors to mean a panorama of things. The Cheetah team defined agility early in the project as flexible, scalable and adaptive processes that could morph quickly in a rapidly evolving Medicare and Medicaid marketplace. Agility manifested itself in several critical ways for the project.

Process

Process was the first opportunity to introduce agile thinking. NAS could not design, develop and deploy workflows as they had in the past. There simply was not enough time. The Cheetah team began the project by creating a new development methodology. The Cheetah development process was planned as a rapid, reusable framework for design, development and deployment of agile workflows.

Within each category of design, development and deployment, agile concepts were put in place. For example, workflow architects, designers and subject matter experts collaborated to create an innovative means to quickly work through business requirements. Architects worked in concert with developers and implementation engineers to create a clever and flexible architecture giving all involved a head start with their respective tasks.

Business

Cheetah would affect 350 business users in thirteen different departments. When the users logged in on September 1, 2005 most, if not all, of their paper documents would be delivered to team workflow queues. For this reason, business users were engaged early and often. Executives, managers, team leaders and clerical staff were all involved in design, development and deployment sessions. These staff members were responsible for assuring the execution of key Medicare processes and served as a critical link to the ultimate customer's requirements. Expectations were clear, measured and audited. Cheetah needed to deliver on those expectations.

Cheetah affected the processes that serve a number of stakeholders. They include:

- The Centers for Medicare and Medicaid Services (CMS), the Federal agency that administers the Medicare program
- Over 130,000 Medicare providers
- Over 6.3 million beneficiaries

The NAS mission was clear and stated in the goals of the project. In addition to reducing cost and improving process agility, Cheetah needed to improve performance in each affected process without a negative impact on quality.

Technology

The technical footprint for the Cheetah project was surprisingly small. Existing servers and software were utilized with the exception of the required, additional client licenses - this was by design. NAS's goal was to leverage existing technical platforms. The Cheetah project utilized OnBase workflow software from Hyland Software. Therefore, the impact to the existing environment was modest.

THE IMPACT ON USERS OF THE SYSTEM

Prior to Cheetah, most users received their work in the form of paper delivered from the mailroom via interoffice mail. An intricate system of counting and logging was performed in multiple areas. A team supervisor assigned work manually, and then the actual work began. Clerical staff would review each piece of paper to determine what type of document was received and then manually performed the appropriate actions. Finally, work was tallied, checked-in and filed. Now imagine this happening for 350 people in 13 different areas, simultaneously. Managing security, privacy, quality and timeliness was a significant feat.

Cheetah has changed that model subtly, yet radically. The goal of Cheetah version 1.0 was to expand the scope of workflow at NAS while creating an environment in which business users could absorb the change. Cheetah would change how users did work, but not what they did. While small process re-design was implemented, the project scope and timeline called for more intensive redesigns to be part of later Cheetah versions.

The most significant change for users was the absence of paper. Mail was scanned and classified in the mailroom. Digital images were delivered to the workflow engine for distribution based on the work type. Users could log in and begin working. After they completed their electronic checklist, the user could simply move to the next item in the queue. Gone was the physical movement of paper, logging, counting, tallying productivity and other paper-based activities. Performance was improved, reducing costs while quality was increased and process changes were less traumatic. The key themes of Cheetah—Performance, Cost, Quality and Agility—found their way into every piece of mail received and every job completed.

THE NEW SYSTEM CONFIGURATION

NAS uses Hyland Software's OnBase product suite. The following OnBase software modules comprise the NAS system.
- Archival API
- CD Authoring
- COLD
- Concurrent Client
- Disconnected Scanning Module
- Document Import Processor
- E-Forms
- EDM Services
- Multi-User System
- Outlook Integration
- Production Document Imaging
- Virtual Print Driver
- Web Server
- Workflow Concurrent Client
- Workflow Server

- Workflow Workstation Client
- Workstation Client

NAS utilizes server hardware from various manufacturers including IBM, Compaq and HP for the OnBase server environment. Individual Servers are dedicated to run the following OnBase applications:

- OnBase DIP/Print
- OnBase Workflow
- OnBase Print
- OnBase File/Print Sharing
- OnBase COLD
- OnBase Web
- OnBase SQL

For document scanning, NAS utilizes the OnBase Production Document Imaging module with six production-level Kodak scanners.

THE BIGGEST HURDLES OVERCOME

As with any project of this size, scope and short deadlines Cheetah encountered a number of hurdles. Fortunately, the team was able to quickly address each challenge they encountered.

Management

Communication: Communication is often a challenge in project teams; Cheetah was no exception. A proactive approach was taken, via a formal communication plan, communicating information widely and consistently throughout the project. The communication approach was a huge success and the team learned that communication could be beneficial even earlier, with greater frequency and more end-user interaction.

Planning: Management Guru Tom Peters is right about project planning. He states that most projects are 10 percent planning and 90 percent execution. Peters argues for a Wow! Project that is 30 percent planning, 30 percent selling (communication), 30 percent execution and 10 percent celebration/hand-off. Cheetah's 20 weeks included a full eight weeks of planning, and we learned that more would have been valuable. NAS saw significant angst from the designers and programmers when they were informed programming would not start until planning was complete in mid-June. In retrospect, the planning was close to the right amount, but more would have definitely made the project deliverables richer and the user experience even smoother.

Business

Assumptions: Don't assume anything, ever. It is easy to say and difficult to live. Make no assumptions about end-user technical literacy. NAS users are a fairly technology-friendly group, but everyone involved needed to wrap their minds around new technologies in a way that reduced fear of change. The team needed to make fewer assumptions and confirm all assumptions, twice.

Resource Changes: Every project loses resources due to a number of factors. Even with the short time frame of the Cheetah project, the team was not immune to this phenomenon. The project confirmed the NAS policy that backups for key spots need to be identified and contingency plans need to be in place for replacing key team members.

Technology

Infrastructure: Do not take infrastructure for granted. New software and hardware can stress even the healthiest of systems. Serious planning should be done with regard to computer systems and the impact of new systems.

COST SAVINGS

As of July 31, 2006 NAS has conservatively saved $175,000 over the last eleven months as a direct result of the Cheetah project. Additional versions of Cheetah will likely produce more dramatic savings due to planned process redesigns. NAS as a whole has conservatively saved $5.6M through the use of workflow. Ongoing savings resulting from workflow are approximately $3.2M per year.

This information is based on a savings model which was created in March of 2006 and represents savings from the following cost categories:

- Full-time equivalent staff labor and benefit costs
- Temporary staff costs
- Facility/Real estate costs
- Archival and storage costs
- Print, photocopy and fax costs
- File cabinet costs
- Shipping costs
- Paper and supplies
- Other

INCREASED REVENUES

NAS has won additional Medicare contracts due, in part, to technical innovations deployed in the Cheetah projects. In late 2005, NAS was awarded a $100 million contract in new services from CMS. On July 31, 2006, CMS announced that NAS was awarded a Medicare Administrative Contractor contract valued at $28.9 million for the first year and a potential of $182 million over five years. While there is no way to determine precisely what role Cheetah and process innovation played in NAS' selection, it certainly did not have a negative impact.

Productivity improvements

In addition to impressive financial returns, NAS achieved significant improvements in other qualitative measures including:

- Quality/Accuracy
- Ability to audit processes
- Disaster recovery
- Workload management
- Internal Controls/Compliance/Risk reduction
- Consistency
- Improved communication
- Ease of training/quicker productivity

Cheetah succeeded in delivering workflow to every operational area. The last of the 20 workflows went into production August 26, 2006 - four days ahead of the deadline. The project was on time, on budget and set a high standard for achievement by the NAS OnBase team.

IMMEDIATE AND LONG-TERM PLANS TO SUSTAIN COMPETITIVE ADVANTAGE

Additional versions of Cheetah are planned for future releases that will focus on leveraging new capabilities in the workflow software.

Groupo Financiero Uno, USA

Gold Award 2005, North America; nominated by Ultimus, USA

EXECUTIVE SUMMARY

Grupo Financiero Uno, headquartered in Miami, FL, is the leading financial service provider for Central America, with locations in seven Latin American Countries, including Mexico, Guatemala, El Salvador, Honduras, Nicaragua, Costa Rica and Panama. The company realized that with its continued success and steady growth, it was about to face a major challenge with its credit card approval process. It was taking 15 days to process a single request due to the many manual administrative tasks and approval cycles. Additionally, the approval process was highly susceptible to human error, including applications sitting in in-boxes for extended periods of time and often getting lost in the shuffle.

Not wanting to lose valuable customers or the potential revenue of bringing on new customers, Grupo Financiero Uno chose to turn to Business Process Management, specifically, the Ultimus BPM Suite, to automate its approval processes. The Ultimus BPM Suite eliminated nearly all of the paperwork and brought Grupo Financiero Uno's process time down from more than two weeks to less than 3 days. In fact, today Grupo Financiero Uno is now able to process 470 percent more credit card applications and credit card disputes with the same number of staff per year while client growth continues to clip along at 30 percent year-over-year.

OVERVIEW.

As the largest issuer of Visa credit cards in Central America, Grupo Uno found itself cutting into its profit margins through inefficient operations and decentralized business processes. Everything at Grupo Uno was done manually, including credit card approval processes which initially took 15 days due to the many administrative tasks and approval cycles that needed to be finalized before the process was complete. Applications were physically handed to an analyst as they went through information checking, verifying of policies and looking for references via external bureaus. This system had an incredibly high rate of error with paper sitting on desks for days and sometimes weeks or often getting lost. Basic data entry processes took 16 people per country to complete and those 16 were behind with the sheer amount of data that needed to be entered.

When it became apparent that continued growth would cause further lag times and would require increased overhead such a significant number of new employees to accomplish the task, the company looked into a way to eliminate these manual processes to better allocate employee resources and synchronize them with more vital activities. The result was an immediate improvement in overall employee and customer satisfaction. The company selected Business Process Management (BPM) and the Ultimus BPM Suite to create the corporate-wide solution.

The Ultimus BPM Suite is an independent BPM platform that automates any process incorporating people, applications and organizations. Through the use of the Ultimus BPM Suite, Grupo Uno eliminated nearly all of the paperwork involved in the credit card approval process and brought that process down from 15 days to less than 3 days.

With the Ultimus BPM Suite, Grupo Uno has been able to operate at a sustain growth rate of 30 percent for two years without hiring additional personnel for the credit card approval process; the ROI attained from just one of the six countries using Ultimus has justified the investment for the entire region.

THE KEY BUSINESS MOTIVATIONS BEHIND THIS PROJECT

About three years ago Grupo Financiero Uno began reviewing its technology needs to determine if there was a better way to conduct its business. A major business motivation that Grupo Uno was looking to achieve was to eliminate much of the paperwork and reduce process time to increase customer satisfaction and employee retention. By introducing the automation of processes and integration with Web services, Grupo Uno would more than double its processing capacity.

In seeing how processes could be implemented in an efficient and optimal manner, employees gained a much better understanding of the importance and value of businesses goals and objectives for their organization. Additionally, through the efficiency of transitioning paper to automated processes, only one person is now required to manage the process as opposed to what originally took 16 people. This allowed for the other 15 employees to focus on other areas of the business that they normally would not be able to touch upon. The result for these employees has been greater satisfaction in their work by focusing on more meaningful areas of the business as opposed to tedious hours spent on data entry processes.

In addition to higher employee satisfaction, the ability to respond quickly to customer requests is the backbone of any organization. Already established as a leader in the Latin American financial services market, Grupo Financiaro Uno saw BPM as an opportunity to increase efficiencies and remain competitive. A major business driver behind this project was the idea of increased customer satisfaction. By automating processes customer applications could be completed faster with less room for human error. The project steered away from literal paper trails that often resulted in delays and processing errors and instead resolved customer requests quickly and accurately using the Ultimus BPM Suite software.

THE KEY INNOVATIONS

Business-Describe the impact on the way the firm engages its customers, partners and suppliers etc.

Grupo Uno's use of the Ultimus BPM Suite has impacted the level of satisfaction that their customers are receiving. Since the project was implemented customers have been receiving credit card approvals at faster rates and information is accurate now that human error has been removed. The mere fact that the bank is processing 470 more credit card applications and increasing its revolving credit accounts with more than a 30 percent growth rate is a strong testament to the power of BPM. However, since the bank can now process more credit applications, this means that the bank can opt for more financially sound loan management than before. In other words, the bank can be more selective in its approval process. The end result is a positive effect on Grupo Uno's bottom line – the most important measure for any business decision.

Process-with before and after schematics of the process

Grupo Financiero Uno's credit card approval process initially took 15 days, as there were many administrative responsibilities and approvals that needed to be finalized before the process was complete. With the Ultimus BPM Suite, the process is down to less than 3 days because it cleared out many of the bottlenecks that the company was previously experiencing. With numerous paper forms and many signature approvals, the traditional way Grupo Uno was doing business was highly inefficient.

Ultimus also helped to increase Grupo Financiero Uno's organizational productivity and responsiveness, reduced costs and cycle times, and improved visibility and accountability, while still delivering the lowest total cost of wnership.

Technology-showing the architecture of the new system

The Ultimus BPM Suite is the only business process Suite that enables automated business processes to be deployed without completely defined process maps. Instead, the system allows processes to be adapted in real-time by process experts to address changing business conditions quickly and easily. Ultimus changes the dynamics of process discovery and provides the shortest time to value possible when implementing robust process-based solutions.

Now in its seventh generation, the Ultimus BPM Suite is the most feature rich product on the market, with enhancements driven from real experience gained from working with more than 1500 customers on thousands of processes. It provides:

- A collaborative process modeling & implementation environment
- Flexible integration and workflow capabilities
- An innovative rules engine capability
- Powerful management tools
- Easy to use Web interfaces for process participants

The Ultimus BPM Suite is ideal for use with processes that involve a mix of people and systems. as the BPM Suite is designed to support cross-functional BPM teams. Process Owners and Business Users can graphically model their processes without having to be experts in any specific modeling methodology. Analysts can take those models, refine them, and create automated solutions without any programming. When complex integration is required, developers can implement functions, or services, using .NET or Web Services that can be easily linked into processes without being embedded in them, abstracting the process analyst from the need to know how to write complex code.

Process Experts create rules in a graphical environment and manage the change associated with running processes. Finally, users, managers, and administrators can adjust day to day task assignments and activities without ever impacting the process itself. For Grupo Uno Ultimus helped reduce the typical application backlog while providing an environment that is geared toward improved collaboration with business teams. By clearly separating different aspects of process automation into manageable pieces, alignment of process responsibility with business responsibility is possible without technology constraints.

THE IMPACT ON USERS OF THE SYSTEM

Improving the IT component was vital to improving business processes at Grupo Financiaro Uno. Implementing a BPM solution meant facilitating multiple jobs helping to achieve more quantifiable results. This practice allowed for both business executives and the IT director to focus on other areas of business that they normally would not be able to touch upon.

Grupo Uno established the best practice of communicating new technology to business users in order to emphasize the advantages it would bring to the organization. By implementing BPM, users now escape the chore of having to manually complete application processes. Because of this technology users can enjoy more satisfaction from their work by focusing on tasks that are important and part of what they were hired to do instead of slogging through the mundane drudgery of data entry..

THE NEW SYSTEM CONFIGURATION (TYPE OF SOFTWARE, SERVERS, ETC.)

Now in its seventh generation, the Ultimus BPM Suite is the most feature rich product on the market, with enhancements driven from real experience gained from working with more than 1500 customers on thousands of processes. It provides:

- A collaborative process modeling & implementation environment
- Flexible integration and workflow capabilities
- An innovative rules engine capability
- Powerful management tools
- Easy to use Web interfaces for process participants

The Ultimus BPM Suite is ideal for use with processes that involve a mix of people and systems since the BPM Suite is designed to support cross-functional BPM teams. Process Owners and Business Users can graphically model their processes without having to be experts in any specific modeling methodology. Analysts can take those models, refine them, and create automated solutions without any programming. When complex integration is required, developers can implement functions, or services, using .NET or Web Services that can be easily linked into processes without being embedded in them, abstracting the process analyst from the need to know how to write complex code.

For Grupo Uno Ultimus helped reduce the typical application backlog while providing an environment that is geared toward improved collaboration with business teams. By clearly separating different aspects of process automation into manageable pieces, alignment of process responsibility with business responsibility is possible without technology constraints.

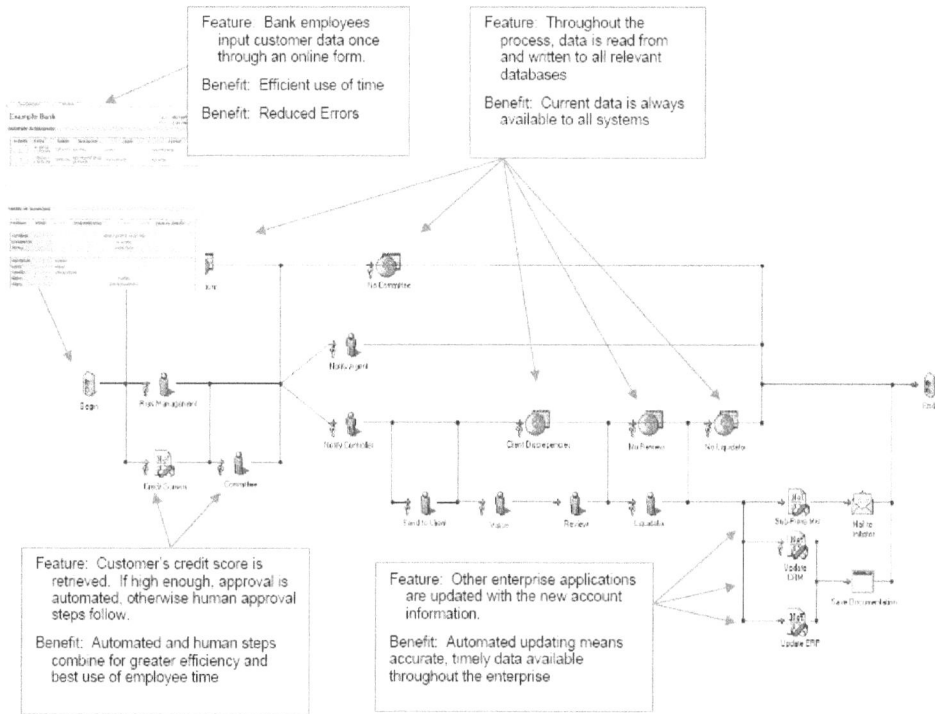

Feature: Bank employees input customer data once through an online form.
Benefit: Efficient use of time
Benefit: Reduced Errors

Feature: Throughout the process, data is read from and written to all relevant databases
Benefit: Current data is always available to all systems

Feature: Customer's credit score is retrieved. If high enough, approval is automated, otherwise human approval steps follow.
Benefit: Automated and human steps combine for greater efficiency and best use of employee time

Feature: Other enterprise applications are updated with the new account information.
Benefit: Automated updating means accurate, timely data available throughout the enterprise

THE BIGGEST HURDLES OVERCOME

Management

The major hurdle that stretched along the management side of the organization was how employees would adapt to this new technology. Employees needed to adjust to working in an environment where the processes that were already accustomed to had been automated leaving them to focus on other aspects within the business.

Prior to implementing the Ultimus BPM Suite the management at Grupo Financiero Uno, management found that employees were spending much of their time on processing applications rather than focusing more on the customer service aspects of the business.

During the Ultimus BPM Suite implementation, the management team at Grupo Financiero Uno was forced to review its business objectives. The evaluation helped the management team determine which processes to automate and to plan out how they would be done. Also, the team needed to focus on what areas the staff could spend more time working on.

After the implementation, the management team felt more confident with its new automated processes. The team saw an increase in both customer and employee satisfaction along with an increase in ROI and productivity.

Business

Prior to the implementation Grupo Uno reviewed customer satisfaction and how manual processes were slow and prone to human error. By transitioning from paper to automated processes, now only one person is required to manage the process as opposed to what originally took 16 people. The remaining 15 employees are able to focus on other areas of the business, and in many cases, business responsibilities for which they were originally hired.

Technology

During the deployment of Ultimus' BPM Suite, Grupo Uno learned that planning ahead was a crucial effort in the success of the project. The technology creates a smoother more efficient style of workflow; however, much more is involved than merely implementation. The company leveraged the Ultimus BPM methodology to select which processes would be automated and when they would be automated. Processes were selected that were critical to governmental compliance standards and have the most significant impact across the entire organization.

BENEFITS

Cost Savings

Grupo Financiero Uno, a well-known international banking institution, was able to continue 35 percent yearly growth while also reducing operational cycle times by 650 percent without increasing headcount.

Increased Revenues

- Grupo Uno saw solid ROI within three months of deploying its first Ultimus-based processes.
- Grupo Uno can now process more than 1000 credit card applications a day, up 470 percent. In the past it took the company 15 days to process a credit card application. One thousand credit card approvals equates to approximately one million dollars in profit.

Productivity Improvements

- Ability to process 470 percent more credit card applications and credit card disputes with the same number of employees per year.
- Client Growth continues at more than 30 percent each year.
- Credit card approval process initially took 15 days, and has been brought down to less than 3 days.

COMPETITIVE ADVANTAGES GAINED AND HOW WE MOVED COMPETITIVE GOAL POSTS FOR OUR INDUSTRY.

Grupo Uno's use of the Ultimus BPM Suite has made them a force in the Latin American banking industry. The bank now ranks in the top 25 banks throughout all of Latin America. The organization is using Ultimus to improve business processes through automation, integration and human-workflow across multiple locations in multiple countries.

This initiative has built a strong foundation for innovative thinking at Grupo Uno. The introduction of BPM has proved to be worthwhile from both a business and IT standpoint. The technology has bridged the gap between both departments creating a vision of how processes can be easily and efficiently streamlined through automation.

The project was able to prove to executives that steering away from the paper processes and establishing an automated business process model saves the unnecessary time involved with the standard signature process. Executives can now see that with an automated system there is less room for error and faster operational processes are attainable and changes can be implemented faster than with traditional custom software applications. The overall initiative has inspired executives to explore the resources available in both the business and IT departments in working together to build a more advanced 21st century approach within the business sphere.

IMMEDIATE AND LONG-TERM PLANS TO SUSTAIN COMPETITIVE ADVANTAGE

Because of the success the Ultimus BPM Suite has brought Grupo Financiaro Uno, the company is continuing to extend the products' capabilities to other areas in the business. As a leading financial services provider in Latin America, it is important for Grupo Uno to stay ahead of the curve and continue to automate processes that keep the company accelerating its competitive advantage.

Since the initial implementation of the Ultimus BPM Suite, Grupo Financiero Uno has also leveraged the use of Web Services. Currently, the organization is working with more than eight Web Services that include adherence to credit card policies, credit scoring, and importing external credit bureau information. Since the automation of these Web Services, each of the branches across seven countries in which Grupo Financiero Uno operates has more than doubled its processing capacity.

Section 4

Pacific Rim

Asia Vital Component Co. Ltd. Taiwan

Silver Award 2006, Pacific Rim; nominated by Flowring Co. Ltd., Taiwan

EXECUTIVE SUMMARY

The article describes the BPM planning and implementation of AVC (Asia Vital Component Co. Ltd.) using BPM suite. The processes covered in the article includes: PDP (product design procedures), QIT (quality issue tracking), MAS (material approval system) and OA (office automation). The target workflow applications integrate legacy ERP/PLM/PDM application system and work together to provide smooth and quick product design activities coordination among R&D teams (from AVC and business partners), as well as the compliance with environmental protection regulation (i.e. RoHS).

OVERVIEW

Company Profile

Asia Vital Components (AVC) is one of the largest cooler/thermal component suppliers throughout the world. AVC designs and manufactures components such as heat sink, DC fan, heat pipe, heat plate, and notebook thermal module to provide cooler solution for CPU, notebook, desktop PC, and servers. The customers include major computer or CPU vendors: AMD, Asus, Dell, HP, IBM, Intel, LG, Samsung, Siemens, Sony, Toshiba and so on. AVC shares over 35 percent and 20 percent of the worldwide market on the *desktop PC cooler* and *notebook thermal module* respectively. The revenue of AVC reached USD$296 million in FY2005. As a leading CPU thermal solution provider, AVC has taken out more than 200 patents worldwide.

AVC has near 9000 employees that are mainly spread in Taiwan and China. The head office of AVC is located in Taiwan. It operates an R&D center and manufacture factories in Taipei, Shenzhen and DongGuan (Southeast China), Shanghai and Suzhou (East China), and Beijing (North China) with total production floors of 192,661 m². AVC also operates four sale offices in Japan, USA (for North America), Brazil (for Latin America), and Germany (for Europe).

Project Information

During past three years since 2004, AVC consecutively kicks-off several internal projects to design and implement workflow application systems based on BPMS, following the first successful BPM process deployment in 2004. The positive outcome of these internal projects forms the BPM infrastructure of AVC to serve the business need of both the employees and business partners.

The PDP, QIT systems ensure the quality and time-to-market of AVC's thermal product design, so that AVC can continuously keep the market leading edge on the thermal product line, and obtain the technical partnership with Intel and AMD to jointly work on the roadmap of next-generation CPUs.

The MAS system ensures AVC to produce environment-friendly products by controlling the use of hazard substances in the material to comply with the Europe regulation of RoHS (Restriction of the use of certain Hazardous Substance in EEE).

The OA workflow applications enable AVC employees to perform daily HR and G&A activities over distributed R&D center and manufacture factories.

2 MOTIVATION AND PROJECT BACKGROUND

2.1 Business motivation

In the AVC's BPM-related internal projects, the underlying business goals are defined to:

- Coordinate the product design and manufacture activities across multiple factories and business partners.
- Provide stronger support on the supply-chain operation between business partners.
- Ensure the manufacture processes comply with stronger environment protection regulations such as RoHS and WEEE.
- Establish the enterprise-wide BPM infrastructure to catch up with the rapid growth of organization, while preserve the legacy IT investment.

As the rapid business growing in AVC, it confronts the challenges to satisfy the customers with sophisticate business processes and product design coordination. To react to the business processes change, AVC can consider the solutions to modify the existing ERP or PLM application system. Because AVC has already deployed ERP system and PLM system to meet the basic requirement of business operation, it can decide to customize the business logic inside ERP and PLM system according to the business change.

The solution is not preferred because at conception the software providers of ERP and PLM contain limited business process architecture to implement complicate and flexible business processes. Besides, even if the ERP or PLM vendors claim to embed the simple workflow solutions in the application systems, they are usually specific to the underlying application domains. Adopting the kind of workflow solution leads to less general enterprise BPM architecture.

With above consideration, AVC decides to adopt BPMS to react to business processes adjustment and varying market environment. The rationales are as the following:

- BPMS provides canonical enterprise architecture and standards to implement process-oriented applications, either intra-organization or inter-organization processes. The effort to implement flexible workflow applications can be reduced by BPMS's rich support on enterprise organization, routing capability, ready-to-use process portal, etc.
- The business scenario that involves functionalities of existing ERP or PLM still can be mainly implemented by BPMS's workflow through bi-directional (BPMS to ERP, BPMS to PLM) information exchange mechanism provided by EAI (Enterprise Application Integration).
- ERP's or PLM's domain-application-oriented workflow functionalities can work with BPMS to obtain more powerful application scenario without confliction.

2.2 Application domain

AVC starts to design and implement the workflow application systems based on BPMS since 2004. The workflow applications built during 2004 to 2006 can be categorized as the following:

- Product development procedures (PDP)
- Quality Issue Tracking (QIT)
- Material Approval System (MAS)

- Office automation (OA) workflows that cover common human resource (HR) and general and administrative (G&A) activities.

Beside the business process definition and implementation, AVC also concerns about the need of specific GUI (i.e. process portal) for different stakeholders of the business processes. It decides to design different process portals for the following types of users:

- The general OA workflow users. They come from departments with various degree of proficiency in computer. They need more general and easier GUI to operate the workflow application system. The OA application modules are deployed under BPMS's standard enterprise process portal.
- The R&D teams. They have advanced computer proficiency therefore the GUI can be more complicated to provide flexible operation and present more concrete and clear information in terms of product design management. General workflow task list has limited capability for them to track complicated and inter-related product design tasks. The PDP, QIT and MAS modules are deployed under the portal.
- The business partners. Their participants contribute to product design but need to be limited to some proper information exposure for AVC's internal workflow processes. In this kind of portal, business partner can exchange product design material and understand the rough product development progress. The *supplier service network* (SSN) and *customer service network* (CSN) modules are provided under the portal.

3 INNOVATION AND BENEFITS

3.1 Key innovation

The key innovation of AVC can be described in the business, process, and technology aspects. It can be summarized as the following:

- [Business] Establish the collaboration environment to bring up the whole industry to obtain the partnership and secure business opportunity with major CPU vendors.
- [Process] Injects design review principle (DR1, DR2, DR3, DR4, ATS) into the PDP process definition to ensure formal product development processes.
- [Process] Injects 8D (Eight Disciplines) into the QIT process definition to ensure formal problem solving and management processes.
- [Process] Apply the process technology to ensure the product manufacturing process comply with the RoHS.
- [Technology] Integrate BPMS with ERP and PDM application system through EAI and Web Services under heterogeneous IT environments for different types of end-users.

3.1.1 Business aspect

Because of AVC's leading position in the thermal solution, in FY2004 to 2005 AVC wins the contract (*An-Hsin Project*) from Department of Industrial Technology in Taiwan to demonstrate the innovation about product design collaboration in its industry segment. AVC brings the suppliers, partners, and customers together to conduct the R&D design collaboration. Under this innovation demonstration, AVC integrates several companies from the mold and dies industry to conduct a collaborative design plan with Intel to obtain improved CPU and chassis thermal solution. The scope of collaboration contains Intel, 33 international vendors or channels from PC and notebook industry, and 20 suppliers from the mold and dies industry.

The benefit of establishing the collaboration environment can bring together the whole supply-chain in the thermal solution industry to become an efficient virtual thermal component design team. In consequence, the suppliers, partners of AVC and AVC itself form a competitive team to keep closer partnership with major CPU vendor such as Intel.

3.1.2 Process aspect

Process enforcement and consistency are challenges for AVC for its quick growth. When AVC spawns new branches or design teams it should ensure the product development process or problem solving and management are consistent over all teams and branches. Before the process definition and deployment, the junior branches or design teams take more time to reproduce the management processes from the senior teams. After the processes are implemented in BPMS, the policy enforcement and team reproduce for product development activities are quicker and easier. With the explicit process flow guidance, checklist in each workflow activities, junior teams learn to practice product review techniques and problem solving/management principles from daily performance of workflow activities work instead of solely studying the company policies.

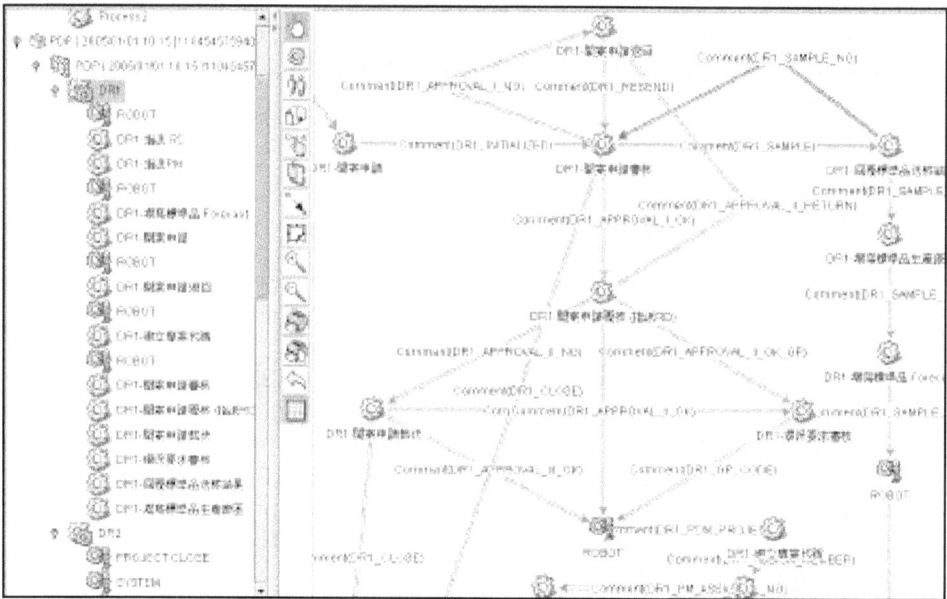

Figure 1. PDP process model diagram

For product development, AVC implements the PDP (product development procedure) processes to guide the product development life cycle. In the process modeling for PDP, it covers

- the artifacts to operate in the BPMS workflow,
- the artifacts to interact in the PDM/PLM system,
- the duty and workflow activities of customers,
- the duty and workflow activity of suppliers
- throughout the main PDP life cycle.

(1) DR1 : Project opening and kick-off

(2) DR2 : Cost analysis and product plan

(3) DR3 : Trial-run and prototype

(4) DR4 : Pilot-run for mass-production

(5) ATS : Approved for mass-production

Figure 2. PDP Project List

For problem solving and management, AVC implements QIT process to adopt 8D that originates from Ford's TOPS (Team Oriented Problem Solving) program. The AVC's QIT system implement several sub-processes to handle problems reported during IQC (incoming material check) processes, problems reported during factory manufactures, and problems raised by the customers.

Figure 3. Customer Complaint Disposal Report in QIT

For RoHS compliance, AVC implements MAS processes to work with the suppliers to ensure the material from the suppliers should be approved by following hazard substance check processes before applying the material into the BOM of the product.

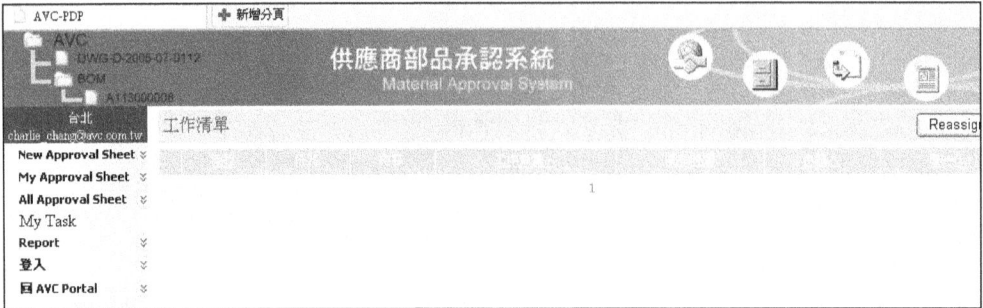

Figure 4. MAS end-user screen dump

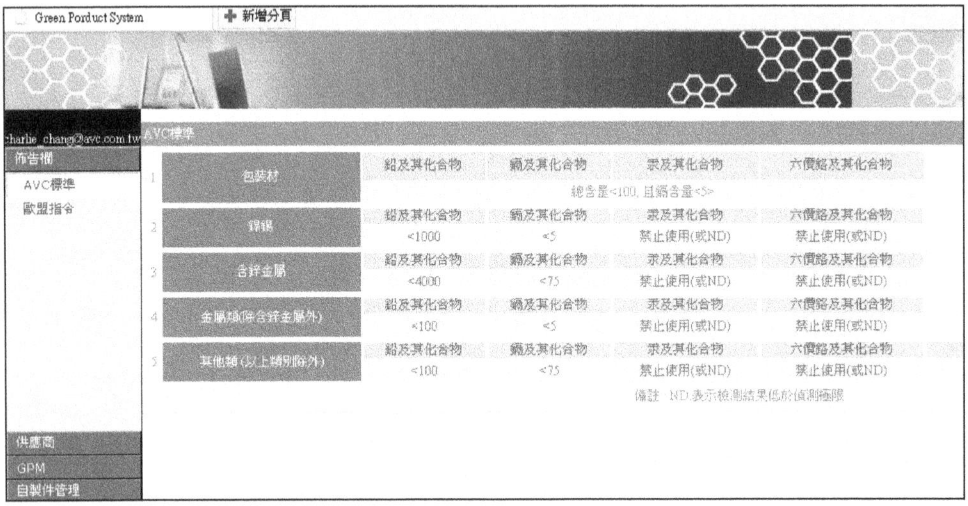

Figure 5. Green Product and RoHS Screen

3.1.3 Technology aspect

In terms of technology innovation, AVC's project achieves a successful BPMS integration with ERP and PLM through the following technical innovations:

- Integrate BPMS with ERP and PLM through Web Services and EAI technology to bring the functionalities of ERP and PLM into BPMS.
- Apply Java technology and Web Services to integrate with backend BPMS's workflow engines.
- Apply ASP.NET and JSP to quickly construct Web-based process portal for different types of end-users. For example, implement *CSN* for customers, *SSN* for suppliers, *engineering portal* for R&D staffs, and *AEPP (Agentflow Enterprise Process Portal)* for general enterprise users.
- Single sign-on solutions that integrates customers, suppliers, and employee accounts. Therefore accounts under CSN, SSN, engineering portal, and AEPP are consolidated into one logical view.
- Extensive use of sub-process and process chaining (relaying) to decompose one complex processes into several smaller and manageable sub-processes. The decomposition enables flexible adjustment for business processes for future business processes changes.

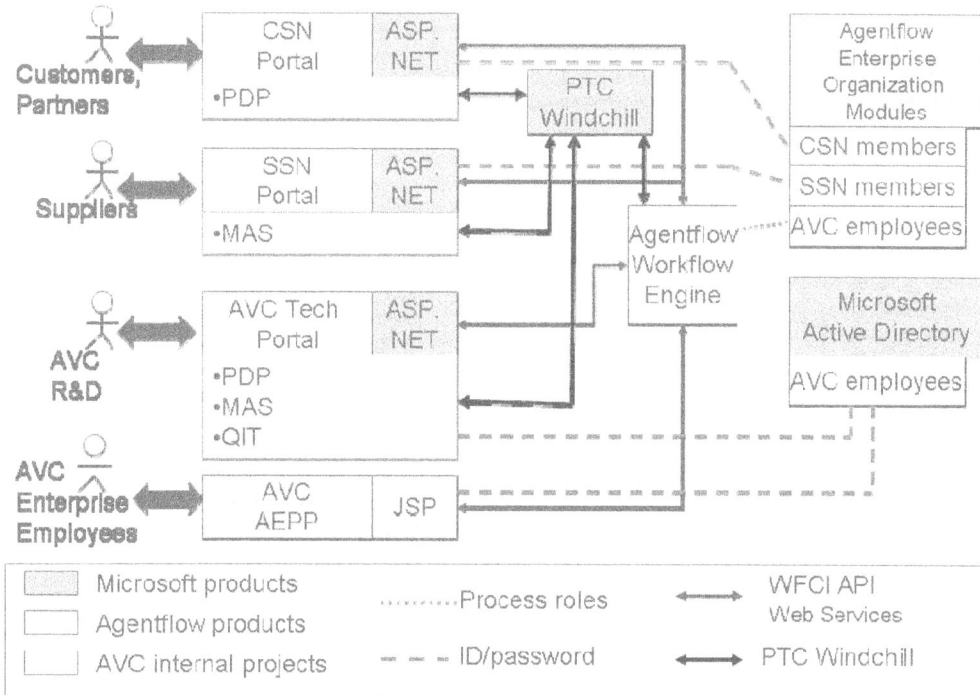

Figure 6. AVC processes deployment architectures

3.2 Users impact and benefits analysis

The impacts and benefits of different roles in the AVC's BPMS deployment can be analyzed in the following sections.

3.2.1 AVC OA users

Roles	OA users
Impacts	• Operation experience • Response time and traceability
Before	• Separate software applications for OA and G&A activities without application integration • Slow process time and hard to trace the progress
After	• OA and G&A application are collected into one single portal with single-sign on capability. • OA and G&A activities are enhanced by workflow to reduce the process cycle time • The progress of process can be traced and alerted
Benefits	• Smooth and easier OA and G&A applications experience • Quick and reliable OA and G&A business operation

3.2.2 AVC R&D users

Roles	• AVC R&D users
Impacts	• Product development • Design collaboration • Problem solving and management
Before	• Process inconsistency and discrepancy among different design teams • Need extra effort to lookup information from ERP/PLM for inte-

		grated product development procedures
		• Much more effort to deploy sophisticate R&D rules and procedures in junior design teams or newly spawned branches
After		• Prevent process inconsistency and discrepancy by implementing checklist and state verification in the activities of automated BPMS processes
		• R&D engineers have a consolidate view of product development status on AVC tech portal, in which the information from BPMS workflow, ERP and PLM is weaved together for easy management
Benefits		• Quick learning cycle for new teams to follow product development procedures
		• Best practices for product development and problem solving procedures in AVC can be embedded in the workflow processes to be shared and enforced in the whole enterprise
		• Obvious and comprehensive product development monitoring and control

3.2.3 AVC customers and business partners

Roles	AVC customer and business partner
Impacts	• Customer and partner relationship • Design collaboration and time-to-market
Before	• Inefficient design collaboration activities for exchanging draft standard specification • Not familiar with the work style to work as a virtual design team across enterprise boundary
After	• Collaborative CSN portal for customers and business partner to exchange the design documents and reflect the progress of product development
Benefits	• Virtual design team provides more powerful R&D capability to increase the supply-chain's overall competency in the CPU thermal solution • Influence and first-hand information on industry standard for guarantee early kick-off of product design and quick time-to-market • Secure the business opportunities for the whole supply-chain with major CPU vendors such as Intel

3.2.4 AVC Suppliers

Roles	AVC Suppliers
Impacts	• Material approval for RoHS compliance • IQC in QIT system
Before	• No application system to support the supplier interaction with AVC
After	• Suppliers use MAS system to follow the approval process and track progress for RoHS materials • AVC uses QIT system to notify the supplier and track the issues solving for unqualified material

Benefits	• Careful handling and checklist on supplier material used in the product so that the final product is compliant with RoHS regulation, reduce the risk of shipping non-compliant products • Establish supplier-side quality management system to increase the product quality

4 SYSTEM DEPLOYMENT / EXPERIENCE SHARING

4.1 System configuration

The components for the new workflow system are illustrated and summarized as the following:

Purpose	Platform	Software	Description
Database	Intel server with 2GB RAM Microsoft Windows 2000	Microsoft SQL server 2000	Work as the data storage for BPMS
Legacy ERP	Intel server Microsoft Windows 2000	MATIC (from domestic ERP vendor)	ERP systems for AVC
PDM/PLM	Unix platform	PTC Windchill	PDM/PLM systems for AVC
BPMS (workflow)	Intel server Dual CPU 2GB RAM 80GB Disk *Microsoft Windows 2000	Flowring Agent-flow 2.2	Standard workflow management features Application access control Provide APIs through Java RMI or Web Services for external program integration
J2EE container JSP container Web server	Intel server Dual CPU 2GB RAM Microsoft Windows 2000	Jakarta Tomcat 4.1.24 Agentflow AEPP	JSP/Web server Agentflow Process Portal works as the end-user GUI Web Services provider
Microsoft .NET server Active Directory server	Intel server Dual CPU 2GB RAM Microsoft Windows 2003	ASP.NET platform	ASP.NET Web server AVC's CSN, SSN, R&D tech portals are hosted on the machine

Table 1. Servers Deployed in the AVC Workflow Systems

The major workflows in AVC include PDP, QIT, MAS and OA. All of the workflows are implemented in Flowring's Agentflow BPMS suite. The suite contains both design-time and run-time tools. The design-time tools include PDE (for process modeling), ORG (for organization structure modeling) and e-Form (for defining abstract data structure, visual presentation, GUI event-handling, binding for form-field and database). The run-time tools include PASE (work as routing engine that provides core workflow primitives) and AEPP (Agentflow Enterprise Process Portal, implemented as web applications running in JSP container to interact with end users).

Because of AVC's decision on providing different GUI for different type of end-users, the deployment plan has to include the development of 3 additional process portals for customers, suppliers, and R&D users. Only the general users use the standard GUI provide by Agentflow. The programmers in AVC's development team are very familiar in Microsoft ASP.NET solution for building portals and related web application to interact with end users, therefore the following technical decisions are concluded to reduce the programming effort (i.e. man-month) and ensure on-time delivery to the end-users:

- Use PDE for all the process modeling in the AVC's workflow applications
- Use PASE as the backend routing engines (i.e. PASE) for all of the routing services
- Use AEPP as the standard GUI for OA-oriented users. Because of the operations are relatively simple, AVC implements workflow forms in *Agentflow e-Form tool* to save a lot of programming effort
- Use ASP.NET to implement portal for suppliers, customers, and R&D users, because the operations in Web UI are complicated. AVC implements portal and workflow forms in Microsoft ASP.NET. The interaction between workflow servers and ASP.NET applications are through Agentflow's Web Services and COM components. For example, the work-list is provided by workflow engine for ASP.NET programs to render the Web display. The workflow form is implemented by ASP.NET programs to interact with users for data collection, and the data record is then sent back to workflow engine via Web Services for persistence into database.

The integration with ERP/PLM is achieved by calling APIs in Agentflow PASE script or Microsoft ASP.NET script.

The single sign-on is provided by synchronizing account information from workflow servers to Microsoft Active Directory. The organization information (e.g. login ID, internal member ID, roles, permissions in workflow applications) needed for process execution is stored in the Agentflow's ORG module. The information needed for login authentication from all portal users is obtained from workflow servers via synchronization and then stored in Microsoft Active Directory.

4.2 Solving system deployment hurdles

The deployment of workflow application systems is not merely to overcome the technical issues. For business challenges in AVC such as constructing a collaborative R&D environment in workflow, building a MAS system to ensure the compliance with RoHS, the AVC IT team has to get advises and business scenario from the senior users and domain expert to make the processes more practical. The following sections summarize the common hurdles and solutions in AVC's work.

Management Hurdle

Cross department communication overhead and efficiency -- some departments set lower priority or have little awareness on the new workflow systems deployment.

Solution

- High level manager commitment to re-state the importance of the new workflow system deployment
- Hold cross-department meeting to have formal decision on the responsibility of cross- department activities.
- Assign and empower an member as the process owner to have enough authority on cross-department communication

Process Hurdle

Business processes or rules are modified to reflect real-world change without considering ripple effect on other existing application system.

Solution

- Apply requirement change control and notification to all process members.
- Change to critical process activities or business rules needs second thoughts or to confirm it again by group meeting

Technical Hurdle

Legacy ERP data transfer -- data consistency and integrity issues.

Solution

- Refines legacy ERP database by repair incomplete or incorrect data records to maintain the data consistency and integrity
- Add more code in the application systems to check the data integrity when inserting new data records
- Update/fetch ERP data through middleware instead of direct SQL query, to obtain better and flexible data format/type manipulation

4.3 BENEFITS ANALYSIS

4.3.1. Cost savings

The most observable cost savings in AVC appears in OA's operation cost reduction and the telecommunication cost for distributed R&D teams. For example, in a routine work of HR department, the HR specialist reduces his work from 3 hours to 30 minutes by the employee leave application. According to the data reported from AVC, the OA-related processes significantly reduced by 60 percent in employee's work hour. A very conservative calculation below can roughly estimate the direct cost saving in OA-related processes in terms of employee's working hours.

In AVC there are about 9000 employees, every 1 employee issues 4 OA-related application forms every month in average. Before the deployment, the employee pays (30 minutes = 0.5 hour) to fill the form as tracking the progress for each application. The effort is reduced by 60 percent after the deployment. Using the lowest man-hour rate NTD $200 as the calculation base, the cost saving per year can be obtained by the following calculation:

(hour rate: 200) * (0.5 hour) * (4 applications) * (12 months)

(reduced effort: 60 percent) * (employee count: 9000) = NTD 25,920,000

4.3.2. Increased revenues

The increase in revenue and net income of the enterprise are not entirely contributed by the workflow application deployment, however we can use it as indirect ROI information. The following table depicts the revenue and net income continuous growth of AVC after the workflow application deployment.

Year	Month	Revenue	Year	Month	Revenue	Growth (percent)
2005	6	826,893	2004	6	686,447	20.46 percent
2005	7	741,377	2004	7	576,496	28.60 percent
2005	8	744,200	2004	8	626,843	18.72 percent
2005	9	848,714	2004	9	703,574	20.63 percent
2005	10	906,671	2004	10	684,803	32.40 percent
2005	11	890,550	2004	11	755,825	17.82 percent

2005	12	971,568	2004	12	755,371	28.62 percent
2006	1	593,754	2005	1	736,472	-19.38 percent
2006	2	610,244	2005	2	558,886	9.19 percent
2006	3	993,899	2005	3	796,772	24.74 percent
2006	4	929,892	2005	4	760,209	22.32 percent

(Unit: NT$ thousand) Growth rate is compared with the same month of previous year.

4.3.3. Productivity improvements

The significant productivity improvement in AVC is the average product development cycle. Based on AVC's statistics, they have more than 1000 PC or notebook vendors request AVC to design specific thermal solution. It is common for AVC to have more than 200 concurrent design projects for customers. For each design project AVC has to conduct at least 5 iterations of design reviews that involve members from distributed R&D team, material supplier, and customer-side engineers. Before the deployment of PDP project, AVC needs 120 days in average to complete a customer design project. It is reduced to 90 days after the deployment.

4.4 Core competence

The core competence of gained from the BPM initiatives help AVC to keep the leading edge in providing total thermal solution. By the processes flexibility for design and manufacture, the process-enabled QMS, the process-enabled CSN (customer service network) and SSN (supplier service network), and well-coordinated R&D teams, AVC get the weapon to maintain its core competence in the following aspects:
- Ability for highly vertical & horizontal integration
- Ability to provide full-range of product lines : heat sinks, DC Fans, Heat pipes, chassis, Serial ATA Cable and Connectors, Bare Bone assemblies (Level 5)
- More than 270 well-coordinated staffs in the R&D team, providing customers with excellent engineering services, from fan simulation, design, prototyping, testing, folding to production.
- Ability to provide dedicated task force for key customers
- Competitive in price for
- In-house solution
- Multiple production sites
- Economy production scale
- Reliable quality & on-time delivery
- Global logistic services

5 CONCLUSION AND FUTURE PLANS

AVC's BPM initiative reflects the general challenges in its industry segment:
- **Enterprise growth**—Need to react to employee growth, product lines extension, and geo-locations expansion.
- **Time to market**—Need to provide quick response to market by shorten product design cycle.
- **Quality improvement**—Need to establish quality management system, through well-defined product design review and issue resolve process
- **Partner relationship**—Need to provide smooth business operation environment for both vendors and customers.

- **Regulation compliance**—Need to refine the manufacture process to comply with RoHS, WEEE.

AVC develops PDP, QIT and MAS processes on the BPMS platform to tackle above business challenge and obtains positive result as shown in the article. Based on previous success in applying BPM solution to tackles business challenges, AVC is more confident on several foreseeable business challenges where BPMS can play important role. For example, AVC understand the BPMS can help them to build more universal and flexible QMS (quality management system) that satisfies most power brands in PC and notebook industry. Because at present they have to operate separate production lines with different QMS methodologies requested by the power brands. In the future AVC can utilize BPMS to increase the QMS flexibility of production lines so that the production lines can be quickly adjusted and assigned to make production for other power brands.

Similar case also appears in MAS that deals with RoHS compliance for *green product*. Some power brands in PC industry also require AVC to have more regulations and rules for their green products. Thus, in the MAS workflow application, AVC needs to add more flexibility in the processes with the help of BPMS.

The ability of AVC to utilize BPMS platform in quickly adjusting the business operation and design/manufacture procedures to support customer's needs is the strong power to keep AVC's leading competency in the thermal component industry.

KTF Co., Ltd., Korea

Gold Award 2006, Pacific Rim; nominated by HandySoft

INTRODUCTION

The telecom market is faced with a sharp increase in the number of service subscribers to such a degree that demand exceeds supply. In the past, the industry's information systems consisted mostly of calculating a customer's telephone traffic and sending a bill. But severe competition and the growing availability of products in the market space has forced the providers to leverage state-of-the-art technologies to improve customer service and satisfaction. In order to remain competitive, information systems had to address this sharp change to customer focus.

A leading telecoms carrier based in Korea, KT Freetel Co. Ltd., (KTF) concluded that creating customer satisfaction-oriented processes that were integrated with back-end company systems would enable them to more flexibly and spontaneously attract, serve, and keep customers who are sensitive to new technology and service.

One of KTF's goals was standardization of the company's core business processes. KTF knew that automation of its core processes could maximize business efficiency. Another goal was to embrace a Business Process Management (BPM) and workflow platform making it visible as an enterprise asset, and promoting standard processes throughout the organization. Promoting the BPM & Workflow Platform within all business units provided a common framework for process improvement, and allowed KTF to focus more on process standardization. KTF also established process consolidation as a goal, and used the BPM & Workflow Platform to integrate business processes wherever possible, allowing human resources to be utilized more efficiently.

THE CHALLENGES

KTF identified and categorized their list of challenges as a Business, Information Systems, or Organization challenge:

- **Business:** Due to a lack of standardized work methods, individual experience and knowledge was a key dependency in daily operations, which lead to many errors. To improve the process, KTF needed a common language that could be shared among team members. Namely, the demand for continuous improvement in work processes and standardization was increasing. In order to adapt to rapid changes in their business environment, KTF needed to create a very visible process and a strategic method for change management.
- **Information Systems:** Maintaining and increasing customer numbers was one of KTF's prior goals. They built CRM and CTI technology-based call centers using independent, commercially available technologies. But KTF found that their call center system could not deal with their dynamic and rapidly changing business environment. They desperately needed an integrated, process-based application.
- **Organization:** KTF had experienced significant growth in a very short period of time. Therefore, they needed to set up and standardize processes that previously were not even considered in the organization's original vi-

sion. In addition, KTF needed to build cooperation among teams to make the processes more flexible and rational.

THE IDENTIFIED TASKS

The tasks that KTF identified in order to meet these challenges can be summarized as follows:

- **Create processes** that were a corporate asset by making them visible.
- Integrate system and human resources based on the defined processes.
- **Secure work transparency and productivity** using clearly defined business rules and a work system that was integrated with existing and new systems.

THE CORE PROCESS IMPROVEMENT GOALS

KTF needed to set up a systematic process and introduce tools to deal with customer demands for various services and to remain competitive. KTF divided their BPM & Workflow installation goals into four categories:

I. Core Process Standardization and Build-Up

- Set up the processes to be shared among team members.
- Minimize work errors through process standardization.
- Facilitate transition of work.

II. Core Process Automation and Management

- Create a faster work process by setting up a Work-Portal with current work status and To Do List.
- Maximize work efficiency by changing the system from a pull method to a push method.
- Prevent work delays in advance by setting up a real-time monitoring system to check work progress.
- Shorten work hours.
- Reduce simple/redundant work.

III. Process-Centered Rearrangement of Resources

- Secure agility and flexibility through a safe transition from the existing systems into the new process-centered system including integration with and connection to a transactional system.
- Strengthen cooperation among team members through process-centered work.
- Set up an efficient management base to discern and align major IT and human resources.

IV. Process Improvement through Work Management History

- Pinpoint and solve process problems through work management history that includes monitoring and statistical indices.
- Secure business transparency through process monitoring.
- Test work performance through development of a process management index.

CORE PROCESS CLASSIFICATION, ANALYSIS & PRIORITIZATION

KTF first started to introduce BPM & Workflow in 1999 and drove to apply BPM & Workflow to all of its processes. The IT team (e-Management Team) led the move gradually to expand BPM & Workflow beyond a process-by-process productivity tool to a company-wide system to increase work efficiency and convenience by setting up a user-oriented portal.

The e-Management team's first step in deciding which processes to automate first was to classify core processes according to function and business areas. As a result, they divided all processes in the company into mega processes and then further into process chains that relate directly to the business areas:

Mega Process	Process Chain	Process					
Strategic Planning Sector	Business Planning	Company Value Assessment					
	Six Sigma Team	Six Sigma Assignment Mgmt (BB)		Six Sigma Assignment Mgmt (GB)			
Business Support Sector	Purchase Team	Purchase Money Request Invoice	Purchase Request Form	In-Stock Confirmation	Bidding Process Report	Bidding Result Contract	PT Technology Evaluation
Financial Management	Financial Planning	Financial Report Internal Control					
	Investor Relations	Public Notice Control					
	Accounting Team	Corporate Card	Purchase Invoice	Sales Invoice	Travel Fare		
	Asset Management	Real Estate Rental Mgmt	Idle Facility Rental Plan				
Ethics Management	Intellectual Property	Intellectual property right management					
Information Service Sector	AP Operation Team	Security related service request		OA machinery request		4-yr expired notebook request	
	e-Mgmt Team	SR mgmt development/service		Integrated account mgmt			
Marketing Sector	Marketing Strategy	Team Value Assessment	Network-based product development				
	Marketing Support	New sales item additional service request					
	Subscriber Service	VOC center	VOC conference	Wrongful sales VOC			
	Marketing Business	Purchase invoice (HQ)					
New Business Sector	New Business Strategy	Team Value Assessment					
Network Sector	Network Strategy	Team Value Assessment	Global roaming service start				
R&D	OSS	Base station repeater					

Mega Process, Process Chain & Process Classification

Beyond the Mega Process and Process Chain categories, processes are further broken down into 77 detailed processes. For example, in the process chain, Purchasing is broken down further into *Purchase Invoice, Purchase Request Form, Warehousing*, and *Contracts*.

The KTF e-Management Team, departmental management, and the BPM & Workflow Platform solution provider chose core processes based on these criteria and multiple discussions. BPM & Workflow were applied to the core processes according to the criteria shown in the table below and on the effectiveness and accessibility of the processes involved.

Criteria	Detail	Contents
Process	Process Significance	Is it a core process that contributes to cost, customer, or quality improvement?
	Related Organization Set Up	Are there many process-related teams and workforce that will use the process?
	Standardization Need	Is there a need to strictly define the process and related controls so that they follow standardized rules?
	Need To Manage Change	Is there a need to oversee the process for continuing process improvement?

Criteria	Detail	Contents
Workflow Handling	Automation Request	Is there a need to automate work, distribution, or workflow based on work guidelines?
	Communication	Is there a need to improve communication between teams and person in charge to carry out the work?
	Work Precision Upgrade	Does work have to be repeated due to frequent errors?
Process Management	Work Speed Upgrade	Is there a need to speed up the work process?
	Work Control Tightening	Is there a need to monitor the work process in real time?
Information Systems	Related Systems	Are there various systems related to the process?
	Soft Copy Information Management	Is there a need to manage soft copy data (files, etc.) that accompany or are related to the process?

When choosing processes for BPM & Workflow initiatives, the teams considered the above criteria and then prepared a list of process details.

After understanding the business sector and process details, the priority of BPM & Workflow projects was decided by analyzing process effectiveness and accessibility. In addition, KTF knew that introducing BPM & Workflow would be very different from previous work methods and they expected users to be resistant to change. Therefore, they wanted to also focus on processes that would have the most positive impact not only on the company overall but on those people actually doing the work.

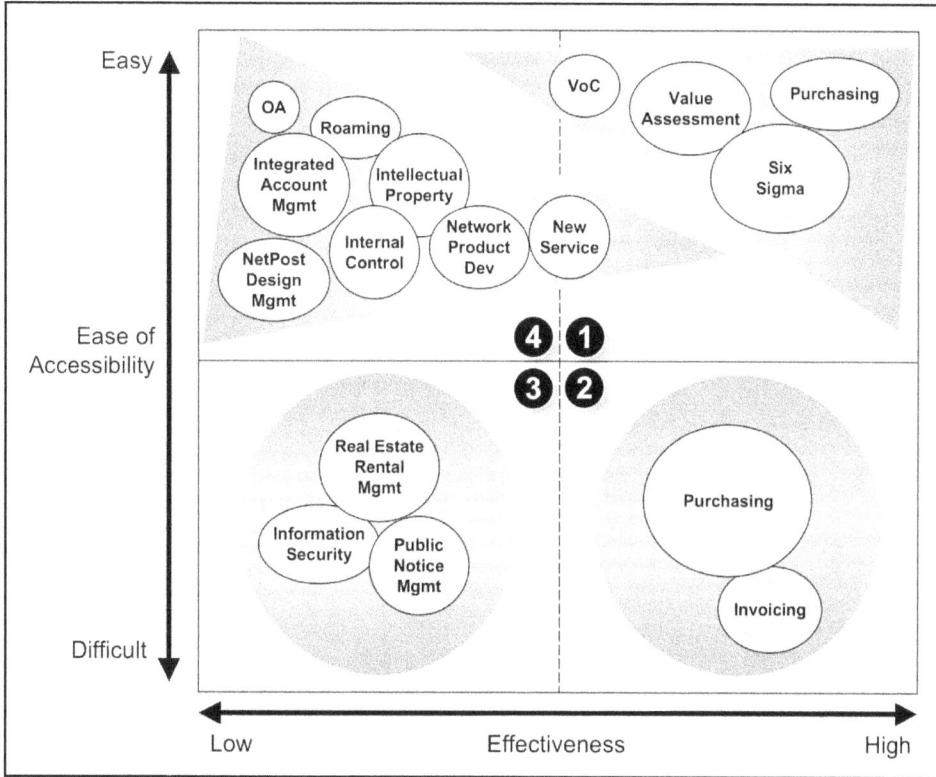

BPM & Workflow Application Target Process Prioritization

As a result of the teams' analysis, the first sectors to which process improvements were applied were part of the Purchasing, Value Assessment, and Six Sigma sectors. They identified Purchasing and Invoicing as the main areas that could benefit from BPM & Workflow as those users needed a transparent and speedy work system.

The latest sectors to which the process improvements were applied were Oversight and Performance Assurance (OA) and Integrated Account Management.

The BPM & Workflow process application was expanded in nine sectors and plans are underway to further expand to all company systems.

THE PROCESS PORTAL—THE WAY PEOPLE WORK AFTER BPM & WORKFLOW

By using BPM & Workflow, IT resource integration centered on process and secured system flexibility through the integration of back-end systems and presentation of those system capabilities to users through the BPM & Workflow Platform-powered FreeNet portal.

Better Management through Separation of Processes and Applications

KTF approached BPM & Workflow by splitting business processes and application logic, thus reducing the burden of always having to account for process change and variation within applications. The separation afforded KTF a more simplified approach to application development, which increased development productivity and reduced maintenance. This approach also yielded more simplistic application logic that could be componentized for more optimal maintenance.

Ease of Access to Knowledge and Information

KTF maximized access to internal and external company knowledge by instituting a portal to facilitate online collaboration. Web-based user interfaces could be customized to meet individual user needs. Users were pleasantly surprised to find that multiple applications required for completing work could be consolidated into a single screen, providing a single point of access for information required across several applications. The BPM & Workflow Platform also provided the capabilities to attach files and associate comments for community sharing and collaboration.

Centering all Systems on BPM & Workflow

Prior to embracing the BPM & Workflow Platform, KTF utilized ERP (SAP), FreeNet (Enterprise Knowledge Portal) Intranet, e-HR, CReaM (CRM), and other systems as stove-piped technologies. Users had to connect to each system individually to conduct work. All the distinct systems are now centered on BPM & Workflow, allowing KTF to respond to diverse business environments, as well as rapidly changing management strategies and goals.

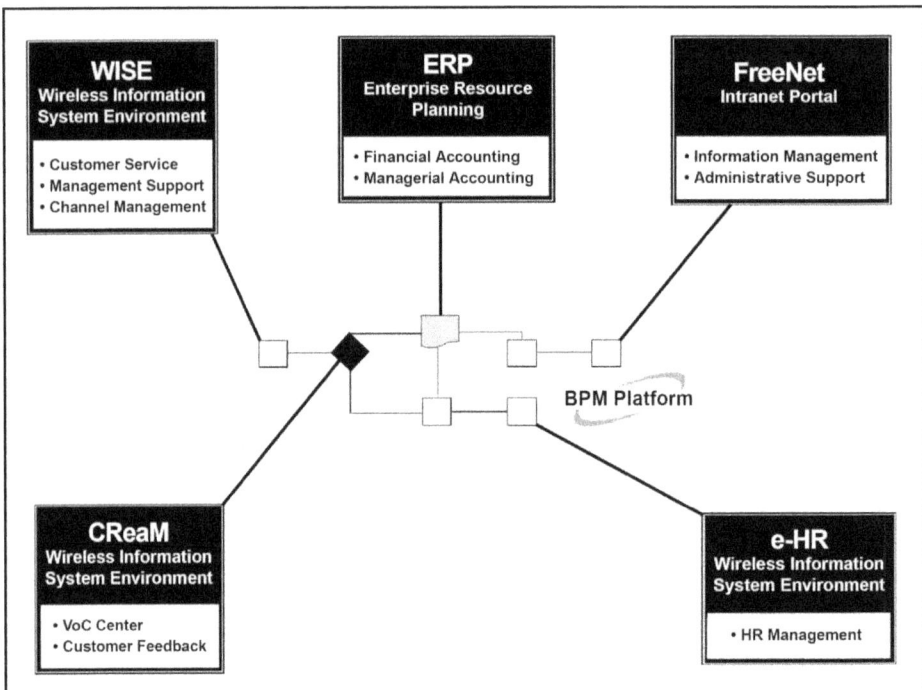

Centering All Systems on BPM & Workflow Platform

The BPM & Workflow Platform serves as a technology footprint, allowing users to work in an integrated work environment. Under this situation, if resources change, if goals change, or if applications change, everything is managed through processes, providing maximum flexibility.

Before KTF embarked on its BPM & Workflow initiative, much of a typical worker's productivity was influenced by factors related to finding work, logging in to multiple systems, locating lost work, finding work inherently related to several business units, and managing changes in existing work. And, with most work being conducted offline, productivity was reduced even further through efforts to share work with others for collaboration. Workers spent significant time searching individual systems for work or information; and once a search was completed, there was little information about how it related to other parts of the organization.

The BPM & Workflow Platform provided a clear and simple approach to improving resource productivity. Although the platform enhanced many aspects of workflow, it also provided a management framework for linking all systems associated with Sales, Subscriber (Customer) Support, and Financial Management. By integrating all of these systems, work is delivered automatically to the appropriate resource, while providing visibility into resource collaboration. By exposing resource input for all work deliverables, work is processed more efficiently among all groups within the organization, while at the same time sharing feedback between all resources. This type of collaboration helps teams work more effectively together.

KTF employees can access all their work through FreeNet, the KTF intranet. This KTF BPM & Workflow portal enables users to see the number of work items that must be completed, all future work, work that must start now, work that is currently being processed, etc. Each user can see the assigned worklist in the "Work Space Full Screen":

The BPM & Workflow Platform-Powered Work Portal

Employees can look up progress of their work assignments by viewing the status of work, as well as search for specific work within the portal. Even if the work is from several different systems, FreeNet provides users with a single point of access to work categorized by priority of completion. Users no longer have to log in and log out of each system. All login information is handled seamlessly by the BPM & Workflow Platform.

A Closer Look at a Process Improvement Example

The VoC subscriber claim (customer care) process shown in the process flow diagram below was developed from March of 2005 to March of 2006 as a process expansion and improvement on the VoC process that was originally developed in August of 2004 to January of 2005.

This process was engineered to optimize an off-line, manual process that could not handle customer claims effectively. The CReaM CRM system can initiate the process automatically, distributing work to each team as required, while providing access to each system seamlessly.

Telemarketers receive the VoC from CReaM, and the VoC automatically links to the BPM & Workflow Platform, where it is routed to the "Operational Head Office", "Handling Organization", and "Middle/Completed" activities which display all work within the FreeNet portal. Once a process is completed, it can be retrieved for informational purposes to assist with knowledge support.

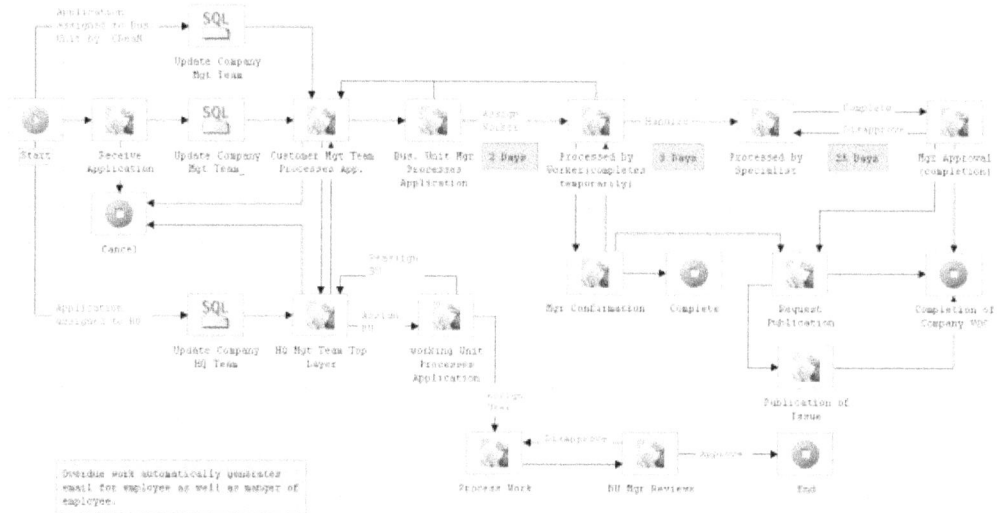

The Automated VoC (Subscriber Care) Process

VoC Process Automation Benefits

A summary of the benefits of utilizing the BPM & Workflow Platform for the VoC process is provided below as they apply to Management, the A/S Center, the IT Team, and customer satisfaction.

Team	Effect
Management	<ul><li>VoC process standardization eliminated the arbitrary prioritization of employee worklists. Standardization of the VoC process also increased the efficiency of work processing, and minimized educational training for new workers.</li><li>Provided visibility into the VoC process which is very critical to achieving customer satisfaction goals.</li><li>Increased customer data collection which prevented</li></ul>

Team	Effect
	potential customers from leaving. For example, it is possible to classify data as a complaining customer, or VIP, and the system can come up with a strategic marketing plan for each customer. • VoC-related teams such as A/S center and the IT team now operate within a unified communication platform.
A/S Center	• Absolute guarantee that registration of feedback on VoC is transferred to IT team. • Customer feedback can be updated using prior VoC knowledge.
IT Team	• Excessive use of VoC is prevented. • Visibility into VoC in customer transfer process. • Systematic analysis on each employee based on VoC performance.
Customers	• Fast feedback and response to customer complaints. • Improved customer service.

The Overall Results

As KTF introduced BPM & Workflow, the following key business innovations, both quantitative and qualitative effects, were noted:

Quantitative Effects of BPM & Workflow Initiatives
- Reduced work cycle times.
- Prevention of work delays through automatic work notification.
- Use of electronic data (invoices, purchase request forms, order forms, etc.) resulting in minimized paperwork.
- Electronic document transfer reduced work feedback time and prevented redundant input of identical data.
- Real-time, step-by-step management allowed better collaboration of work between related departments.
- Reduced claim response times increased workers' productivity.
- Process designs can be easily understood and changed quickly and easily in the work environment.

Qualitative Effects of BPM & Workflow Initiatives

Work Process Standardization
- Standardization of work processes on the BPM & Workflow Platform.
- Standardization through user authority setup and business rule application.
- Users are able to easily perform tasks without relying on a manual.
- All parties in a process from start to finish can take the work through a standard process and they can clearly see the object and contents of the work.
- Exceptions can be automatically flagged and follow-up measures can be automatically initiated according to pre-defined business rules.

Work Process Status Monitoring Improvements
- Work process detail management and tracing of the work according to the defined process strengthens work transparency.
- Progress status monitoring, automatic work notification, and process visibility improves management levels.

- Process status such as due date, emergency, delay, etc., can be checked continuously.
- Company cooperation system is set up to respond to customer demands in real time.
- Simplified reporting function enables easy inspection of process efficiency.
- Ability to introduce new services in a timely manner through fast-paced work processes.
- Work management, work negotiation, and managerial functions are improved.
- Ability to manage work load, bottle-neck incidence, and problem type by each unit.

Statistical Data
- Process and unit work-related data is automatically collected.
- Work collaboration improved.
- Communication with workers on meeting agenda and work instructions are sent instantly through e-mail and notifications.
- Upon completion of previous work, the work is transferred to the worker's work list in real time.

Measurable Benefits

The following measurable improvements were directly recorded as a result of the BPM & Workflow Platform's being deployed at KTF:

Savings	Outcomes
Cost Savings	- Shortened work hours, ~**10-15 percentage** cost reduction. - Easy to see the work progress, which reduced idle work hours: **20 hours/month**. - Reduced labor costs required to improve the process: **10 million won Korean/ month**.
Increased Revenues	- Product development time span was reduced, improving product settlement rate: Annual average product development case: 0.15 ➜ 0.18. - Work adoption period was reduced by over 10 percentage. - Knowledge proficiency period was reduced by over 10 percentage.
Productivity Improvements	**Quantitative Productivity Improvement** - Work process period: 15 days ➜ 10 days. - Data collection period: five days ➜ real-time. - Per unit work process average hours: 48 hours ➜ two hours. - Average claim settlement period: 15 days ➜ 11 days. - Cost to settle one claim: three million won ➜ 2.2 million won Korean. - Customer claim on quality reduced: 100 cases/month ➜ 65 cases/month. **Qualitative Productivity Improvement** - Existing off-line and paper-based settlement and product development applications were automated. - Product development process is now transparent, making

	forecast on product development schedule possible.
	• All requests for product development and related feedback are unified into the BPM & Workflow Platform, thus facilitating communication and minimizing any confusion over requests.
	• Product development process participation result leads to career history and liability management.
	• All requests for product development processes and applications are now standardized.

BPM & WORKFLOW MOVING FORWARD

KTF will continue to grow its business by applying the BPM & WorkFlow solution. KTF expects that this strategy will continue to drive KTF's lead in the industry and strengthen the company's competitive edge in the following ways:

- Continuously monitor operations, and incorporate user demands in order to maximize applications through exhaustive analyses.
- Further expand BPM & Workflow to the cut-off process between core systems.
- Continuously monitor processes in order to improve existing processes.
- Create and manage an expert group in each core area to activate culture and cooperation around the BPM & WorkFlow solution.
- Promote the BPM & WorkFlow solution through continued highlights of benefits.
- Manage and operate an expert BPM & Workflow group that can carry out process optimization by studying and collecting process data, while managing and refining those processes.
- Establish strategic goals and CSFs (Critical Success Factors) based on KPIs (Key Performance Indicators) linked with processes and continuously analyze process performance.
- Through the analysis of process performance, create a database on customer-related information such as customer service, quality, cycle times, and costs, and utilize the data to lay a foundation for making fair judgments on each department and employees.
- Define the knowledge required for each process, and find out from where the knowledge comes. Then supply the knowledge just-in-time at point of need. Accumulate the results of the process to create a useful knowledge base for the organization.
- To deal with prior internal financial and audit controls, link the BPM & Workflow system with Internal Controls Assessment according to utility accounting reformation laws.
- Set up an Early Risk Warning system for operational risk management.
- Secure process agility to set up a base for the "Real-Time Enterprise."

CONCLUSION

With over 2,500 employees and annual revenues of $5.6 billion USD, KT Freetel Co. Ltd., is Korea's second largest mobile communications company. In order for a telecom company like KTF to gain a competitive advantage within today's rapidly changing world, it must have strong technical skills that can meet international standards, and it must be able to manage its internal and external resources efficiently and flexibly. However, introducing new technology can cause companies to overlook their ultimate goal and key benefits of each information system and individual resource. This can result in decreased competitiveness that opens the company to the risk of lost opportunities.

KTF realized that in order to exceed customer expectations and make customer-oriented service a priority, an investment in and commitment to BPM & Workflow was necessary. Through BPM & Workflow, KTF aimed to automate and standardize operational processes, reengineer inefficient workflows, improve work cycle times, and provide a platform designed to foster continued process improvement. KTF selected BizFlow® by HandySoft (www.handysoft.com) as their BPM and workflow solution.

BizFlow gave KTF the ability to integrate KTF's existing FreeNet (Enterprise Knowledge Portal) and ERP (SAP) systems. In so doing, KTF was able to maximize flexibility in IT resource utilization by applying the same resources against standardized, and consolidated processes. A configurable UI with menus based on operation type was a plus with the users. User familiarity and efficiency was improved through delivery via a user-friendly portal.

Since implementing the BizFlow solution, internal operating efficiency has been steadily rising, allowing KTF to better manage its resources, and cut operating costs where gains could be realized. By establishing better management over its core operating processes, KTF has been better able to quickly and efficiently cope with operational changes in a flexible manner and sustain competitive advantage in the crowded telecom market space.

Max New York Life Insurance, India

Finalist 2006, Pacific Rim; nominated by Newgen, India

EXECUTIVE SUMMARY

The company operates in a fiercely competitive and rapidly growing Life Insurance industry in India. The advent of several private insurance players—most of them collaborations involving international Insurance giants—has broken the monopoly of the monolithic state insurance agency—Life Insurance Corporation of India. With most of the new players in the Insurance market offering more or less the similar type of basic products, key differentiations can be achieved through automation of processes that enhance customer service. As a result, Max New York Life (MNYL) became one of the earliest insurance players in India to adopt Business Process Management (BPM). The phased implementation of BPM solution has enabled the company to rapidly expand its customer base, continuously enhance product offering, and stay well on course of realizing its vision of being the most admired life insurance company in India.

OVERVIEW

MNYL is a joint venture that brings together two conglomerates—one India's leading multi-business corporation and the other a Fortune 100 company with 160 years of experience in the Life Insurance business and ranked number one in Life Insurance sales in the USA. With a paid-up capital of over Rs. 732 crore (USD 180 million), workforce of over 5000 people, and offices in 120 Indian cities with over 27,500 direct agents as the primary channel of distribution, the company is geared towards exponential growth.

The company has implemented the BPM solution for three of its most crucial processes—Policy Owner Servicing (POS), New Business Acquisition and Claims Processing.

In the prevalent process, the customer used to send a new proposal form or policy-owner request to the nearest General Office (GO) in the form of a request letter accompanied with supporting documents. All these documents were sent by post/courier to the Home Office (HO) on a daily basis. The HO, on receiving these documents, intimated the concerned GO and forwarded the application to the concerned department for a quality check at the HO. In case any discrepancies were found, the GO was notified and the agent/customer was contacted for clarifications and additional documents, if needed. Applications were then forwarded to the New Business or POS department. Similarly, the claims were sent to the Claims department.

MNYL concluded that they needed to immediately automate these processes by implementing a BPM platform. The system included a workflow solution, an enterprise document management solution, an image capture and indexing solution, and record-management solution.

The process for POS was rolled out at the HO in a record time of four months and subsequently in 37 GOs spread across Indian sub-continent. Further, other processes were rolled out. The GOs are given Web-access to OmniFlow. With numerous worksteps and several hundred rules defined for routing, this solution has been designed to handle the complexities of multiple requests with ease. Integration with Ingenium, the core insurance application, enabled the company to make quick decisions. The workflow system is designed to cater to each specific worktype, providing a user-friendly desktop, with documents and relevant information from Ingenium displayed side-by-side on a split-screen.

Once the system was implemented, MNYL witnessed rapid, all-round gains such as reduction in turn-around-time, improved productivity, reduced operational costs, and so on.

KEY BUSINESS MOTIVATIONS

- Reduce Delayed and Faulty Processing
  - Delay in processing of application, as documents were physically transported to HO from various GOs
  - Delay in catching discrepancy in documents as verification could be done only at HO where all the physical records were maintained
  - Slow movement of relevant files across departments for processing requests
  - Limited automation and poor workflow capabilities
  - Poor integration of existing IT systems, such as Ingenium and POSTracker
  - Ensure minimum duplicate data entry for data already available in Ingenium
- Easier and Better Document Management
  - Difficulty in storing and managing huge number of physical documents
  - Risk of misplaced or worn out documents
  - Inability to instantly track status of request(s) due to time involved in searching relevant document(s)
- Adherence to Compliance Issues
  - Adherence to guidelines laid by IRDA, India's insurance regulatory authority, was mandatory, failing which invited heavy penalties and loss of reputation. These guidelines include claims settlement within 30 days from receipt of all documents and other SLAs.
  - Signature verification, though critical for servicing requests, could not be enforced
- Handle Increasing Workload
  - Burgeoning business transactions demanded a reliable system for operations
  - The system involved 29 different worktypes, which were set to increase, thus making system highly complex to be handled manually
- Correctly Measure Productivity
  - Since the process was manual and involved factors beyond user's control, it was difficult to measure user productivity
  - Supervisors were dependent on spreadsheets to collate data and make decisions for optimum resource utilization
- Reduce High Operational Costs
  - Recurring costs on sending documents by post/courier and storing and photocopying documents were increasing with the burgeoning business

SYSTEM CONFIGURATION

BPM Software: Consisting of OmniFlow, OmniDocs, OmniCapture and Records Management system.

Additionally, multiple service centers across India have Remote Image servers installed for managing the locally scanned images.

The OmniFlow Server, implemented using server-side Java technology, abstracts the complexity and configuration of the underlying OmniFlow Database and DMS Engines. It is implemented as the middle tier Transaction Server. Processing Servers and Configuration Server are responsible for managing workitem routings, workstep expiries etc.

The Process Modeler is a tool provided for defining business processes and rule-based workflow. The OmniFlow Workdesk and Web Client send transaction requests using XML while the Web-based Process Manager is used for administration, reports, monitoring various business processes.

Newgen OmniFlow Server provides a middle tier framework for Workflow Management Application Programming Interfaces (WAPI) for building enterprise automated work management systems to provide computerized support for the procedural automation of business processes.

- Platform: J2EE
- Database: SQL Server
- Servers: Dual processor, high-end servers with 2-4 GB RAM

THE SOLUTION

The solution is composed of the following products:

- OmniFlow, a platform-independent, scalable workflow solution that enables automation of organizational business processes
- OmniDocs, an Enterprise Document Management solution for creating, capturing, managing, delivering, and archiving large volumes of documents and content
- OmniCapture, a production grade Scanning and Indexing System for large-scale conversion of paper documents into electronic images, indexing, and seamless upload of these images to Document Management and workflow Systems
- Record Management System, the complete Web-enabled record management solution. The system provides the functionality to transfer document details to records and apply record policies on them. It manages physical records as if they are electronic records.

Solution For Policy Owner Service (POS) Department

- The solution was deployed at the HO in a record four months and subsequently in 37 GOs spread across Indian sub-continent. The GOs are given Web-access to OmniFlow. With more than 70 worksteps and several hundred rules defined for routing, this solution has been designed to handle the complexities of multiple requests with ease. Integration with Ingenium, the core insurance application, enabled the company to make quick decisions.
- The request, along with supporting documents, is scanned using OmniCapture at GOs, introduced into the workflow at HO and sent for further processing. Physical documents are sent to the Application Service Center (ASC) at HO for storage. The entire process is depicted below.

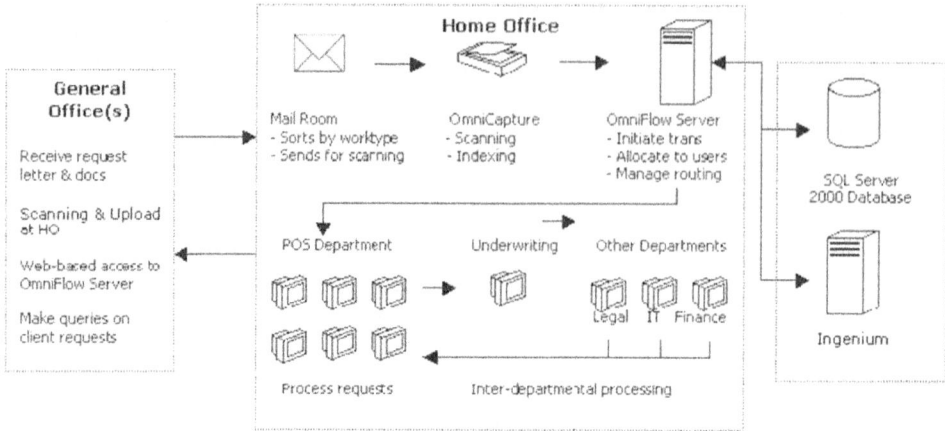

The workflow system is designed to cater to each specific worktype, providing a user-friendly desktop, with documents and relevant information from Ingenium displayed side-by-side on a split-screen, as shown below, while maintaining system security and data integrity.

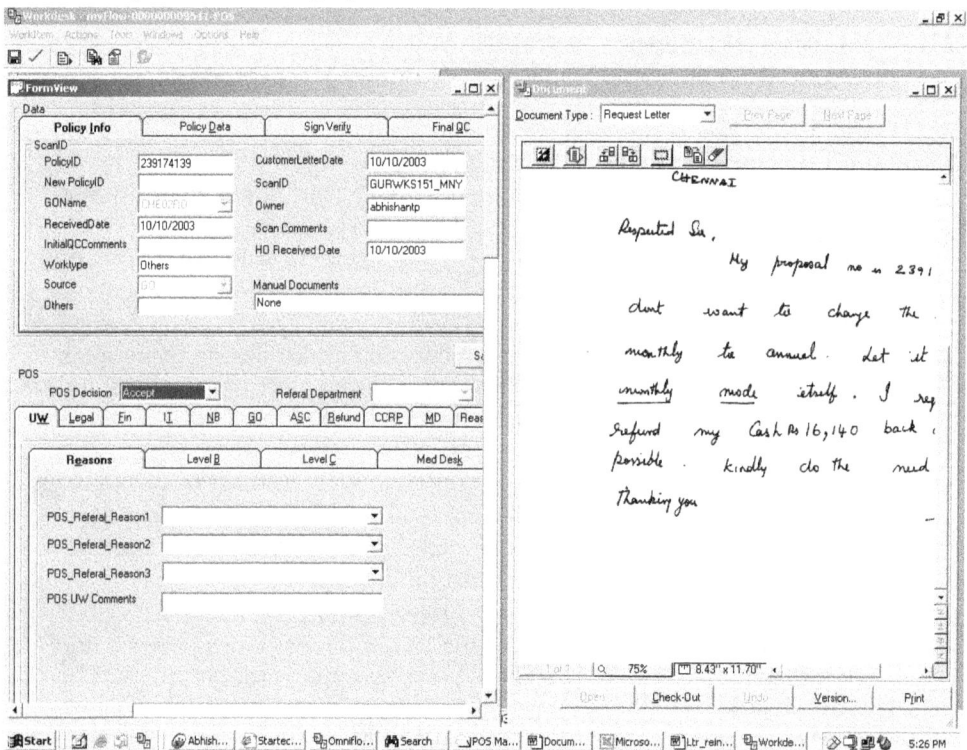

Solution for New Business Acquisition

The centralized solution was deployed at the HO along with 18 GOs. Over 50 smaller branches spread across the Indian sub-continent have been provided Web-access to OmniFlow through CITRIX environment. With over 150 worksteps and hundreds of rules defined for routing, this solution was designed to handle the complexities involved in issuing new policies. Further, integration with Ingenium, the core insurance application, gave the company a competitive edge by providing the relevant core business logic such as underwriting for faster deci-sion-making.

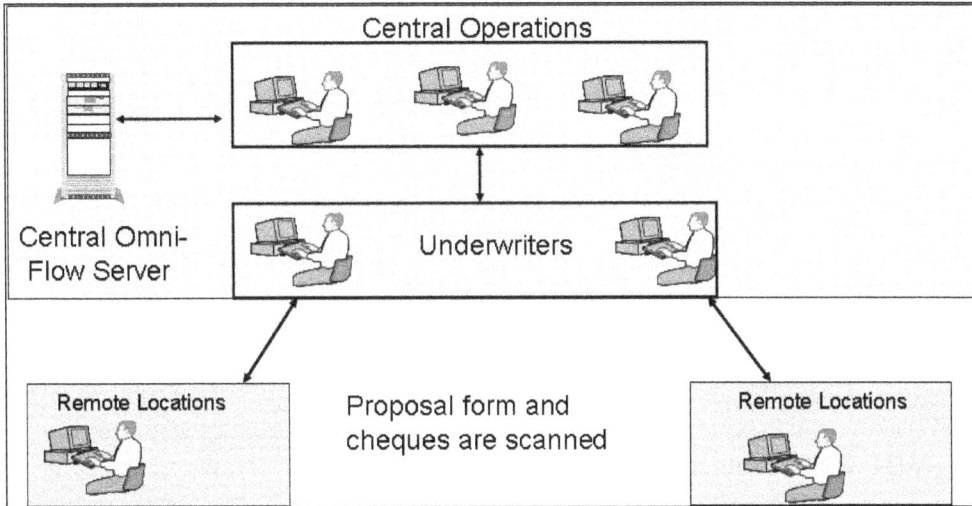

On an average, a branch usually receives 30-40 proposal requests along with supporting documents each day. However, number of requests might go up to 250 per day during peak time. These are scanned at nearest GO using OmniCap-ture and introduced into the workflow. The physical documents are sent for stor-age to the Application Service Center (ASC) at HO. The movement of physical documents is tracked using Record Management System (RMS).

The scanned proposals are immediately available for processing. Users perform data entry, quality check, underwriting, and other activities in Ingenium using the OmniFlow interface. Relevant Ingenium screens are launched from the Om-niFlow desktop using a silent Login and authorized users perform the requisite actions. Ingenium automatically generates various documents such as response letters, counter offers, and request for additional information. These auto-generated documents are attached to the corresponding workitem in OmniFlow and forwarded to the relevant workstep. All the documents are centrally managed at OmniDocs repository to ensure round-the-clock availability. The status of each proposal is readily available at all branch offices and agents at the mere click of a button.

Since underwriting for new policy issuance is a highly confidential process, the documents related to underwriting are secure and available only to authorized underwriters.

Solution for Insurance Claims Processing

The company may receive death claim intimations in the form of a let-ter/fax/email from a nominee, an assignee, the court or the Income Tax depart-ment. Non-death claims, which include critical illness, waiver of premium in case of disability, etc., are, however, filed by the insured person herself. Once the claim is registered and the relevant details captured for processing and reporting, a de-tailed assessment is done. The claim may be settled in part or full, or in some cases, repudiated. The claim amount is calculated and the claim passes for set-tlement. The case may also be reopened at a later date, if the beneficiary chal-lenges the decision of the insurance company.

To maintain strict compliance with IRDA guidelines, the solution provides built-in features reminding users at regular intervals informing them of pending actions and the timeline for the same.

KEY INNOVATIONS

Overall Technological Innovation

The solution provides users at HO and GOs with a secure, easy-to-use interface for instant access to policy documents and quick action. This is in stark contrast to the earlier system, which was slow and an impediment to collaborative working. Seamless integration with Ingenium—the core insurance application, leverages strengths of existing legacy system to enable end-to-end process automation.

Overall Business Innovation

The solution, as a result of implementing process workflows, made personnel involved in processing of Insurance documents more accountable, and therefore, made immediate impact in their productivity. Moreover, the solution enables MNYL to rapidly expand its product portfolio and reach distant geographies.

Overall Process Innovation

Prior to implementation of Workflow for processes such as POS, New Business and Claims, the maximum cases that could be handled at every GO was around 40-50. After the implementation of Workflow automation, each GO can easily handle more than 250 cases every day, with ability to further ramp up the number of cases it can handle if the need arises. Collaboration enabled right mix of centralized and decentralized execution of tasks within the processes.

IMPACT TO THE COMPANY

- Reduced Operational Costs
  - Parallel processing at branches and HO lead to reduced communication costs and time
  - 70 percent reduction in costs of retrieving documents
  - Daily costs of return courier for 10 percent discrepancy cases eliminated
  - Savings on printouts and photocopies for approximately 500 pages per day
  - Savings on reduced number of phone calls from GOs to HO and vie versa for status enquiry
  - Savings on underwriting effort and cost
- Turn around time drastically reduced
  - For customer request to POS, turnaround time approximately reduced by 45 percent to 3.7 days from 6.7 days
  - New Policies being issued in as less as 24 hours
  - Immediate availability of documents for instant processing
  - Quicker resolution of discrepancies at the GOs itself
  - Slickly defined workflow using OmniFlow ensures action-oriented worksteps, resulting in zero time delay in transfer of documents
  - Instant response to customer queries using online search facility
  - Better handling of fraudulent claims
  - 50 percent reduction in duplicate data entry required for existing data in Ingenium
- Easier and more accurate assessment of Productivity
  - Complete audit trail to lend more visibility to the entire process, making easier performance monitoring

- Properly defined work automatically arrives to allocated personnel, making lag time zero. The client registered about 40 percent increase in productivity for New Business.
- Processes can be molded easily to suit business requirements and enhance productivity
- Easier document management
  - Automated and highly convenient storage and management of documents with the help of OmniDocs
  - Convenient and quick tracking of documents and customer requests with help of RMS
  - Reminders to users when the timelines are about to expire and when they do expire
  - Quick signature verification
- Managing Increased Workload
  - Optimized workload distribution by automatic allocation of 80 percent simple requests and manual allocation of 20 percent complex requests
  - The system involved 29 different worktypes, which were set to increase, thus making system highly complex to be handled manually
- Integration with core Insurance Systems
  - Reduced data look-up time from up to 15 minutes to zero due to integration with company's core insurance system, Ingenium
  - Minimum duplicate data entry as data already available in existing insurance system can be accessed instantly anytime
  - Improved MIS standards

AcBel Polytech, Taiwan

Silver Award 2005, Pacific Rim; nominated by Flowring, Taiwan

Establish the ISO 9001 quality assurance, product design support, and global customer support applications by integrating the workflow platform with AcBel's legacy ERP system

ABSTRACT

The intention of this case study is to present the business process modeling and implementation effort that was invested in the past years to deploy an integrated information systems at AcBel. The goal of the target information system is to enhance and extend the capability of AcBel legacy ERP system by introducing a full-function workflow system. From the functional view, it constructs a software system for AcBel's ISO quality assurance system, and provides computer-guided standard operating procedures for the product design and manufacture processes.

Furthermore, AcBel extends the internal customer support functions of the legacy ERP system with the help of Flowring's Agentflow process portal to create new Web-based global customer support system. The ability to operate a global product after-services system becomes one of the critical successful factors to keep secured long-term cooperative relationship with the top ten famous computer suppliers such as IBM and Apple computer.

The deployment of the workflow infrastructure also makes AcBel users work together without geographical limit through the connection of the Web-based workflow applications.

OVERVIEW

Company overview

AcBel Polytech, a strategic alliance member of the Kinpo group, is the top five power conversion devices design and manufacturing company in the world. Nowadays, AcBel has its manufacturing factories in Taiwan, China and the Philippines. It also operates 13 regional offices, 20 warehouses, and 11 after-services centers in Asia, northern America, and Europe. The company has achieved revenue of NT$ 12.4 billion (US$ 380 million) in FY2004, with market capitalization US$ 237.3 million (as of August 31, 2005). It envisions a world where every laptop, every IA product in people's daily lives as well as every telecom system and every workstation for industry use are powered by AcBel.

Project Overview

In the early stage, from 2002 to 2003, AcBel started to construct the workflow applications to support: (a) the ISO quality assurance system, and (b) the storage system. With the strong demand for the technical support and global after-sale services for major computer suppliers, AcBel continues to invest by adding two new workflow projects (c) CCAR systems, and (d) RMA systems to the same workflow platform from 2004 to 2005.

The ISO quality assurance system is implemented as a set of concrete processes and procedures for activities of AcBel's ISO 9001 quality assurance system. The benefits of the workflow application are two-fold: (1) It helps the organization to enforce the principle of ISO – 'write what you do, do what you have written, and record what you have done'. Because the practices of ISO processes are guided, tracked and recorded by the workflow systems, when required procedures are ignored or incomplete the workflow system can remind relevant stakeholders to correct it. (2) It reduces the annual ISO audit effort by enabling check the ISO related activities electrically, because the process activities and related records are kept in the workflow systems. The ISO audit team can then assert that the process activities do not violate the documented ISO quality polices. Before that, the audit team has to pay much time to review piles of papers records.

The *storage system* consists of several workflow applications to manage the documents and drawings generated in the product life cycle. The storage system serves the design engineers by providing history product design information as the knowledge database for designing whole new product models or making minor modification to existing product models. It also serves as a more user-friendly front-end for engineers to look up the legacy ERP database for available components or parts.

The *CCAR (Customer-complaints Corrective Action Request) system* implements the problem management functions. The main workflow process enables the design and manufacture team to practice 8D problem management techniques (e.g. http://www.semiconfareast.com/8D.htm) to handle the design defects.

The RMA (Return Material Authorization) system implements the customer support system for global after-service centers to manage RMA requests from the customers. The RMA workflow interacts smoothly with the legacy ERP database through the middleware provided by the workflow platform to find available replacement of the RMA request. It is then used tracks the logistics/shipping/billing of each RMA application.

Common Workflow Platform

All the four systems are built on single workflow system, therefore the ISO system, storage system, CCAR system, and RMA system share the common benefits of the workflow platform, with only one-time deployment effort:

1. Unified login account, application deployment mechanism, access control, and aggregated work item list. This means new workflow applications can be added into the platform with no additional cost.
2. Linked workflow process for several plants spread in Taiwan, China, and Philippine through the network. This means engineers in geographically separated plants can work collaboratively on the same product design project, logically sharing the common workspace.
3. Controlled and secured expose of legacy ERP database to external plants by using Web-based workflow applications as the front-end. This means the functions of the legacy client-server ERP system can be extended through the Web-based GUI front-end of the new workflow platform to expose information to external business partner

KEY BUSINESS MOTIVATION

Because most power conversion products of AcBel are equipped into the personal computers, notebooks, and telecommunication devices for daily use, the design and manufacture processes of these products should be carefully handled to ensure the human safety. Therefore international safety standards such as **CSA, UL, ITS, TUV, CE** mark are necessary for AcBel product to sell worldwide. Sophisticated design and manufacture procedures and rules are also necessary for AcBel to follow in the everyday design and manufacture activities.

In addition, AcBel has established the mature business management processes that are certified by the ISO 9001, TL 9000, ISO 14001 and OHSAS 18001 international standards. This means that AcBel's processes have considered the quality assurance, environmental management, and occupational health policies.

As the world-class power conversion product designer and manufacturer, AcBel has described its strategy in the company publication: "...increase productivity by improving the process, enforce the quality policy. Aggressively improve the design, plan, and management of processes. In addition, continuously perform quality improvement to double the productivity ..." Thanks to existing standard operation procedures and best practices that have already been documented and formalized (approved) during previous ISO 9001 standard initiative, the team can reduce the effort to compose the requirement for the target software applications. AcBel has set the following concrete missions for the new workflow systems:

1. To construct the software systems for the quality assurance system (ISO system). The new application system needs to implement the required functions in the workflow process to enforce the process stakeholders to perform required procedures described in quality and safety documents of the international standards
2. To establish the internal design support system (Storage system) to manage history design sheets and document, also integrate components and parts database in the legacy ERP
3. To establish the external technical support system (CCAR system) to provide problem management mechanism to collaborate with design team members of top computer supplier companies
4. To establish the global after-sale services system (RMA system) to provide support for global service centers operation (e.g. components repair or replacement logistic)
5. To extend the life-time of the investment on the precious legacy ERP system that contains about 3000 programs that perform AcBel's distinctive business models and rules.
6. To introduce a new workflow platform to enhance the ERP system in terms of workflow process control and Web access

KEY INNOVATION

Overall Business Innovation

The typical innovated features provided through the system contribute to the stakeholders in different business aspects. From the aspect of enterprise internal management, the ISO system:

1. Can work as the core of enterprise quality procedures life-cycle management, to enable the continuous quality improvement mission of the enterprise.
2. Can enforce and monitor quality-related activities by the workflow system. Implementing the ISO quality assurance procedures as an executable computer system, the quality-related activities can be easily enforced, monitored, audited on the workflow system.
3. Can remind the activity performers and his/her managers if some required activities are not performed at the right timing.
4. Can record and archive the artifacts as the evidence of performing quality-related activities.
5. Enables ISO audit team members to check the quality activities and tangible evidences electrically to increase the audit efficiency and coverage.

Also from the aspect of internal enterprise management, the *storage system*

1. supports the product design engineers to manage the design document during the whole product life-cycle.
2. can track and list the product models affected by some component specification modification.
3. seamlessly integrates the parts and components database in the legacy ERP system for product designer to lookup availability of parts or components conveniently.

From the aspect of business partners, the innovations provided by the *CCAR system* are:

1. extending the problem management system to support AcBel's business model on working together with engineer team members from top computer supplier.
2. implementing 8-D (eight-disciplines) problem management systems into a workable workflow applications to make the problem handling progress transparent to business partners.

From the aspect of customers, the *RMA system* enables Acbel to:

1. provide global after-sale services to handle component repair and replacement.
2. provide real-time progress tracking of RMA requests.
3. dispatch of RMA requests to proper departments or repair centers.
4. quickly response the customer's request by integrating real-time warehouse information to find available replacement and possible shipping date.

Overall Process Innovation

The following are the overall process innovation in this project:

1. The SOP documents defined in AcBel's previous ISO certification initiatives are used as the basis requirements of workflow applications. It shows that these SOP can dramatically increase the efficiency of requirement gathering and business process definition.
2. It applies a proven process modeling and analysis methodology, as shown in the figure 1, during the development stage by mapping requirements of the workflow applications into proper modules and tools in Agentflow workflow platform.
3. It demonstrates that workflow systems can integrate with legacy ERP system by working merely as the user-friendly GUI front-ends of ERP to simplify end-user operation. Furthermore, the workflow systems can intensely interweave the independent ERP functions and newly developed workflow functions (e.g. routing, timer actions, alert, etc.) to compose a more powerful ERP workflow applications.

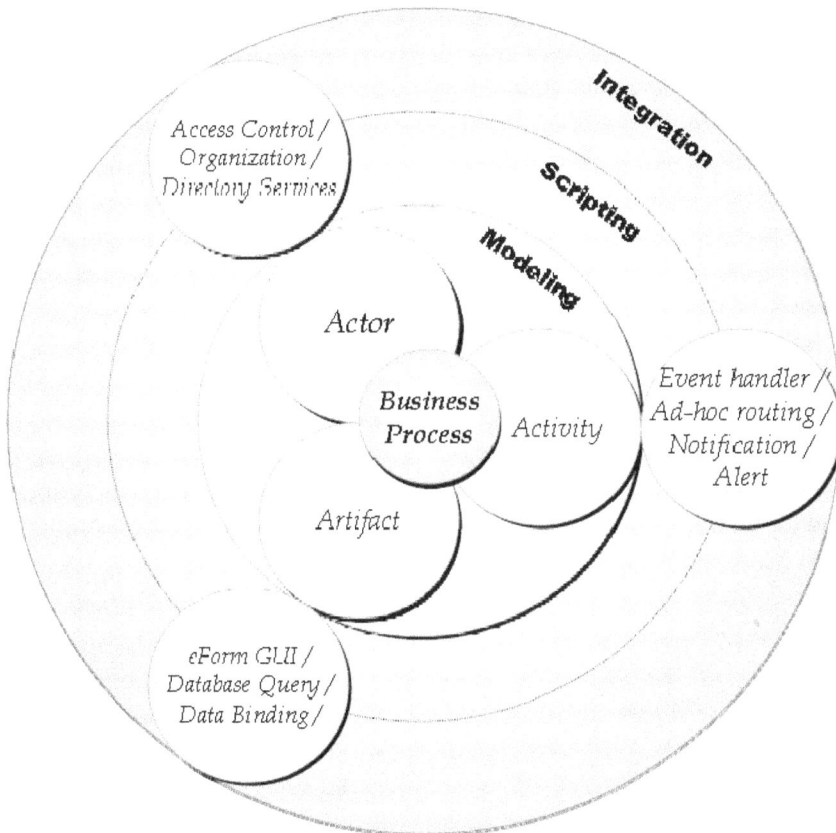

Figure 1. Process Modeling and Analysis using Agentflow's Methodology

Overall Technical Innovation

Most of the innovations mentioned in the section are default functions of Agentflow platform. Innovations found in the technical area are summarized as the following:

4. Integrating legacy ERP through the database middleware embedded in the workflow platform. With the database layer abstract, workflow application designer can easily access legacy ERP database by writing simple script.
5. Provide I18N features in the end users GUI. It also provides support on the difference between traditional Chinese characters and simplified Chinese characters.
6. Provide online transform from several document types to Acrobat PDF file format so that end users can download documents via browsers. It can also optionally set the document's password for protection, or add water mark on the document for security issues.
7. Support attachment file in the e-Form to carry documents through all the activities of process.
8. Integrate with search engine, to perform full-text search on the operational artifacts (documents)
9. Reserve a design flexibility for the legacy ERP programs (that are implemented in Delphi) to call Agentflow through Web services

THE DEPLOYMENT RESULT AND IMPACT ON THE USERS

The target system is designed for use with AcBel global employees with 200 concurrent user requests to the workflow systems. With 150 concurrent requests handling capacity, the system configuration allows about 800 to 1000 users to work concurrently in the system with intermittent workflow requests. The privilege to operate the workflow applications are assigned by system's access control mechanism so that only authorized employees can access the controlled system functions.

For the AcBel MIS department, they achieved the goal to deploy the workflow platform as the enterprise infrastructure for current and future BPM initiatives. Newly workflow applications enable AcBel to provide better services for business partners and end users of the power conversion products. Legacy ERP application systems designed in traditional client-server architecture are connected to Web through the workflow system's Web-based architecture. Thus the legacy ERP system extends the life-time and is powered with the workflow capability with the new workflow software architecture. The consequences are: (1) MIS team members increase their productivity in developing new Web-based applications that need to utilize ERP data and workflow process control mechanism. (2) MIS team reduces the end-user training effort by the unified Web-based workflow operation GUI. (3) MIS team can reduce the effort on daily workflow administration routines with the help of standard workflow administration tools.

For normal end users in AcBel workflow system environment, the deployment provides them with the following functions for the daily work:

No	Category	Functional description	Before-and-after comparison
1	General/ common features	Single sign-on for all applications Web access to application systems Workflow-enabled applications Process tracking and monitoring facilities Process history query Process performance report Personal process administration tool	Before: Users must install and periodically upgrade client programs to access ERP applications. Hard to track the progress of requests. Hard to transfer ownership of selected tasks, sometimes the user adopts the unsafe workaround to share his/her login account After: Users can access the applications through standard Web browser without installing/upgrading client programs. System actively sends progress notification to users. Users can monitor/review the progress/performance of requests processes Better access control and the user can transfer the ownership of selected tasks to colleagues (by using *task delegation* setup dialog)
2	ISO System	Implementation of ISO 9001 quality assurance systems Life-cycle management for quality system manual Full text search on quality	Before: Human procedures to follow the rules defined in the ISO 9001 quality systems. It is tedious and error-prone. Manually query the rules in the

		manuals Access control on documents distribution	quality system manuals After: Process enforcement for quality assurance system Automatically check every execution steps to ensure no required steps are ignored Automatic activity record for future audit Quickly obtain the relevant quality system rules from the set of quality system manuals Automated procedures to distribute/renew/revoke quality system document to/from all stakeholders, with better access control
3	Storage System	Implement automated product model design process Design sheets / document management and approval PDF output with password and watermark protect Scanned image files are routed with workflow attachments	Before: Design team members manually archive the design document Hard to search history designs and retrieve the design document for non-HQ design team Hard to find out all affected design model for adjust the design, if the specification of components or parts change After: Storage for design sheets and related documents is centralized to avoid lost All the design documents for a new product model is approved by the managers and other stakeholders through the workflow Easy to find out all the product models that are affected by the change of specification. Thus, relevant model design modification can be executed to keep the design of product line consistent
4	CCAR System	Provide the workflow applications for the problem management, so that stakeholders in the system can : Online submit design problems Review problem report forms Dispatch the problem to corresponding departments by the criteria (e.g. process defect, workmanship defect, or	Before: The product design team has no automated problem management systems to support the design activities. Problem reports are handled by manual processes Lack the problem tracking and monitoring tools to point out overdue cases After: Product design team works with

		design defect) Organize re-action plan Perform failure analysis and calculate failure cost Provide permanent solution and change the SOP Maintain the problem knowledge base and guidelines	the help computer-aided problem management workflow systems to standardize the problem reaction procedures and shorten the problem reaction cycle-time Managers of the product design team can have clear view on the overall problem solving status History problem solving guidelines reduce the effort to solve similar problems
5	RMA System	Provide members RMA services center to product repair and replacement service Circulate the RMA documents through the stakeholders of the RMA workflow Dispatch the RMA requests to proper handling department Arrange the replacement logistic Provide billing and accounting information for RMA requests Perform goods check-in / check-out / transfer management among warehouses	Before: No direct software support in the RMA services center, so the customers get slow response for the RMA request RMA progress tracking are handled by manual/paper work RMA business rules are complex to follow without software support. After: RMA service routines are standardized by the RMA service workflow application The real-time ERP information for the RMA is summarized and brought the RMA service stakeholders through the workflow platform. Thus RMA service specialists can answer the customers based on the information RMA requests can be tracked from the global service centers via Web browsers RMA service workflow is integrated with the billing and accounting systems of the ERP systems, reduce manual routine work to input the RMA billing information to the ERP system

Figure 2. Screen for end users to select workflow task from the work list

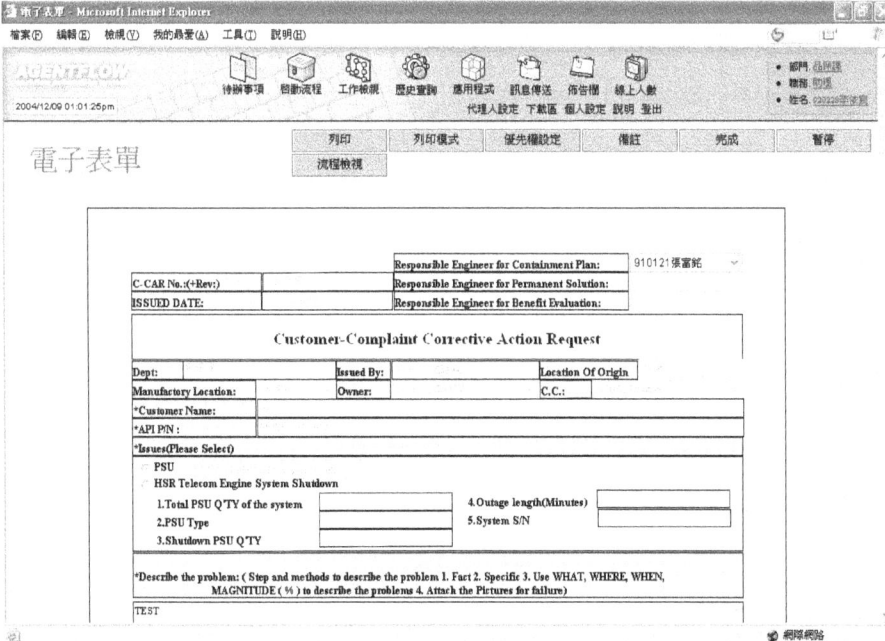

Figure 3. End users use Web GUI to interact with the CCAR process via eForm

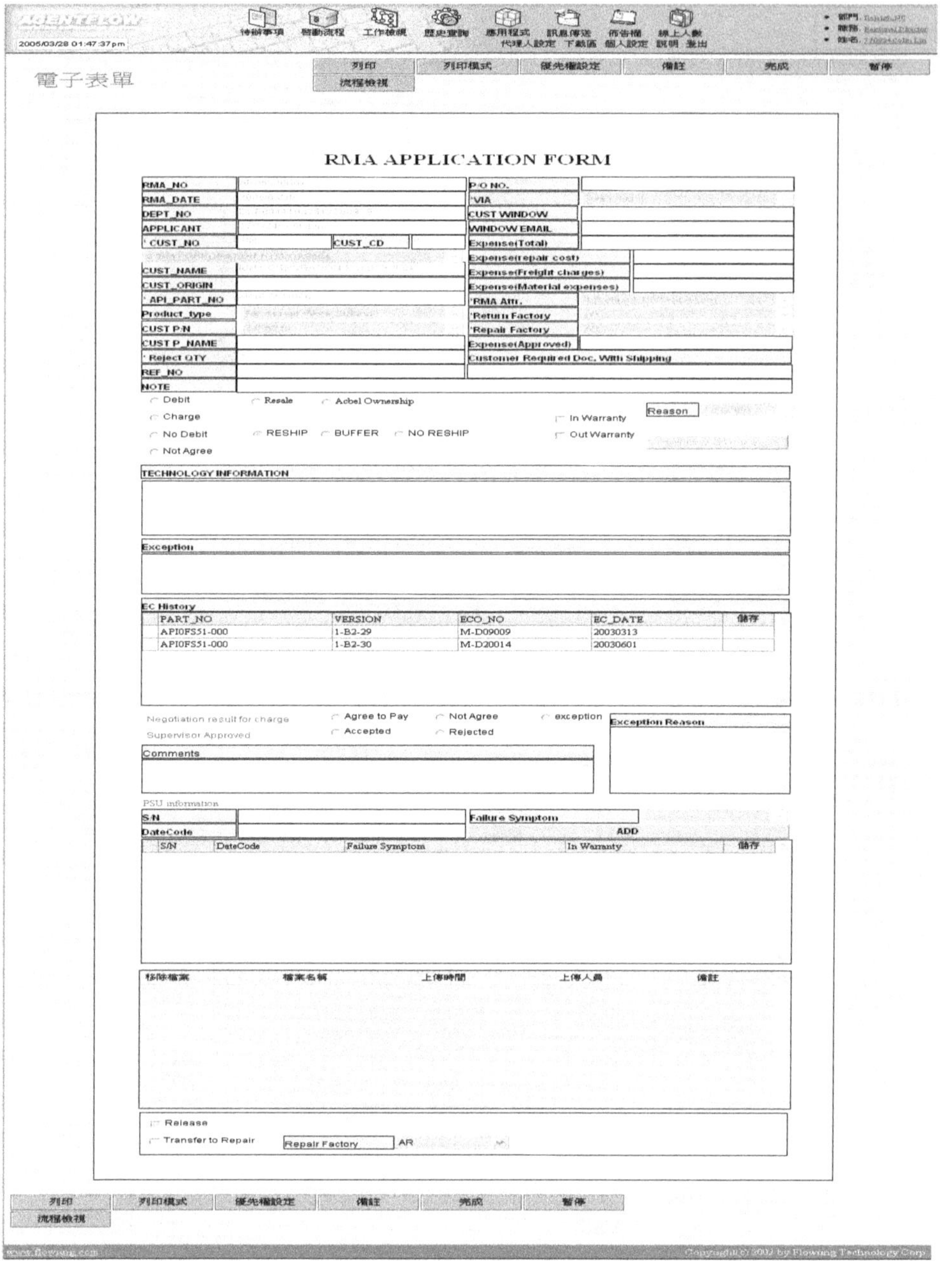

Figure 4. End users use Web GUI to interact with the RMA process via eForm

SYSTEM CONFIGURATION

The components for the new workflow system are illustrated and summarized by the following table and figure:

Purpose	Hardware/OS	Software	Description
Database Server	IBM RS6000 AIX Unix 4.3 External RAID	Oracle 8.1.7	Work as the data storage for the legacy ERP and new work-flow servers

Legacy ERP Server	Intel PC server Windows NT 4.0 Dual CPU 1GB RAM 40GB HDD	N.A.	ERP systems developed by AcBel MIS in Delphi
Workflow server	Intel PC server Windows 2000 Dual CPU 2GB RAM 80GB HDD	Flowring's Agentflow servers, version 2.2	Standard workflow management features Application access control Provide APIs through Java RMI or Web Services for external program integration
Web server / JSP server	Intel PC server Windows 2000 Dual CPU 2GB RAM 80GB HDD	Jakarta Tomcat 4.1.24 Flowring's Agentflow Process Portal, as JSP Web applications	JSP/Web server Agentflow Process Portal works as the end-user GUI Performs applet-view to HTML-view real-time transform

Table 1. Servers Deployed in the AcBel Workflow Systems

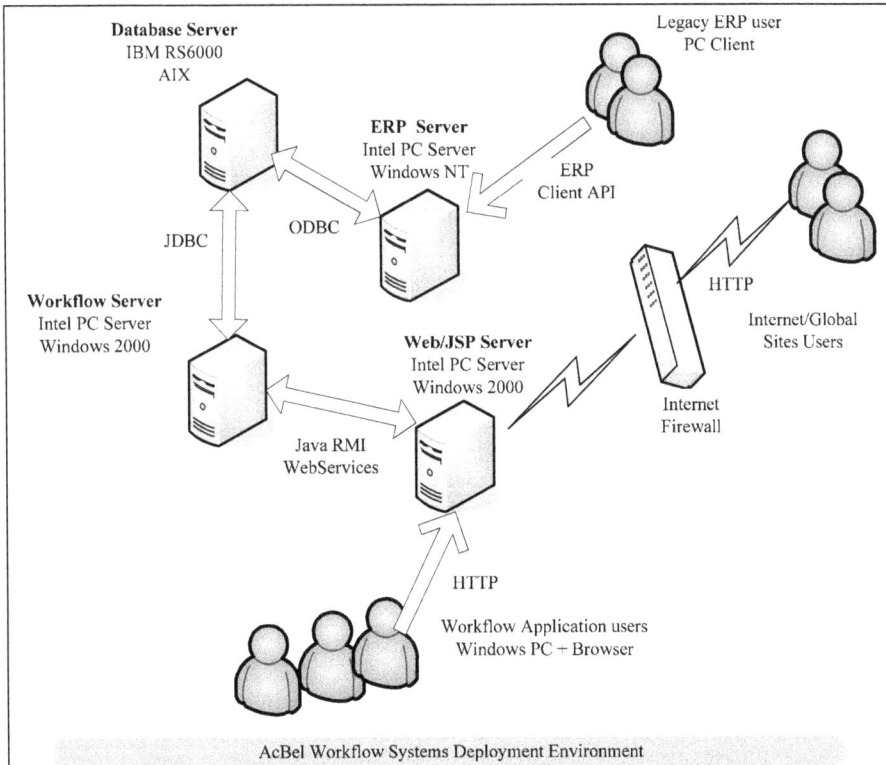

Figure 5. The AcBel Workflow Systems Deployment Environment

The workflow application systems *ISO, Storage, CCAR and RMA* are implemented in Flowring's Agentflow workflow systems. The design-time tools are used to specify application's process definition and event handlers. An e-Form design tool is also provided for the programmer to design the layout of the form and GUI event handlers, if the application need to provide GUI to interact with the end users involved in the process. The process definitions of these workflow applications are stored in the database, and then loaded by the workflow run-time server to interpret the process definition. The end users operate the applications through the unified Web-based workflow GUI. Under the workflow application infrastructure, future workflow applications can be easily added and operated in the same manner.

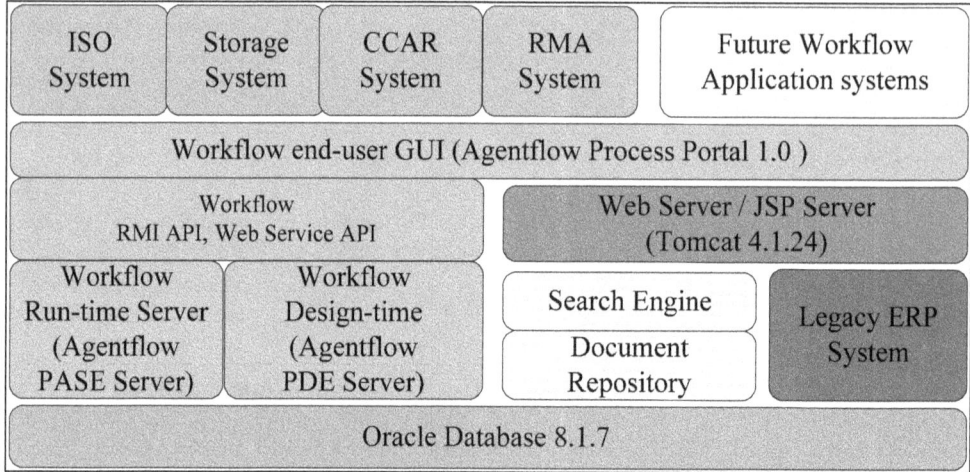

ISO System	Storage System	CCAR System	RMA System	Future Workflow Application systems
Workflow end-user GUI (Agentflow Process Portal 1.0)				
Workflow RMI API, Web Service API		Web Server / JSP Server (Tomcat 4.1.24)		
Workflow Run-time Server (Agentflow PASE Server)	Workflow Design-time (Agentflow PDE Server)	Search Engine / Document Repository		Legacy ERP System
Oracle Database 8.1.7				

Figure 6. The Modules of AcBel Workflow Application Systems

SOLVING SYSTEM DEPLOYMENT HURDLES

To deploy workflow application systems into an enterprise is not merely to overcome the technical issues. It also involves the introduction or enforcement of newly defined business process and enterprise culture. Therefore the workflow systems may not always work well in the real-world on the first or second deployments. Adjustment in terms of business process and technical solutions are needed. Sometimes it also needs high-level manager's decision to clarify ambiguity or select alternatives to push the project to the next iteration sooner. The following table summarizes the categories of common hurdles and their solutions we met when working with workflow systems:

No	Category	Hurdles	Solution
1	Management	Due to team members transfer, new process owner sometimes has new ideas or different policies on business processes	Check the contract and scope of work to clearly explain the necessary work in the stage, reserve the process design flexibility design to allow the new ideas be implemented in the new stage Hold meetings to make sure the new policy still confirms to previously defined project policies or strategies.
2	Management	Cross department communication overhead and efficiency -- some departments set lower priority or has little	High level manager commitment to restate the importance of the new workflow system deployment Hold cross-department meeting to

		awareness on the new work-flow systems deployment	have formal decision on the responsibility of cross- department activities. Assign and empower an member as the process owner to have enough authority on cross-department communication
3	Process	Business processes or rules are modified to reflect real-world change without considering ripple effect on other existing application system	Apply requirement change control and notification to all process members. Change to critical process activities or business rules needs second thoughts or to confirm it again by group meeting
4	Process	Lack of version control so that running workflow applications can not match up-to-date business rules	Define a step-by-step workflow application version upgrade check/approval procedures to match the new business rules
5	Technical	Document repository contains large size design sheets, it is slow to transfer whole engineering design sheet over the leased line	AcBel MIS guides external sites users to view the design sheets by installing CITRIX remote screen display solution
6	Technical	Legacy ERP data transfer -- data consistency and integrity issues	AcBel MIS refines legacy ERP database by repair incomplete or incorrect data records to maintain the data consistency and integrity Add more code in the application systems to check the data integrity when inserting new data records Update/fetch ERP data through middleware instead of direct SQL query, to obtain better and flexible data format/type manipulation
7	Technical	We understand that the workflow e-Form can be implemented as pure JSP/HTML programs, However in some cases we need to apply Java applets for smooth/sophisticated GUI operation. The applet download are slow over low bandwidth network	Turn on Agentflow's real-time *apple-to-JSP* screen translation feature at the Web server, so that only the HTML view of the e-Form is transferred to the client browser Carefully study Java JAR file cache mechanism, by applying JAR version control feature to reduce unnecessary applet class file download
8	Technical	Reuse the process template, program template, GUI component to reduce the development cost and effort	Apply the re-use features provided by Agentflow workflow platform: Application process template and pattern e-Form GUI plug-in component Manage site-level or enterprise-level business rules in the *Script library*

BENEFIT EVALUATION

The ROI of the workflow applications can be measured from several direct and indirect factors. For realistic benefits analysis, we discard the method to directly compare the quarterly or yearly cost because it may not reflect the facts well especially when the enterprise is in quick growth stage. In this case study we calculate by formula to estimate the saving on business activities. By reviewing the history records, we count the occurrences (or simply estimate the percentage) of events of which the cost can be eliminated (prevented, or avoided) by the deployment of the workflow application systems.

Cost saving formula

A : the occurrence counts in the history records
B : the occurrence counts that can be eliminated in the history records
C : the saving percentage in occurrence = B / A * 100 percentage
D : average cost per occurrence
E : the cost saving in the cost category = D * A * C

The following table is the cost saving calculation based on the above formula using the selected history records from the sampled department. By selecting history records in FY2003, we can calculate the direct saving in FY2004 on the following cost categories, assuming no business growth in the department.

	A Sampled occur.	B Saved occur.	C Saved percentage	D Avg cost per occur.	E Saved Cost
International phone call, fax	800	300	37.5 percentage	$120	NT$36,000
Foreign Traveling	50	20	40.0 percentage	$50,000	NT$1,000,000
Document delivery (UPS, Fedex, ...)	550	260	47.3 percentage	$800	NT$208,000
Failure Cost due to Design Defects	40	25	62.5 percentage	$100,000	NT$2,500,000
					NT$3,744,000

Although the increase in revenue and net income of the enterprise are not entirely contributed by the workflow application deployment, we can use it as an indirect ROI information. The following table depicts the revenue and net income continuous growth of AcBel after the workflow application deployment since 2003.

	FY 2003	2004 Q1	2004 Q2	2004 Q3	2004 Q4
Revenue	10,302	2,638	2,973	3,127	3,684
Net Income	1,315	387	348	479	238

(Unit: NT$ million)

GAINED COMPETITIVE ADVANTAGES

After the deployment of the workflow application system, AcBel gains more competitive advantages in the following aspects:

1. More mature and quality process control on design and manufactures
2. Shorten the cycle-time of the design problem solution or technical support requests
3. Reduce the number of design defects, and consequence loss in material and manufacture
4. Continuous product design knowledge accumulation. Rich design knowledge base contribute to the quick time-to-market of new product models
5. Global and complete RMA system enables global end-users support. It secures the products orders from top computer supplier company
6. Enforcement of SOP on several enterprise activities. It reduces the ambiguity and communication overhead.
7. Automatic business process workflow enables the new team members to involves in the team workspace sooner with business operation guidance designed in the applications
8. Transparent workflow tracking and monitoring on process progress. It satisfies both the business partners and customers.

LONG-TERM PLANS TO SUSTAIN COMPETITIVE ADVANTAGES

Based on previous successful deployment of workflow platform and applications, AcBel continues to utilize the platform to increase the service quality and response speed by making more business processes operated under the support of software applications. The following are the long-term policies or plans that sustain AcBel's competitive advantage:

1. Hold the policy of continuous improvement on the quality system
2. Expand the workflow applications to more business activities such as KM, CRM, SCM
3. Enhance the IT infrastructure to ensure the capacity to serve more company members and various business processes
4. Investigate and integrate more software platforms and components into the enterprise IT infrastructure to reduce the development cost and deployment cycle
5. Extend the business process to include B2B business partners by inviting them to join AcBel's process as one of the stakeholders.
6. Extend the business process and enterprise IT infrastructure to include B2B partners by inviting them to perform application-to-application interaction, achieving more flexible B2B processes.

Samsung Heavy Industries, Korea

Gold Award 2005, Pacific Rim; nominated by HandySoft Global, Korea

EXECUTIVE SUMMARY/ABSTRACT

Due to a dramatic increase in the quantity of orders received since 2000, **Samsung Heavy Industries** (SHI) realized the necessity of implementing business process management (BPM) technology for more efficient management and monitoring of our international shipbuilding operations. Today, the implemented BPM system has improved and efficiently manages not only processes such as order placement management, contractor process management, production management, and quantity management related to shipbuilding outsourcing, but has also improved the business processes related to the materials supplied to subcontractors of the various shipyards. Using this system, the *e-ouTEr Assembly Management System* (**e-TEAMS**) processes were visualized. This visualization allowed us to optimize the fabrication management process, enable employees to manage and monitor the priority and status of various business processes in real-time, and provide an alarm notification function for process delays. e-TEAMS was the first instance of the application of BPM technology supporting business processes in the Korean shipbuilding industry.

CORPORATE OVERVIEW

Established in 1974, **Samsung Heavy Industries** (SHI) currently has 8,572 employees worldwide. SHI maintains four business units comprised Shipbuilding, Offshore, Digital Business, and Engineering & Construction, and puts its main focus on the shipbuilding and offshore business. In Korea, SHI operations include the Geoje Shipyard, the Suwon Plant, and the Daeduk R&D Center. SHI operates eight overseas facilities including a ship block factory, SHI Ningbo factory in China, and has an extensive global network comprising of a number of successful overseas branches. In response to a rapid growth in the shipbuilding industry since 2000, we adopted a strategy for industry dominance and continuous gross revenue increase through 2006. At present, the company is processing three years' worth of orders for 127 ships, for a total of $9.6 billion in revenue by 2007.

In order to achieve our goal of becoming the world's leading shipbuilding company, we formulated a strategy for maintaining global competitiveness, developing an improved business model, and cultivating a new corporate culture. To these ends, we are now dedicated to becoming a *Digital & Shipbuilding industry leader*, striving for flexible sales and marketing, simultaneous collaborative design, collaborative production management, customer-centered quality service, and innovative business management. In addition, we are implementing collaborative support using personalized portal technology, improved process management using BPM, and effective knowledge management.

After careful consideration of various commercially available BPM solutions, we selected HandySoft's BizFlow BPM platform and began implementation between October 2003 and April 2004.

We use a 16-step business process for any given job, from the selection of the partner company to the settlement of the account after the delivery. With the previous system, users were able to locate jobs; but the current BPM system is more efficient because jobs are given to the users with predefined rules. In the past, the data was provided in text-only format; but the new BPM system displays the entire 16-step process at a glance, as well as the priority and status of each process, whether it is on-time, earlier than scheduled, or delayed. This has significantly improved business productivity.

Outer-assembly management of ship blocks is a complex process and, frequently, there are changes, corrections and adjustments made during the process. With the introduction of the BPM system, our process management became more efficient, and the on-time completion ratio of outsourced production has improved. Also, the development of an Improvement Request System using BizFlow is nearing completion at SHI; this system will address the problems and challenges that arise in design processes at production facilities. We are further planning to apply this system to other business processes, in order to fully utilize the advantages of BPM technology.

KEY MOTIVATIONS FOR INSTALLING A BPM PLATFORM

The shipbuilding business is capital-intensive, involving many processes and requiring cutting-edge production technologies. Among these technologies, information management is more important than anything else. As the global economy recovers and strengthens, it is reasonable to expect increased international trade volumes, increased marine oil exploration and use of natural gas, and, as a result, increased demand for shipbuilding. As the Japanese shipbuilding industry has declined amid increasing Chinese competition, Korea is expected to lead the world in shipbuilding for the foreseeable future.

Following our strategy of industry dominance and accommodating the increased production capacity required by favorable market conditions, we developed large block fabrication methods and expanded the outsourcing of block fabrication. However, we recognized that industry leadership also entailed strengthening the company's core competencies in sales, design, and production technologies—as well as internal information management, communications, and collaboration with our global industry partners.

Why did we implement the BPM technology?

SHI's Geoje Shipyard has a production capacity of 40-50 ships per year, and Geoje enjoys an excellent internal production management system. However, with an expanded production schedule of 52 ships for 2006, Geoje's collaboration with outsourcing companies has recently become a production management priority.

The single most important factor calling for improvements in our work environment was the sudden increase in outsourced fabrication volume. SHI recorded an outsourced fabrication volume of 150,000 tons in 2002, but this volume more than doubled to 320,000 tons in 2004, placing a substantially heavier load on the outsourced contractors.

In addition, our decision to implement a large block fabrication system increased the number of work items to be managed. This increase in the number of work items and the order volume significantly strained the systematic management of the production schedule, creating schedule conflicts between internal and outsourced production. The resulting delay and confusion only exacerbated problems that arose in material supply and outsourced production delivery.

The lack of calculation and verification of special order volume, delays and failure in delivering designs, and unclear assignment of internal and outsourcing production tasks created situations in which orders were not issued in a timely fashion. The increase of in-yard shipping and management costs, production delays stemming from delays in material supply for the outsourced contractors, and the lack of systematic management of the materials called for a new internal control system.

We wanted to streamline communications with outsourced contractors and create an internal control system for easy management of our business processes. With these considerations in-hand, we turned to BPM technology to standardize and visualize the entire business process from order placement to account settlement.

What is SHI's goal with BPM technology?

SHI planned to standardize the business process related to outsourced production through the implementation of a BPM platform. The processes — ranging from contract signing to account settlement — will be shared internally and with outsourcing contractors. Using the visual step-by-step management system, total collaboration with outsourced contractors will be established.

The goals of implementing the BPM system are management of the business processes, management of outsourcing and designs generated through the network, management of the segmented production process, and transparent contract and account settlement processes.

- Business Process Management (BPM)
  - Standardized business processes and graphical step-by-step progress status
  - New task notification (provide portal site for process management for individuals)
  - Improved process management using task-start notification and delay alarm
  - Problem prevention through the registration and sharing of prior problems and solutions
- Material and Network Design Documents Management
  - Material supply system and supporting IT system management (including VMI)
  - Supply management of raw materials, subsidiary materials, and rigging and finishing materials (management of on-time delivery and part shortage records for each pallet)
  - Online design drawings management
- Segmented Production Process Management
  - Process commencement and completion records management
  - Daily progress management per WBS
  - Work transfer records management using e-TEAMS
- Transparent Contract Terms and Account Settlement Management
  - Pre-assignment of outsourcing contractors based on work volume
  - Build-to-order order system
  - Online management of delivery confirmation and account settlement based on inspection records and work transfer documents
  - Electronic tax documents integrated with e-certification based on the received inventory amount

Why did we choose BizFlow?

To achieve our goal of becoming a Digital & Shipbuilding industry leader, we carefully reviewed several BPM products for their ease-of-use and seamless system integration. Our BPM project team (consisting of seven staff members) reviewed and assessed likely BPM platforms over a period of six months, from October 2003 to April 2004.

HandySoft's BizFlow Business Process Management platform received the highest rating in its potential to satisfy our business requirements and deliver a fully integrated BPM technology platform.

The following were the selection criteria for SHI's BPM technology initiative:
- Server performance and the structures proven at a reference site for a large number of users and the given system environment.
- Reference sites for similar implementations.
- Does it satisfy the detailed requirements for the workflow of Samsung Heavy Industries?
- Does it meet the business environment and corporate culture in Korea and does it provide user-friendly interface for visual process monitoring?
- Does it provide template modification functionality that enables changes to the processes on the fly?
- Does it provide various search functions for completed processes and does it provide detail view functions for search results?
- The capability of the vendor to successfully complete with skilled technical staffs and implementation experiences.
- The possibility of consistent technical support for system upgrades, optimization, and expansion of the functions in terms of financial stability and the technological capability.
- Integration and interface with the current and planned infrastructure.
- Does it provide refined and easy API for the expansion of processes in the future?

THE OVERALL BUSINESS INNOVATION

Prior to implementation of the BizFlow BPM system, an analysis of problems and possible improvements for SHI's business processes was performed. We interviewed 28 outsourcing contractors in September 2003, and identified problems related to the outsourcing contractors. Starting in October 2003, our BPM project team conducted five workshops with a total of 80 employees over a period of a month and a half, defining likely business process improvement targets. The project began on October 24, 2003, and took six months to develop and test applications and train end users.

The quantitative and qualitative achievements of SHI's business innovation using BPM are as follows:

Quantitative Effects

The quantitative effects can be summarized by looking at process improvements:
- Increased Reputation and Credibility (with Collaboration System):
  - Automatic generation and transfer of the POR data in each process
  - Increased reliability between the companies because of the automatic generation of the delivery confirmation based on the actual results
  - Transparent management of the account settlement process using electronic delivery documents
- Process Synchronization
  - Real-time management of work processes among various departments
  - Task and problem management for each staff member
  - Management of the workloads, bottlenecks, and problem types
- Minimization of Paperwork
  - Electronic data processing of the work schedule, order requests, work transfer documents, delivery documents, account settlement agreements, and material check-out documents

Qualitative Effects

The qualitative effects can be summarized by looking at the increase in productivity:

- Business Process Improvement
  - Efforts and Time reduction in order placement, POR, delivery document management , and daily progress management
- Decrease in production cost
  - Increased productivity with increased outsourcing volume
  - Reduction in management time
  - Increase in the outsourced production
  - Reduction in the material selection and searching

THE OVERALL *TECHNOLOGICAL* INNOVATION

SHI achieved three major technological innovations with the new BPM solution:

- Work processes were centralized with the work portal. User convenience was significantly improved by introducing easy-to-use, one-point access to the various current systems. SHI can now provide the optimum work environment, the Work Portal, with the implementation of integrated work environment, where file attachment and various electronic communication exchanges are available.
- Development productivity was improved and repair and maintenance was made easier with the separation of business processes from application logic, which simplifies necessary application developments. Furthermore, the simplified application logic made modular application components possible.
- Future expansion was made possible by the selection of the standardized integration method between existing systems and the database.

Other technological achievements can be summarized as follows:

- Progress monitoring and user interface enables tracking of various processes and histories.
- Graphic map of progress monitoring shows each process progress using graphs and statistical data.
- The "change" function can dynamically change processes on the fly.
- Team members can design processes by themselves.
- Document management was automated using routing function.
- Work request and results management processes were completely automated.
- Business process bottlenecks were eliminated.

THE SYSTEM USERS AND WHAT THEIR JOBS NOW ENTAIL COMPARED TO PRE-INSTALLATION

The status of the BPM system can be summarized as follows:

Criteria	Details
Total users	600
Concurrent users	50 (average), 200 (Peak Time)
Installation location	Samsung Heavy Industries : HQ, Geoje shipyard Outsourcing contractors
Outsourcing block fabrication process	Annual total completed transactions : 23000 cases Average monthly pending transactions: 2000 cases

Compared with the previous system, the current BPM system is more complete, systematic, and automated. It provides a simplified workflow as well as management of all processes related to the outsourcing through the integration of existing systems including materials, production, and design systems.

Previously, users had to rely on their best judgment when navigating through the system; but the current system actively displays data to the user with predefined rules, making navigation much easier. The integration of various interdepartmental processes shows all processes in a single screen, preventing delays and reducing time required for corrective actions.

The Geoje Shipyard staff and outsourcing contractors employ user IDs and passwords to access the process portal, **mySingle**. The big difference between the old system and the new one is that users had to "find their way" to their processes in the past, whereas the new system automatically presents processes to the users on-screen.

With the prior systems, users logged in and "found their way" by clicking through menus. For other tasks, the user had to go back to the main menu, starting from the beginning. Now, with the login to the *mySingle* system, integrated with the BPM system, the tasks are presented with the tasks for the day and to-do items presented clearly in advance.

In addition, data integrated with each system is presented on the screen with a single click. The data used to be presented in text only, but the new system shows all 16 processes in a single screen. Each process is shown as on-time, early, or delayed using numbers. The system uses client-server architecture for internal users, and outsourcing contractors can access the system through the Web.

The major functions of new application are as follows:
- Electronic Management of Outsourcing Contractors & e-TEAMS Quantity Assignment
  - Early assignment of contractors based on standardized contractor information (production jobs, factor, manufacturing method, etc.).
  - Automatic calculation of e-TEAMS volume using the interface with the legacy system.
- Material Supply System Management (Creating N/W Design Document)
  - Carrying out of function according to the material supply system.
  - Issuing electronic transfer documents using barcodes and e-TEAMS information.
  - Transfer function using barcodes on the carrying-out documents.
  - Creation of design documents through the network drawing.
- Segmented Process Management for Each Business Process Unit
  - Segmented process management function, integrating the material receipt information.
  - Real-time progress management function integrated with the inspection records.
- Transparent Account Settlement Using Electronic Delivery Documents
  - Electronic delivery (delivery details) document request/receipt/authorization function.
  - Real-time shipping and receiving, and account settlement management function.
  - Electronic tax documents.
  - Correction request function for additional tasks or mistakes.
  - Correction request and account settlement agreement.

The following screen captures are provided for easier understanding of the BPM system:

Process Management

- Graphic presentation of the outsourcing process and real-time management of process progress.
- Maximized productivity through sharing of the status information among staffs and departments.

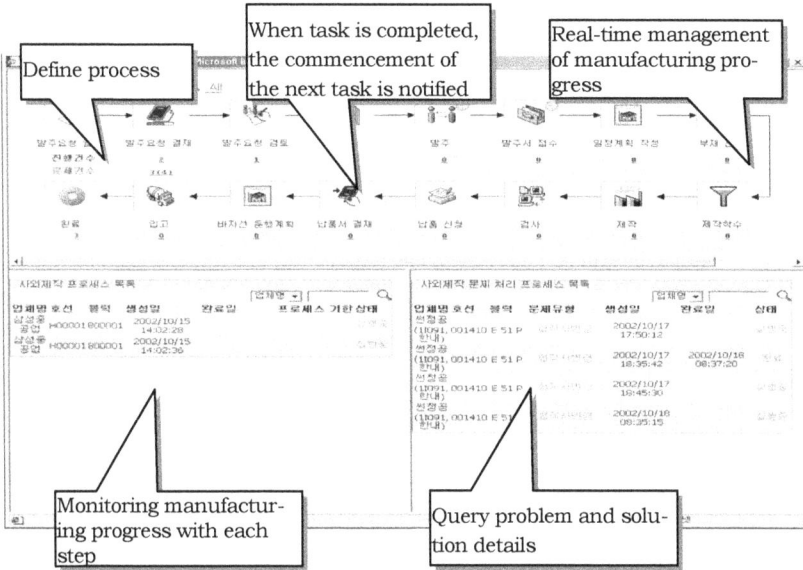

Define process

When task is completed, the commencement of the next task is notified

Real-time management of manufacturing progress

Monitoring manufacturing progress with each step

Query problem and solution details

Individual Staff Task Management:

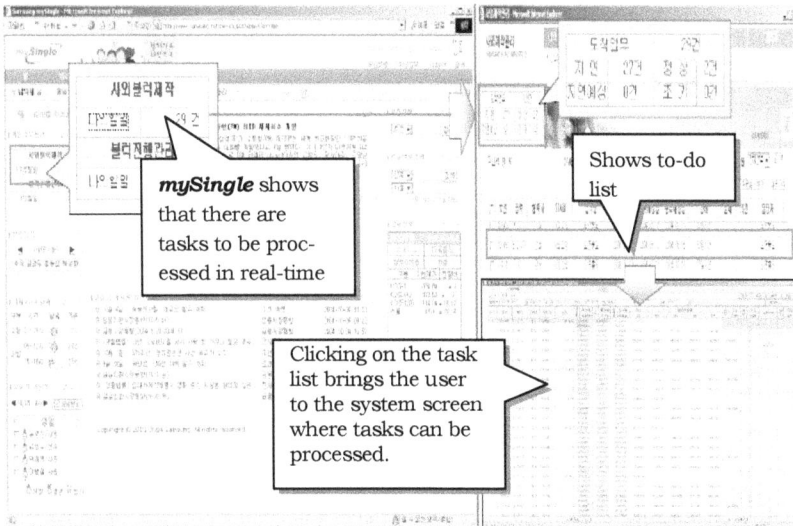

mySingle shows that there are tasks to be processed in real-time

Shows to-do list

Clicking on the task list brings the user to the system screen where tasks can be processed.

- *mySingle* automatically recognizes the tasks to be processed.
- Portal function for processing individual's tasks.
- *mySingle* shows that there are tasks to be processed in real-time.
- Clicking on the task list brings the user to the system screen where tasks can be processed.

Alarm System Management

- Block fabrication process management is reinforced using work commencement notifications and delay warnings.

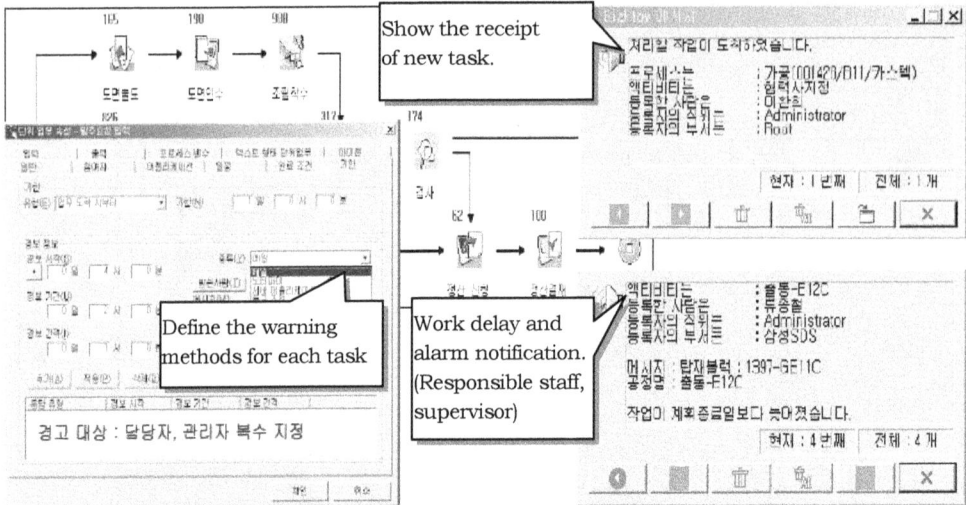

Show the receipt of new task.

Define the warning methods for each task

Work delay and alarm notification. (Responsible staff, supervisor)

경고 대상 : 담당자, 관리자 복수 지정

Problem Registration and Sharing Management

- Notes and problems for each business process step can be registered and managed so that staff members can share the information and prevent/solve problems early on.

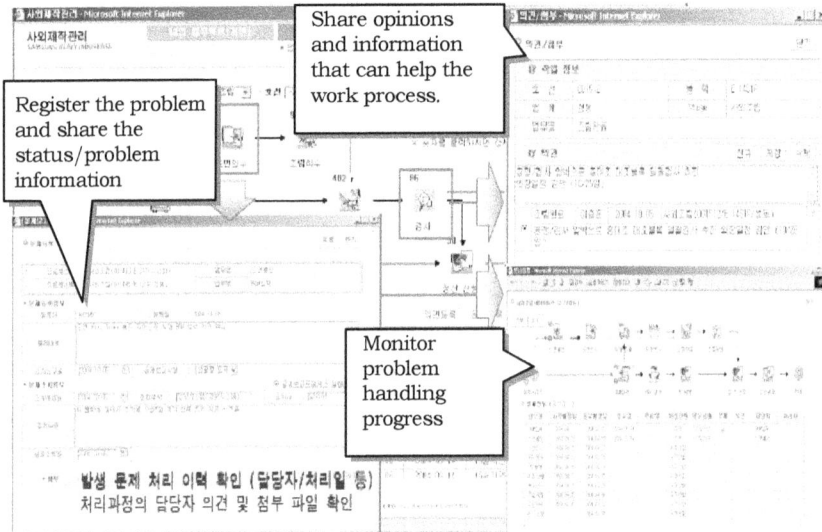

Share opinions and information that can help the work process.

Register the problem and share the status/problem information

Monitor problem handling progress

발생 문제 처리 이력 확인 (담당자/처리일 등)
처리과정의 담당자 의견 및 첨부 파일 확인

Result Analysis Management

Processed task result information can be used to analyze the work load, bottlenecks, and problem types for each work unit to achieve optimized business process.

협력사별 분석 그래프

업무 단위별 분석 그래프

지연 일자별 분석 그래프

Work Processing Result Analysis. Number of items processed, delayed items, process time, problem types, etc.

다양한 레포트 기능 지원

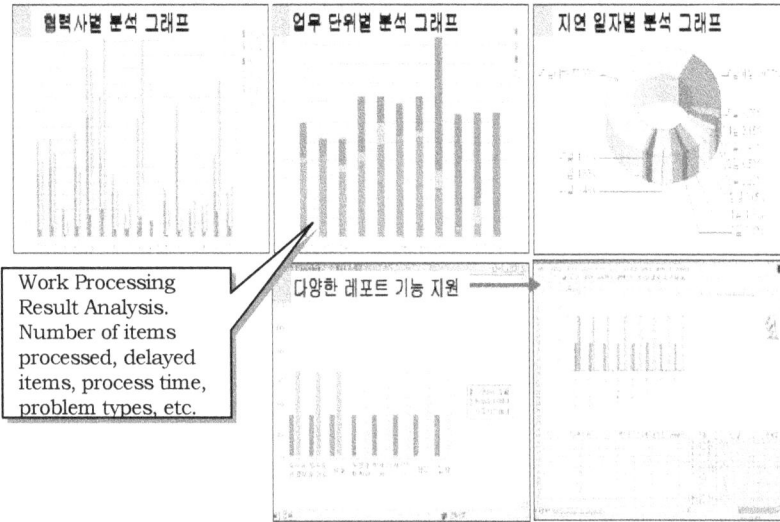

THE BIGGEST HURDLES OVERCOME IN MANAGEMENT, BUSINESS AND TECHNOLOGY

Obstacles and solutions of implementing the BPM system are categorized as follows:

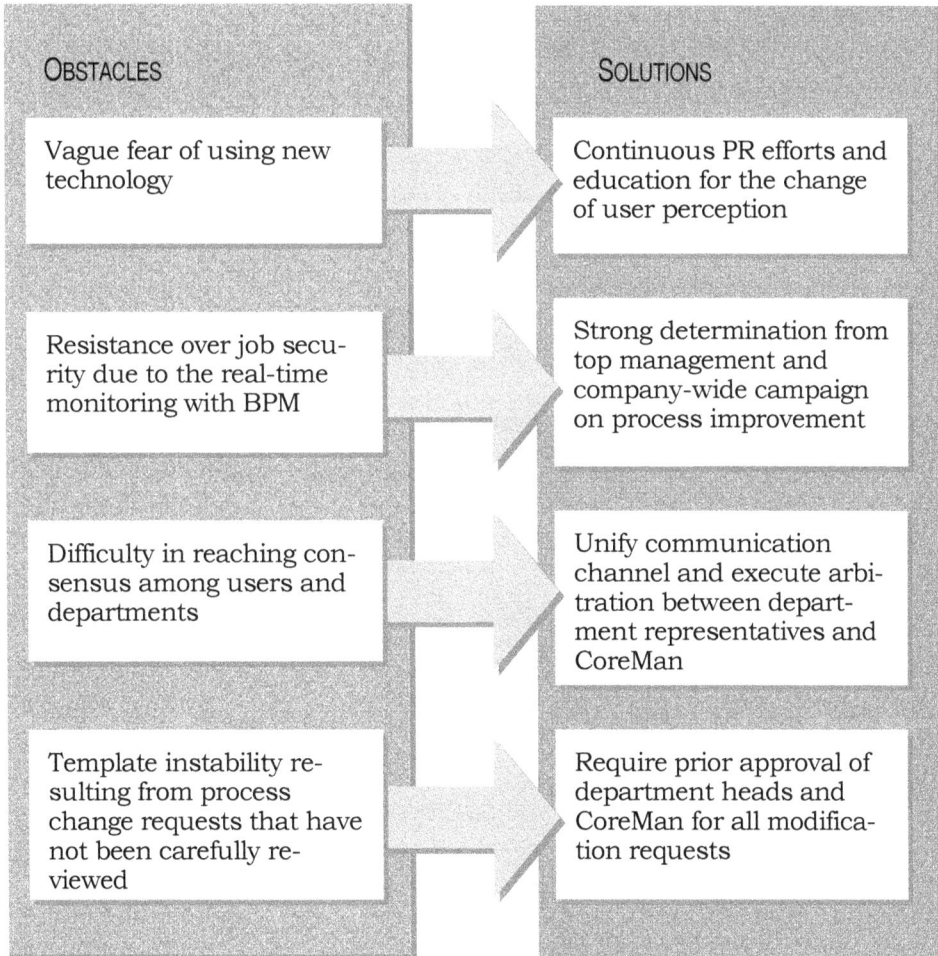

OBSTACLES	SOLUTIONS
Vague fear of using new technology	Continuous PR efforts and education for the change of user perception
Resistance over job security due to the real-time monitoring with BPM	Strong determination from top management and company-wide campaign on process improvement
Difficulty in reaching consensus among users and departments	Unify communication channel and execute arbitration between department representatives and CoreMan
Template instability resulting from process change requests that have not been carefully reviewed	Require prior approval of department heads and CoreMan for all modification requests

Explanations of initial and ongoing efforts to address obstacles encountered before, during, and after BPM implementation are outlined below:

First, the central considerations prior to application of the BPM system:
- Management of the process progress using monitoring functions with an easy-to-use user interface.
- Providing graphic statistical data related to the process progress history.
- Flexibility for changes to the process in progress.
- Integration with the existing systems, resulting in easier work and reduction of labor costs.

Next, the obstacles addressed during implementation of the BPM system:
- Preparation of the usable process through effective analysis of the business process.
- Tight interface with the existing system.
- Drawing a user-friendly interface system.
- Prevention of system speed reduction due to the addition of many functions.

Finally, the items to be managed continuously:
- Continuous improvement of the process by monitoring its progress history.
- Increase in the process management capability of the actual users.
- Examination of the possibility of connecting processes of subsidiaries and outsourcing contractors.

THE NEW SYSTEM CONFIGURATION

The following is the network and hardware diagram of the BPM system:

BPM Server Specifications (including DB Server)

Category	System Configuration
BPM Server	<ul><li>IBM RS6000<ul><li>12 CPU</li><li>28 GB Main Memory</li><li>ESS SHARK DISK 1 TB</li></ul></li></ul>

BPM System Software and Application Interface Components

Category	Model	Version	Usage
OS	AIX	4.3.3.11	System operation
DB	Oracle	8.1.7.4	BPM data repository
BPM System	HandySoft's BizFlow	8.7.1.4	
Language	Java, JSP		

COST SAVINGS, INCREASED REVENUES, AND PRODUCTIVITY IMPROVEMENTS

The results obtained by Samsung Heavy Industries using the BizFlow BPM platform are summarized in the table below:

Category	Improvement Details

Cost Savings Shown in USD per year	• Process improvement
	  • Order- and POR-related time reduction: $163,000
	  • Product delivery doc management time reduction: $196,000
	• Cost reduction
	  • Management time reduction: $845,000
	  • Increase in the outsourcing production volume: $2,520,000
	  • Material selection/search time reduction: $338,000
	• Total cost reduction of US $4.4 million a year

Increased Revenues	• Currently, there are three years' worth of orders. To meet the increase in order volume and to solve the problems related to increased volume such as production space, facilities, and labor, integrated outsourcing block fabrication can be used to implement continuous collaboration with contractors. The market share is expected to increase continuously, contributing to an increase in net profits.

Productivity Improvement	• POR generation time reduction
	  • **Before** Data gathering: seven days; POR generation: 10 days
	  • **After** Data gathering: one day (automatic generation); POR generation: one day
	• Daily operation time reduction
	  • **Before** Operation info gathering: four hours; paperwork: one hour
	  • **After** Operation info gathering time: one hour; No paperwork
	• Reduction of time in delivery document & account settlement
	  • **Before** Delivery document issue seven days; settlement: four days
	  • **After** Delivery document issue: one day; settlement: one day
	• Segmented process management
	  • **Before** Results were managed manually
	  • **After** Results are managed electronically
	• Transparent account settlement process based on inspection results
	  • **Before** Account settlement based on manual result compilations
	  • **After** Transparent account settlement based on inspection results (electronic delivery records and tax documents)

COMPETITIVE ADVANTAGES GAINED

The outsourcing production process was complex, entailing frequent changes that made management difficult. The competitive advantages we achieved resulted from efficient management of the process, and improved ratio of on-time outsourcing production process completion. The *e-ouTEr Assembly Management System* (e-TEAMS) was the first application of BPM technology in the Korean shipbuilding industry, and we expect our market share to make gains through differentiation from the competitors and increased customer satisfaction.

The competitive advantages obtained through the integration of the BPM system, our existing system and the Web interface are as follows:

First, the improvement of the corporate image:
- Improved corporate competitiveness
- Maximization of the PR effects
- Becoming the leader in the industry for IT system implementation
- Streamlined communication channel and collaboration system with contractors

Next, the creation of the new business relationships:
- To achieve a competitive advantage with low-cost labor, the company is strategically restructuring the e-TEAMS to suit the needs of SHI Ningbo in China, in order to accommodate its expansion of production capacity.
- Outsourcing contractors are planning a collaborative implementation of ERP system with us, through integration with SHI's e-TEAMS.

IMMEDIATE AND LONG-TERM PLANS TO SUSTAIN COMPETITIVE ADVANTAGE

By expanding the application of our BPM system as outlined below, we will strengthen our leadership in the industry and improve our competitiveness.

Our short-term plan for application expansion is as follows:
- Integration of disconnected business processes between existing systems using the BizFlow BPM system.
- Project-wide systematic management using a portal site based on the BPM system.
- Integration of personal tasks with portal functions using *mySingle* and legacy system.

Our long-term plans for application expansion are:
- Extend BPM technology to affiliated companies.
- Develop application of outdoors process management for shipyard.

In the future, we plan to apply the BizFlow BPM system to all business processes at Samsung Heavy Industries for process visualization, making the BizFlow BPM system an even more valuable asset. We will not only expand our application of the BPM system to various business processes among partners, but will also make the BPM technology a framework for our IT system.

Section 5

South America

Allianz, Vehicle Insurance Operation, Colombia Division

Gold Award 2006, South America; nominated by Bizagi, Colombia

EXECUTIVE SUMMARY

This document describes the successful implementation of the Allianz Colombia BPM model on the vehicle insurance division "The Power on Your Side." Today, the system has literally given the power to third parties involved on the business; engaging agents, brokers, CNCs, call centers, work shops, lawyers and the back office in more than 1.500 activities starting from the underwriting of the policy until the disbursement of a claim. This has increased the integration, visibility, productivity and profitability of the whole operation of the auto-insurance Allianz Colombia division.

THE DRIVING FORCES BEHIND THE PROJECT

"The Power on Your Side" began in 1999 when the Automobile Insurance Division CEO Aaron Ossias—looking forward to reduce costs, increase the quality in customer service, increase productivity and visibility—enforced a transition to establish an operation where third parties (suppliers, outsourcing, distribution channels, etc.) involved on the Allianz Auto Insurance business played a major role in the operation.

Allianz Colombia project leaders identified that there were two core processes that could be remodeled in order to obtain a cost reduction and an efficiency increase in customer service. Those processes were the underwriting and the claims/disbursement process.

The project was launched nation wide, with the integration of more than 100 workshops, 395 agents, 65 CNC and several external lawyers' offices.

Innovation to Reduce Complexity

Empower the third parties in the development of an optimized and integrated operation system was not an easy job. The system was implemented in a series of phases that began with the automation of all the claims process in 2003. This one included more than 84 principal processes, sub process, modules and multiple sub process for a total of 1171 activities. The implementation included three principal kinds of claims; Collision, Loss and third party insurance. One case may have multiple combinations of these processes depending on the existence of a damage, robbery, injury, etc. These combinations resulted in more than 17 kinds of processes increasing the complexity of the system.

The need of integrating all the car shops, external lawyers, outsourced and internal information of the auto insurance claims process was a big challenge in order to make a clean process for the final client and for Allianz. The commitment and the training strategy of the organization played a major role to successfully make everybody interact with the system and embrace all the parties on the process.

Implementation of the Process Claims

The process began with the call center; they receive and charge the information from the policy owner and the claim. The system locates and assigns a work shop according to the information taken from the client and the internal information allocate it through BizAgi from the different system organizations.

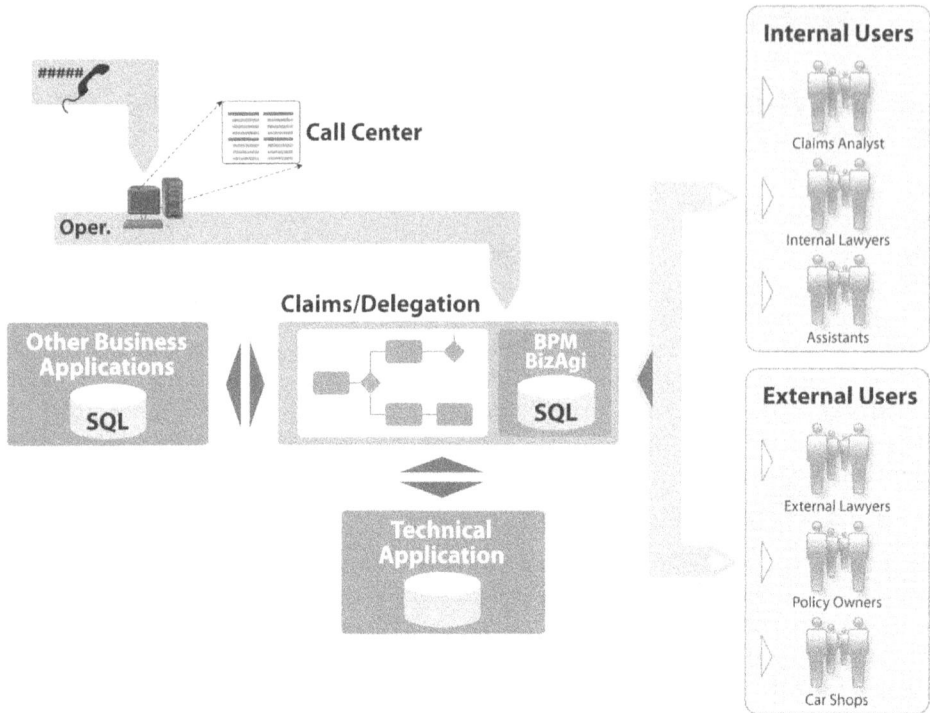

The workshops' participation on the process allowed them to actively offer a better service to the owners of the policy. Updated information about costs of repair, status of the repair, car damage evaluation, etc. are included on the system on time basis so the insurance company and the final client can successfully track the status of the claim process.

Thanks to the integration made through BizAgi with the car shop system, the claim user is also able to look via Internet the pictures of the car taken on the car shop and an estimate of the reparation end date.

At the same time, external lawyers are notified via web on the pending legal tasks of the process; the tasks included in the process have the necessary information to let the external lawyer start the correspondent subsequent legal activity. All legal information generated around a claim has to be charged on the system (visits to the courts, conciliation meetings, etc.). The implementation also allows that in the moment of a decision on the court, the system is able to proceed according to what the law implies.

This information offers Allianz two big benefits: On one side, all the activities done by the external lawyer are effectively send through BizAgi to the payments system of Allianz; enhancing the exact disbursement according to the amount of services of the outsourced. On the other side, BizAgi allows a constant flow of information between the third party and the system; increasing the visibility for the client, the claims analyst and the agents who are now able to measure number and amount of their claims.

On the internal side of the company, the claims analyst receive all the organization via web so they not longer have to worry for the status of all the documentation and the assignation of tasks according to an old and not pragmatic process schema. Their labor was significantly concentrated now on the evaluation and analysis of all the claims cases.

The main factors that allowed the successful implementation and integration of the third parties on the process were two: Concentration on maintaining always the big picture of the auto insurance business, and focusing on the consistency of the information and the contact points with the client and the organization. This allowed analyst to focus on core business areas and process.

IMPACT ON THE CLAIMS PROCESS

Competitive Advantages on the claims process due to the implementation of BizAgi:

- Claim evaluation via Internet (workshops and lawyers charges information and pictures for clients, agents and Allianz follow up)
- Reduction on time for the repair process decreasing the devolution end date car claim.
- Exact payment for third parties like car shops and external lawyers
- Reduction on times (from three to one day claims analyst)
- Reduction of unnecessary job positions (data assistants and operators)

Benefits:

- 100 percent operation control.
- Total unification of processes.
- Development of business rules and politics standards.
- Service Optimization

Underwriting

The second phase of "The Power on Your Side" involved the organization and optimization of all the vehicle policy issue at Allianz. The project began as part of the effort to reduce costs and increase the competitive advantage of the auto insurance line in the Colombian market. The project team and the direction of the line identified that the issue system could delegate the major operation of the quotation and the endorsement to the third parties involved in the operation. Those parties are all the distribution channels for the vehicle line (brokers, agents, CNC and Car shops).

The policy issue and underwriting involved more than 400 activities in more than 13 process and sub processes divided in:

- FYP policy
- Endorsement
- Individual Renewal
- Group Renewal
- Pre-renewal Individual
- Pre-renewal Group
- Consultancy and activation of the policy
- Group policy Negotiation
- New Group Business
- New Individual Business
- Inspection
- Group business renegotiation.

The system enhances the broker to quote and endorse almost all new individual car policy without the support and help of the underwriting analyst or assistance of Allianz. This feature gave the third parties the autonomy and efficiency to deliver a fast and excellent client service.

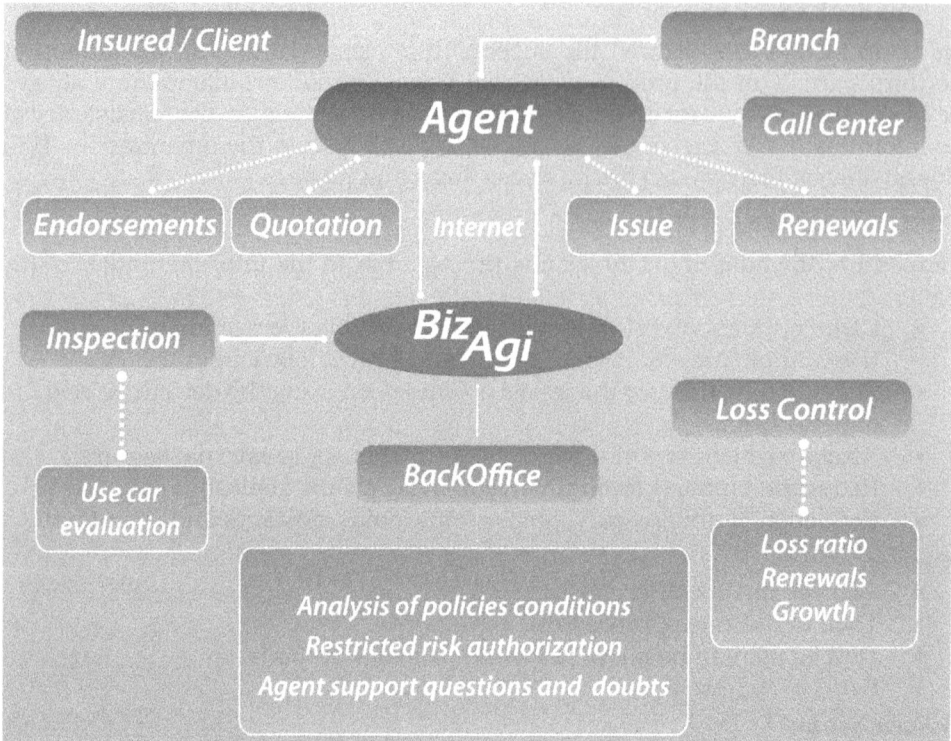

The process began with the insurance agent or CNC who work with the Internet portal to charge all the vehicle information and the coverage selection. The system, through different business rules developed in BizAgi (according to the coverage and conditions of the products), establish if the coverage choice of the agent and vehicle information are correct.

Following the analysis, the system allows the agent to analyze the quote according with the information charge. The agent or the broker is immediately ready to print an insurance application form to the client. Once the application is complete the system interacts with the different internal and external systems of the company making a risk analysis for the application and finally issuing the policy. BizAgi allows the agent to check all the documents and send alerts for the receipt and policy payment.

ISSUES

The implementation of the underwriting process included the creation of the endorsement process; in this process a group or individual policy already issue, could be modified at different levels: Data of the policy, data of vehicles for group policies, or new vehicles to add in group policies.

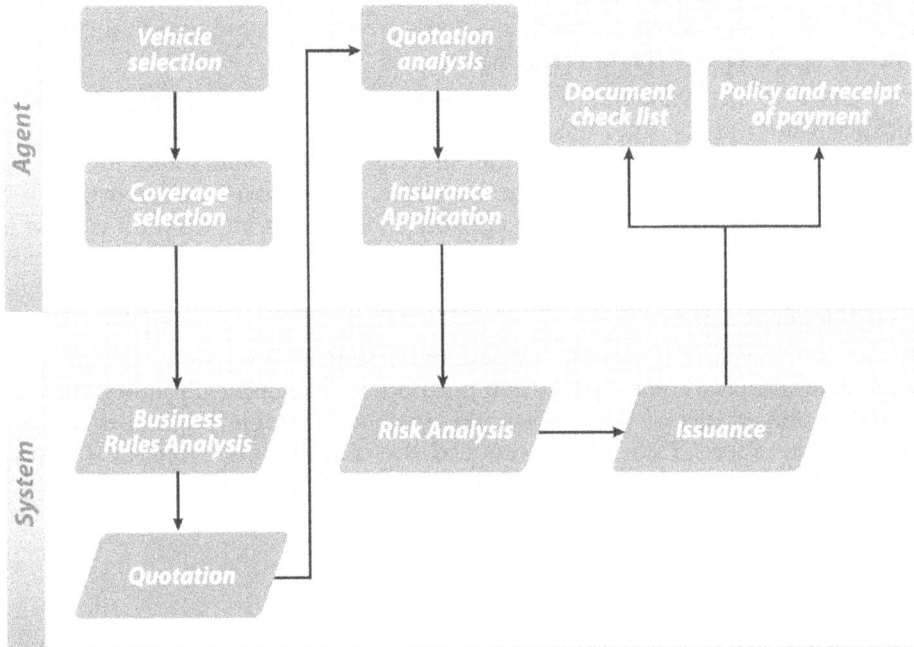

Adding new vehicles to an already-issued policy through the system enhanced the agents' ability and the insurance company to reduce documentation and times of approval. In this process, the insurance company delegates most of the tasks to the agent reducing their participation to the analysis and approval of the changes as seen here.

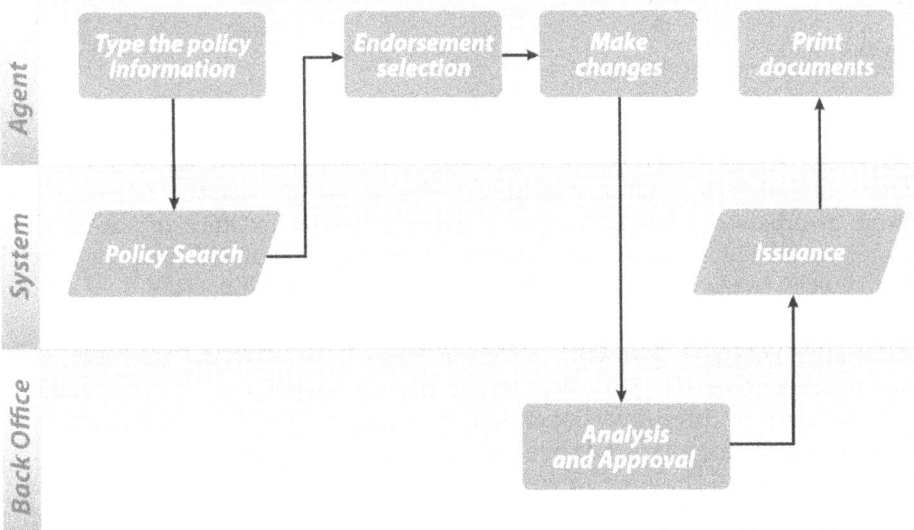

The Backoffice is integrated to the Renewal, pre-renewal and re-negotiation of policies processes through the endorsement as seen on diagrams three and four. The renewal processes are generated automatically close to the maturity date of the policy; the system creates pending tasks to internal and external users who are in charge of contact the policies owners.

For all cases, BizAgi validates all the vehicles information (coverage, conditions, insurance value, policy age, risk evaluation, robbery information, maturity and expedition dates, etc.) and at the same time all the risk validations for the business (total value of the policy on the business, Profit and Loss analysis for the total group policy, total risk of the group policy, etc.). This information is open and clean for the agent and the insurance company enhancing the reduction on service times, costs at backoffice operations and profitability of the business obtaining a better client service.

The implementation of the quotation and endorsement process for group policies enhanced Allianz and their distribution partners to automatically charge the basic information for groups of vehicles in one single and simple process through the use of a quote sheet. This feature reduced the underwriting time for a group of 1000 vehicles from two or three weeks to seven hours (one day).

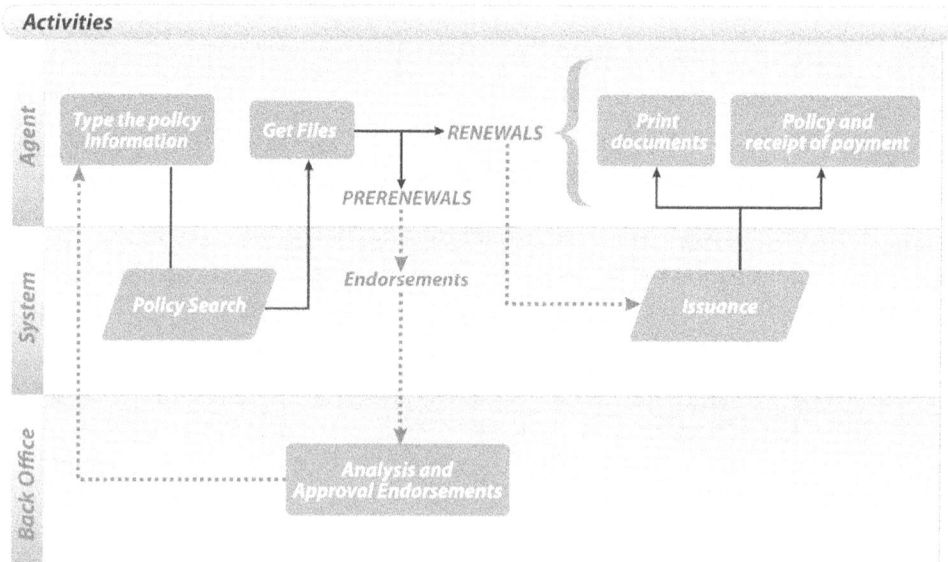

System integration and manage of information in groups allowed Allianz to handle large numbers of vehicles in group policies. The BackOffice or the broker is now able to add or modified the coverage on group using different criteria like kind of vehicle, brand, model, circulation zone, coverage value, etc.

Impact on the Underwriting Process

- Single Policies Underwriting: This is the time between the quotation and the reception of the physical policy, without inspection. Time reduction from two or three days depending on the amount of work that could have the insurance office to five minutes.
- Fleet Policies Underwriting: This is the time between the quotation and the reception of the physical policy, without inspection. Time reduction from two or three days depending on the amount of work that could have the insurance office to three hours depending on the amount of vehicles.

- Renewals: This is the time between the automatic renewal done by the core system, and the physical reception of the policy. Time reduction from two or three days to immediately.
- Endorsements: This is the time between the agent's requirement and the reception of the physical document. Time reduction from one or two days depending on the amount of work that could have the insurance office.
- Inspection: This is the time between the generation of the inspection order and the reception by the workshop, and the time between the sending of the information by the workshop, and the reception by the insurance company. Reduction time from one to three days depending on the city to immediately.
- The reduction of time was accompanied by a reduction of unnecessary jobs (more than 10) increasing the productivity and efficiency of the whole operation area.
- The reduction of costs and times, and the increase of efficiency in client service and policy issue are beginning to represent increase of revenues for the vehicle insurance line.

Basic System Configuration

Hardware Components

1 Server	Xeon 2.5Ghz	36GB	2 GB	Web Server
1 Server	Xeon 2.5Ghz	36GB	2 GB	Application Server
1 Server	Xeon 2.5Ghz	70GB RAID	2 GB	Database Datawarehouse
1 Server	Xeon 2.5Ghz	200GB RAID	1 GB	File Server

Software Components
- Windows 2000 or Windows 2003
- IIS - Internet Information Services
- .net Framework v1.1
- SQL Server 2000 or SQL Server 2000
- Enterprise if there is Data base Cluster
- SQL Server 2000 Service Pack 3
- SQL Analysis Services 2000
- SQL Analysis Services 2000 SP3

COMPETITIVE ADVANTAGE

Previously the insurance vehicle line of Allianz was just beginning to develop a continuous improvement of their processes. The integration of indicators and measure standards to the claims process system with BizAgi (unknown information before the implementation and in course of implementation at this time) will allow the organization to truly optimize their processes and improve their efficiency reducing costs, times and improving client service.

At this moment, most of the underwriting individual processes have been implemented and executed, but still some of the processes on the group policy issue project have not been definitively implemented. The automation of the group underwriting processes will allow Allianz to effectively reduce the difference on the share of participation in the vehicle insurance portfolio between the individual and the group policies. The goal of Allianz Colombia division is to reach a 50 percent share in order to decrease the dependence on the group policies as it is today in the organization and in the market industry standard.

At the same time, the complete automation of the underwriting process will bring the company the opportunity to measure the efficiency, the increase of productivity and the increase on the new and renewal policies issued due to the system implementation.

Allianz have reached competitive advantages in the industry by the increase of productivity, efficiency and client service through the implementation of BizAgi in the project "The Power on Your Hands". It is the only insurance company that effectively engages all its partners in the efficiency of the operation; but this is just the beginning. Allianz and their partners are finding the way to develop the continuous improvement through the measure and analysis of their integration process operation. This will bring to the multinational firm the way to sustain and increase the competitive advantage already reached.

METROVÍAS, Argentina

Finalist 2006, South America; nominated by PECTRA Technology, Inc., USA

EXECUTIVE SUMMARY

METROVÍAS is a company that operates a major public transportation net in Buenos Aires city, Argentina. The net comprises five subway lines, two streetcar branches and one railroad branch. Nowadays, METROVÍAS has 3,000 employees working on 70Kms of rails through 108 stations and yearly carries 300 million passengers in its 692 cars.

METROVÍAS started operating on January 1st 1994 facing the challenge of changing a traditionally deficit activity into an efficient and profitable business. By applying modern and competitive entrepreneurial criteria, according to the theories of contemporary management, METROVÍAS strives to turn the service into a customer-oriented one.

Taking into account a strategic need, in 2002 the company decided to carry out process reengineering, based on technological innovation, facing important projects. The first project was based in optimizing the organizational structure, taking advantage of all the knowledge and information that flow within it, and updating and making more efficient the existent technological infrastructure. The second one, launching the first smart card for electronic payment of subway tickets in Latin America, thus implementing the first electronic wallet, which replaces cash and is also used for commercial transactions.

In order to do so, METROVíAS acquires PECTRA BPM's set of tools working it as an integrator for all applications.

"The integral solution offered by PECTRA BPM has provided us with major benefits, not only to our employees, but also to 300 millions passengers per year we assist," President of METROVIAS, Alberto Verra states. "The amount of rejected debits decreased by 40 percent, due to PECTRA; and nowadays the reload procedure, was reduced from 72 hours to five minutes."

OVERVIEW

In 1993, through a tender organized by the State of Argentina, METROVÍAS wins the concession of the passengers transportation public network, that entailed a total investment in remodeling and improvement works for about 1,800 millions dollars. Hence, the company committed to operatively and commercially explode trains and associated facilities and to carry out an investment program.

METROVÍAS started operating on January 1st, 1994 facing the challenge of changing a traditionally deficit activity into an efficient and profitable business. By applying modern and competitive entrepreneurial criteria, accordant to the theories of contemporary management, METROVÍAS strives to turn the service into a customer-oriented one.

Today, METROVÍAS integrates the Nova Metro Benchmarking (www.nova-metros.org), a program of international railway benchmarking, made up of a consortium of thirteen medium sized metro systems from around the world - Buenos Aires, Dublin, Glasgow, Hong Kong (KCRC), Lisbon, Montréal, Naples, Newcastle, Rio de Janeiro, Santiago de Chile, Singapore, Taipei and Toronto; and also

METROVÍAS is an active member of Alamys (www.alamys.org), Asociación Latinoamericana de Metros y Subterráneos.

Taking into account a strategic need, in 2002 the company decided to carry out process reengineering, based on technological innovation, facing important projects. The first project was based in optimizing the organizational structure, taking advantage of all the knowledge and information that flow within it, and updating and making more efficient the existent technological infrastructure. The second project launched the first smart card for electronic payment of subway tickets in Latin America, thus implementing the first electronic wallet, which replaces cash and is also used for commercial transactions.

In order to do so, METROVíAS acquired PECTRA BPM's set of tools working it as an integrator for all applications.

THE KEY BUSINESS MOTIVATIONS BEHIND THE PROJECT.

In 2002 the company decided to carry out process reengineering, based on technological innovation. "METROVÍAS has a mayor strategy mission statement: *efficient management in terms of quality and costs*; that is why we sought to improve the operability and to control each position inside the company in a more efficient manner," President of METROVÍAS Alberto Verra states.

METROVÍAS operates according to an integrated strategy:
- Communicating the strategy and the objectives in clear terms.
- Monitoring the global business strategy.
- Get into focus actions and resources according to critical factors of success.
- Balancing the objectives of short term with the long-range.
- Aligning group and individual objectives to strategic objectives.
- taking advantage of all the knowledge and information that flow within it, and updating and making more efficient the existent technological infrastructure

"The main objectives were to optimize the organizational structure taking advantage of all the knowledge and information that flow within it, and updating and making more efficient the existent technological infrastructure, Verra adds. "Since 2000, we had been working to approach all administrative and management systems from a process-centered point of view (Business Process Management). Hence, a project aiming to define every process took place," Alberto Verra explains. "A new release of ERP systems arises from that project, and so we acquired PECTRA to put that brand new process-centered philosophy into practice." "Also, within the framework of this modernization project, we aimed to implement a technological solution based on the concept of smart cards which were able to replace cash for paying subway tickets and also commercial transactions at associated shops," Verra adds.

The critical economic situation and the lack of cash availability made this project be brought forward, achieving milestones as pre-paid journeys with automated reload through debit or credit card. That was METROVÍAS' answer intended to maintain and to increase the urban transportation market share, by offering the chance of paying journeys without using cash. METROVÍAS faced the challenge of doing massive the use of the new smart card for accessing subway service and for making commercial transactions at associated shops. In order to do so, METROVÍAS developed with PECTRA BPM Suite the infrastructure needed to support the processes. It is worth pointing out that the administrative and management processes of the company involve more than 900 people in continuous interaction. Prominente S.A. (distributor of PECTRA Technology for Argentina) started up the project on May 2002.

THE KEY INNOVATION

Business

"The capability of PECTRA Technology to systematize the most critical processes, enabled the generation of added-value to the business by allowing us to model evaluation instances –Strategic Planning Process– and to digital document management within the organization," Verra highlights. BAM (Business Activity Monitoring) tools of PECTRA BPM Suite allowed improving commercial processes by virtue of real time-available information, accessing in minimal time to the most important business variables for the decision making.

The global project was defined in 2002. It aimed not only to implement PECTRA BPM Suite, but also to change the whole system schema in which PECTRA BPM Suite became the core resource, working as an integrator for all applications, for example, enabling access to the corporate gate, the access point for all systems.

The definition of new business strategies due to the non-stable Argentinean political and financial situation, generated new projects of high technological content

The PECTRA BPM Suite-based infrastructure created, allowed modeling new projects under PECTRA BPM Suite framework. Therefore, a series of projects exclusively based on processes began to come up at METROVÍAS that were rapidly implemented. "As we already had the entire infrastructure organized on PECTRA and the process-centered philosophy well embraced, all those projects took advantage of PECTRA BPM Suite to model, survey, document, develop and implement processes," Verra points out.

It is worth mentioning the market release of the first electronic wallet for means of transport in Latin America, MONEDERO.

MONEDERO
7965 8150 0079 5875
03/03   03/06

The subway users would be able to conveniently pay for their journeys and even buy and pay services at associated shops without using cash. Hence, MONEDERO, the pre-paid smart card, re-loadable through credit and debit cards, was implemented in the beginning of 2003. In order for the passengers to enjoy the benefits of this system, they just need to register at the corresponding subscription points that enable MONEDERO card. The card is issued with no charges at all, even in case of renewal.

1. Acquisition of a non-reloadable card paid cash or through debit card with a pre-determined amount equivalent to 30 journeys. The card must be discarded once the credit is empty.
2. Acquisition of a reloadable card paid cash or through debit card with a pre-determined amount equivalent to 30 journeys; once the credit is consumed, the card is automatically reloaded with the same amount while going through the pinwheel.

The last step was the deployment of new features for the card that allows not only the payment of journeys but also the feasibility of shopping and paying services at associated shops, thus becoming the first electronic wallet in Latin America.

A wide range of shops (associated shops) nowadays offers acquiring and reloading cards through cash and debit or credit cards and also the chance of buying products. Users of the system of transportation count on an extensive range of products to acquire at the shops, called "Subtexpress" (some 40 on the whole Buenos Aires), like phone cards, music CDs, products of esthetics and personal hygiene, food and beverages, books, photo, audio and video, cleaning, etc. In addition, passengers may acquire or reload cards at the ATMs or through the site www.pagomiscuentas.com. The Banelco network has 3,393 ATMs in Argentina.

Some Data about the Project Success

- 25,000 smart cards issued in the first three months.
- 55,000 refills carried out in the same period.
- 1,250,000 people traveled through the transportation net in the same period.
- 8,000 requirements were attended at the contact center.
- 25,000 visits at the website.
- 1,000,000 of daily transactions were processed at that time.

Process

The schema of METROVÍAS' process model comprises Operative Processes (the business core), and some other Assistant Processes that contribute to the company operation.

"Train Traffic"; "Ticket Sale"; and "Customer Service"; were identified as main Operative Processes. "Strategic Planning and Management Control"; "Planning of Operative Cycle—Budgets"; "Maintenance Plan Generation"; "Purchase Planning"; "Supply Management"; "Purchase Management"; "Stocktaking"; "Quality Assurance"; "Administrative Management"; and "Human Resources Management" were identified as Assistant Processes.

"By optimizing the Assistant Processes, we have achieved the improvement of the information related to business results. Thus, by better knowing, analyzing and optimizing the operative models, we have obtained a complete perspective to get the most of the service and to make it more efficient, allowing to build up user loyalty," Gonzalo Rueda, Development Manager of Prominente S.A. states. "Defining processes considered as sequences of activities linking suppliers and customers, was an important benefit, generating added-value for the inputs and getting outputs that meet both customer's and enterprise's needs," he concludes.

The process-oriented schema enabled the segmentation of the organization into key areas. "PECTRA Designer tool based on a friendly graphic methodology certainly contributed to this perspective," Gonzalo Rueda points out. "The organization was defined as a macro process and critical processes, those contributing with added-value, were identified. The subprocesses were then defined in great detail within the macro process. This allowed us to identify procedures, activities and technological solutions supporting the path and optimizing functions."

Since the deployment of PECTRA BPM SUITE, the working dynamics has drastically changed. This new way of working entails several advantages: business process-centered work, namely working with a map of sequences; process automation (workflow) and nearly all tasks automated; better organization of the whole management at the company. The tool even allows the processes to be carried out automatically, through "robots" that perform the entire process orderly and in a timely fashion.

"As for the smart card, we had to deal with many automated activities: transactions over different systems had to be automatically generated from an event of a single instance, for example, a customer's call," Verra explains. "METROVIAS had to disable a card whose owner claimed to have lost. It also had to return, some credit back feeding all administrative and customer service systems in order to notify the customer. All of the latter is achieved through PECTRA."

Every complaint jointly launches action plans under a PECTRA network from customer service. Therefore, reengineering of all involved processes was performed. "With PECTRA this reengineering was easy, workable and fast. We took advantage of PECTRA's features and the process modeling itself; the information and the business rules have been centralized at this network containing every issue related to disabled cards and customer service throughout the year," Rueda highlights.

Technology

"It was a very ambitious project that entailed a major infrastructure change. New servers were acquired and the database schema was changed to working with SQL schemas," Gonzalo Rueda explains. A PECTRA BPM Suite-based basic infrastructure was created, allowing modeling of new projects under PECTRA BPM Suite framework. Also, many systems, not belonging to the administrative project, were added at this point. The project comprised from modeling of surveyed processes itself and their update to centralized deployment of administration on PECTRA BPM Suite and the new versions of involved systems.

"Once surveyed, every process was design through PECTRA BPM Suite, enabling the integration with the ERP (Enterprise Resource Planning) system that controls METROVÍAS' administrative processes, which started running on the workflow tool," Rueda comments. "The ERP solution was implemented for every single area or department within the organization, in accordance with specific interaction needs."

"As we had already all the infrastructure organized on PECTRA and the process-centered philosophy well embraced, all those projects took advantage of PECTRA BPM Suite for modeling, surveying, documenting, developing and implementing processes," Verra points out.

"As there were major modifications, the processes were in constant change. PECTRA BPM Suite greatly helped to overcome these suddenly changing scenarios, facilitating the modification and deployment of processes with little time-consuming efforts. That is one of the greatest benefits that PECTRA reported for these constant changing projects," Gonzalo Rueda states. "PECTRA assisted us integrate applications in a faster and easier way, creating an independent connection with each application with no need for an integration tool. From that moment on, we came up with new ideas to be carried out through PECTRA," Rueda explains. "Many non-existing features were then implemented, such as compliance with credit cards, a specialized contact center, easy handling of processes that required excessive supervision in the past, and many others features whose optimization, automation and control procedures PECTRA enabled."

"The smart card deployment was a complex change, mainly because some risks were taken facing a cultural pattern embodied in the way of payment for most of trains and subway users," Gonzalo Rueda comments. "There was also a change for METROVÍAS' personnel, as the working environment shifted, and so their usual working tools did. It was a major change and people take their time for adopt the new system. There were no delays and. PECTRA was successfully implemented, becoming the foundations over which we started working on this project," Verra remarks. The deployment of this smart card, called MONEDERO, took place during a critical period, by the time the country was experiencing a deep economic crisis. It had been planned to be carried out six months later, but the circumstances made it to be brought forward. In addition, there was an important diversity of systems to be integrated and non-existing technologies to be developed at METROVÍAS.

"We had also to homologate the system with Visa Electron debit card in order to implement an automated debit system for MONEDERO," Gonzalo Rueda comments. Nowadays MONEDERO is compliant with the most important credit and debit cards in the market: American Express, Diners, MasterCard, Visa, and all local cards.

Pinwheels located at subway stations are in charge of taking off the credit for a journey from the magnetic cards and eventually reloading them in case the passenger has subscribed the automated debit system described above (modality 2). A resident system at the pinwheels identifies the kind of card and performs the corresponding transaction, storing the new balance of the card and eventually reloading it through specific hardware.

That information stored at the pinwheels is periodically sent throughout stations' computers. These computers running on MS Windows 2000 Server workstation access the pinwheels by SMNP and they extract information from transactions, which in turn is sent to METROVÍAS' Back Office System for further processing. Computers located at subway stations works also updating the records of blacklisted cards (those cards disabled due to robbery or loss). Banelco's back office system receives these transactions and sends them to METROVÍAS' back office system for further processing. A web-enabled application is used for physically handing in the sold card to the passenger. That application associates the PIN MONEDERO number with the corresponding transaction registered in the back office system.

THE IMPACT ON SYSTEM USERS AND THE IMPACT IN THEIR JOBS

The users of PECTRA BPM Suite are nearly 900 across the entire company. Prior to BPM tool deployment, the working routine was the same as any typical office, where a person carries out a certain task while some other does another, and so on. If these tasks are not well coordinated, it is common to perform repeated actions and—consequently—waste of time, because the lack of coordination results in disorder and delays for achieving milestones. "With PECTRA BPM Suite we have taken advantage of its feature to automate work, helping to coordinate tasks and people—and turning the process fully automated in cases of no intercession of people, with the consequence of a decrease in errors and costs," Alberto Verra remarks with satisfaction. "In conclusion, it enabled to organize the work of the personnel, saving time and money."

"As for operative issues, PECTRA BPM Suite allowed to organize user's tasks, systems accesses, and all matters concerning the new administrative system, which has been built up onto a process-centered philosophy and has been modeled on PECTRA BPM Suite," Verra adds.

"Basically, it offers several working options. The same user with an specific assignment, can contribute in different organizations of the same Holding Company, or work in an independent function such as MONEDERO. It is a great benefit for

METROVÍAS, especially for the Informatin Systems area, which used to deal with a myriad of users, roles, etc.," Gonzalo Rueda comments.

Users have a friendly and intuitive interface, PECTRA Digital Gate, which provides access to all the information.

"There are about 900 PECTRA users at METROVÍAS, and the very solution itself has collaborated a lot with the administration system," Rueda comments.

"The system users do not require any special training, besides the two-four weeks that should take to instruct them according to their profile. Nevertheless, it depends on the complexity of the application that PECTRA integrates. The utilization of PECTRA Digital Gate and the integration with our ERP did not require a longer training than the three weeks planned," emphasizes Verra.

THE NEW SYSTEM CONFIGURATION.

Regarding the infrastructure, the general design was meant to mainly guarantee:
- Continuous availability of all services
- Information Security Control
- Simplification of tools
- Simplification of platforms
- Simplification of administration procedures
- Reliability on fast transactions

The implemented architecture is as follows:

Cluster
- Hardware: two HP Blade BL40 with four CPUs dual core, with 3.0 Ghz each and memory of four GB Ram. Two HD of 36 GB, Storage shared in a SAN (EVA3000) of two
- Software: Windows 2000 Advance (MS), SQL Server 2000 Enterprise (MS)

PECTRA Technology
- Hardware: two DL360 Net Server HP with two PCU of 2.8 GB dual core, two GB RAM and two HD of 36 GB
- Software MS Windows 2000 Server, PECTRA 2000 Server, MS IE 5.5.
- PECTRA's database is located in the Cluster, next to ERP's database.

Citrix Metaframe
- Hardware: seven BladeBL20p HP with two CPU at 3.0 GB, with two GB RAM and two HDs of 36 GB.
- Software: MS Windows 2000 Server, Citrix Metaframe XP, Feature Release three, Load Balancing, MS IIE 5.5, along with all libraries needed for the proper functioning of the systems: Cristal Report, OCX of stocktaking, Fox, PECTRA Integrator).

MONEDERO solution

The infrastructure compose of 400 intelligent pinwheels and 70 servers processing one million transactions a day, connected by optical fiber through subway stations.

The above mentioned infrastructure and the selected platform (MS Windows NT 2000 and MS SQL Server database) make this solution unique at worldwide level.

MONEDERO uses PECTRA BPM Suite as platform, enabling the integration of all applications compounding this solution. Card transactions are recorded into a MS SQL Server 2000 database in Cluster, on MS Windows 2003 Advanced Server platform. Approximately 1,000,000 transactions a day are handled, including consumptions and reloads of cards. Another database MS SQL Server 2000 in

Cluster on MS Windows 2003 Advanced Server platform stores data related to customers, commercial accounts and administrative processes. Every system is integrated with PECTRA BPM Suite, platform on which the electronic wallet solution is based. Each administrative and management process has been design and implemented into PECTRA, resulting in nearly 200 processes for the whole solution.

Hardware infrastructure: the hardware for implementation comprises 18 servers; among them, four compounds two clusters:

The database of transactions is installed on two clustered servers with four CPUs at three GHz with four Gb RAM, with storage SAN of 2TB. The database of administrative systems is installed on another two clustered servers with four CPUs at three GHz with four Gb RAM, with storage SAN of 2TB. PECTRA BPM Suite is installed in two CPUs of three GHz and twoGb RAM, where PECTRA's services run; PECTRA's engine and CRM run on another CPU at 3.0 GHz with two GB RAM. The Accounts to Collect system and the applications for Points of Purchase and Reload are installed on seven servers, each with two CPUs at 3.0 GHz with 2.5 Gb RAM. Citrix Mainframe with 250 users is also installed on these servers, granting access to users of administrative systems.

MONEDERO's website and its Consultation system are installed on one server with CPU at 800 MHz, with 512 Mb RAM. The web service for card reconciliation and the applications for the Card Server are installed on one server with CPU at 500 Mhz, with 256 Mb RAM and one X25 communication card to exchange data with banking systems of credit and debit cards.

Seventy five PCs with CPU at 800 Mhz and 128 Mb RAM running on MS Windows 2000 Professional platform make up the subway stations' computers.

Hardware infrastructure is interconnected via Ethernet network with IP routing. A firewall secures the network and incoming and outgoing communications of Internet and X25 networks. An additional security layer is used: SSL (Secure Sockets Layer) with public key digital certificates.

Hardware and associated services are continuously monitored by highly qualified personnel, through specific software for managing and monitoring data networks. All existing information in the databases is kept secured on a daily basis with batched backup systems to ensure its integrity.

Computer Center counts on its own source of power supply that guarantees the functioning on 24by7 modality. The facility is also protected by automated systems for fire detection, video surveillance, intelligent air conditioning systems, and permanent security guard.

THE BIGGEST HURDLES OVERCOME DURING THE PROJECT

"There was no significant obstacle, just the typical ones of any technological project: issues that were solved, adjustments, improvements and reductions, completely normal situations for projects of such importance," Gonzalo Rueda comments.

METROVÍAS has always backed and fully supported the project, collaborating to solve any possible issue and to prevent any obstacle that may delay the deployment, from the very moment that the company decided to optimize the whole organizational structure, modernizing and making the existing technological structure more efficient.

"One obstacle we had to overcome when we started implementing the smart card was facing another scenario at Urquiza railroad. We realized that most users of this railroad line, do not operate through banks; they just lack credit or debit cards at all. The train crosses some areas where residents have low incomes," Gonzalo Rueda states. "Nevertheless, the studies carried out by METROVÍAS, showed this service would serve users to manipulate money in a very convenient rechargeable card for low transactions of money (30 journeys = $21 = USD 4.00). However, they did ask for this service because, noticed by promotion campaigns, they knew that the journey fare was lower if paid through this card," explains Rueda. "That forced us to implement a truly electronic wallet: a card that they may load and use either to travel or to pay for products and services," he summarizes.

QUANTIFY ANY BENEFITS ACROSS EACH SUB-CATEGORY

"The integral solution offered by PECTRA BPM has provided us with major benefits," Alberto Verra states.

Among them:
- Reduction in operative costs
- Optimization of Human Resources
- Increase in the efficiency of business operations
- Agile dynamics and flexibility in the operations
- Fluent intercommunication among areas
- Higher levels of customer satisfaction
- Secured access to relevant business information
- Better controls
- Improved management

In addition, it allowed obtaining:
- Standardization of business processes
- Optimization of stocktaking administration
- Efficient processing of purchase orders
- Solid foundations for corporative growth or increase of demand
- Transparency in pipeline of operations
- Follow-up of operations

In turn, the integration of PECTRA with ERP tool enabled:
- Information on management for every single step of processes
- Pre-defined queries and reports
- Access to information automatically gathered by several means: e-mail, pagers, and others
- Reports of forecasts, balances, and financial scenarios
- Multidimensional queries: Sensors, Control Board, Process Performance

"PECTRA allowed decentralize administrative activities that used to be carried out through costly efforts repeatedly dedicated to the same task. By analyzing the cases in question and those effort-consuming situations and their causes, we were able to automate those processes through action plans and reduce METROVÍAS administrative tasks," Alberto Verra points out. "In addition, it gave us the control over the processes, by detecting delays, bottlenecks and failures in the distribution of tasks, considering optimal variables defined as parameters for our business during the simulation stage," he adds. Another significant consequence of having developed that process-centered philosophy is that every new project, such as MONEDERO, is already embedded into this philosophy by having been fully integrated into PECTRA.

The Contactless card, manufactured with a chip, permits the access the subway by simple proximity to the card reader. Its most important advantages: a safer way of doing payments, avoids frauds, and it expedites the flows of passengers

"Regarding the smart card, time savings in reloading resulted in money savings," Verra highlights, "Also, it allowed us to better organize the everyday work."

The following results have been obtained from deployment:
- Subscription Points Systems centralized and interconnected with credit cards companies
- Interconnection Systems with the existing smart card to process transactions
- Control Systems with records for blacklisting and fraud
- Monitoring and follow-up events Systems generated by the Contact Center
- Control Boards for ROI and financial indicators
- Control modules with management indexes
- Website for consultation, subscription and usage check

"The amount of rejected debits decreased by 40 percent with the automation of accounts to collect due to PECTRA," Alberto Verra emphasizes.

"On the other hand, the reload procedure used to take 72 hours. After optimizing the process through PECTRA BPM Suite, the reload at pinwheels takes only five minutes nowadays," Rueda adds. "The reduction in that gap is very important to these systems that work logically off-line, given the fact that a pinwheel through which 10 people go through every minute can certainly not be on-line. And the reload made at those pinwheels is money to be collected as soon as possible," Gonzalo Rueda explains.

Besides, a rejected debit used to entail a notice for the customer. Nowadays, the customer is automatically notified through an e-mail sent by PECTRA.

"At present, we can easily come up with the automation and configuration of business rules as the business itself evolves," Verra comments. "It is just about letting an automated circuit (process) flow towards and from the credit card. When the circuit comes back, an action is performed, sending each transaction in order and deciding the next node to follow whether or not the transaction has been collected. That means added-value for our business."

"The centralized subscription register system connects to a transactions server that communicates with the credit card companies and carries out the subscription approval. The same system is responsible of generating, through a pre-defined process, the periodical statements for the credit card companies," Gonzalo Rueda explains.

PECTRA has been integrated with company's CRM for the administration of the Contact Center, which is available to passengers Mondays to Saturdays from 8 AM to 10 PM.

"That integration with the Contact Center means a significant improvement, especially for handling events like card loss. PECTRA automates that process, triggering different mechanisms to fulfill the requests of users, such as disabling cards in case of, for example, robbery or loss. Also, it keeps the remaining credit of the lost or stolen card and adds it to the user's profile. As the whole process is automated, there are few errors. In addition, PECTRA inputs the Contact Center with detailed information, so that when a passenger contacts the service, all related information is available. That is due to the feature of event follow-up that complements the automation process: date of last transaction; rejected attempts of consumptions with the card. All this information gets available and helps a lot to better meet user's expectations during the contact," Verra emphasizes. PECTRA works fully integrated to the Contact Center, with an average of 50 action plans automatically triggered per day updating all the information at the back office.

All the above has provided METROVÍAS with clear advantages:
- More control on sales of tickets
- More speed for transactions
- A large volume of information on statistics about journeys and consumptions

Another important benefit for the customer was the release of MONEDERO website allowing the passenger to access diverse information regarding the card usage: balance check, consumptions and other transaction, and promotional information such as sale discounts and marketing campaigns.

"The relevant fact is that the website has been carried out through PECTRA components, with an exclusive login for each user, who directly registers in PECTRA's database. Thus, each user is assigned to a profile that allows him/her to access all the features," Gonzalo Rueda describes.

"People truly appreciate this service. Users are pleased avoiding delays at ticket offices, as they may directly go through the pinwheels and just use the transport means," Alberto Verra summarizes.

Nowadays, MONEDERO has about 300,000 users; there are nearly 30,000 registered users in the website and 300,000 active cards, at a growth monthly ratio of 10,000 new users.

Summing up, the main advantages of the smart card follow:
- Optimal transactions speed
- Reliability
- Lower rates in holidays
- Null issue or maintenance charges
- Easy payment method for many products and services
- No need of cash
- No delays at ticket offices

COMPETITIVE ADVANTAGES GAINED AND HOW YOU MOVED COMPETITIVE GOAL POSTS

METROVÍAS has managed to elevate the standards of service in the industry for the transportation of passengers. A poll of image and satisfaction carried out in 2004 by one of the most prestigious agencies of the country, Mora & Araujo, thus declares it. On it, there were interviewed 917 subway passengers, 630 train passengers and 180 bus passengers. It's determined the following conclusions: METROVÍAS is the transportation net with better image. Comparing the data of different providers of transportation service, METROVIAS appears heading the Argentina ranking with an 85 percent of users answering to be "very satisfied" with the service offered.

According to the quality and service that distinguish the subway, some characteristic are very related to the deployment of MONEDERO, as "queues in ticket offices," "efficiency on consults," "ease in using services," "innovation," " ticket price in relation to service offered," and "on-line information service" that allows passengers to have information of frequencies, state of service, and cards reload, among others.

It is possible to appreciate in this whole solution how doing a proper use of technology, companies can add value to massive services for the community, not only increasing its quality, but also gaining in efficiency and saving costs.

The amount of passengers transported in 2005 (including combinations and franchises) were increased in a 4.42 percent respect the preceding period, passing from 357.11 million to 372.89 million.

The kilometers traveled by car decreased in 2005 to 40.79 million (1.54 percent less than previous year, that was 41.43 million). PECTRA BPM Suite has allowed knowing the evolution of the demand with precision, the way METROVÍAS has adjusted the offering to the real needs of the demand without affecting the service quality.

The company has an organization of pyramidal type, with heads by area, being the direction and administration of the company in charge of eight regular directors and eight acting directors. The strategic-operating decisions are adopted for the managers of the different areas.

PECTRA has allowed them an internal control, integrating all information systems and giving all the information on time for the decition making.

SHORT-TIME AND LONG-TIME PLANNING TO KEEP THE OBTAINED COMPETITIVE ADVANTAGE

"PECTRA is included for the short and long-time system planning in order to support METROVIAS everyday operation tasks," Alberto Verra states.

For METROVÍAS "PECTRA has become the foundations over which we implement all the information system, and whenever a new project comes up, it is designed, modeled and documented through PECTRA," Verra remarks. "The new project is implemented on PECTRA Technology, and we have planned our work this way over the next years."

As for the short-time planning, "We must implement newer releases of PECTRA, extending the scope of the tool until reaching new processes that nowadays are being manually carried out, simple processes that already exist and that are part of an automation plan," Alberto Verra comments. "PECTRA easily allows the deployment without allocating development work what is a major advantage," he adds.

The smart card is a project that will enable different options and uses not restricted only for transportation issues.

"PECTRA has provided us with a myriad of benefits and features that perfectly fits in our commercial strategy and vision, and is the reason why we have broadly implemented it all throughout our processes," Alberto Verra points out. "PECTRA BPM Suite has revealed a brand new perspective for us to face new challenges. By these days, it allowed us to start up METROSHOP (a credit card) in just 20 days, what becomes a great achievement for our company," he highlights.

Grupo Pão de Açúcar

Silver Award 2006, South America; nominated by iProcess, Brazil

EXECUTIVE SUMMARY

This paper describes the experience of the implementation of workflow technology in Grupo Pão de Açúcar (GPA), the largest retail group in Brazil. Motivated by the necessity of adjustment to the Sarbanes-Oxley act, and of acceleration of critical processes execution, GPA began the usage of workflow technology. There are three developed workflow systems: the first, Investment Approval Workflow, being deployed in May, 2005. The benefits of workflow technology were quickly perceived, with the reduction of 80 percent of average process time and great increase of control effectiveness. For this reason, GPA is not only expanding the use of workflow technology, but also connecting IT and process disciplines, building a solid path into BPM direction.

OVERVIEW

Grupo Pão de Açúcar (GPA) previously known as Companhia Brasileira de Distribuição (CBD) is a strong and complex company that runs a great amount of business processes. Their business is based on a multiformat structure, with a balance between supermarkets and mega stores operating in 15 of 26 Brazilian states. GPA has 554 stores, 12 distribution centers and around 63 thousand employees.

In order to achieve greater control, higher agility, better efficiency and lower operational costs, GPA has decided to automate business processes using workflow technology.

The Investment Approval Workflow (IAW) was the first application of the workflow technology proposed by the company. The IAW solution has provided GPA the necessary flexibility in defining the approval group of each kind of document, without losing the basic idea that rules the responsibilities of their managers. Workflow has boosted agility and transparency resulting in 80 percent of total time savings. Paper documents have been replaced by electronic documents having review and approval activities controlled by a workflow engine. Its most common interface is e-mail that contains messages supplying the approver with the information needed for the decision making, demanding less time and effort in training the executives on using this technology. The following results where achieved within this past year: 50 users and near R$ 30 million on investments approved using the Investment Approval Workflow, distributed on around 250 instances of process for investments such as equipment acquisitions, software upgrade, construction and reform of stores and administration and security services.

The success of applying this technology at GPA has inspired the company to automate two other important business processes. The Resources Control Workflow (RCW), created to support the IT department, implements a complex process of approval and execution activities for access and restriction control for systems and technology resources of the company. This fulfills an important requirement of the Sarbanes-Oxley act. This workflow grants people restricted access to information and resources designated for their positions. The exceptions must be approved and acknowledged by the proper manager. The Workflow for Outsourcing Management (WOM) supports the company on selecting, transferring and releasing workers from third parties, focusing on their competences. Executives receive the necessary information about costs related to these operations for their cost centers. Both projects followed the Investment Workflow regarding the approval flexibility expected for these processes. The WOM started production in May, 2006, and RCW is predicted for Q3 2006. Since they are outside the Awards' deadlines, they will be referenced only to allow a better comprehension of GPA's strategy.

GPA already has plans for raising investments on workflow solutions - on the enclosure of this paper, four new projects were under development.

KEY MOTIVATIONS FOR WORKFLOW SYSTEM IMPLEMENTATION

GPA is one of the most admired companies in Brazil, building a history of excellent customer service, innovation and social responsibility. GPA was founded in 1948 as a grocery store, and 60 years later has more than 500 stores. Its success has been recognized by several recent awards such as "The most admired retail company," "Excellence in E-Commerce," "Retail Community Service Award," "100 Best places to work" and "50 Best places for women to work".

Many factors, both internal and external, collaborated for the implementation of workflow technology at GPA. The following subsections illustrate the main motivations.

Sarbanes-Oxley Act compliance

Since the association of GPA to the French Casino Group, the company started to have shared negotiated at New York Stock Exchange and thus was affected by the requirements of Sarbanes-Oxley act. This means that many processes, specially those involving financial impact, had to be adjusted for an additional level of control, with a higher formalism of the exchanged information and total traceability.

As it is known, workflow technology offers excellent resources to implement this additional level of control. To GPA, it was specially important: i) guarantee of process integrity offered by the workflow technology; ii) the automatic and accurate recording of every execution step of the process; iii) the substitution of request and answers through e-mail by organized and well documented interactions through the workflow system. These functionalities where decisive for GPA's decision to employ workflow technology for the automation of processes related to the Sarbanes-Oxley act.

Tougher competition requires new levels of agility

Since 2000, when GPA became the leader of Brazilian retail market, the company has been constantly challenged to maintain its position. This pressure is made by Carrefour (today in second place) and especially from Wal-Mart, which due to a series of acquisitions (as happened to Bompreço, leader in the northeast of Brazil, and later to SDB, leader in south Brazil), have been aggressively expanding in the market. It is important to observe that currently the difference of sales between GPA (first place) and Wal-Mart (third place) is less than R$ five billion (US$ 2.28 billion) - in 2004 the difference was near R$ 10 billion (US$ 4.56 billion).

To maintain its current position and expand activities in the Brazilian market, GPA has announced an investment plan of R$ 1.5 billion (US$ 684 million) for 2006-2007, entirely financed by internal cash flow. This investment is directed to the opening of 16 to 20 new hypermarkets, 40 to 60 supermarkets, renovation of existing stores, infrastructure and technology.

In this environment of daily frantic competition and heavy growth rate, business processes have to work in their best performance, without giving chances for flaws or delays. The Investment Approval process is one of the most critical, since most part (if not all) of the R$ 1.5 billion (US$ 684 million) investment will be analyzed through this process. In other words, the whole strategic plan execution could be slowed (or even halted) if this process' performance is low. This was exactly the situation in the end of 2004 - Investment Approval process was slow, unreliable, uncontrolled and totally paper-based.

Under these circumstances, GPA evaluated that workflow technology could be an allied, increasing process speed and reducing the risk of failures. Thus, GPA saw on workflow technology a bridge to reduce the distance between strategy definition and its execution.

Preparation for Process Management Implementation

Historically, the vision over processes is not a preponderant element to the management style of GPA. This is motivated for many reasons, but mainly by a deep respect for the hierarchical structure. Despite that, the awareness about the importance of process management has been growing.

The beginning of the use of workflow technology is a direct result of the increase of this awareness. By choosing workflow technology for implementing certain systems, instead of software development traditional techniques, GPA's IT department made a significant bet on the process concept. Thus, GPA saw on workflow technology the most adequate way to obtain IT support for several of their processes.

KEY INNOVATIONS

Business

The introduction of workflow technology transformed the vision of GPA about the company's processes. The following topics describe the main innovations obtained by the technology under the business focus.

Powerful process configuration tools give power to business process owners

Defining business activities for process automation is always an important matter of reflection. A detailed mapped process may cover every step needed to maintain the process integrity, but any need of change may turn into complex and expensive work. On the other hand, a superficial mapping process might not guarantee the desired integrity. To support GPA on achieving the best benefits of the workflow technology, flexibility and integrity have to walk hand in hand.

This way, IAW solution enlightens this question. The necessary and specific steps of the business process, such as document review or specific operations related to business rules (whose definition is needed to guarantee process integrity) are designed and controlled by the workflow engine. Supporting the business process automation, a key application was built to allow the process owner to define rules for investment approval, where approval roles (such as directors and managers) are organized on different flows. These flows are used by the workflow system to identify the next approver in the chain according to the nature and value of investment. This allows the process administrator to update workflow definitions for approval, giving the organization the possibility to make fast moves into new rules for business processes - in other words, putting process control into process owner's hands.

The following picture shows the application where users can configure the approval steps for a certain kind of investment ("Tipo: Projetos") when requested by a certain business area ("Núcleo EV: Informática"). Process owners can define approval order, approver role (e.g. "Diretor Executivo"), authority limit (e.g. R$100.000) and other parameters.

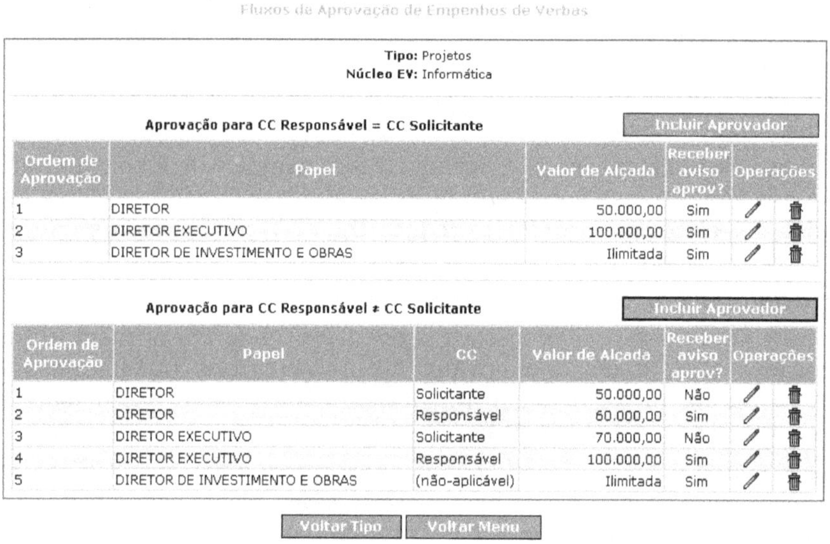

Fluxos de Aprovação de Empenhos de Verbas

Tipo: Projetos
Núcleo EV: Informática

Aprovação para CC Responsável = CC Solicitante   Incluir Aprovador

Ordem de Aprovação	Papel	Valor de Alçada	Receber aviso aprov?	Operações
1	DIRETOR	50.000,00	Sim	✏ 🗑
2	DIRETOR EXECUTIVO	100.000,00	Sim	✏ 🗑
3	DIRETOR DE INVESTIMENTO E OBRAS	Ilimitada	Sim	✏ 🗑

Aprovação para CC Responsável ≠ CC Solicitante   Incluir Aprovador

Ordem de Aprovação	Papel	CC	Valor de Alçada	Receber aviso aprov?	Operações
1	DIRETOR	Solicitante	50.000,00	Não	✏ 🗑
2	DIRETOR	Responsável	60.000,00	Sim	✏ 🗑
3	DIRETOR EXECUTIVO	Solicitante	70.000,00	Não	✏ 🗑
4	DIRETOR EXECUTIVO	Responsável	100.000,00	Sim	✏ 🗑
5	DIRETOR DE INVESTIMENTO E OBRAS	(não-aplicável)	Ilimitada	Sim	✏ 🗑

Voltar Tipo   Voltar Menu

Figure 1. Process owners can define different flows for the approval chain, according to the kind of investment and to the requesting area.

Higher process agility

Process agility was one of the most important aspects that led to the decision of implementing workflow technology in GPA. It is important to note that retail market dynamics demands GPA to work on constant pressure, where decisions have to be taken fast and deadlines are very strict. Thus, it is possible to say that workflow technology, if correctly applied, may perfectly fit to this culture.

Before the use of workflow technology in the Investment Approval process, documents where exchanged from one approver to another in paper. Apart from the risk of lost or misplaced documents, people who created the document were also responsible for setting and following physically the steps of approval for an investment. A document might be left behind for further evaluation on some approver's desk for days. With the replacement of paper by a digital document and the establishment of a flexible control for approval flow definition, it is the workflow engine that manages the delivery and approval results for the process, coordinating the exchange of the document between the involved people with safety and agility. The paper submission to approvers has been successfully replaced by an e-mail notification for approval, reducing significant time dispended on exchanging paper from one hand to another.

With no need of the physical process, workflow also made it possible for the employee to execute any activity of the investment approval process wherever he/she might be, breaking the barriers of time and place.

This solution also brought to the daily routine of the executives involved on the process the concept of different priority and time expectation for the process activities. Based on this, important or urgent investments may be rapidly approved and its execution may happen without compromising strategic plans of the company. Critical activities now have deadlines monitored by the workflow system, which takes pro-active measures to avoid process delay, such as sending notifications to the approver and to the responsible for the process. During one year of system usage, it was possible to identify an average reduction of 80 percent on the necessary time for approving investments on GPA.

Improved safety of the approval process

An important innovation brought by IAW was the assurance that each investment request will be directed to the right person, and approved only by him/her. Before workflow, approval safety relied on signature validation, what is (optimistically speaking) a fragile mechanism. IAW validates user permission using a single sign on control, virtually eliminating the risk of fraud.

Another important benefit was improved process confidentiality. Before workflow, strategic investment decisions of millions of dollars were carried through the company in paper documents, with fragile security. Considering the level of competitiveness in the retail market, this is a very risky and vulnerable approach. The IAW solved this issue by introducing the concept of virtual process, replacing paper documents by secure Web applications, guaranteeing that information will be known only by people which are supposed to know it.

Collaboration improves decision making

The fact that the investment requester is involved in the beginning of the process for review and the possibility for approvers to submit their doubts or other questions to any other workflow user increased the collaboration along the process. Every comment is recorded and is available for the next approvers. Many of them contain new information that may have positive or negative influence in the decision making. This improves the quality of the final result of the process. Considering the high value of a typical investment, increased collaboration may lead to significant savings.

Control and continuous improvement

The use of workflow technology allowed the IAW team to follow and control possible bottlenecks of the business process, and using this information, to improve the process. The most important enhancements to the process were: a) the possibility of having approvers submitting questions to any other person involved on the process; b) the optional involvement of staff workers in the process, so they could provide other relevant information to support decision-making.

Process

Workflow technology deeply changed the Investment Approval process. The table below shows the main changes:

Topic	Before	After
Document creation	Using a spreadsheet model	Custom Web application
Approval group definition	Informal definition. Approval group and approver order were known only by the typewriter, who had to print their names in the document	Set of user-configured rules define the order and roles involved in the approval

Media	Paper. The spreadsheet was printed and submitted to approvers	Digital. Information is automatically sent to requester for review and after to approvers
Process control	Manually made by the typewriter, demanding effort to call and remind approvers and to check process status	Electronic, with the possibility of monitor process status anytime
Approval task	The document was delivered to the approver, who could approve immediately or leave with the secretary for further evaluation	Approval tasks are submitted directly to approver's e-mail inbox. System is responsible to send new alert messages if the approver takes too long to fulfill the task
Comments about the document	There was no space for commenting. Some managers used to justify the rejection in the document body.	Every comment is registered and the comment history is presented to the following approvers, allowing effective collaboration improvement
Typical process time	Five to 40 days	Less than five days

With the substitution of the paper document by a Web application, information is all united on a single document, containing data related to the investment and each approver's comments. The electronic document goes to a review, at the beginning of the process, and this information cannot be changed after the final review. This way, the consistence of information is guaranteed. The fact that the all the information is provided by the workflow system also offers to approvers better possibilities for the decision making. Searching the system, the approver may access other details about the document, comments of past approvers and other investments approved or rejected that could affect his/her decision.

The picture below shows the main parts of the process.

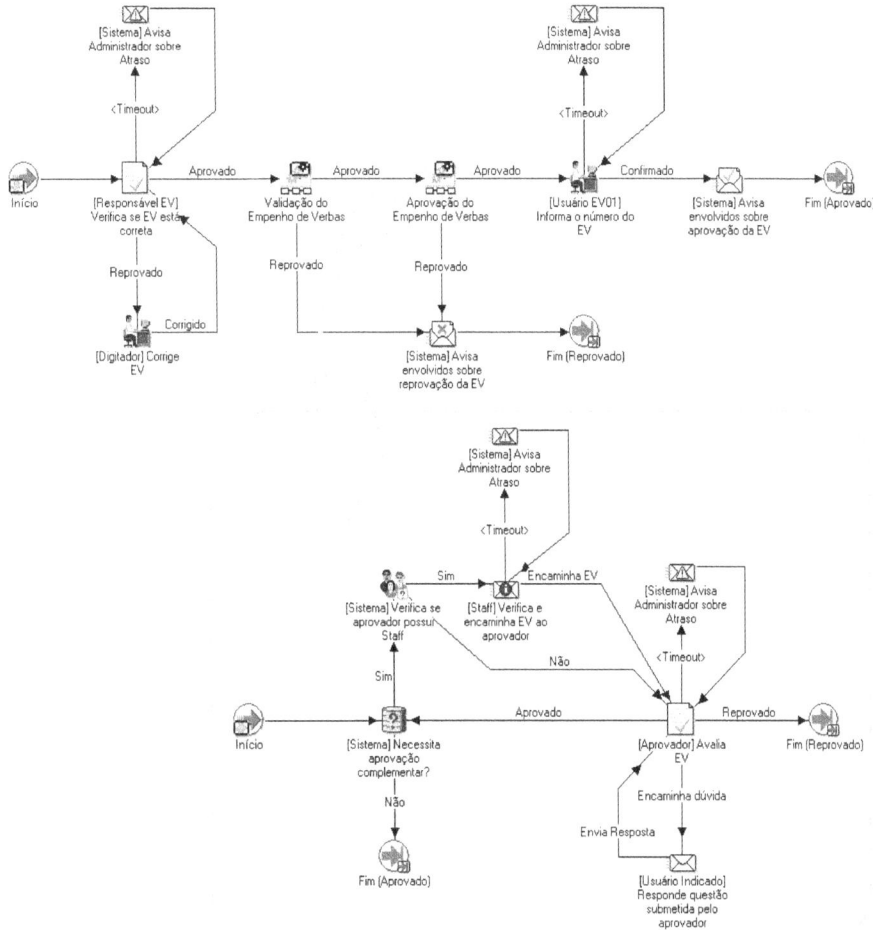

Figure 2. Graphical workflow for Investment Approval Workflow

Technology

Under the technology focus, two aspects stand out: simplified user interaction and the technologic structure built to support the flexibility of the approval flow definition.

One-click Approval

Although IAW is used by a restrict group of users, these people are, mostly, managers and directors of several departments and areas of the company, whose time to interact with the system is limited and whose requirement level regarding interface usability is very high.

Counting on the strong practice of communication through electronic mail, already implied in the daily routine of these users, it was adopted the concept of one-click user interaction. With a simple click on the application, accessible from the e-mail, the user may approve or reject the investment. He/she may also ask a question to another user, having the request and answer registered on a list of comments. In fact, e-mail was pointed by users as one of the most important usability features, demanding less time and effort for training the executives on using this technology.

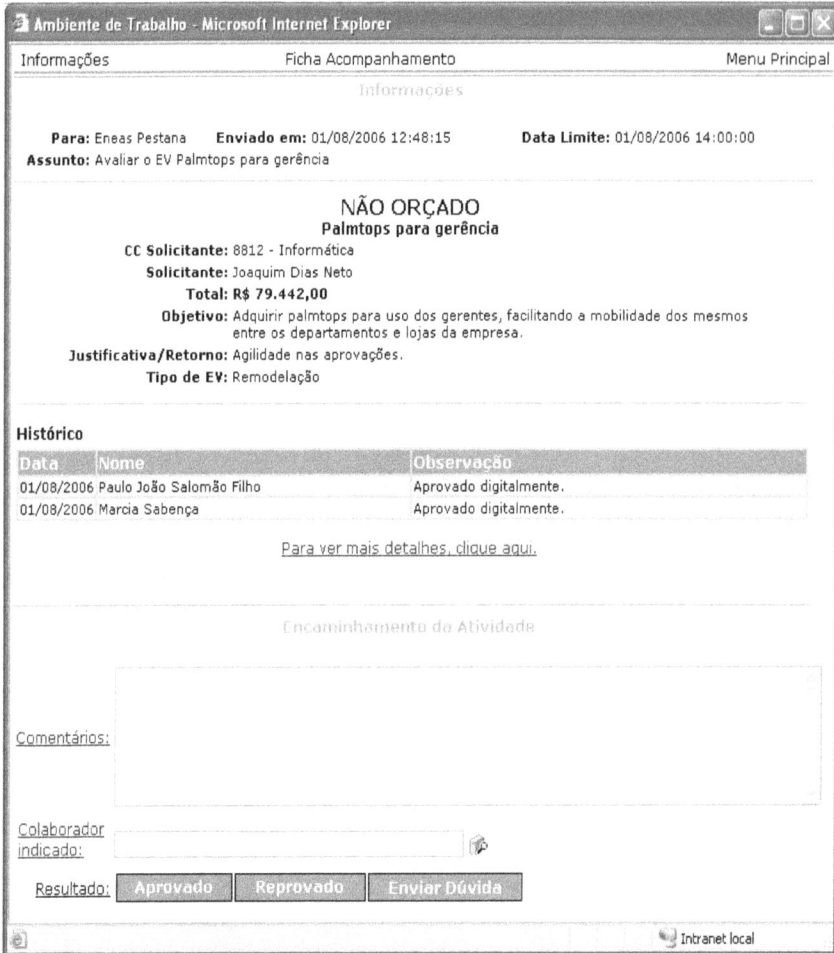

Figure 3. From his/her e-mail inbox, user receives summarized information about the process and may, in one click, decide to approve (Aprovado) or reject (Reprovado) the investment or to send questions (Enviar Dúvida) to another user (Colaborador indicado).

THE IMPACT ON USERS OF THE SYSTEM

Workflow usage at GPA has had several impacts on users. The most important are:

- greater organization at work, because one can easily check his or her worklist to see pending activities
- transition from paper documents to electronic documents, allowing several data validations, easing cooperation and speeding the process
- process transparency, making full history available and allowing one to know who's delaying the process
- greater awareness about task deadlines due to work item information and to alerts

THE NEW SYSTEM CONFIGURATION

GPA adopted Oracle Workflow as platform for workflow development and deployment.

The system infrastructure combines:

- Workflow Server: IBM Server running AIX, Oracle Database Server 9.1.2, Oracle Workflow Server 2.6.3 and Oracle HTTP Server 1.3.22.
- Workstations: Intel (several speeds), 32 to 512Mb, running MS Windows (98, 2000 or XP), Microsoft Internet Explorer up to version 5.5, Mozilla or Mozilla Firefox browser, Microsoft Outlook, Oracle Workflow Builder (only Process Analyst).
- E-mail server: Microsoft Exchange Server.

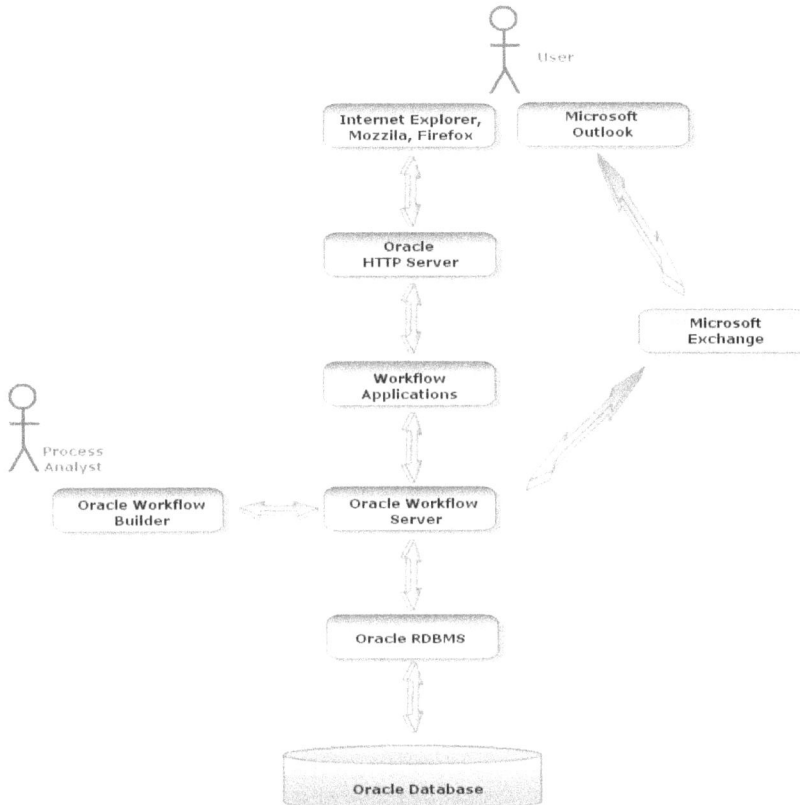

Figure 5. Global System Architecture

THE BIGGEST HURDLES OVERCOME IN MANAGEMENT, BUSINESS AND TECHNOLOGY

Management and Business Hurdles

In a broad sense, management and business hurdles where related to the challenge of supplying the special needs of the system users. Most of them are senior managers and directors, professionals that usually have a very high level of requirement about systems. In fact, their expectation was nothing less than perfection: the system had to be intuitive, easy to use, bug-free and stable. Ironically, due to their daily responsibilities, their involvement in system development (analysis, design, prototyping and tests) was very low. Naturally, it was a huge challenge to meet this expectation with almost no user participation.

These hurdles were overcome by a combination of actions. First, user interface was kept simple and was based on the preferred user's software: e-mail. To avoid the need to log in the system (seen as an unacceptable time loss by users) workflow authentication was integrated with GPA's portal authentication. As a result, workflow-user communications works on a very natural way, with zero hour training, and the fulfillment of these expectations was fundamental for the easy and quick acceptance of these users.

Technology Hurdles

The main technology hurdle was certainly related to the requirement of a flexible definition of the approval steps. A previous unsuccessful attempt to use workflow technology to map and control every possible route for the investment approval process created a negative impression about the technology, turning it into an important issue to overcome. In fact, due to this frustrated experience, several managers where skeptic about the viability of using workflow technology. Some of them even held positions such as "Workflow is not for GPA". As aforementioned, the solution was to build a sophisticated (yet easy to manage) mechanism for approval flow definition.

Another important hurdle overcome was the development model introduced to GPA. Due to the geographic distance between GPA (in São Paulo) and iProcess, workflow consultant placed in Porto Alegre (south Brazil), the development of IAW system required a distributed development approach. This work model was new for GPA, a company used to have its consultants working onsite. For this new approach to work properly, some important aspects had to be observed:

- project management based on Project Management Institute (PMI) practices
- more precise definition of project phases and artifacts, reducing risks of scope misinterpretation
- detailed project planning to assure that workflow analyst can complete his/her work in two-three days
- weekly conference calls to ensure that both parties are synchronized
- analyst presence during homologation and initial production phases, and software test team prepared for remote cooperation

These actions have achieved the desired results, and distributed development has had a great success. Currently, all GPA workflow systems are being developed by iProcess, who has been considered a reference for distributed development among GPA's technology consultants.

COST SAVINGS, INCREASED REVENUES, AND PRODUCTIVITY IMPROVEMENTS

The major benefits obtained with the implementation of workflow technology were process agility and the establishment of clear control over processes. Given the strategic nature of these processes, these benefits are essentially intangible, being difficult to measure by the traditional techniques of Return On Investment. Among the main benefits are:

- Agility in decision making reagarding investments. Many investments are often of several millions of dollars. The time-consuming on approving these investments may represent slowness on implementation of the defined strategies or, even worse, slowness on responding to the competition. Thus, the 80 percent reduction in the average time for investment approval, obtained with the workflow system developed, has a wide range strategic impact.
- Safety of approval process. Using the workflow technology has significantly increased the security of the approval activity on eliminating the paper or e-mail signatures due to authorized access to the workflow system. This fact gets especially relevant when, as it was already said, approval involves

expressive value. On such scenario, it is easy to identify the return obtained with the elimination of risks of this nature

- Establishment of Preventive Controls. On a complex company as GPA a single fail over the security access to information systems may result in high financial loss. The discipline obtained through systems like the Resources Workflow eliminates these loss risks on guaranteeing the process integrity as prevention.
- Guarantee of the adoption of new processes. The use of workflow technology was fundamental so the new Workflow for Outsourcing Management could be quickly adopted by every participant. Without workflow technology, there would be a greater effort from the managers to guarantee that every involved part could comprehend the new process and follow the execution rules.

COMPETITIVE ADVANTAGES GAINED

On an environment of highly competition as the Brazilian retail market, companies must look for - and sustain - every possible competitive advantage. And, certainly, the major competitive advantage earned by GPA with the usage of workflow technology was the improvement of the governance policies. Due to the Sarbanes-Oxley act, this improvement became not only an action directed to the refinement of management strategies, but a fundamental element for the business continuity. The non-adjustment for the SOX requirements might bring brutal impacts to the company, as the impediment of having ADRs in the American market, what would have heavy financial effects (Brazilian interest taxes are historically very elevated, usually becoming unfeasible to take expressive resources in the country). Thus, the described workflow implementations collaborated for striking this strategic aim.

IMMEDIATE AND LONG-TERM PLANS TO SUSTAIN COMPETITIVE ADVANTAGE

With the success of the first workflow systems, GPA plans to increase investments on this technology. Besides these three workflow systems described in this paper, the following systems are in the initial steps of development: Marketing Events Approval Workflow, Reimbursement Workflow and Travel Workflow. Beyond these workflows there are other processes being evaluated, motivated by the adjustment for the Sarbanes-Oxley act and the increasing of operational efficiency.

On a broader way, workflow technology is expanding awareness of business process management at GPA. Historically, process management hadn't found, in the retail industry, a fertile field for action. The main reason for this is that return of investment on processes is usually long-term and thus may be seen as incompatible to the extreme dynamics of the retail market. By bringing fast and tangible benefits, workflow technology is breaking this scenario and shows the advantages of business processes management approach.

A new and important sign for the increasing strength of this movement was the recent incorporation of GPA's Process Office to the IT department. From now on, IT and process professionals begin to study and define together mechanisms for integrated work between these disciplines, building an effective path to the implementation of the BPM concept. Certainly, nowadays, few initiatives may bring so much value to a company.

La Voz del Interior, Argentina

Gold Award 2005, South America; nominated by PECTRA Argentina, SA.

1. SUMMARY

La Voz del Interior is the most prestigious regional newspaper in the Argentine Republic. It is currently owned by the Grupo Clarín, the main mass media holding in Argentina, and one of the most important mass media organizations in the Spanish-speaking world.

With a history spanning more than 100 years, La Voz del Interior tops the list of the daily newspapers that are edited in the interior of the country, and is ranked third in Argentina, vis-a-vis advertising revenues. Its average daily circulation is 60,000 copies (Mondays to Saturdays) and 85,000 copies on Sundays.

With a view to carrying out the distribution process of third-party materials, which is provided by the country's most renowned publishing houses, La Voz del Interior acquired the set of BPM (Business Process Management) tools from PECTRA Technology Inc.

Due to the successful implementation of the solution, which showed excellent results, the company has optimized the distribution of additional material and achieved significant cost-reductions and tighter control in the traceability of its processes.

2. OVERVIEW

La Voz del Interior is a century-old newspaper founded on the 15th of March, 1904 in the city of Córdoba, Argentina. The newspaper chose this name because it wanted to become the "voice" that would address the entire country from the city of Córdoba, the geographical heart of the Argentine Republic.

It is currently owned by Grupo Clarín, the main mass media holding in Argentina, as well as one of the most important mass media organizations in the Spanish-speaking world. Grupo Clarín, together with the daily newspaper La Nación (Buenos Aires) and Grupo Vocento (Spain), have formed CIMECO (Compañía Inversora en Medios de Comunicación), the first graphic media network in Argentina, of which La Voz del Interior is part.

La Voz del Interior currently tops the list of the daily newspapers edited in Córdoba, one of the most important newspapers in the interior of the country, and is ranked third in Argentina, vis-a-vis advertising revenues. Daily circulation is above 60,000 copies (Mondays to Saturdays) and 85,000 copies on Sundays.

From that historic "sheet" of only six pages to today's edition, more than 100 years have gone by. During those years, the region witnessed significant social changes and the newspaper did not remain indifferent: it moved forward embracing technological innovation.

Today La Voz del Interior has become a modern organization. The networks that link computers together have definitely changed traditional workspaces. Digitalization is standard procedure in all types of tasks, including the treatment and filing of pictures and advertising design.

The newspaper is printed using a state-of-the-art Goss Headliner press, which allows them to print 60.000 copies per hour, with automatic regulation of inks and colors. These features guarantee higher printing quality.

The plant is located in an 11-hectare site, in the northern area of the city, next to the international airport. It not only contains the printing press but offers additional services, such as a maintenance workshop, a paper store-room, its own power generator, lunchrooms and conference and meetings rooms. Total investment reached 20 million dollars.

There is a 4,000 square-meter building next to the press that operates as the company's headquarters since April 2000, housing the Managing Director's office, the News Room, commercial departments and the company's Admin and the Board of Directors offices.

Since 1996, La Voz del Interior is published on the Internet and it has become the web site showing most hits in the interior of the country, with number of visits to the web page growing significantly, at an average daily rate of over 40,000 hits.

"Early in 2004, and following a considerable reduction in the activities of a large distributor in Córdoba, a group formed by the most prestigious publishing houses in the country, such as Perfil, La Nación, and Clarín, offered to take over the distribution of third-party materials to the interior of the country. Consequently, the need arose to have a new Business Division. This had very little in common with what we had been doing for over 100 years, which was to produce newspapers," explains Eng. Marcelo Rizzi, Systems Manager of La Voz del Interior.

3. The key motivations behind installing this workflow system.

The newspaper "La Voz del Interior" needed to create a new Business Unit to carry on with the operation. And they did it overnight. "First, we established a work circuit with conventional tools: e-mail, text editor, spreadsheets, etc.; and then we polished up the circuit with those tools and nothing else, because our priority was to solve the market need problem first. We had found a great business opportunity, and there was no time to waste; the market would not allow for it," said Marcelo Rizzi.

However, time brought up those problems that result from out-of-control processes, such as important economic damages and security problems, among others. Then the main question arises: "How are we going to manage this?" said Rizzi about the situation that had been reached. "It's what I call 'to try to extinguish a fire with gasoline': you start making changes that make the situation even worse, like hiring more people. The same scenario is much more complicated when the communication networks include too many people."

When faced with this uncertainty, all different users focused on their own processes without taking into account the impact of their actions on the process in general. This caused constant lack of information, lack of coordination, multiple-control exercises that had no effect, excessive delays and, most important, lack of control over stock. Ultimately, information had no quality and processing costs rose considerably. This put everybody on alert and many thought that the Business Unit incorporated to La Voz del Interior could not be profitable.

Thus, the main objective of the organization is to optimize and be able to carry on with all third party product distribution for the city of Córdoba and the rest of the province, that is to say, reception of requests, product delivery and distribution in different formats such as magazines, videos, books, special documents, supplements, CDs, etc.

La Voz del Interior has historically been a means of communications that only handled the production and distribution of the newspaper (single-product) and some supplements.

In the case of newspapers, the relationship with the different points-of-sale is simple: at the end of the day all unsold papers are returned to the organization, which acts as a simple final recipient. But when dealing with the delivery of third party products, the organization acts as a distributor, an intermediary of sorts. "Points-of-sale return the products, and we have to give this same product back to our provider, with all the back and forth that it entails.

"That is why we had a very important problem at hand: we did not know whether we were going to make or lose money," said Marcelo when describing the uncertainty of those days. "Then we started to think of a suitable solution."

"At La Voz del Interior we knew about PECTRA Technology, and we knew someday it would come in handy. Process-orientation seemed to be the best solution. At that point, aware of our problem, we knew that a BPM solution would help us a lot," emphasized Marcelo Rizzi. "Then we put our imagination to work. We scheduled several meetings with prospective users of said processes, we designed real flow and ideal flow, and from that moment on we started developing the first processes, designed by the users themselves."

The acquisition of PECTRA Technology coincided with the implementation of the Systems Plan (*Plan de Sistemas*), launched for the first time in many years by La Voz del Interior. In this plan that encompassed the years 2004/2005/2006, directors draw up future strategies based on which management offices formed committees with the users so that, based present and prospective requests, they could make suggestions regarding what could be done with the current technology and what was necessary to acquire.

A solution focused on BPM (Business Process Management) was then internally suggested, because process-by-process management allows for a clear definition of objectives, in this case, to obtain better profitability from third party product distribution processes. "We held six meetings to define all distributor-related processes. We were not sure about it, because everything was new to us," explains Marcelo. "That is why we sketched a few simple charts that we later turned into PECTRA diagrams."

During the meetings held between La Voz del Interior Systems Management and PECTRA Technology engineers, the actual process was understood and the performance of the tasks was analytically described. A comprehensive solution aimed at solving the needs specifically related to the administration and managements of third party products was presented. Then, the process were studied, analyzed, designed, documented, developed and implemented. Only four processes were fully identified:

Request and reception of products: Its main objective is to monitor product requests to each provider. It takes into account the request for products, the reception, the initial arrival of products to storage and it sets expiration dates in order to determine its further management. This process solves product forecast as well as product registration that have no previous request order.

Product distribution: Its main objective is the follow-up of product distribution to the different customers.

Points-of-sale and cash sales: The latter is a store owned by La Voz del Interior located downtown that is mainly used as secondary storage so other points-of sale have fast and easy access to it in case they need more items of the product. Additionally, this process allows stock movement tracking when distribution is under way.

Return of products: Its main objective is the follow-up and monitoring of all returns coming from points-of-sale and cash sales (cash and carry).

Customer complaints: This process records complaints coming from points-of-sale to determine its validity. Note: Points-of-sale are persons selling newspapers on their own or in newsstands.

The design of process was based on the following premises:

1. Design and performance of simple and precise processes.
2. Minimization of manual work.
3. Systematization of control points.
4. Traceability in business-related processes.
5. Computerized recording for the proper functioning of processes.
6. Performance of easily audited processes.

"Every process is extremely important for the project. Perhaps, the less critical one is Customer's complaints, but from the business point of view, customer satisfaction is essential," explains Marcelo.

4. THE OVERALL BUSINESS INNOVATION.

Shortly after being implemented, the Business Unit started to show positive results, because not only the main objectives were achieved (to optimize the distribution of the product) but also costs were drastically reduced and there was better control based on traceability of process-by-process management. Generally speaking, this solution allowed the optimization of operative efficiency, thus making good use of all existing resources and satisfying customer needs in a timely and adequate manner.

"Regarding investment returns, we now realize that the tool is going to self-finance as soon as new processes are involved. We started to solve our most critical problems with PECTRA. We now know that volume work may spawn new problems, but this tool has proved that we can easily add new functions and correct other aspects, as needed," added Marcelo. "Today, with the help of PECTRA, we have gone over 100 products and our intention is go ahead and incorporate new processes."

"Alerts, cube reporting, and Business Intelligence tools are extremely important for the user. They are already realizing the enormous potential to perform their own benchmarks or the self-or cross-control between areas. It is also a very useful controlling tool for immediate supervisors. It is there where the best results are being obtained, especially when answering to the reports requested by higher management," said Marcelo Rizzi.

"We worked a year and a half with conventional tools," he comments, "And we had serious problems related to the resources assigned and activities that added cost, like manual controls. For instance, one of the publishers used to send us invoices showing all items sent minus those returned for over a total of 60 different products. Those bimonthly invoices, sometimes with 16 pages, were checked by ticking off emails and spreadsheets, etc."

At that time, from a turnover standpoint, the Business Unit broke even. "We now know that once we implement the tool we will save resources and make money," summarizes Marcelo. "What we save in resources will let us attack the market and sell more. This business is based on sales volume, and PECTRA has allowed us to internally reorganize all information in order to know whether we lose or make money."

"Another of the problems we solved was the elimination of possible error-related losses. When the margin is set too low, the loss of a 21-peso video takes away all profits on the product. There were just too many manual processes in which each of us had to complete a form and then make it match with everything else, as if it were magic. Some products simply disappeared between points-of-sale in the city and the ones located in farther locations, and even between local storages," explained Marcelo.

5. THE OVERALL TECHNOLOGICAL INNOVATION

Before the implementation of PECTRA, processes were distributed in seven or eight parts, and each user would only take care of his/her assigned area.

"PECTRA allowed us to unify them, and we got rid of duplicated tasks and controls.I always say that the only thing that we didn't do was to have a person in charge of photocopying and another person right behind him/her to control the photocopy," remembers Marcelo ironically. "That how we made possible that all vertical know-how be traced horizontally in order to design the best processes."

"The bigger problem on the part of the customers was that they worked in watertight compartments, and when they gathered all information, for management reasons or to return to the provider, they did not know what to return," said Marcelo.

There was a historical clash between the areas involved in these particular processes: "The clash was unavoidable in most of the cases; take into account that we are dealing with a 101-year old company. An example of this was that there were many discussions between supervisors to determine who received damaged goods or goods in perfect conditions. The biggest challenge, then, was to convince all areas that it was important to as one," stressed Marcelo.

One of the peculiarities of these processes is that someone requests a product, a magazine for example, and this product has several editions (N54, N55, N56) with their corresponding publishing dates. Requests were not processed every week, and some products could arrive without being requested in cases when historic quantities are used. Then, the process has two possibilities: request and reception, the latter not always scheduled. Therefore, if there is no one there to receive it, someone has to be called in to organize the area in order to have space, people and shelves available. Products arrive by different means, sometimes by truck, by plane, or both.

"PECTRA helps us to consolidate and manage information, and specially to monitor product movement through the different areas. For instance, when delivering to points-of-sale, when returning from points-of-sale, or when moving between storage areas.

"It is a quite complex process, and if there is any problem, PECTRA allows us to track the product in a simple manner, and this way we are able to see who handled it, what points were covered and where the product is. In this way, we can take corrective measures immediately. Also, it helps us avoid serious problems, such as delayed arrivals and task delegation when the person in charge does not show up, etc.

"Some vendors have an expiration date, others don't. Some are strict and would not negotiate about expired goods, some are not. Some have web sites where you can upload information, some don't. For instance, in the process of returning products, we need to let the vendor know in advance about the edition and amount of returned products, and we need to negotiate how many of the expired goods are going to be returned. It is important to know how much money is lost when the expiration dates are not negotiated with enough time. Once the period has expired, the vendor does not acknowledge the cost of the product. This way, we now have access to accurate information, thus allowing the vendor to acknowledge the returning products," indicates Marcelo.

In many cases, the warehouses did not know for sure the quantity of products being carried.Sometimes shipping documents did not match, because there had been losses. In some other cases, the products suffered accidents, like getting wet or deteriorated, and to take on their cost was a great problem.

"This was made worse during the billing process, because debit notes were listed instead of credit ones... it was chaos. Besides, the more products we distributed, the worse the operation got, until it became unsustainable," Rizzi said. "Today, this tool allows for early detection. All discrepancies are detected long before they become a problem. In the past, with the way things were done, we had to wait until last minute. Now we have online management and control, and we are able to detect mistakes in a timely manner.

"On the other hand, with a standardized process, it is not only possible to work homogeneously and obtain the desired results, but it is also easier to train a new user as we can instantly provide them access to all documentation and manuals and avoid wasting time and resources in staff training," explained Marcelo. "What is more, their performance during the first days may be the same as an experienced user. From a communication standpoint, another very important benefit is that we all speak the same language. It is possible that the users, engrossed in their daily routines, do not realize about this; but I can see now that there is a unified language."

PECTRA has allowed the users to define processes and working styles. If we want to have the same success expectations today, we must work as indicated by the process. If we go outside the process, we will not get the results expected. It is possible that today some users think that without this tool the process may be easier or simpler. But they forget about tomorrow. If it happens that we have 50 more products, that working style will become a complete chaos. And we are aware that if we don't do it right, somebody else will, and that is why we need to optimize our processes," stated Marcelo.

At a strategic level, this tool allows them to know whether the business is profitable or not. And in the future, they will be able to evaluate if it is convenient to invest or not. At the operative level, and after improving the process of distribution, users are starting to use other features of the tool. They request more information through management reports, alarms, etc.

"The tool is easy to use by technicians. All users have access to the tool through a web browser. They enter directly into the Digital Gate (its user friendly and very intuitive interface)," explains Rizzi.

"These processes have crucial importance. And this is simply because they have to relate with other processes. These types of circuits are very difficult to touch in a completely technology-dependant means of communication. One has to be sure to be walking on steady ground. For instance, at an automotive production plant, if the LAN collapses, car production does not stop. I'm not saying it is not important and that it is not necessary to get it back to work again, but in a newspaper, if we have this kind of problem we cannot do one thing, because everything is 100 percent digital content... and then there is no newspaper. There is a credibility and trust issue in which the news industry is based on, especially for newspapers. And I'll mention again the car analogy: if a BMW is delivered two days late to the car dealer... I don't think anybody would stop buying BMWs... my opinion about BMW won't change. However, in the case of a newspaper, being available every morning builds up the credibility. It is the essence of the media. If one day the paper is not out, that day you lose your business," Marcelo says.

6. IMPLEMENTATION.

Implementation began seven months ago. The Systems area decided to organize an intensive 15-day training course for all the users, and teach them the skills they needed for their specific tasks, as well as providing them with general view of the rest of the tasks involved. This would guarantee that the users would have an overall vision of the project and its processes.

"When training was over, we said: 'Right, the first product we get from now on, we load it into the system.' And the product came. We started working and we found some errors. We corrected them. And we kept on trying with the following product. This is how this works. Everyday you get new products. It's like a chairlift, the next one to arrive, I'll take it," explains Marcelo, commenting on the early stages of implementation. "Later on, we corrected a problem with a vertical module, called Stores, and from then on, we haven't stopped.

"The greatest advantage we got from PECTRA Technology, which is extremely important for us, is its consulting and technical support services. Its response level has always been very good, and we are very pleased with the results," he adds.

7. THE SYSTEM USERS AND WHAT THEIR JOBS NOW ENTAIL COMPARED TO PRE-INSTALLATION.

Today, there are 13 users involved in the processes, working in 3 different areas:
- Storage Facilities/Warehouses and Despatch.
- Distribution
- Product Management.

These processes comprise some 25 activities and are integrated with different processes that originate in the admin and operative areas of the company.

"The change in our work methodology has been significant. However, we have planned for a gradual transition to help users adapt to the new system. We have thoroughly analized each of the problems they encounter, to ensure that the circuit works in optimal conditions. We are being able to provide solid answers to each of the users' requirements, with a view to improving the processes."

Furthermore, PECTRA enables real-time objective performance assessments, for example, if users despatch the products in due time and form.

"Employees are already carrying out controls such as these, and readily accept them. Ever since their training began, they have regarded PECTRA as an ally, as a solution that helps them perform their tasks more easily. We even worked with the Human Resources area so that their people could get to know the tool and in that way help the Systems area in promoting BPM technology internally, and having users adopt it without any problems. Users are quick to see how this works: today, anyone who understands that by placing orders using this solution they will get a quicker and more secure answer, will convince other employees that this system is much more effective and efficient than the phone, for example," adds Marcelo.

"We are well aware that incorporating the process-based work methodology is a matter of time. Nobody regards PECTRA as the enemy, we all think of it as an ally. The biggest problems to be solved were age-old differences between areas, but PECTRA is helping to eliminate these disagreements. The cultural change is huge. This is a new mentality."

8. The biggest hurdles overcome in management, business and technology.

"We haven't had any major obstacles to implement the tool, other than the normal delay of wanting to start in Summer, when our company's activities slowed down a little, so we had to push things forward to Autumn," says Marcelo.

This was the organization's first experience in IT tools that provided process-based work methodologies. Regarding the process culture, as a company, they are just starting. "However, everybody knows that we have to adopt this process-based methodology. At Systems meetings, we are beginning to see the need for processes, especially in the accounting and admin areas. Basically, admin desperately needs to integrate with the rest of the organization," says Marcelo.

"Regarding technology, it is very common in software engineering that if the tool performs well, you look for problems to improve it, if performance is faulty, you highlight the problems to make it better. The truth is that users saw great potential in the tool, which is why they started to demand more from it," explains Marcelo.

9. The new system configuration

The new workflow tool has a web site (Digital Gate) that supports all the interface and publication layers on an Internet Information Server 5.0. PECTRA Technology engines use COM+ services provided by Windows 2000 and the distribute transaction services provided by Microsoft DTC (Distribute Transaction Coordinator). The systems Database is managed by an SQL Server 2000. Connectivity is architectured on a 100 Base T switch to the system's server. The server runs on Intel CEON MPS (MultiProcessor) technology, with Windows 2000 operative system. It has two 2.4 GHz and 1 GB RAM processors. For storage, it uses a RAID 5 disks. Installation is integrated with data stored in an ORACLE 9i database. Integration of both platforms is carried out through Providers.Net.

Users access via browser (Internet Explorer 6.0), physically distributed in 4 specific locations: main plant, printing plant (200 meters from the main plant), offices in Barrio Alta Córdoba (10 km. from the plant) and in Colón Street, the city's downtown.

10. Cost savings, increased revenues, and productivity improvements.

By implementing PECTRA, and its BPM (Business Process Management) technology, La Voz del Interior achieved the following benefits:
- **To cut costs and to shorten** follow up and control **times** of third-party products. It also enabled a clear definition of the objectives to be achieved and an efficient delimitation of responsibilities for all the parties involved.
- **To increase efficiency** in the execution of business processes.
- **To increase service quality** both for clients (sales points) and product distributors.
- To minimize steps.
- **To eliminate** tasks that do not add value.
- **To increase** the effectiveness and quality of available information.
- **To eliminate** redundant controls.

- **To verify** the status of the different storage facilities/warehouses on-line.
- **To define alerts** for due-date activities.
- To specify notifications for pending activities.
- To improve Security.
- **To trace activities** by means of an accurate traceability model.
- **To control operations** in a simple way and in real time.

11. Immediate and Long-Term Plans to Sustain Competitive Advantages.

"Currently, with PECTRA, we have more than 100 products running," adds Marcelo, who explains that the plan is to move forward and to add new products. "There is a political and Management decision to continue adding products because nobody wants to go back to the status quo previously, to the sort of chaos we had before. Today we need 'to manage' and this tool is a great asset. This first implementation stage has triggered the promotion of this process-based work methodology internally, which I find is extremely useful for the organization."

"Being able to load the process into a computer, and not to store it inside our heads, is very important. Today we haven't implemented quality control in our processes but with PECTRA it is going to be easier to do. Without any doubt, it is impossible today for La Voz del Interior to add and distribute new products without PECTRA Technology's contribution. We know it and we are completely sure about it. In the future, the idea is to integrate other processes within the organization and then add third-party suppliers, as is the case with La Nación, where we want to implement electronic invoicing. We've had talks with them and they've agreed. At the moment, we're working on how to do it," concludes Rizzi.

Universidade de Santa Cruz do Sul, Brazil

Silver Award 2005, South America; nominated by Cryo Technologies, Brazil

ABSTRACT

The University of Santa Cruz do Sul (UNISC) based on the commitment to keep its characteristics of a Community University—an institution of not-state public nature—expressed by administrative and financial transparency, democratic management and its insertion in community's life, searched through the use of Workflow technology to afford a tool to its managers that guarantee the essential characteristics so that the information becomes a strategic resource. This technology allowed the accompaniment and the management of the work flows and the access to information on a safe, online and integrated form, reflecting transparency and agility in processes and also reduction of people and paper's traffic.

INTRODUCTION

It is intended, thru this document, to present the main organizational impacts from the implantation of Workflow technology in guiding Projects of Research and Extension in UNISC.

So, to start with, motivations that took UNISC to automate processes of guiding Projects of Research and Extension are enumerated, presenting, in general lines, characteristics of the University and how Research and Extension work.

After that, business innovation is presented thru implantation of Workflow technology, the description of processes of guiding projects before the use of technology and after the implantation, detaching adopted technological solution. In sequence, the main impacts in users of this solution, the detailing of new system's configuration and the obstacles faced to implantation are presented. Also the benefits with implantation of new technology are quantified, in that it says respect to reduction of costs, increase of profits and improvements of productivity. Finally, we present competitive advantages and UNISC plans to consolidate this technology as a competitive advantage.

MOTIVATION

UNISC is a university located in the city of Santa Cruz do Sul, state of Rio Grande do Sul, in southern Brazil. Having about 12.000 pupils distributed in 42 courses of Graduation, 25 courses of Post Graduation Lato Sensu and 5 courses of Post Graduation Stricto Sensu, and a campus headquarters with 47.973,62 m2, UNISC is widely recognized as one of the main universities of this region of performance, contributing strongly for the development of regional economy through population qualification, foments to research and maintenance of appraised extension programs to the community, being distinguished, mainly, by programs in health area.

The research developed by UNISC and other Brazilian universities consists of a set of activities aiming at the introduction of innovations techniques in productive process (new products, methods of production, materials, etc.), enclosing since initial conception until the tests of its effective use. The "project of research" is a document that defines, in details, the planning of the way to follow the construction of a scientific work of research, in accordance with established deadlines and goals.

The activity of extension understands planning and development of processes that make possible the interaction between university and community as courses, events, seminaries and lectures, as well as, to create a space of democratic exercise into the community itself, where the processes of quarrel, reflection and exchange of knowing are privileged. The activity of extension can be:

- Circumstantial—they are prompt activities and the hour-activity of the teachers are not used;
- Continued—activities that normally take a superior period than six months, involves teacher's hour-activity and are evaluated by the Assessor Committee of Evaluation—CAA.

The Assessor Committee of Evaluation has the attribution to elaborate merit analysis and emit evaluation of all projects of Research and Extension—Continued and on the requests of scholarships of internal university programs, as Program UNISC of Scientific Initiation and Program UNISC of Scholarship of Extension.

In this direction, some important facts of Research and Extension activities become especially important for UNISC:

- Ministry of Education and Culture of Brazil (MEC), determines that Brazilian universities must apply, at least, 2 percent of its operational budget in research (art. 3° of portaria MEC n° 637, of 13 of May of 1997), with sights to keep its legal credential with Brazilian Government;
- Law n° 9394 of 20 of December of 1996 makes use of Lines of Direction and Bases of National Education—LDB, where in its art.52, II and III, is recommended that 1/3 of the total number of teachers of the university must be part of Integral Time Regimen—TI and that 1/3 has title of Master and Doctor;
- Art.11 of UNISC Teacher Career Plan establishes that teachers in Integral Time Regimen—TI (40 weekly hours), Partial Time—TP (30 and 20 weekly hours) must fulfill, from the total of its working hours:
  - 50 percent for activities of teaching;
  - 30 percent for Research, Extension and/or Administration; and
  - 20 percent for class preparation.
- One of the main principles of UNISC is to group together education, research and extension.

Considering these aspects, UNISC Rectory, the superior executive office that manages, co-ordinates and controls all university activities, understood, as a key process of the institution, the Management of Projects of Research and Extension of the university. So, it launched guidelines of direction that searched the mapping, revision, optimization and automation of this process, with focus to increase the quality of this key-sector in the university, as well as contributing for the generation of a competitive differential. In the objectives glimpsed with the process were:

- Improvement of quality and agility of internal processes;
- Better control on expenses and investments in programs of this area;
- Reduction of operational costs;
- Regulating the prominence of UNISC in front of many education institutions and agencies.

From July to December of 2004 the management of these projects was totally automated, through the joint use of Workflow technology and system of Management of Activities of Research and Extension—GAPE (complex form web), developed internally.

INNOVATION

Business

Significant changes in organizational and cultural order after the implantation of Workflow technology associated with GAPE system follows.

In evaluation of teachers, proceedings adopted before this implementation were very bureaucratic, the projects of Extension were filled in form through a text editor, in paper form and for Research they were filled in electronic form. Many of them were felt upset when the request of data changes filled in the electronic form, caused by typing error and also they alleged the unfamiliarity with fields to be filled. With the unification of forms, allows teachers to selects which type of project he desires to submit, and is qualified for fulfilling only the relative fields to the selected type. Also an on-line manual of main fields of the forms was available.

With implementation of web form, through GAPE system, consulting projects is totally online, what was done previously in paper is available any time and can be accessed trough the Intranet. So, the projects files in paper were totally eliminated.

Another important aspect was the development of rules of budgetary calculation in electronic form, where, besides allowing teacher to get the esteem value of its project before submitting it to the responsible sector for validate this task, also consists the percentage of 30 percent of work hours of teachers, destined the Research and Extension, not allowing that they enter with projects beyond this percentage. This control, previously, was done in a total manual form.

In the same way that the fulfilling of forms was uneasy to teachers, the directing flow also, therefore projects of Extension were directed of total manual form, already of Research, the flow was partially automated. With automatization of proceeding of directing projects, or either, those effected steps of manual form had started to pass through automatically of a responsible one to another, fit to the teacher to be worried in effecting its tasks and following where point of the proceeding is its project.

Previously the deadline were not respected, for example, 90 percent of projects were directed for elaboration of budgetary calculation in the last week, causing a high number of budgets done per day, by manual form, leading to a degree of physical and mental consuming of employees of this sector.

With automation, transparency in processes was possible, where the teacher can follow all proceeding (fig. 01), knowing accurately with who is the project and access information about them and the date where it was appreciated. The Head of Department consults the projects, approved by the CONPPEX—Council of Research, Post Graduation and Extension, in which the teachers of the department still participate as coordinating or integrant and projects directed for it (fig. 02) and still, the Pro-Rectories possesses the graphical vision of flow progress (fig. 03), indicating activities/tasks already done, which task is active at that moment and which are hanging, contributing for the management of process, beyond they possess analysis reports of each task execution time and the number of projects that are in determined task.

Detalhamento do Fluxo

Cod.	Tarefa	Data de Início	Horário	Data de Fim	Horário	Status	Resultado	Responsável
8461	**Criação de Novo Projeto/Atividade**	27/01/2005	15:10:41	27/01/2005	15:10:41	✓	Concluído	IEDA DE CAMARGO *Professor (DEPTO EDUCACAO)*
8462	**Efetuar Cálculo Orçamentário** *Efetuar cálculo orçamentário.*	27/01/2005	15:10:41	28/01/2005	17:07:16	✓	Concluído	JULIA FERNANDA AREND *Funcionário do Setor ORCAMENTO/PREST.CONTAS)* Revisor de Orçamento (SETOR ORCAMENTO/PREST.CONTAS)
8594	**Avaliar Orçamento** *Avaliar Orçamento.* *IMPORTANTE: Projetos Circunstanciais de Extensão com inscrições devem ser encaminhados à PROEXT 30 dias antes do início do período de inscrições.*	28/01/2005	17:07:16	01/02/2005	10:15:58	✓	Concluído	IEDA DE CAMARGO *Professor (DEPTO EDUCACAO)*
8731	**Anexar Documentos** *Anexar documentos (.doc, .pdf, .rtf, .xls, .xrm, .src, .txt, ...).* *IMPORTANTE: Projetos Circunstanciais de Extensão com inscrições devem ser encaminhados à PROEXT 30 dias antes do início do período de inscrições.*	01/02/2005	10:15:59	02/02/2005	11:40:42	✓	Concluído	IEDA DE CAMARGO *Professor (DEPTO EDUCACAO)*
8829	**Aprovar Projeto** *Avaliar o projeto acessando o link.*	02/02/2005	11:40:43	02/02/2005	16:54:51	✓	Rejeitado	SUSANA MARGARITA SPERONI *Professor (DEPTO EDUCACAO)* Chefe de Departamento (DEPTO EDUCACAO)
8831	**Aprovar Projeto** *Avaliar o projeto acessando o*	02/02/2005	11:40:43	02/02/2005	15:06:17	✓	Aprovado	ANGELO HOFF *Professor (DEPTO ED FIS E SAUDE)* Chefe de Departamento (DEPTO ED FIS E

🔲 WorkFlow   🖳 Local intranet

Fig. 01—Flow Detailing

Meus Projetos e Atividades

🔲 Criar Nova Atividade / Projeto

Protocolo	Título	Tipo	Estado	Preenchimento
☑	Análise e Implantação de Sistemas de Produção Agroecológicos na Região do Vale do Rio Pardo, RS	Pesquisa	Novo	Pendente
☑	Instalação e monitoramento de rede de estações meteorológicas no Vale do Rio Pardo (Estação UNISC)	Pesquisa	Novo	Pendente
☑ 2403	Os direitos e deveres individuais e coletivos na Construção da República Federativa do Brasil: uma aproximação do conhecimento dos direitos e deveres constitucionais na comunidade local e regional	Pesquisa	Encaminhado	Concluído

Projetos e Atividades que Participo

	Título	Tipo	Estado	Preenchimento
☑	As espécies da Família Vespidae no Sul do Brasil	Pesquisa	Novo	Pendente

Projetos e Atividades que os Docentes do INFORMATICA participam

Protocolo	Título	Tipo	Estado	Preenchimento
☑ 1927	PORTAL MESOSUL - CAPACITAÇÃO PARA CRIAÇÃO/MANUTENÇÃO DA PÁGINA DE CADA COREDE	Extensão	Aprovado	Concluído
☑ 2193	Linux I	Extensão	Aprovado	Concluído
☑ 2040	Semana Acadêmica do Curso de Matemática Licenciatura e Licenciatura em Computação: Uma aventura pela interdisciplinaridade.	Extensão	Aprovado	Concluído

Fig. 02—Consulting the department head

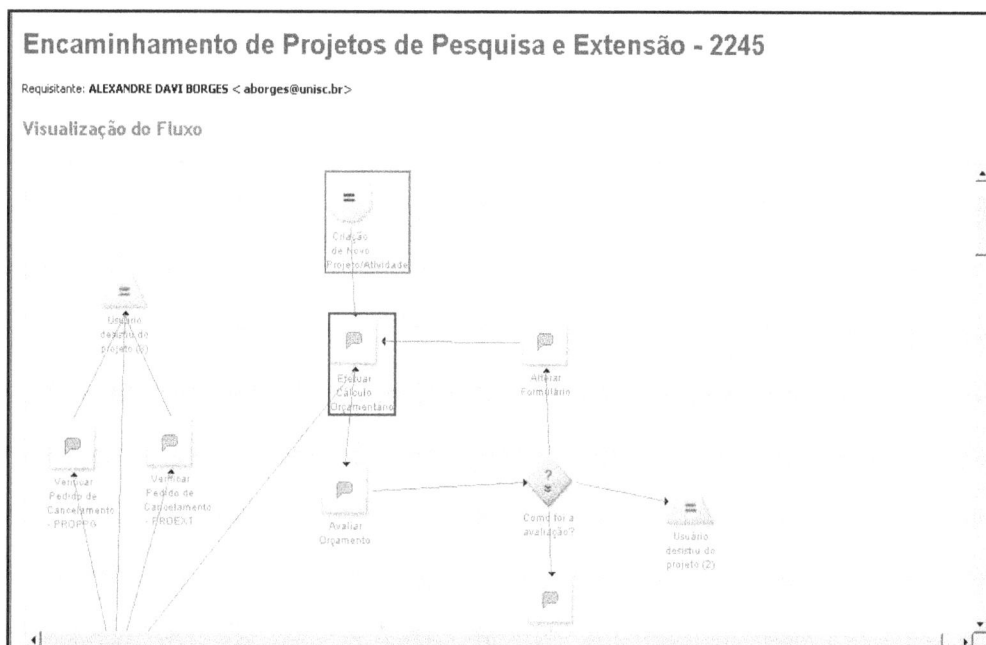

Encaminhamento de Projetos de Pesquisa e Extensão - 2245

Requisitante: **ALEXANDRE DAVI BORGES** < aborges@unisc.br>

Visualização do Fluxo

Fig. 03—Flow's Graphical Vision

Another innovation was the sending of the necessary documentation for the evaluation of the CAA in electronic archives and the available of direct access to Workflow system for evaluation of the projects. Before, this documentation was sent in paper, attached to the directing form of the project, generating difficulty in organize documentation for each commission and in the manuscript of the papers for the members of the commissions.

After the approval of the project, printed copies was done and distributed to the people and the sectors that would have to execute it, what, many times did not happen on a synchronized way. As the distribution process, now, is made automatically, through the sending of e-mails, it is guaranteed that the same ones received at the same moment.

With the implantation of the adopted solution, still was possible:

1. Trustworthiness of data filled in the form, therefore has the register of the proponent of the project and also which are the other responsible ones for the tasks;

2. To avoid that the teacher direct the project again after thirty days of the approval of the budgetary calculation, where the values can be unbalanced, was available the automatic cancellation of the flow and the project in the tasks To Evaluate Budget, To Modify Form and To Annex Documents, with sending of notification, for e-mail, in 15° day, later in 28° and 30° day;

3. Sending e-mail to people responsible for the task, informing the receiving of a new task and the alert of time.

With the joint use of Workflow technology with GAPE system, the elaboration of any statistics is possible, identifying "bottlenecks", for example, among other information for the planning of the Institution and the continuous analysis of the process.

The adopted technology allowed the administration of the information and the knowledge on the functioning of the process, as well as the rules that control its proceeding. Another important point to detach is the use of Workflow technology as a process of knowledge externalization, because in process execution are registered explicit information that previously was not registered, that were with the person who executed the activity and were lost with the time, for example: register of the messages changed between the tasks and time and date of the execution of the task.

Processes

1. Before the implementation of Workflow technology:
   1. Extension projects were directed for approval on the following way:
      a) Teacher fills form of guiding project, using a text editor;
      b) He sends this paper to Sector of Budget and Rendering of Accounts (SOPC), who make the budgetary calculations manually and returns a rough draft of the budget to the teacher;
      c) The teacher types the budgetary data in the form and, if in accordance with the budget, he prints, signs and directs it to SOPC again to revise the typing and sign it;
      d) After the signature of SOPC, teacher submits to approval of respective(s) department(s);

      (i) If the project will be inter-departments (involving more than one department), it must be submitted to approval of respective department's chief;

      e) Having the department(s) approved the project, it is conducted to Extension's Coordination, that makes the conference of the required documentation;

      (i) The documents must be annexed (in paper) to the project's form: descriptive project, Curriculum Lattés, work planning of scholarship students; report of previous project; report of scholarship holders of previous project and registration fiches of scholarship requests;

      f) The Coordination of Extension only accepts the project if it is with all the attached documentation, moment where the project receives a protocol number, which is sequential per year, for example: 059/2003. At this moment the Coordination of Extension directs:

      (i) When necessary, copy of the project form to Legal Assessor ship—AJUR—for elaboration of corresponding legal instrument;

      (ii) When projects are continued, the complete documentation (in paper) of the project is sent to Assessor Committee of Evaluation—CAA (external agency);

      (iii) When circumstantial projects, copy(is) of the form are sent to:

      1. Project's Proponent;

      2. Post Graduation and Extension's Secretariat, when the project has candidate students;

      3. Pole of Technological Modernization, when the project will have interface with this sector;

4. Accounting Sector—Area of Costs, for the countable codification;

5. Financial Sector—Treasury, when the project will have values less than R$ 2.000,00 (U$ 860);

g) For appreciation of Research and Post Graduation Council of UNISC—CONPPEX, the Coordination of Extension emits a report of all Circumstantial and Continued Projects, after the validation of CAA;

h) If CONPPEX report is:

(i) Approved with budgetary alterations: the Coordination of Extension conducts it to SOPC to do alterations. These alterations are made manually at the side of the field that must be modified and it is subscribed;

(ii) Approved, approved with suggestions or still approved with budgetary alterations: the Coordination of Extension collects the signature of Pro-Rector of Extension and Communitarian Relations in the project form;

(iii) To be re-elaborated: the Coordination of Extension returns the documentation to the proponent to re-elaborate the project.

i) The Coordination of Extension communicates the proponent about the result of evaluation and send form copies for the same sectors cited in the item (f) (iii), above;

j) The last stage of the process culminates with the typing of information, contained in the extension form, for register in the System of Management of Research and Extension Projects—SGPE. The form and the documentation are filed away at Coordination of Extension;

k) If the teacher desires to redirect the approved project for alterations or cancellation, he must fill the form, designating the option "Redirected" and submit the flow again (SOPC, Head Department...).

2. The research projects were directed by the following way:

a) Teacher fills electronic form in Intranet. At this moment, project pertinent information automatically is updated in the database that stores data of all extension and research projects (SGPE);

b) When the electronic form is fulfilled, the teacher sends the project for budgetary calculation through the option "to submit". This action generates an automatic electronic message for the SOPC;

c) The calculation of budgetary prevision is done through Excel spread sheet and returned, to the proponent, by e-mail. The SOPC makes use of two working days to conclude the budget;

d) After approval of budgetary prevision, the teacher prints a copy of the electronic form and a copy of the archive with the calculation of budgetary prevision, attaches demanded documentation (descriptive project, Curriculum Lattés, work planning of scholarship students; report of previous project; report of scholarship holders of previous project and registration fiches of scholarship requests) and submit the project for Department(s) approval;

e) From this stage, the proceeding is identical to the one of Extension, described previously;

f) If it's necessary to re-conduct the approved project for alterations or cancellation, the teacher must formally request to the Coordination of Research the release of the form for alteration, which is effected by system (SGPE). In this case, the proponent designates the option "Re-conduct" in the form, updates the form and again submits it to the approval flow.

AFTER IMPLEMENTATION OF THE TECHNOLOGY

In July, 2004, the Assessory of Organizational Development and Sector of Informatics of UNISC had initiated data-collecting of process requirements. In this stage, the coordinators of Pro-Rectory of Research and Post Graduate (PROPPG), Pro-Rectory of Extension and Communitarian Relations (PROEXT), Pro-Rectory of Administration (PROAD), SOPC, Legal Assessor ship (AJUR), Sector of Accounting and Committee of Ethics in Research (CEP)—UNISC had participated.

Trying to minimize the impacts of a culture change with implantation of a new technology, during the definition of business rules and flow, some teachers considered as participant and opinion builders were invited to give suggestions.

To start the process of automation, it had two moments of socialization of new systematic in UNISC; the first one was in July 2004, to the teachers who worked in definitions and to responsible sectors involved in some tasks of the flow and the second one, in August 2004, like a seminary to all teachers of university. The entrance of projects by the automation flow was initiated in October 2004.

The flow drawing of Guiding Research and Extension Projects, developed in software Orchestra, is met in fig. 04.

Technology

The new technological solution for Guiding Research and Extension Projects processes automatization was elaborated on the platform of Orchestra, developed by Brazilian company Cryo Technologies.

The Orchestra is a BPMS—Business Process Management Suite—that allows modeling, configuration, execution, administration and monitoring processes. Its interface is friendly and allows the users to shape and configure its processes through dragging and dropping tasks and elements of connections.

The Research and Extension process was easily implemented and automation into the Orchestra by a mixed team formed by representatives of technical and business areas of UNISC and consultants of Cryo Technologies. The Orchestra, for using the notation of Casati&Ceri for flow modeling, created the need of some small modifications in process drawing, initially mapped using software Microsoft Visio.

In a first moment, the mapped flow was drawn inside the new tool by the consultants and people of UNISC business area. It was necessary just one week to place and configure all the tasks and conditions associated to the process inside the system. This involved more than 120 process stages mapped and the possibility of involvement of more than 200 actors registered in cadastre to execute tasks or to initiate processes.

After the flow being shaped and configured, the work of the technical team that aimed at the integration of the flow of Workflow with other systems of the institution started. The main focus of integration, however, was GAPE system, internally developed for management of research and extension projects, integrating all the information about project participants, budgetary target of research and extension and calculations.

The GAPE is constituted by a complex form WEB responsible for maintenance and management of project related data. It was defined, that the proponent of the project would have to enter with its data on GAPE system and this, automatically, generates the beginning of an approval process that could lead up to four months to be concluded. During the time of development of this process, diverse stages of synchronization had been drawn in the Orchestra, which stated searching and sending date for GAPE system.

Is important to detach that, with intention to facilitate use for users, the interface of the two systems was integrated; the entrance started to be thru Orchestra, controlling conditions, tasks, times, responsible people and, when necessary, showing a direct link to data form of GAPE system.

Users impact

The optimization, improvements and profits of time in using Workflow technology associated with GAPE, in this process, had reflected in users, mainly for:

1. Avail information in electronic way, preventing loss of time in searching and localization activities in paper to supply information to the interested parts in the process;
2. Avoid manuscript papers handling, increasing productivity;
3. Reduce the flow of people who circulate in sectors and Pro-Rectories, allowing the use of this time to another activities;
4. Eliminate involvement of Pro-Rectories people in registering projects in database, providing the creation of the project in this base;
5. To diminish involvement of Pro-Rectories people in distribution of the project to sectors, allowing that all receive at the same time;
6. Eliminate the need of sending documents in paper form to the members of Assessor Committee of Evaluation—CAA (external agency), therefore direct access to Workflow system was available for evaluation of the projects and its respective attached documents;
7. Speeding up and organizing activities developed by CAA, allowing that the obtaining of ideas and notes for the projects were made on simultaneous form to Coordinators of Pro-Rectories, qualifying evaluation work between the Committee and UNISC;
8. With the definition of budgetary calculation rules, contemplated in GAPE system, the teacher, after the data entry, gets the estimated value of its project before submitting for budgetary calculation;
9. With this functionality, SOPC validates budgetary calculations with no need of manual calculation. By this way, there was a reduction in people flow in this sector, what previously difficult concentration and involves other employees in subject and still, avoid the pressure done by the teacher in way the budget be done in that right moment.
10. Give transparency to the process; the teacher follow the points of proceeding of its project;
11. Provide projects on-line consultation to teachers, Heads of Department, Pro-Rectors and Coordinators of Pro-Rectories.

Configuring the new system

The Orchestra, used as base for process modeling and execution, was developed on Microsoft platform, as characteristics below:

- Microsoft Technology NET
- Programming language C#.NET
- Multiple-tiers with transactional objects.

Currently, the application is running in a Windows 2003 server with the following configuration:

- 2 processors Intel Pentium 4 Xeon 2.4Ghz
- 2 GB of RAM
- 1 disk of 34GB
- Operational system Windows 2003
- 1 connection with Storage Hitachi

Concerning to the database, it is being used SQL Server 2000, base for other internal systems of UNISC. The database of Workflow system is running in a SQL Server 2000 in Windows environment with the following configuration:

- 2 processors Intel Pentium 4 Xeon 2Ghz
- 2 GB of RAM
- 2 disks of 17G
- Operational system Windows 2000
- 1 connection with Storage Hitachi

Besides that, currently the system communicates directly with two other UNISC applications:

- Rubi/Ronda: system for Human Resources (RH) control, developed on platform SQL Server 2000. It communicates directly with Workflow system, supplying information about register of UNISC employees and its profile of performance. The integration is done thru setting appointments of Stored Procedures.
- GAPE: system developed on platform J2EE and database PostgreSQL/SQLServer. The GAPE system initiates the process of guiding through a call to Workflow system using WebServices. Once the process is instantiated, diverse automation tasks mapped in the flow are initiated by the Orchestra in execution time to synchronize information with GAPE system and to control permissions of access. These communications are done through Web Services, simple solicitations HTTP, and use of Linked Servers in SQL Server for communication between the databases. The control of transactions between the applications is done by DTC (Distributed Transaction Coordinator) from Windows of Workflow system database server.

OBSTACLES

Following, we detach the main obstacles faced during the collect of information needs and automation:

a) Management

1. Concern of Pro-Rectories, agencies that make the management of Research and Extension in UNISC, if the project would be really evaluated and authorized by all and still, distributed to teachers/sectors that must execute it;
2. Difficulty of Pro-Rectories visualizes, during the phase of development, the benefits with the implantation of the technology.

b) Business

1. Standardization of the process, mainly in definition of execution time of each task and also business rules, since previously projects were sent in paper and by hands to people, and sometimes the stages of the proceeding, fulfilling necessary fields and times of execution of the activity, were not respected;
2. It was a moment of changing organizational culture, because process was automated, and users were afraid by not using the paper anymore and the project being passed through electronic media;

3. The flow could get 200 users more than as actors of different tasks of application; however, for the correct application of the involved business rules into the flow, it would be necessary to map the functions of each one of these users as well as map the hierarchic structure of the area where they were placed. As this information did not exist in consistent way in no other system of the university, a task-force was necessary to collect and register manually all this data.

c) Technology

Being the project about implantation of an already consolidated tool of BPM, the biggest technological obstacles to the project refer to questions of solution adaptation to the environment NET and integration with other systems of the institution:

1. The automatization of the process on the platform of Orchestra was the first implantation of system in technology NET inside the university, what generated some environment problems at a first moment and expectation about the performance at the moment of the entrance in production;

2. The necessity of integration of the two systems in different environments (Orchestra in environment Windows and GAPE in Linux environment) was a great obstacle won. In first place, GAPE system was being developed by an independent team, parallel to the automation of the flow, generating necessity of constant interaction and revision of business rules and interfaces involved in the two systems. In second place, the necessity of using the resource of distributed transaction, which would be controlled for Microsoft DTC, started to present problems caused from a bug in the software related by Microsoft. This problem forced modifications in both platforms.

Quantification of the benefits

1. Reduction of Costs
   a) Elimination of paper archive, saving occupation of physical space;
   b) Economy of, approximately, U$120,000.00 and six months of development of new systems due the use of the ready base of the Orchestra;
   c) Reduction of impressions number, since the form until necessary documentation for evaluation of CAA. In average, by project, it was printed, until come at Pro-Rector office, 44 pages of form and 130 pages (attached documents). Considering 85 projects of Research and Extension, received by Pro-Rectories between days 10/12/2004 and 04/02/2005, we are speaking of a reduction of 14,790 copies, approximately.
   d) Expedite and manage the activities developed by CAA, generating time economy, of assessor hours, hosting and feeding members of the committee.

2. Increase of profits
   a) With the validation, in data entry, of the percentage of 30 percent referred to hour-activity of teachers with integral and partial time regimen, we may close working hours destined to research projects and extension, not being allowed directing projects beyond this percentage. This number of hours is searched in the system of payment of Human Resources sector, in an integrated way;
   b) Using Workflow technology with GAPE system, it is possible elaborate any statistics over the process, identifying "bottlenecks", for example, from other institution planning information and continuous analysis of process;

   c) Workflow technology allows administrate information and knowledge about processes functioning, as well as the rules that control its proceeding.

3. Improvements in productivity

   a) Assurance that project documents will not be lost and was sent (in electronic way) for the people and sectors that must do the tasks/activities or even authorize it;

   b) After the project approval by CONPPEX, distribution for the proponent and sectors that are involved in execution is done in automatic way. The information that the project may be initiated is distributed in the same hour for all the involved ones;

   c) The proponent, on receiving the e-mail informing that its project was approved and can be initiated:

     (i) Have the certainty that the Legal Assessor ship elaborated the contract, if the project needs it;

     (ii) Receives the information from the necessary countable codes for any expenses.

     (iii) The number of impressions with this functionality reduced, in average, 24 copies by project. Considering the projects that had been sent between days 10/12/2004 and 04/02/2005, for these sectors, we are talking about a reduction of 543 copies, approximately;

     (iv) Reduction of the averaged time of guiding projects.

COMPETITIVE ADVANTAGE

Considering that:

1. A university needs, also for legal force, to invest in knowledge production (research) and in practical application of this knowledge to the community in which it meets inserted (extension);

2. A significant volume of financial, technical and human resources is conceded for activities of research and extension;

3. These activities, when well articulated and developed, are configured as an important competitive differential for the university, adding to its name qualifying of quality, innovation and insertion;

The investment in an application that income in a bigger optimization and management of these activities, providing automatic integration between areas, controlling instantaneously the allocation of contractual hours for different projects and allowing to the managers the professionalized administration of human resources, available technician and financial, for sure, adds a competitive differential to the institution.

If a university institution not only detaches for the quality of its education, but also for the level of excellence of its activities of research and extension, any process that improves, that organizes, that in such a way allows the integrated insertion of different actors of the activities ends as those of support, will contribute decisively for the improvement of the quality of these activities, becoming, by this way, a competitive advantage on those institutions that still had not reached this level of excellence in its processes.

PLANS AT MEDIUM AND LONG TIME TO KEEP COMPETITIVE ADVANTAGE:

Following the philosophy that process automation improvement organizes and provides automatic integration between areas of the institution, UNISC is prioritizing the implementation of Workflow technology in critical and decisive processes.

In this direction, beyond automation of Guiding Research and Extension Projects, related in a brief form in this document, the following flows had been automated, using software Orchestra in set with other systems:

1. Flow of Redirecting Research and Extension projects for Alteration and/or Cancellation;
2. Flow of Budgetary Control of the Sectors;
3. Flow of Accompaniment of the Projects Approved for the Committee of Ethics to monitoring the course of Projects of Research Approved by the Committee of Ethics, Conclusion Works and Projects of Santa Cruz Hospital and Community.

We are in phase of definition and validation with involved sectors, of the following processes:

1. Flow of request of purchases, for the directing of material purchasing solicitations and contracting services;
2. Flow of directing for approval of Post Graduate Lato Sensu courses;
3. Process of recruitment and selection of staff;
4. Evaluation of employees performance;
5. Request of scholarships Scientific Initiation Program (PUIC), Extension Scholarship Program (PROBEX) and Support Program to Social Development's Extension Projects (PAPEDS).

In conclusion, the great benefits gotten with the first project of automation of process inside UNISC, had contributed for the consolidation of a management's strategy of processes in wide scale that will reach similar results in other flows of the organization.

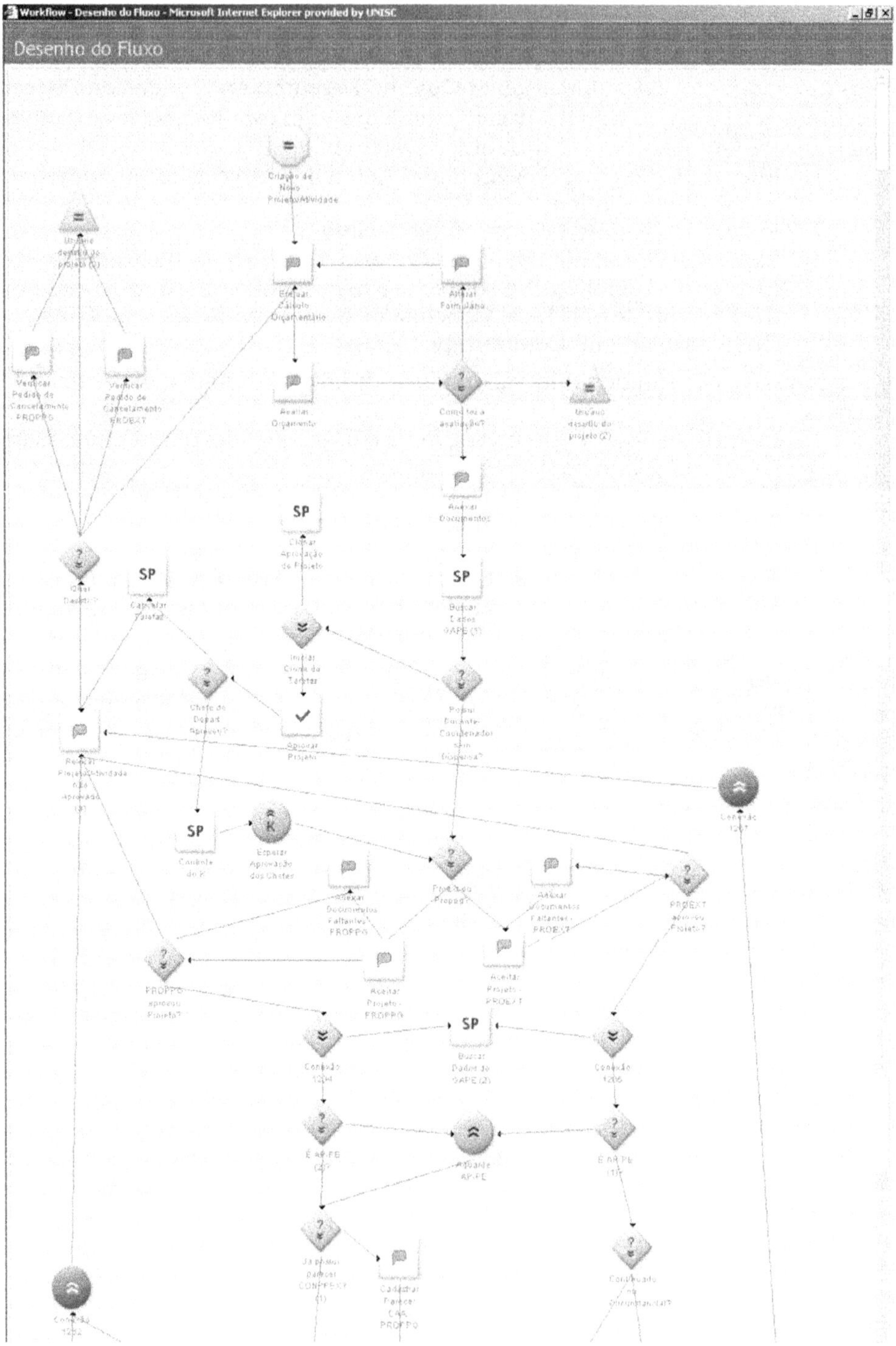
Workflow - Desenho do Fluxo - Microsoft Internet Explorer provided by UNISC
Desenho do Fluxo

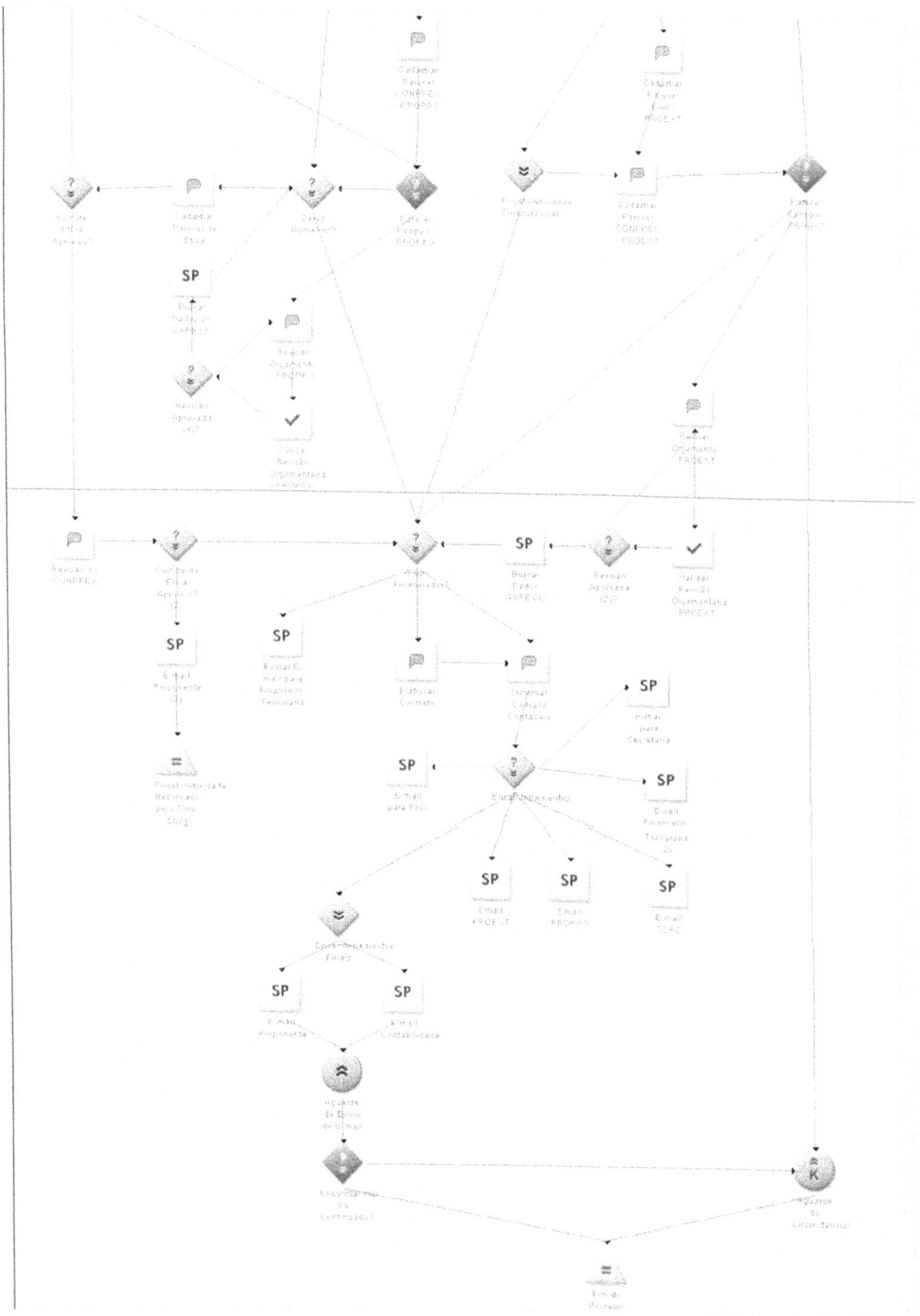

Fig. 04 – The flow drawing in software Orchestra

Section 5

Appendix

Appendix

Awards Winners, Nominees and Nominators

INTRODUCTION

LAYNA FISCHER

About the Excellence Awards

Company	Future Strategies Inc	2436 North Federal Highway, #374
Title	Publisher	Lighthouse Point, FL. 33064
E-Mail	layna@futstrat.com	
URL	www.futstrat.com	
Phone	[954] 782-3376	

Case Studies

Section 1: Europe

BARCLAYS FRANCE

2006 Finalist

Contact	Hubert Locqueville	183 avenue Daumesnil PARIS 75012
Title	COO	France
E-Mail	hubert.locqueville@barclays.fr	
URL	www.barclays.fr	
Phone	+33 +33 155 784 200	

Nominator W4

Contact	Francois Bonnet	4 rue Emile Baudot Palaiseau 91873 Palaiseau Cedex
Title	Marketing Product Manager	France
E-Mail	francois.bonnet@w4global.com	
URL	www.w4global.com	
Phone	[33] 1 64 53 19 12	

W4, one of the leading European software vendors specialized in « Business Process Management », supplies more than 270 customers, serving more than 1 million people. For almost 10 years W4 has been widely acclaimed for its expertise in Human Workflow, which guarantees transparently, via its functional architecture, task follow-up and traceability: who does what, when and how. Whatever the particular need, there is a package available allowing customers to take full advantage of the powerful W4 technology.

MODELO CONTINENTE HIPERMERCADOS PORTUGAL

2006 Gold Winner

Contact	Miguel Ângelo Santos	Rua João Mendonça, 529, Matosinhos 4460-501
Title	Director of Management Information & Web Center	Portugal
E-Mail	mangelo@modelocontinente.pt	
URL	www.modelocontinente.pt	
Phone	+351-22-0161005 ext.16866	

Nominator   **iProcess**

Contact	Vinícius Amaral	Rua Washington Luiz 820/301, Porto Alegre, RS, 90010-460
Title	Diretor de Negócios e Tecnologia	Brazil
E-Mail	vinicius.amaral@iprocess.com.br	
URL	www.iprocess.com.br	
Phone	+55-51-3211-4036	

Integrator   **Tlantic SI**

Contact	Reginaldo Back	Av. Ipiranga, 6681, Predio 96E – Tecnopuc, Porto Alegre, RS 90619-900
Title	Director	Brazil
E-Mail	rback@tlantic.com.br	
URL	www.tlantic.com.br	
Phone	+55(51)3320-1622	

TELENOR NORWAY

2006 Silver Winner

Contact	Jon Omund Revhaug	Telenor Fornebu Snaroyveien 30 Fornebu 1331
Title	Senior Business Advisor	Norway
E-Mail	jon-omund.revhaug@telenor.com	
URL	www.telenor.com	
Phone	+47 (99) 24 49 15	

Nominator   **auSystems (now Cybercom Sweden South AB)**

Contact	Göran Lindh	Dockplatsen 1 Malmoe S-211 19
Title	Business Area Manager	Sweden

E-Mail	Goran.Lindh@cybercomgroup.com	
URL	www.cybercomgroup.com	
Phone	[46] 40 665 92 73	

Cybercom Group is an IT/Telecom consultant company with about 1200 consultants based in offices in a number of countries in Europe and Asia with a majority in Sweden.

Cybercom is a high-tech consulting company that concentrates on selected technologies and offers business critical solutions, primarily to the telecom sector. Using IT, we help customers get results. We are experts in the latest technologies. And we serve leading enterprises that are on the cutting edge of technology. Cybercom is a key partner for customers that assertively invest in enterprise solutions (including BPM), portal development, billing solutions, or embedded systems. Cybercom also provides expertise, advice, and services within all aspects of procurement, implementation, and operation of telecom networks and systems.

We have been active in the system integration and process management area since 1995, and are a Tibco partner since 1997. We are currently running 7 parallel EAI/OM project (size 2-20 persons) within in Business Unit Process Management & Integration (PM&SI). PM&SI employs 50 dedicated EAI developers and architects. In several projects competence is also brough in from other parts of the company.

The largest customers include companies such as Sony Ericsson (handsets, mobile content), Ericsson (telecom equipment), Nokia (handsets), Telenor (telecom), TeliaSonera (telecom), Tele2 (telecom), Millicom (telecom), Teracom (telecom/TV), ASSA ABLOY (industry), Reuters (finance), SEB (finance) and Swedbank (finance).

Section 2: Middle East Africa

AMMAN CHAMBER OF INDUSTRY JORDAN

2005 Gold Winner

Contact	Abeer Al-Fawaeer	Zahran Street 2nd Circle P.O. Box 1800 Amman 11118
Title	IT Manager	Jordan
E-Mail	Abeer.fawaeer@jci.org.jo	
URL	www.jci.org.jo	
Phone	+962 (6) 4643001	

Nominator   *Telaterra Software LLC*

Contact	Nourah Y. Mehyar	Ba'oneh Street - Jabal Weibdeh P.O Box: 927954 Amman 11190
Title	Chief Operating Officer	Jordan
E-Mail	nourahm@telaterra.com	
URL	www.telaterra.com	
Phone	[962] (6) 4733505	

PAYMENTCENTRIC JORDAN

2006 Gold Winner

Contact	Sameer G. Mubarak	P.O Box: 911641
		Amman 11191
Title	General Manager	Jordan
E-Mail	smubarak@paymentcentric.com	
URL	www.paymentcentric.com	
Phone	+962 6 4618080	

Nominator   Telaterra Software LLC

Contact	Nourah Y. Mehyar	Ba'oneh Street - Jabal
		Weibdeh
		P.O Box: 927954
		Amman 11190
Title	Chief Operating Officer	Jordan
E-Mail	nmehyar@telaterra.com	
URL	www.telaterra.com	
Phone	[962] (6) 4733505	

TRACKER SOUTH AFRICA

2006 Silver Winner

Contact	Andre Ackerman	Stenemill Office Park 171
		Republic Road
		Darrenwood
		Gauteng 2194
Title	Financial Manager	South Africa
E-Mail	aackerman@tracker.co.za	
URL	www.tracker.co.za	
Phone	+27 11 380-0300	

Nominator   TIBCO

Contact	Marco Gerazounis	Pebble Beach Bldg.
		Fourways Gold Park
		Roos St.
		Fourways,
		Gauteng 2191
Title	Country Manager	South Africa
E-Mail	mgerazou@tibco.com	
URL	www.tibco.com	
Phone	[27] 11 467 3111	

TIBCO Software Inc. (NASDAQ:TIBX) provides enterprise software that helps companies achieve service-oriented architecture (SOA) and business process management (BPM) success. With over 3,000 customers, TIBCO has given leading organizations around the world better awareness and agility—what TIBCO calls The Power of Now®. TIBCO provides one of the most complete offerings for enterprise-scale BPM, with powerful software that is capable of solving not just the challenges of automating routine tasks and exception handling scenarios, but also the challenges of orchestrating sophisticated and long-lived activities and transactions that involve people and systems across organizational and geographical boundaries.

NEDBANK LTD SOUTH AFRICA

2005 Silver Winner

Contact		135 Rivonia Road
		Sandton
		Johannesburg
		Gauteng 2021
Title		South Africa
E-Mail		
URL	www.nedbank.com	
Phone	+27 (11) 295 6382	

Nominator   TIBCO Software

Contact	Marco Gerazounis	Pebble Beach Bldg.
		Fourways Gold Park
		Roos St.
		Fourways, Gauteng 2191
Title	Country Manager	South Africa
E-Mail	mgerazou@tibco.com	
URL	www.tibco.com	
Phone	[27] 11 467 3111	

TIBCO Software Inc. (NASDAQ:TIBX) provides enterprise software that helps companies achieve service-oriented architecture (SOA) and business process management (BPM) success. With over 3,000 customers, TIBCO has given leading organizations around the world better awareness and agility—what TIBCO calls The Power of Now®. TIBCO provides one of the most complete offerings for enterprise-scale BPM, with powerful software that is capable of solving not just the challenges of automating routine tasks and exception handling scenarios, but also the challenges of orchestrating sophisticated and long-lived activities and transactions that involve people and systems across organizational and geographical boundaries.

Section 3: North America

NORIDIAN ADMINISTRATIVE SERVICES LLC US

2006 Finalist

Contact	Kevin Erickson	4510 13th Avenue, NW
		Fargo
		ND 58121
Title	Director of Information Technology	USA
E-Mail	kevin.erickson@noridian.com	
URL	www.noridian.com	

Phone	+1 701-282-1292	
Nominator	**Green Square, Inc.**	
Contact	Michael Hurley	10835 S. Hoyne Avenue Suite 300, Chicago IL 60643
Title	Process Philosopher	USA
E-Mail	mike@greensquareinc.com	
URL	www.greensquareinc.com	
Phone	773-445-0084	

GRUPO FINANCIERO UNO USA

2005 Gold Winner

Contact	Erick Holmann	7801NW 37th St Miami, FL 33166-6503
Title	BPM Regional Coordinator	USA
E-Mail	eholmann@grupo-uno.com / erick.holmann@citi.com	
URL	www.grupo-uno.com	
Phone	011 (505) 254-4864	
Nominator	**Ultimus**	
Contact	Franz Schubert	15200 Weston Parkway Suite 106, Cary NC 27513
Title	Marketing Communications Manager	USA
E-Mail	fschubert@ultimus.com	
URL	www.ultimus.com	
Phone	919-678-0900	
Integrator	**PAN Communications**	
Contact	Lindsay Soulard	300 Brickstone Square, Andover, MA 1810
Title	Junior Associate	USA
E-Mail	ultimus@pancomm.com	
URL	www.pancommunications.com	
Phone	978.474.1900	

HASBRO USA

2006 Silver Winner

Contact	David Adams	1027 Newport Ave. Pawtucket RI 2862

Title	Senior Manager of Operations - US	USA
E-Mail	dadams@hasbro.com	
URL	www.hasbro.com	
Phone	+1 (401) 431-8204	

Nominator **Lombardi Software**

Contact	Wayne Snell	4516 Seton Center Parkway Suite 250, Austin TX 78759
Title	Senior Director of Marketing	USA
E-Mail	wsnell@lombardi.com	
URL	www.lombardi.com	
Phone	+1.512-383-8200	

Lombardi is a leader in business process management (BPM) software for companies, systems integrators and government agencies. We offer award-winning BPM technology, know-how and services to help our customers become Process-Driven. Lombardi products are built on open standards and provide ongoing prioritization, planning, visibility and control of business processes, increasing the speed and flexibility with which organizations can manage their business process activity and decision-making. Lombardi is behind some of the largest, most successful BPM implementations in the world. Our Teamworks BPM software suite helps companies to design, execute, and improve their business processes. Teamworks for Office™ makes it easy for anyone to participate in business process management using the familiar Microsoft® Office System products. Lombardi Blueprint™ is the only on-demand collaborative process planning tool that enables companies to map processes, identify problems and prioritize improvement opportunities. Our customers include leading financial services institutions, insurers, manufacturers, healthcare, telecommunication, retailing and public/government agencies. For more information, visit www.lombardi.com.

CHESTER COUNTY HOSPITAL USA

2006 Gold Winner

Contact	Ray Hess	701 E. Marshall Street West Chester PA 19380
Title	Vice President, Information Management	USA
E-Mail	rhess@cchosp.com	
URL	www.cchosp.com	
Phone	+1 610-431-5260	

Nominator **Siemens Medical**

Contact	Jonathan Emanuele	51 Valley Stream Parkway Malvern, PA 19355

Title	Product Manager	USA
E-Mail	jonathan.emanuele@siemens.com	
URL	www.medical.siemens.com	
Phone	+1 610-219-9006	

Integrator   **TIBCO**

Contact	Don Plummer	4 Cambridge Center 4th Floor, Cambridge MA – 02142
Title	Alliance and OEM Sales	USA
E-Mail	dplummer@tibco.com	
URL	www.tibco.com	
Phone	+1 617-499-4402	

Section 4: Pacific Rim

ASIA VITAL COMPONENT CO., LTD. TAIWAN

2006 Silver Winner

Contact	Jimmy Teng	7F-3, No 24, Wu-Chuan 2 Rd., Hsin-Chuang City, Taipei County, Taiwan – 24892
Title	Director of Information Management Division	Taiwan
E-Mail	jimmy_teng@avc.com.tw	
URL	www.avc.com.tw	
Phone	886-7-815-7612	

Nominator   **Flowring Technology**

Contact	Yang Chi-Tsai	12F, No. 120, Sec. 2 Gongdao 5th Rd. Hsinchu City Taiwan 30050
Title	VP and CTO	Taiwan
E-Mail	jjyang@flowring.com	
URL	www.flowring.com	
Phone	[886] (35) 753331	

KTF CO LTD., SOUTH KOREA

2006 Gold Winner

Contact	Kyung Eun Lee	KTF, 7-18 Shincheon- Dong, Songpa-Gu Seoul, Korea 138-240
Title	Manager/e-Management Team	South Korea

E-Mail	kelee@ktf.com
URL	www.ktf.com
Phone	+82-2-2010-0993, Mobile : +82-10-3010-1658

Nominator   **HandySoft**

Contact	Robert Cain	1952 Gallows Road, Suite 200 Vienna VA 22182
Title	Product Manager	USA
E-Mail	rcain@handysoft.com	
URL	www.handysoft.com	
Phone	[1] 703-442-5635	

HandySoft Global Corporation is leading the way for companies worldwide to develop new strategies for conducting business through the improvement, automation, and optimization of their business processes. As a leading provider of Business Process Management (BPM) software and services, we deliver innovative solutions to both the public and private sectors. Proven to reduce costs while improving quality and productivity, our foundation software platform, BizFlow®, is an award-winning BPM suite of tools used to design, analyze, automate, monitor, and optimize business processes. By delivering a single-source solution, capable of improving all types of business processes, HandySoft empowers our clients to leverage their investment across whole departments and the entire enterprise, making BizFlow the Strategic Choice for BPM.

ACBEL POLYTECH TAIWAN

2005 Silver Winner

Contact	Jeffrey Jiang	No.159, Sec. 3 Tam-King Rd., Tamsui Town, Taipei county - 251
Title	MIS	Taiwan
E-Mail	jeffrey_jiang@APITECH.com.tw	
URL	www.apitech.com.tw	
Phone	+1 886-2-2621-7672	

Nominator   **Flowring Technology**

Contact	Yang Chi-Tsai	12F, No. 120, Sec. 2 Gongdao 5th Rd. Hsinchu City - 30050
Title	CTO	Taiwan
E-Mail	jjyang@flowring.com	
URL	www.flowring.com	
Phone	886 (35) 753331	

MAX NEW YORK LIFE

2006 Finalist

Contact	Amit Kumar	3rd Floor, DLF Square, DLF City, Jacaranda Marg, (Phase II] Gurgaon Haryana 122002
Title	Group CIO – MNYL & MHC	India
E-Mail	amit.kumar@maxnewyorklife.com	
URL	www.maxnewyorklife.com	
Phone	+91-124-2389273	

Nominator	***Newgen Software Technologies Ltd.***	
Contact	Hareish Gur	D-152, Okhla Industrial Area, Phase I, New Delhi- 110020
Title	Head-Marketing	India
E-Mail	hareish@newgen.co.in	
URL	www.newgensoft.com	
Phone	+91-11-26815467 / 8	

SAMSUNG HEAVY INDUSTRIES KOREA

2005 Gold Winner

Contact	Bong-won Ko	530, Jangpyeong-Ri Sinhyeon-Eup, Geoje-Si Gyeongsangnam-Do 656-710
Title	Senior Manager	Korea
E-Mail	bongwon.ko@samsung.com	
URL	www.samsung.com	
Phone	+1 82-55-630-5603	

Nominator	***HandySoft Corporation***	
Contact	Robert Cain	1952 Gallows Road Suite 200 Vienna VA 22182
Title	Product Manager	USA
E-Mail	rcain@handysoft.com	
URL	www.handysoft.com	
Phone	703-442-5600	

HandySoft Global Corporation is leading the way for companies worldwide to develop new strategies for conducting business through the improvement, automation, and optimization of their business processes. As a leading provider of Business Process Management (BPM) software and services, we deliver innovative solutions to both the public and private sectors. Proven to reduce costs while improving quality and productivity, our foundation software platform, BizFlow®, is an award-winning BPM suite of tools used to design, analyze, automate, monitor, and optimize business processes. By delivering a single-source solution, capable of improving all types of business processes, HandySoft empowers our clients to leverage their investment across whole departments and the entire enterprise, making BizFlow the Strategic Choice for BPM.

Section 5: South America

ALLIANZ COLOMBIA BPM COLOMBIA

2006 Gold Winner

Contact	Marcela Gaitan	Cra 13 A No. 29-24 Piso 10 Bogotá Cundinamarca
Title	Directora de Proyecto	Colombia
E-Mail	maria.gaitan@colseguros.com	
URL	www.allianz.com	
Phone	+57 571 - 5600601 Ext.1028	

Nominator — Bizagi - Vision Software

Contact	Federico Ramírez	Cra. 7a # 71-52 Torre B Of. 1302, Bogotá, Cundinamarca
Title	Marketing and Commercial Analyst	Colombia
E-Mail	federico.ramirez@bizagi.com	
URL	www.bizagi.com	
Phone	+57 1 3170049	

As the result of over 18 years of experience in process automation technologies, our company developed the BizAgi® Business Process Management System. BizAgi® is now a leading BPM Solution specialized in the financial sector with a strong presence in Latin America and Europe where it is being used by some of the most important financial institutions. BizAgi® allows process owners to automate or modify complex and dynamic processes faster and more flexibly than any other solution in the market. This is due to a concept called The Relational Process Model. This model fuses the relational data model with modern process theory allowing BizAgi® to automate processes without programming using a Model Driven Architecture and a Data Driven Process Engine.

METROVIAS ARGENTINA
2006 Finalist

Contact	Alberto Verra	Bartolome Mitre 3342
		Capital Federal,
		Buenos Aires
		C1201AAl
Title	President	Argentina
E-Mail		
URL	www.metrovias.com.ar	
Phone	+1 011 5368 6800	

Nominator   PECTRA Technology

Contact	Fabio Rocca	2425 Wst Loop South
		Suite 200
		Houston
		TX - 77027
Title	Manager	USA
E-Mail	frocca@pectra.com	
URL	www.pectra.com	
Phone	(713) 335 5562	

PECTRA Technology's award-winning Business Process Management system, PECTRA BPM Suite®, is a powerful set of tools enabling discovery, design, implementation, maintenance, optimization and analysis of business processes for different kinds of organizations. PECTRA BPM Suite® is an application that automates the processes and the most critical tasks in the organization, generating optimum levels of operational effectiveness. It fulfills all requirements demanded by today's organization, quickly and efficiently. Furthermore, it increases the return on previous investments made in technology by integrating all existing applications. Based on BPM technology it incorporates the concepts of: BAM (Business Activity Monitoring) providing management with user-friendly graphic monitoring tools, to follow up any deviation in the organization's critical success factors, with capabilities to control and coordinate the organization's performance by means of graphic management indicators; WORKFLOW offering powerful tools to automate and speed the organization's business processes, improving communication and work-flow between people working in different areas; carrying out the work more efficiently and producing customer satisfaction, lower levels of bureaucracy and cost-reductions in day-to-day operations; EAI (Enterprise Application Integration) enabling integration with all existing technologies in the organization, regardless of their origin or platform, coordinating them to help the organization achieve its goals more efficiently; and B2Bi (Business to Business Integration) enabling the control and coordination of each and every link in the organization's value chain, providing robust tools for business process management, and enterprise application integration, making it possible to totally integrate suppliers, clients and partners in an easy and flexible way.

GRUPO PÃO DE AÇÚCAR (GPA) BRAZIL

2006 Silver Winner

Contact	Paulo Salomão	Rua Manuel da Nobrega, 930 São Paulo SP - 04001-003
Title	IT Coordinator	Brazil
E-Mail	paulo.salomao@grupopaodeacucar.com.br	
URL	www.grupopaodeacucar.com.br	
Phone	+55 (11) 388-69283	

Nominator   iProcess

Contact	Vinícius Amaral	Rua Washington Luiz 820/301 Porto, Alegre RS 90010-460
Title	Diretor de Negócios e Tecnologia	Brazil
E-Mail	vinicius.amaral@iprocess.com.br	
URL	www.iprocess.com.br	
Phone	+55-51-3211.4036	

LA VOZ DEL INTERIOR ARGENTINA

2005 Gold Winner

Contact	Marcelo Rizzi	Av. La Voz del Interior 6080 Córdoba - X5008HKJ
Title	System Manager	Argentina
E-Mail	mrizzi@lavozdelinterior.com.ar	
URL	www2.lavoz.com.ar	
Phone	+54 3514757322	

Nominator   PECTRA Technology

Contact	Federico Silva	Boulevard Las Heras 402 Córdoba - X5000FMR
Title	Marketing Manager	Argentina
E-Mail	fsilva@grupoprominente.com	
URL	www.pectra.com	
Phone	+54 (351) 410 4400 ext. 9400	

UNIVERSITY OF SANTA CRUZ DO SUL BRAZIL

2005 Silver Winner

Contact	Magali Carolina Ellwanger	Av. Independência, 2293 Bairro Universitário

		Santa Cruz do Sul
		Rio Grande do Sul
		96815-900
Title	Process Analysis Coordinator	Brazil
E-Mail	carol@unisc.br	
URL	www.unisc.br	
Phone	+55 51 3717 7353	

Nominator   **Cryo Technologies**

Contact	Rafael Bortolini	Av. João Abbott, 473, cj. 305 Bairro Petrópolis Porto Alegre Rio Grande do Sul 90460-150
Title	Project Director	Brazil
E-Mail	rafael@cryo.com.br	
URL	www.cryo.com.br	
Phone	+ 55 51 3019-3532	

Cryo Technologies´s Orquestra BPM suite is an award-winning software focused in human-centric BPM (Business Process Management), providing a complete set of tools to manage the entire process life-cycle. Orquestra BPM is helping the leading South American organizations, both on private and public sectors, to achieve greater control and transparency over their primary business process, with cost reductions and better overall performance. Orquestra BPM is 100% web-based and empowers business analyst to design, automate, execute, monitor and optimize their business process, at great development speeds and lower costs, using innovative and user-friendly features.

Additional BPM and Workflow Resources

- AIIM (Association for Information and Image Management)
  www.aiim.org
- AIS Special Interest Group on Process Automation and
  Management (SIGPAM)
  www.sigpam.org
- BPM Focus (previously WARIA)
  bpmfocus.org/
- Business Process Management Initiative
  www.bpmi.org *see* Object Management Group
- IEEE (Electrical and Electronics Engineers, Inc.)
  www.ieee.org
- Institute for Information Management (IIM)
  www.iim.org
- ISO (International Organization for Standardization)
  www.iso.ch
- Object Management Group
  www.omg.org
- Open Document Management Association
  infocentrale.net/dmware
- Organization for the Advancement of Structured Information
  Standards
  www.oasis-open.org
- Society for Human Resource Management
  www.shrm.org
- Society for Information Management
  www.simnet.org
- Wesley J. Howe School of Technology Management
  attila.stevens.edu/workflow
- Workflow And Reengineering International Association (WARIA)
  www.waria.com – now BPMFocus
- Workflow Management Coalition (WfMC)
  www.wfmc.org
- Workflow Portal
  www.e-workflow.org

Index